Remaking the Democratic Party

Hanes Walton Jr., Pearl Dowe, and Josephine Allen explore Lyndon Baines Johnson's experiences as a Democratic candidate, in both congressional and presidential elections, and his transformative leadership of the Democratic Party. Along with Walton's previous work on Bill Clinton and Jimmy Carter, this book advances a theory of the native-son phenomenon in U.S. elections. The Johnson case study demonstrates that a southern native son can win the presidency even without the localism (i.e., an alliance of friends and neighbors) so evident in the elections of his fellow southern Democrats Clinton and Carter.

Johnson's ability to transform the Democratic Party also demonstrates that leadership shouldn't be defined solely as domination over the national committee. Indeed, Johnson was ridiculed for his apparent lack of control over formal party politics. Yet he excelled at leading the party's policy agenda. Both as a senator and as president, Johnson advocated for—and secured—liberal social welfare and civil rights legislation. By challenging elitism, conservatism, and white supremacy, he not only broke with his own party's traditions, he also pushed the Republican Party to react against the Democrats' new ideology. Thus, Johnson set the terms for the partisan battles that continue today.

Remaking the Democratic Party makes four contributions to our understanding of U.S. elections and the U.S. presidency: a detailed analysis of Johnson's elections, a general theory of the native-son phenomenon, an examination of Johnson's party leadership, and a general understanding of the ways in which a president can direct his party without controlling the national committee.

Hanes Walton Jr. was Professor of Political Science at the University of Michigan.

Pearl K. Ford Dowe is Associate Professor of Political Science at the University of Arkansas.

Josephine A. V. Allen is Professor Emerita of Social Work at Binghamton University and Professor Emerita of Policy Analysis and Management at Cornell University.

Dr. Hanes Walton Jr.

Remaking the Democratic Party

Lyndon B. Johnson as a Native-Son Presidential Candidate

Hanes Walton Jr.,

Pearl K. Ford Dowe, &

Josephine A. V. Allen

University of Michigan Press ★ Ann Arbor

First paperback edition 2018

Published in the United States of America by the
University of Michigan Press
Manufactured in the United States of America
♾ Printed on acid-free paper

2021 2020 2019 2018 5 4 3 2

A CIP catalog record for this book is available from the British Library.

Library of Congress Cataloging-in-Publication Data

Names: Walton, Hanes, 1941– author. | Ford, Pearl K., 1972– author. | Allen, Josephine A. V., author.
Title: Remaking the Democratic Party : Lyndon B. Johnson as a native-son presidential candidate / Hanes Walton, Jr., Pearl K. Ford Dowe, and Josephine A. V. Allen.
Description: Ann Arbor : University of Michigan, [2016] | Includes bibliographical references and index.
Identifiers: LCCN 2016009191 | ISBN 9780472119943 (hardcover : acid-free paper) | ISBN 9780472122110 (e-book)
Subjects: LCSH: Johnson, Lyndon B. (Lyndon Baines), 1908–1973. | Democratic Party (U.S.)—History—20th century. | Presidents—United States—Election, 1964. | United States—Politics and government—1963–1969. | Political culture—Southern States.
Classification: LCC E847 .W35 2016 | DDC 324.973/0923—dc23
LC record available at https://lccn.loc.gov/2016009191

ISBN 978-0-472-03705-6 (pbk. : alk. paper)

from Hanes Walton Jr.

To my oldest son, Brandon Michael Walton, who traveled with me to the Lyndon Baines Johnson Presidential Library in Austin, Texas, and the University of Texas at Arlington Library to help collect rare election return data for this work and thereby sharpened both his and my own research skills and talents. Thanks for the help and the company on the long drives.

from Pearl K. Ford Dowe

To my beloved husband, Alfred Dowe Jr. You have been a loving and supportive partner as I pursue my dreams.

from Josephine A. V. Allen

To my son, Damani James Partridge, with love and sincere appreciation for your care and support. Your intellect, your indestructible faith in the good, your creative vision, your warmth and your belief in the beauty of all life are genuine sources of hope for a brighter tomorrow.

Foreword

I can still remember key points of many of the classroom lectures that Professor Hanes Walton Jr. presented in his courses at Savannah State College, a small historically Black college in my hometown where I earned my undergraduate degree in political science. Those of us who majored in political science were fortunate to have Professor Walton in small classes. His lectures were always lively, funny, engaging, and packed with important observations. In his course, "Black Politics," Walton explained the experience of African Americans within the various institutions of government. Walton often emphasized the key role of the American presidency. He explained that under the Constitution, the office of the president held great powers. Walton revealed the important role that presidents played in the lives of African Americans. Walton discussed this in his pioneering textbook, *Black Politics: A Theoretical and Structural Analysis*. "The American chief executive," Walton observed, "is in a position to affect the lives and life-styles of black Americans. The best proof of this is the significant advances that black Americans have made under some presidents and the equally significant reverses they have had under others."[1] In his lectures, Walton explained that very few of the U.S. presidents have been allies in the struggle for racial justice. Walton, however, always singled out President Lyndon B. Johnson. Walton taught us that President Johnson contributed significantly to the African American quest for universal freedom.

In this book, *Remaking the Democratic Party: Lyndon B. Johnson as a Native-Son Presidential Candidate*, Hanes Walton, Pearl Dowe, and Josephine Allen argue that President Johnson used the institution of the presidency to establish policies that significantly aided African Americans in their struggle for equality. Democratic Party leaders, especially southerners in the U.S. Congress, tried to stop LBJ's civil rights policies; they could not. These policies ultimately remade the Democratic Party. Today, the Democratic Party is home to the large majority of the African American electorate and its progressive allies. Johnson transformed the Democratic Party. Walton, Dowe, and Allen use the "native-son" concept to explore how Johnson was able to accomplish this significant task.

Remaking the Democratic Party completes a trilogy of volumes by Hanes Walton on how recent, successful Democratic southern native-son candidates for president fared in their native states. In his first volume, Walton focused on the votes received by Jimmy Carter in his election in Georgia; the second volume concentrated on Bill Clinton's elections in Arkansas.[2] Each volume explores how Carter and Clinton benefited significantly by gaining votes in the region and states of their births. A candidate for public office whose electoral appeal derives from his home state is called a "native son." Using county-level election returns from Georgia, Arkansas, the southern region, and election returns from the nation, Walton persuasively demonstrated the significant ways in which Carter and Clinton's "native-son" candidacies shaped modern presidential elections. Building on the works of his former professor, Harold Gosnell, and works by V. O. Key Jr., Walton's earlier books on Carter and Clinton developed new insights and findings about the impact of native-son candidacies on presidential elections. This book continues the line of research Walton initiated in his work on Carter and Clinton with a focus on Lyndon B. Johnson as a southern native-son Democratic candidate.

In 1960, Senator John F. Kennedy of Massachusetts, the Democratic nominee for president, tapped Lyndon Johnson to be his vice presidential running mate because they needed to win southern states. As Johnson's biographer, Robert Caro, put it, "Johnson's job was to hold the South—or, to be more precise, since Eisenhower had won five of the eleven states of the Old Confederacy in 1956, to win it back."[3] Kennedy's southern native-son vice-presidential strategy was successful. Caro underscored the important role Johnson played in Kennedy's victory.

Before Johnson was nominated, Republican strategists had been confident—a confidence bolstered by poll results—that Nixon would hold all of the former Confederate states that Eisenhower had carried in 1956—Texas, Louisiana, Florida, Tennessee, and Virginia—and would pick up the two Carolinas, for a total of seven. In the event, it was Kennedy who carried seven, while Nixon won only three southern states. Texas and Louisiana were brought back into the Democratic column, and both Carolinas stayed there—by very narrow margins. Together, the Carolinas had 22 electoral votes, Louisiana 10, and of course there was Texas's 24—a total of 56 votes. Kennedy defeated Nixon with 303 to 219 electoral votes. Had those four states gone Republican, Kennedy would have had 247 electoral votes—and Nixon would have had 275.[4]

The modern Democratic Party began nominating a southern native-son vice presidential candidate in the 1928 election as a strategy to "block the Republican sweep of the region."[5] Decades later, after the GOP had developed a significant stranglehold on the South, Democrats developed the southern native-son *presidential* strategy. After 1964 a solid Republican South created a tremendous challenge for the Democratic Party. Democrats had to develop a winning national electoral strategy that took into account the Republican base in the South. A proven Democratic strategy was to nominate southerners as the party's standard bearer. Jimmy Carter and Bill Clinton were the most recent southern Democrats to win the White House. Before Carter and Clinton, however, there was Lyndon Baines Johnson of Texas.

Remaking the Democratic Party concentrates on the native-son variable and builds on the basic procedure developed in Walton's earlier analyses of Carter and Clinton. The focus of this volume is on Lyndon Johnson's campaigns, for Walton, Dowe, and Allen examine aggregate election returns for all 254 counties in Texas. They explore Lyndon Johnson's candidacies for U.S. House of Representatives, U.S. Senate, and U.S. president. In the process, this book provides a historical and political description of Texas politics. Their methodological approach permits Walton, Dowe, and Allen to examine how aggregates, instead of individuals, voted over time for LBJ. With this approach, the authors are able to discern where Johnson's support in Texas came from over time and how it shifted or realigned. In addition, because of Walton's earlier case studies of Carter and Clinton, Walton, Dowe, and Allen are able to compare and contrast the southern native-son variable across three contexts—Georgia, Arkansas, and Texas. For these authors, the comparisons are important because their real purpose is robust theory building of the native-son concept.

Lyndon Johnson's only campaign for the presidency illustrates the appeal of the southern "native son" nationally, beyond the South. Johnson's 1964 victory over Republican Barry Goldwater remains the greatest margin and greatest percentage that any President has ever drawn from the American voter. In fact, in New England, the landslide for Johnson was greater than any other region in the country. Rhode Island, the nation's smallest state, gave Lyndon Johnson a larger margin of victory than any other state, including Texas. Johnson garnered a remarkable 80 percent of the total votes in Rhode Island against Goldwater. He got 63 percent in his native state of Texas.

Just how have southern native-son presidential candidates fared in areas outside the South? An analysis of Rhode Island is revealing. Following the approach employed in this volume, when I break down the aggregate election data by political units and demographic categories, the pattern of the southern native-son electoral support is revealed. The data show that in Rhode Island, Lyndon Johnson's 1964 vote percentage was the strongest among southern native-son Democratic presidential candidates (Johnson, Carter, Clinton, and Al Gore).[6] Al Gore was second, winning 61 percent of the total vote in Rhode Island in 2000.[7] In all the races, the Democratic southern native-son candidate garnered a higher percentage of the vote in Rhode Island than he did nationally. For example, in 1996 Bill Clinton won 59.7 percent of the total vote in Rhode Island, but only 49.2 percent nationally. Gore's 61 percent vote total in Rhode Island was significantly larger than the 48.4 percent he won nationally. In addition, Democratic southern native-son nominees outperformed the GOP nominees in the urban and suburban areas of the state. Again, LBJ led the way. In 1964 Johnson won 86.3 of the total vote in Providence, the state's capital city, and 77.8 percent of the total vote in Warwick, a suburban jurisdiction. No other Democratic southern native-son nominee for president has been able to amass the kind of voter support in Rhode Island that Johnson did in 1964.

A unique contribution that distinguishes this volume on the native-son presidential variable from Walton's earlier work on Carter and Clinton is that he and his coauthors Dowe and Allen persuasively develop a thesis about the capacity of presidents to realign or "remake" their party's agenda and image. Walton and his collaborators make a strong case that challenges one of the dominant theories in the literature about presidential leadership—that presidents are "titular heads" of their party organizations and, therefore, do not have the power to reshape their political parties. Walton, Dowe, and Allen employ the native-son concept and LBJ's record on civil rights to convincingly challenge the "president-as-titular-head" thesis.

As Walton and his coauthors show, President Johnson used the institution of the presidency to put in place policies like the 1964 Civil Rights Act, the 1965 Voting Rights Act, and the Fair Housing Act of 1968, designed to deal with Jim Crow laws. In addition, LBJ launched the Great Society and the War on Poverty to address the material needs of poor Americans, a disproportionate number of whom were Black. Johnson also appointed African Americans to important positions in the federal government. The first Black cabinet member was appointed by LBJ, as was the first Black justice of the U.S. Supreme Court. The authors argue that it was these achievements, led by LBJ, that transformed and remade the Democratic Party. LBJ remade the Democrats into a political party that many of its leaders during that time strongly resisted. The Democratic Party became the party of racial progressives and home for those who wished to advance the quest for freedom that African Americans had fought for since the country's founding.

This book is one of the last that Hanes Walton Jr. authored. He died in January 2013. I am pleased that Professors Dowe and Allen joined him on this project as they were instrumental in bringing the book to fruition. *Remaking the Democratic Party*, like Walton's previous books, makes a tremendous contribution to the political science literature. The scope, nature, and significance of the native-son variable as an important aspect of presidential politics have been critically elevated by this important book. *Remaking the Democratic Party* is great scholarship in the tradition of Hanes Walton Jr.

Marion Orr
Frederick Lippitt Professor of Public Policy
Professor of Political Science and Urban Studies
Brown University

Contents

Preface: On Dr. Hanes Walton Jr.

Dr. Hanes Walton Jr. passed away on January 7, 2013. Walton entered the profession in 1967, which was significant for an African American entering the professorate. Until the 1965 Voting Rights Act, black political participation was severely restricted and Walton set out to study the significance of this new phenomenon, black electoral behavior. He was a complete scholar who specialized in American politics, race and politics, political parties, and elections. Walton began work on this manuscript in 1999, and we are honored that, during the last years of his life, he trusted us to assist in completing this monumental work. We were blessed to have known him and to call him our teacher, mentor, and friend.

Between the second semester of my freshman year and the first semester of my sophomore year (1959–60), my academic and scholarly interest in United States senator Lyndon B. Johnson (D-TX) emerged, which also happened to be the initial year of the sit-in demonstrations in both Greensboro, North Carolina, and Atlanta, Georgia, and especially to coincide with LBJ's capture of the Democratic nomination for vice president. As a rising political science major at Morehouse College, I keenly listened as Professor Robert H. Brisbane, in his assigned readings and lectures, talked about a southerner in such a political position with a liberal easterner, Senator John F. Kennedy, as president. How much power and influence would he have in the forthcoming struggle to integrate the South? We simply speculated.

But in November 1963 our classroom, dining hall, and dormitory speculations became anything but mere speculations and academic exchanges as Air Force One carried the body of assassinated President Kennedy and the newly sworn-in southern President Johnson. Now, what would happen to African American dreams and hopes as promised and captured in President Kennedy's proposed Civil Rights Bill that was launched in part by the sit-in demonstrations? In November, I was now in the initial semester (1963) of Atlanta University's graduate program in political science under the auspices of Professor Samuel Dubois Cook. And many of us were well aware of what happened when President Lincoln had a southern vice president, Senator Andrew Johnson (D-TN). He initially agreed with President Lincoln's suggestive plan to grant limited/partial suffrage rights to qualified freedmen but then later opposed all types of suffrage rights to qualified freedmen in both the federal territories and the states. Clearly this reset the stage for strong opposition in the South and the border states to suffrage rights for African Americans that existed well beyond the four military Reconstruction Acts and the 15th and 19th Amendments. In November 1963 the question for African Americans was whether history would repeat itself with the rise of the first southern president since the Civil War.

Journalist Robert Caro, the Pulitzer Prize–winning biographer of Senator Lyndon B. Johnson, writes in his fourth volume, *The Passage of Power*:

> [O]n the evening of November 26, the advisers gathered around the dining room table in his [LBJ's] home to draft the speech he was to deliver the following day to a joint session of Congress were arguing about the amount of emphasis to be given to civil rights in that speech, his first major address as President. . . . [O]ne of those advisers recalls, "one of the wise, practical people around the table" told him to his face that a President shouldn't spend his time and power on lost causes, no matter how worthy those causes might be. "Well, what the hell's the presidency for?" Lyndon Johnson replied.[1]

What Caro does not say is that, in his first speech to the nation after arriving from Dallas, the new president kept those like myself in great suspense simply because he did not come out for civil rights until the very last statements in the speech. Needless to say, I was not only astounded and captivated but after his remarks was on my way to become a strong Democratic partisan. This southern president would restore our civil and voting rights in America. It was at that moment that I promised myself to one day research and write on the LBJ presidency. Although I would eventually get my master's and doctorate in political science by 1967, my hope to work on President Johnson didn't materialize until 1999.

The University of Michigan's Department of Political Science provided me with a yearlong sabbatical, and I applied for and received a travel grant from the LBJ Presidential Library at Austin, Texas, to travel there and undertake my research project. There I spent the 1999–2000 academic year gathering data and materials on my long-planned Johnson research project. While awaiting my research opportunity, I had chosen to analyze the types of electoral coalitions that had put and then sustained Johnson in office at the congressional, senatorial, vice presidential, and presidential levels. Here was a southerner who remade his political party, region, the Southern Caucus in the Senate, the Senate as majority leader, and passed social justice legislation while the discipline of political science was reinventing its voting behavior methodology from a group-level approach to an individual-level approach. The breakthrough work in political science was launched via *The American Voter*[2] in 1960 at the University of Michigan. This pioneering work used survey methodology and data gathered at the individual level instead of using election return data gathered at the group level. But the older methodology still had viability, especially during those years before 1960 and even in the years since 1960.

Professors Robert Brisbane and Tobe Johnson had taught us at Morehouse College how to use homogenous precinct election return data to analyze candidates' electoral and voting data to explore and assess electoral coalitions at the group level. At Atlanta University, Professor Samuel DuBois Cook, using the V. O. Key Jr. classic, *Southern Politics*, one of a very few books in this period before the sixties, to see how white southern voters aligned with white supremacy candidates or dealigned, and then at times realigned with them. Congressman and Senator Johnson had not been chosen as one of Key's detailed examples. Hence, my need and desire to research this topic. Professor Cook didn't only provide his graduate students with just the stellar research of Professor Key, but also of his mentor; Harold Gosnell. Gosnell's *The Negro Politician* was a pioneering work on how the northern African American electorate voted for African American elected officials in the urban ghetto of Chicago. Key had been one of Gosnell's graduate students at the University of Chicago and had learned and expanded on Gosnell's approach.

But he didn't stop there. On his required readings for the class on the American political process, he listed one of Professor Key's researchers for the *Southern Politics* book, Professor Alexander Heard, who used the same approach as well as some of the data and materials to write his own book, *A Two-Party South?* Like Professor Gosnell's book, this one used election return data in some unique and interesting ways. Thus, this approach, when seen and used in a collective fashion, offered a serious method to analyze and assess Johnson's election coalition of congressman, senator, vice president, and president. And what further cemented my use of this method during my doctorate studies is that I became Professor Gosnell's student during my doctoral studies at Howard University over a three-year period. The use of election return data was the dominant methodology in the discipline of political science for studying elections until the arrival of *The American Voter* in 1960, which launched survey research techniques to allow for research at the individual instead of the group level.

Arriving at the LBJ Presidential Library in Austin, Texas, I soon discovered that not enough survey research data or other materials existed for all of the Johnson elections. To be sure there were a few surveys of several of his elections but not enough to develop a holistic portrait of his supporters. And what little survey data did exist was derived essentially from one of the pioneering polls in Texas that was not highly regarded outside of the state and region or nationally as a poll with highly reliable and trustworthy data. Thus, the absence of this type of survey data meant that the only reliable and trustworthy data had to come from the election return data approach.

Therefore, upon arriving at the library and finding very limited survey data, I had to undertake careful research to try to track down election return data for LBJ's initial special election to the House of Representatives in 1937, as well as the other congressional elections, the senatorial elections, the vice presidential election, and the presidential primaries and presidential elections. Although this sounds simple, it was anything but due to the fact that the state of Texas, like several other southern states, never had or maintained centralized collections of election return data from the sundry candidates in their political process, nor were these data archived and stored in any systematic and comprehensive fashion.

As I soon discovered at the Lyndon Baines Johnson Presidential Library, Texas State Archives, and the public libraries in the city of Austin, whatever election return data existed was essentially collected and published by the Texas Election Bureau, a Dallas-based newspaper syndicate, in a publication series called the *Texas Almanac*.[3] Candidates themselves called in to the Election Bureau and reported their own votes to this body, and then the Bureau would publish said numbers as if they were official. In the state of Texas, this private organization substituted for an official state agency, despite the fact that a State Canvassing Board collected data from some of the state's 254 counties and reported that data to the Secretary of State's office, which did not make such data available in published format. Needless to say, both sources of data have missing county-level votes because neither the counties nor the candidates regularly reported all of their election return data or updated data correctly or at all by the time of the election certification deadline. Sadly, there are missing LBJ elections, as well as missing county-level votes in some elections. In his congressional, senatorial, and presidential elections, primary and general election data are missing. Moreover, in the official microfilmed election return data available at the State Archives at the Texas State Library in Austin, depending on the election, county-level data is missing or is so badly handwritten that it is no longer legible. Hence, at the end of my yearlong research, my election return data was incomplete at the county level or at the state level, or both; it became apparent that I would have to undertake a longer research effort to collect and acquire the missing LBJ election return data. This would take additional time, and I had no idea how much, simply because this data was missing from both the Lyndon Baines Johnson Presidential Library and the United States Senate Library. And it was missing from the Dallas Newspaper Library.

Besides the incomplete election return data record for President Johnson, there was a unique feature to LBJ's elections. He had participated in several special elections, and in "1959, the 56th Legislature amended the state Election Code. The amendment allowed candidates in Texas to run for president or vice president at the same time they were seeking another office. Johnson was able to run for president and seek re-election to his U.S. Senate seat simultaneously."[4] Such elections were not always collected by the Bureau and published in the next *Almanac.* And county-level data were also missing. Finally, I made a request to the United State Senate Library—to no avail as they did not have a comprehensive set of election return data for President Johnson.

Finally, there was the problem, as in most southern states, that the Democratic Party owned the primary election data. Where such data had not been collected and published by the Bureau and was not available in the State Archives, I made a request to the Democratic Party about its availability and possible access to their records. Hence, I learned in a telephone call that the Texas Democratic Party did not have copies of the missing Democratic Party data for President Johnson's primary campaigns. The librarian of the Bureau in Dallas also wrote back and confirmed they had no data available on President Johnson's missing primary election returns.

Upon leaving the Johnson Presidential Library empty-handed, the search led to my researching the papers of his congressional colleagues, especially the Texan and close personal friend, House Speaker Samuel Rayburn, requiring several trips to the University of Houston. I also reviewed well-known election data collections, as well the compendium of the Gallup polls, also to no avail. Eventually, the pursuit and search for this missing data went from a few months and into more than a few years. Finally, I sent a letter to his biographer, journalist Robert Caro, who had his own collection, but I received no response. Therefore, I decided to bring onboard as coauthors two young southern-born and -raised scholars who were and are very well versed in southern politics and who had an interest in the numerous elections of President Johnson.

As luck would have it, I had worked with two such people over my career. One was a former undergraduate political science major of mine who had written a book chapter with me while a senior[5] and was a Howard University doctoral graduate in political science with a specialization in American politics and African American politics. Professor Pearl Ford Dowe had just completed her first book on recent southern politics in Georgia.[6] In this dynamic and penetrating and timely work, Professor Dowe and several of her contributors made excellent use of state-level election return data. And, finally, Professor Dowe, now on the University of Arkansas faculty, was involved in developing and implementing a first of its kind innovative southern politics survey. Thus, I was immensely happy that she had the time and interest to join the project.

Equally lucky is the fact that I had begun a series of research and writing projects with another southerner who had been trained at the doctoral level in quantitative techniques at the University of Michigan and who was a specialist in public policy. Like Professor Dowe, Professor Josephine A. V. Allen is a native of Georgia and was deeply involved in social justice issues that had arisen during the sixties. She too is and was well versed in the impact and influence of President Johnson's social justice legislation, as well as quite knowledgeable about the role of how such election coalitions shaped such issues in southern politics by electing southern "moderates," rare "liberals," and dominant "segregationists" to local and statewide offices in the South and to Congress.[7]

Collectively, we were able to collect from numerous places some complete election data as well as some partial data and report for the very first time missing election return data for President Johnson here in this volume. Such work allowed additional insights into the nature and scope of the election coalitions that elected and reelected Johnson to office and political power, so that he could become the innovative and creative force in southern, regional, and national politics in transforming American democracy and political parties as a nation with a national conscience among mature democracies and as a beacon to those new evolving democracies on social justice issues like civil rights.

Of the three scholars working on this volume, Professor Walton would like to offer his thanks to his undergraduate professors, the late Professor Robert Brisbane and Doctor Tobe Johnson at Morehouse College. Each man is responsible in part for the intellectual richness of this book. Both men were fine scholars and academics in their own manner.

At the master's level there was the ever-erudite professor and later president at Dillard University, Dr. Samuel DuBois Cook. Before, at Atlanta University, his classes and required readings and insights clearly made this volume possible, and his knowledge of social justice issues are at the center of this volume and its research endeavors. In many ways this is a part of his very rich legacy on southern politics.

Finally, at the doctoral level, there were the wonderful insights from the late Professor and Chairman E. E. Dorsey, late Professor Harold Gosnell, late Professor Bernard Fall, and the late Professor N. P. Tillman Jr., who added to their work unique ideas and thoughts on not only southern politics but also on the Johnson presidency. I found it interesting to be in their classes.

Dr. Pearl K. Ford Dowe

I always found President Johnson of interest. I grew up in Savannah, Georgia, and entered public schools in the late seventies. As a young girl I was aware of the challenge of integrating the public schools. This challenge had a direct impact on me and other black children that I grew up in a neighborhood of working- and middle-class black families. Our neighborhood students were often bused several miles away (my middle school was 10 miles away) to schools that resided in middle-class white communities. Very early I understood that our neighborhood was deemed acceptable because we were allowed to attend schools that were considered affluent due to their location and surrounding neighborhoods. As I began to academically mature and incorporate my academic understanding with these types of life lessons and with oral histories of my parents and older Blacks in the community, I realized my generation was not greatly removed from the civil rights movement and the legacy of *Brown v. Board of Education*.

As a result of this understanding I began to know more about the struggles African Americans faced and of the civil rights movement and how it all came about. To truly understand this great social movement, one cannot remove the role of government as an institution that hindered and advanced the movement. I became curious about the Texas president, Lyndon Baines Johnson. My curiosity led me to the LBJ biographies written by Robert Caro. I was enthralled with the complexities of this powerful politician—his insecurities, his knack for the use of obscenities, and intimidation. What I found the most fascinating was his political will. When Hanes approached me about working on this manuscript, I was extremely excited. I was Hanes' student at Savannah State University and I knew he was a master scholar. While I was in graduate school, Hanes informed me that he had begun working on a project on LBJ that would be labor intensive. When Hanes approached me, I knew that he had labored for many years to gather data. I immediately accepted and thought it a privilege to assist him on what could be considered his magnum opus.

My current scholarship focuses on Johnson's legacy—African American political behavior. The incorporation of African Americans transformed society and political behavior. I often teach about party politics and race. To understand the racially polarized voting that exists today, we must revisit the Voting Rights Act and the reinvention of the Democratic Party under LBJ. To not do so would be to dismiss one of the greatest social movements that is embodied within the man himself.

Dr. Josephine A. V. Allen

As a high school student during the Johnson presidency, growing up in a segregated Atlanta, Georgia, I participated in the protests and organizing work of the NAACP Youth Council. We advocated for the benefits of full citizenship and racial/ethnic equality and recognition for citizens, both locally and globally. I followed the courageous positions taken by President Johnson from the signing of the Civil Rights Act in 1964 to the signing of the Voting Rights Act in 1965 to the declaration of a War on Poverty and his vision for the Great Society that were all part of his impressive political career at the national level. While a political science major at Vassar College, during the summer of my junior year I had the opportunity to work as an intern in Washington, DC, in what was then the Department of Health, Education and Welfare. As a result of this experience, I found a substantial calling to champion economic and social justice issues through public policy. After enrolling in the Joint Doctoral Program in Social Welfare Administration and Policy at the School of Social Work and in the Department of Political Science at the University of Michigan, I participated in efforts to increase the recruitment and retention of faculty and students of color as well as to make the contributions of local, national, and global social activists more widely included and recognized across the curriculum.

Through the Black Action Movement, we extended the struggle for equality and social justice at that university. Professors Cedric Robinson, Nellie Varner, Archie Singham, William Ellis, Joel Samoff, Rosemary Sarri, Harold Johnson, and Roger Lind were generous and significant intellectual guides during my graduate education and development in social justice and public policy journeys. I was familiar with Professor Walton's research and publications as well as his professional activities in the development of Black politics and Black political scientists with the founding of the National Conference of Black Political Scientists. When I spent a sabbatical in 2000 at the University of Michigan's Institute for Social Research, Professor Walton and I began collaborating. He very graciously invited me to participate in several projects that captured my interests in social justice, African American political history and activism, with particular emphasis on the experiences of residents of the American South. The invitation to join him on the LBJ project was both greatly appreciated and intellectually exciting. This project captures many critical elements of the social justice emphasis and the history of Black activism and politics that we shared: having grown up in Georgia; having a deep interest in politics; and appreciating the contributions of political figures devoted to social justice and social and economic well-being, both locally and nationally. I am indebted to Dr. Walton. His passion for this work, his commitment to encouraging and promoting students and scholars and his deep love of historical and social justice narratives have been inspiring and I shall continue to pursue the projects we envisioned completing, highlighting the contributions of African American women in politics.

I am currently professor emerita in the Department of Policy Analysis and Management at Cornell University in Ithaca, New York, and Professor of Community and Public and Affairs at Binghamton University in Binghamton, New York. It has been a great privilege to work with Drs. Walton and Dowe on this critical expansion of the native-son theory and to analyze the significance of President Johnson's legislative talent, on this half century anniversary of the Civil Rights and Voting Rights Acts and during the second term of the first African American president. LBJ's remaking of the Democratic Party and his legislation transformed the lives of so many who were not previously allowed to vote, who were denied civil rights, and who during this era have become beneficiaries of the Affordable Care Act and a national health insurance program, President Obama's executive order extending temporary residence to millions of undocumented immigrants, and the restoration of a dramatically faltering economy.

Acknowledgments

In the final stages of preparing the manuscript for the publisher, we would like to thank Dr. Walton's long-time typist, Mrs. Margaret Mitchell, and acknowledge with appreciation the computer skills of Ms. Greta Blake who presented the election return data in a visual statistical manner so that it would be readable and useful to the reader. Clearly, we want to thank them not only for their skills and talents but also for their long dedication on this one project. We also would like to thank Dean Todd G. Shields and Angie Maxwell, both with the Diane D. Blair Center of Southern Politics and Society at the University of Arkansas, which provided resources to produce this manuscript during its final stages. We must also acknowledge Teresa Waddell, Director of Technology for Fulbright College of Arts and Sciences at the University of Arkansas. Ms. Waddell provided necessary technical support during the last revision process. This manuscript would not have reached completion without several graduate students from the University of Arkansas who assisted with preparing the manuscript for press: Misti Harper, Victoria S. Hui, Ethan B. Hunter, Whitley Hall, and Merritt J. Royal. Ms. Royal was a true lifesaver during the final months of completing this work.

Finally, Hanes Walton would like to thank his family, his two sons, Brandon and Brent—especially Brandon, who not only traveled to the LBJ Presidential Library and the University in Dallas but also helped collect some relevant data— his brother, Thomas N. Walton, and his lovely wife, Geanelvin, as well as his brilliant children for their support and encouragement during this long trek to the project's conclusion.

Pearl Dowe would like to thank her family, her husband, Alfred, and daughter, Karen, for their support and love during this long process.

Josephine Allen acknowledges with enormous appreciation the love, care, and support of her late parents, James and Gwendella Allen; her son and his wife, Damani and Sunita Partridge; her granddaughters, Jasmine

Josephine, Mariya, and Jenea; and her sisters, Vynita Thomas and Gerald LaVonne Crowder.

And for any errors found in the work, collectively, we assume full responsibility.

Hanes Walton Jr.
University of Michigan
June 29, 2012

Pearl K. Ford Dowe
University of Arkansas
March 24, 2015

Josephine A. V. Allen
Binghamton University
March 30, 2015

★ 1

Linkages

The Other Native-Son Presidential Case Studies

This Lyndon Johnson case study is a prequel to the initial series of case studies on recent southern presidents James (Jimmy) Carter and William (Bill) Clinton.[1] Ordinarily, this series of studies should have commenced with Johnson, proceeded to Carter, and then moved on to Clinton. Yet the real world of scholarship and analysis is not so neatly organized and structured. Despite the separation of these case studies, they are linked and connected not only because they have emerged from the same region but also because in the pioneering work of Professor Harold Gosnell's *Grass Roots Politics: National Voting Behavior of Typical States* he found that there was a unique feature of group voting behavior in presidential elections that emerged as a larger vote for the native-son candidate.[2] The native son received more votes than expected from his home state under normal circumstances. Later, Professor Gosnell's mentee and student V. O. Key Jr. applied his concept of the native son to his classic *Southern Politics* and renamed it "Friends and Neighbors" voting and also dubbed it "localism."[3] Although this group-level voting characteristic didn't appear in all of the 11 southern states, it stood out as a dominant voting characteristic. If one wanted to analyze the voting behavior of a group for these recent southern presidents, one had to be aware of it and test for it in an empirical manner. Hence, having found this characteristic in the voting for Carter in Georgia and Clinton in Arkansas, one had to analyze the aggregate vote in the Johnson elections for this unique trait.

Following the intellectual emergence of this characteristic in the 1940s, it was placed on the academic shelf due to the rise of *The American Voter* in 1960, which sought to investigate individual-level characteristics via surveys and polling.[4] This new methodology sidestepped the election return data method as well as many of the concepts that were born with that now older methodology. Moreover, it was not until 1976 that another southerner won the presidency, which made it possible for us to revitalize this research agenda. Next came the third southern president in 1992 and 1996. Simply put, there were very few southern presidents.

Hence, 1976 became a major point of departure for this case study series not only because it launched a major participatory event for the senior scholar on this study but also because intellectually, until this point in time, the greatest amount of scholarly research on the native-son variable had been done on local candidates in the South. Although, as we shall see in chapter 3, other scholars had tested the Gosnell/Key variable in other regions of the country, the southern regional variant of this variable dominated the field of political science. Hence, it was essential for us to begin work with a southern candidate.

Second, in 1974 Governor Jimmy Carter of Georgia placed Walton on his Portrait Advisory Selection Committee. Governor Carter selected Rev. Dr. Martin Luther King Jr. as the first African American to have his portrait displayed in the state Capitol. The King family and Andrew Young were invited to the unveiling of the portrait. The Ku Klux Klan marched outside the Capitol in protest, and the three major television networks captured it all for posterity.[5]

Therefore, Walton's insider's perspective on this sequence of events provided him with the opportunity to begin what would become a series of books on native-son presidential candidates with President Carter. His subsequent work on President Bill Clinton emerged because the Carter book came out in the midst of the 1992 presidential primaries, when the Arkansas governor was leading the other candidates for the Democratic Party's nomination. Thus, research for a second book on Clinton began immediately after he had won the presidential election. Despite the two different beginnings of the series, one was ever mindful of President Johnson's position in the native-son chronology. Such is the nature of political science scholarship in the real world.

The Theoretical Paradigm: A Series on the Native-Son Presidential Candidate

Despite their chronological order, these case studies seek to lay the groundwork for an empirically based theory of the native-son variable in presidential elections.[6] Theory building in political science in the postbehavioral era has basically evolved into theory testing at best. The original purpose of developing a solid and well-informed theory has been neglected in favor of case studies and descriptive analyses.

When scholars at Columbia University and later at the University of Michigan launched a series of voting studies, the case studies poured forth. Grand theory building was a major part of these inaugural and pioneering works, but the Columbia group's efforts fell short on this score.[7] At Michigan the "funnel of causality" was introduced as a metaphor and as a guide to grand theory building; but as the early pioneers Angus Campbell, Warren Miller, Philip Converse, and Donald Stokes moved on to other research projects and their efforts to develop a grand political theory ended. The 1968 election study would be the last election study either of them made a major contribution to.[8] Although Miller continued with the Michigan voting model in his 1976 and 1996 studies, these volumes sought to address the standard variables of party, candidates, and issues in new political contexts and times; grand theory building took a backseat to testing.[9] Many of the subsequent case studies that built upon the Michigan model focused solely upon testing their original list of variables, ignoring theory development altogether.[10]

Another series launched by Michigan scholars studied political socialization. Again, while there has been progress and numerous case studies, no overall theory has yet emerged.[11] In fact, work on this concept has stalled, if not collapsed. The originator of this series, M. Kent Jennings, wrote in 2004, "fresh research efforts tailed off. . . . Political socialization came to be assumed, rather than observed."[12]

The third series produced at Michigan resulted in two "quantitative studies of delegate characteristics" at the 1976, 1980, and 1984 national party conventions.[13] Leon Epstein, who analyzed the series, posits that "both books compare the characteristics, notably issue preferences and ideological attributes, not only of Republican with Democratic delegates, but also of each party's delegates with each party's voters . . . Miller and Jennings explicitly put aside the study of convention decision making by delegates" and focused upon "the role of delegates 'as campaign activists.'"[14] However, these two case studies failed to generate any grand theory about regular party campaign activists vis-à-vis issue-oriented reformer campaign activists. Epstein added that "the lesson from the longitudinal data [of Miller and Jennings] is that the relationship is time bound."[15] Yet this series, like the other two, did generate some empirical findings that may eventually lead to more systematic theory development about convention activists.

The three case-study series launched by the University of Michigan pioneers set into motion Gerald Pomper's study covering each presidential election from 1976 to 2000.[16] Each one is an almost self-contained descriptive study with some explanation of what happened in the election under analysis. However, not a single one of these seven case studies comes even remotely close to any theory building. Theory testing, on the other hand, does exist in most of the volumes in the series. From this overview of different series in American politics, a central fact emerges: each is built on case studies, which cover some specific aspect of the political phenomena under analysis. There is theory testing in each of them, and some attempt is made to generate some low-level theory. In nearly every instance there is a set of empirical findings and assumptions, but no grand theory to guide and structure them so that the theory is applicable to another situation. But this is no reason to stop trying.

Linkage: The Carter and Clinton Case Studies

In these case studies on Carter and Clinton, the key variable unique to that particular case was identified and tested, as were the variables essential to understanding the native-son presidential candidate. These variables then were organized into 35 testable propositions and structured into five categories: (1) contextual, (2) national, (3) state, (4) racial, and (5) electoral. (See table 11.2 in the Clinton volume.)[17] These common variables, as well as those that transcend the specific case and can apply across time and place, have been isolated and placed in the table. They have become the bases for the linkage across the case studies.

In addition to common variables, this series has noted the "unique" variables, those factors that are case specific and applicable only to either Carter or Clinton, but which have not been placed among the testable propositions. If they are seen to reoccur in later studies, however, they will be added to the common list. The series has thus generated both common (transcendent) and specific variables as well as formal linkages to the common ones. Some appear in this Johnson case study.[18]

However, the Johnson case is different from those of Carter and Clinton. V. O. Key's *Southern Politics* demonstrated that Texas, unlike Georgia and Arkansas, did not exhibit "localism" or "friends-and-neighbors" voting behavior.[19] Hence, Johnson is unique in that "localism" is not related to the native-son variable in Texas as it is in Georgia and Arkansas. This case-specific reality tells us that a native-son presidential candidate can emerge without the aid of "friends-and-neighbors" voter support. One can only guess what the next case study will reveal on this point.

Although the Johnson study has case-specific variables such as this, it does have common variables as well. Table 13.2 (chapter 13) identifies the unique variables evident in the political context of the Johnson case, utilizing the five categories of testable propositions previously established. These common linkages continue to build across each case study and add to those components that will be used ultimately to develop a grand theory based upon this series.

Throughout this Johnson case study, we refer to the findings from the Carter and Clinton studies, with comparisons and contrasts. At times tabular presentations of these comparisons and contrasts are provided so that the reader can see and discern the relationship and linkages. Nonlinkages also are brought to the reader's attention. In this way the series is connected both theoretically and organizationally.

Ultimately, when there are enough case studies and a representative set of testable propositions, a longitudinal study can be undertaken for the purpose of crafting a broad-based theory about the native-son presidential candidate. Nevertheless, because Johnson came first in the chronological sequence, many of the features of his candidacy set theoretical parameters. Johnson thus serves as a guide to the other candidates, Carter and Clinton. The South generated three Democratic native sons first; this should not be surprising given its long one-party Democratic history. With the Johnson case study, we now have the complete series on these candidates.

This same region has started to generate Republican native sons, most recently President George W. Bush. This should not be surprising given the region's recent realignment to the Republican Party. Part of that story can be found in these case studies of Democratic candidates, especially Johnson, because Texas has produced both of the Republican native sons (the other one is President George H. W. Bush) and the initial Democratic one as well. Hence, the Johnson volume can serve as a guide in the future to the Republican native-son candidates as well.

★ 2

Remaking

What is the impact of presidential leadership? James David Barber, the perceptive presidential scholar, writes:

> The story of our peculiar democracy shows how, from time to time, we have overcome old prejudices and replaced them with new visions. Sooner or later we will shuck off the myths that, in our own experience, prove to serve us ill. Those who tell the story, those who act in it, and those who think through what it yet might mean have the chance to breathe new life into our old adventure.[1]

This insight offers a most thoughtful framework for a robust portrait of presidential leadership. A characteristic feature of presidential leadership is indeed helping the nation to "overcome old prejudices and replace them with new visions," by someone who can "breathe new life into our old adventures" and political institutions. This immediately brings to mind Lyndon Baines Johnson and the Democratic Party.

The Democratic Party provides a link between the domestic crisis of the 1930s and that of the 1960s because it held the presidency in both eras. And these two domestic crises converge in one man, Lyndon B. Johnson. In the thirties he was a bureaucratic and congressional leader as well as a staunch New Deal Democrat; in the sixties he was a presidential leader, and still a New Deal Democrat. The party linked both the times and the leader. And perhaps most important, the man linked the times and the party.

In both roles, Johnson's crisis-based leadership transformed and remade the Democratic Party and through its transformation the Republican Party and some third parties as well. Although the transformation in the 1930s was within his congressional district and later within his home state of Texas, the transformation in the 1960s was regional and then nationwide. The end result was a remade party system, within one presidential term.

Such an alteration of party behavior by shifting the political axis on which the party system revolves is exactly what the popular and scholarly literature suggests cannot be done by a president. As a result, Johnson's unique role in particular, and other presidents' party leadership in general, constitute an underexplored empirical variable in American party politics. Part of the reason for this is embedded in the concept of titular party leadership.

The Concept of Titular Party Leadership

Born in Clinton Rossiter's first edition of *The American Presidency* in 1956, the concept of titular party leadership has traveled far through intellectual space and time. Rossiter's typology categorized the presidency into sundry roles and functions, writing that "the first of these is the President's role as Chief of Party, one that he has played by popular demand and to a mixed reception ever since the administration of Thomas Jefferson." He continued, "No matter how fondly or how often we may long for a President who is above the heat of party strife, we must acknowledge resolutely his right and duty to be the leader of his party. He is at once the least political and most political of all heads of government."[2] Yet, having made this observation, Rossiter concluded that "the party, as we know from the history of a dozen administrations, is more likely to tame him than he is to reshape it."[3] Why? Well, said Rossiter,

> if the opposing party is a roadblock in the path of the President, his own party is at best a drag. . . . Not only must he be careful not to plunge too far ahead or lag too far to the rear of his allies in Congress; he must pay homage to the traditions of his party, select his chief lieutenants from its ranks, act as "honest broker" among its squabbling wings, and endure silently attacks upon his integrity by men who roam the outer reaches of party loyalty. . . . The party that makes him also brakes him—this is the lot, not entirely unhappy, of the modern President.[4]

Rossiter closed his innovative categorization by saying that "the President is the grand sachem of his own party and thus symbol of its hopes and instrument of its principles," but he does not have any power to redirect his party.[5] Hence, he is a titular leader—"the grand sachem of his own party"—a leader in name only.[6]

But no sooner had this concept been created than it came under criticism. In *Presidential Power,* also now considered a classic, Richard Neustadt decried the limitation of the Rossiter categorization and offered another that suggested even stronger support for the "titular party leader" concept: "Lacking popular demand, the natural conservatism of establishment institutions will keep . . . the party organizations quite resistant to reforms that could give [the president] a clear advantage over them." He added further, "Our parties are unlikely to be revolutionized as instruments of government because they are unlikely to be altered fundamentally as voter coalitions differently aligned for different offices in different places."[7] From Neustadt's critical insights, it can be inferred that no president could get the sustained support from the "party-in-the-electorate" to remake and transform his party. To bolster his argument, Neustadt stated that "barring a deep depression or unlimited war, a total transformation is the least of likelihoods. . . . [N]either limited war nor limited depression is productive in those terms."[8] Hence, the concept of the president as only a "titular" party leader remains.

By 1960 these two political scientists had placed this new concept into the discipline's literature and with it the thesis that the president could not transform or remake his political party unless there was some major contextual failure. At best, the president could be only a titular party leader. Soon, however, the concept would pass from its creators into the wider profession, which was on the verge of behavioralism. Before the end of the sixties, the concept would be operationalized so that it could be measured as a functional, if not empirical, variable. In a pioneering article, Ralph Goldman succinctly defined titular party leadership as being composed of "the President and his most recently defeated opponent" coming from "incumbency in the presidency or recent service as the party's presidential nominee [but carrying] no special status in the formal party organization." At this point in the definitional discussion, Goldman declared that "these men are perceived as and expected to behave as leaders of the national presidential parties. Such leadership is indeed 'titular'; it is an elusive political resource for the incumbent, the party, and the nation."[9]

Having created this thin and rather imprecise working definition of the concept, Goldman proceeded to develop a typology of all party leaders (in and out of the presidency) from the first national conventions held by Republicans and Democrats in 1832 through Nixon in 1968 to discern the viability of the concept as well as the "problem" of presidential party leadership. He found not only four types of titular party leaders but also that the president will "seize as many opportunities as possible to exercise his titular leadership in the promotion of party policies and the solicitation of popular support for the party."[10] Nevertheless, titular party leaders, in Goldman's work, have no power because of their informal organizational positions. Goldman agreed with Rossiter and Neustadt, however, that the incumbent president does have more power over the party organization than defeated presidential candidates because the party has numerous semiautonomous units and is highly decentralized. Goldman noted that "party structure at the national level, for example, is a fragmented array of sometimes cooperating, sometimes hostile, sometimes active, sometimes dormant organizational units," which leads to "the incapacity to achieve even a minimal coordination of national party affairs."[11] In a word, presidents have a little more power than the defeated party leaders, but truly little power with which to remake or transform the party. In fact, thirty years after he operationalized it, Goldman revisited the definition of titular party leadership and merely restated it without any modifications: "The President and the defeated out-party nominee are official party leaders in title only . . . [a] title without authority."[12] Although the conceptualization of the term remained static despite party removal from power and upheaval, it had leapt from its originator to the popular and academic sectors of the populace.

Presidential Party Leadership: The Textbook Model

The concept of titular party leadership was popularized when it became included in numerous American government textbooks. Writers of these works took the categorization of Rossiter, Neustadt, and Goldman and passed it on to the next generation of students, particularly younger college students, socializing them into a new way of thinking about presidential party leadership.

American government textbooks tend to take one of three different approaches: pluralism, elitism, or behavioralism. The major elitist American government textbook, by Thomas Dye and Harmon Zeigler, described the concept thusly: "American parties are dominated by small groups of activists who formulate party objectives and select candidates for public office. The choice of party nominees is a choice of party activists, not a choice of the masses of party members."[13] Other than simply noting that the powers of the president include a party leadership role and that the president can control the party through federal patronage and "influence (not control) state and local parties through prestige," there was not a hint that the president could transform or remake his political party or the party system. Although the authors wrote that "technological improvements in the mass media" could strengthen "the role of the president as the party leader,"[14] there was no explanation for this associative statement. In the main, this elitist textbook placed the president as the titular leader of his party in nothing more than a simple management role.

But this was not Dye and Zeigler's last word on the subject. In a 1997 edition, using the same elitist approach, Dye remarked: "Presidents are leaders of their party, but this role is hardly a source of great strength. It is true that presidents select the national party chair, control the national committee and its Washington staff, and largely direct the national party convention . . . [yet] . . . the role of party leader is of limited value to a president, since the parties have few controls over their members."[15] In the 16 years between the two editions, although Dye had not changed his definition, he did shift focus. Now according to Dye, it is the party-in-the-electorate rather than party activists that keep the president as a titular leader. This reversal did not derive from any empirical rendering as much as it did from the fashion in the discipline in the nineties to make the party-in-the-electorate responsible for all weaknesses, inefficiencies, and limitations of the political system.

In contrast, in texts using the pluralism approach, such as a major textbook by Kenneth Janda, Jeffrey Berry, and Jerry Goldman that spans the 1980s and 1990s, one finds these comments about the concept: "Part of the president's job is to head his party. This is very much an informal duty with no prescribed tasks. . . . [N]ational Party Committees play a relatively minor role in national politics, although they are active in raising money for their congressional candidates."[16] Moreover, the textbook added that "American parties have traditionally been so weak that . . . positive trends have not altered their basic character." Remaking and transformation thus are useless because parties are "so organizationally diffuse and decentralized that they raise questions about how well they link voters to the government."[17] However, a textbook of the 1990s noted, "As long as presidents remain in office, they are the chief architects of their political party's fortunes. The Constitution makes no reference to party leadership—indeed, it makes no reference to parties at all—but today's presidents must never forget that their party put them in the Oval Office." It then goes on to say that "a president's every action will either help or hurt that party, and its members will keep a close eye on the president to make sure that their party's ideas and fortunes are promoted." Surprisingly, this text never mentioned the president as titular head of the party organization but suggested that the president must of necessity be a balancer or juggler of roles, simply because "[p]residents who act more like partisans than national leaders are asking for public disapproval."[18] The titular party leader, here, is a tightrope walker.

Another textbook with a pluralistic approach offered in the modern era of divided government the following reflection: "The president often poses as being above partisanship in order to win 'bipartisan' support in Congress. But in pursuing a bipartisan strategy, a president cannot concentrate solely on building the party loyalty and party discipline that would maximize the value of the party's support in Congress. This is a dilemma for all presidents, particularly those faced with an opposition-controlled Congress."[19] This text makes the concept definitely timely. Titular party leadership here is merely a tool in the struggle with Congress.

Other texts sought to be timely by adjusting their definition to match another aspect of the 1980s and 1990s, a period when American politics had shifted from party-centered to candidate-centered politics. One text said, "The president's role as party leader has weakened as the parties themselves have declined in power and influence. . . . In the modern era, the president's role as party leader is more a function of public perception than of party governance." This text, having noted a decline in even "titular" leadership abilities, concluded by noting that "in general the fortunes of the president's party are tied to those of the president. A successful president is a godsend to state and local parties; a failed or failing president can be a crushing burden."[20] Titular party leadership here becomes simply presidential behavior in office. This new twist on an old theme should not come as a surprise, given the rumbling at the time surrounding the possible impeachment of President Clinton.[21]

Using the same titular leadership concept, another textbook merely shifts focus in its definitional bid: "as party leader, the president chooses the national committee chairperson and can try to discipline party members who fail to support presidential politics. One way of exerting political power within the party is by *patronage*—appointing individuals to government or public jobs." To this the authors added: "Presidents also reward loyal supporters in Congress with funding for local projects, tax breaks for regional industries, and other forms of 'pork.'"[22] This is where the authors leave the matter. We are not told how patronage can or cannot affect the president's role as party leader. One thing is certain: there is no discussion of how the president can remake his political party. The unspoken implication is that this is an impossibility.

W. Lance Bennett, in his initial textbook in 1994, took another direction. In his discussion of party leaders, Bennett said, "The American president must balance the role of figurehead with hard-nosed party politician—often a tough balancing act indeed. With the decline of party platforms and the rise of congressional candidates who have their own war chests, the job of rallying parties around a presidential program has become all the more difficult. . . . This makes party leadership challenging, to say the least." Here is the titular concept again, just in a restated form. In closing, Bennett offered the following observation: "Success in the job can depend on how well an individual masters both the ceremonial and party leadership duties of the presidency."[23] While an interesting presentation of the concept, this approach leaves the matter entirely encapsulated within the standard textbook model.

Before we leave the ever changing textbook model, it must be said that one textbook of the nineties omits any discussion of the concept, although it does list it in a table, noting that, as party leader, the president organizes "party support for the presidential program."[24] This text offers the briefest description of the concept ever, reducing the chief of party role to a mere relationship between the presidency and Congress. In this work, the titular party leader concept is almost gone.

Thus, in the half century since it was created, the Rossiter/Neustadt/Goldman formulation has continued to appear, nearly unchanged, in American government textbooks. Although different approaches—the elitist, pluralist, or behavioral—have focused on different features and aspects of the formulation, the basic reality has remained. The president has little power to remake the party. While an incumbent president can reward the party faithful and refill the party coffers, there is no chance that the president can redirect the organization. This is the essence of the standard textbook model. There is no rival idea to be found. The president cannot really express party leadership except in *symbolic* and *ceremonial* ways, which is the point of the "titular party leadership" concept. It has remained static despite the presidencies of eleven individual partisan leaders—Eisenhower, Kennedy, Johnson, Nixon, Ford, Carter, Reagan, Bush, Clinton, Bush, and Obama. Apparently there was nothing in the presidencies of these men or in their times that gave rise to a rethinking of the definition of the concept or its meaning. The question is, why?

Presidential Party Leadership: The Academic Model

Although the popular textbook literature has immobilized the titular party leader concept, the academic literature has on occasion further explored the relationship between presidents and political parties. In 1958, V. O. Key Jr. wrote, "The Presidency provides an organizing center for the party whose congressional and presidential elements ordinarily close ranks for the conduct of the campaign."[25] Yet this proved to be a limited foray into presidential party leadership.

Leading party scholars of the sixties and seventies used an array of behavioral techniques to reveal that the national party organization was highly decentralized into semiautonomous units, each powerful in and of itself.

> We have a variety of national party units for each party, but they are not part of a neat pyramid of power, with the national chair at the top and the other committees and units filling subordinate positions in a party hierarchy. Rather, it is a segmented and pluralized assortment of party units with no clear and precise linkage to each other.[26]

On this structural diversity among the presidential and congressional parties at the national level and their state and local organizations, Samuel Eldersveld and Hanes Walton Jr. explain, "we have a 'co-archy': 'a structure of equal power relationships'. . . . What this means is that there is no central managerial control of the national party, no singular body of power, authority and responsibility. Rather it is a structure of several centers of power and decision making."[27] Regarding the president's party leadership, they noted, "while the president may have a close relationship with, and some control over, the national chair of his party, this has not always been true."[28] This situation is even more of a reality today, given the shift from a party-centered context to a candidate-centered one.[29]

Paul Allen Beck, author of a leading political party textbook, not only echoed the Eldersveld thesis about structural diversity but declared that the executive-led party is harmful in the long run and leads to the decline and disintegration of the party organization:

> [T]he executive-centered party is a coalition of the executive-dominated party in government with the party in the electorate. That alliance, of necessity, bypasses the party organization. The

> identification and localities of voters are not to the party organization but to the party symbols, the meaning for which comes largely from executives and their programs.[30]

Presidents "once in office . . . put the leverage they derive from their position as party leaders into the business of governing, rather than into any concern for the party as an organization."[31] Thus, in Beck's perspective presidential party leadership stops at the national party level, but even this will eventually erode the party's overall organization. Since presidents simply ignore their party leadership role, there is little use in studying it and the titular leader concept, which it generated.

Given the structural realities of the national party apparatus, it took party scholars 27 years to begin publishing on presidential party leadership beyond the titular leader concept. In an innovative and pathbreaking article, Cornelius Cotter broke a static academic tradition. He wrote:

> The record reveals that as president, Eisenhower executed considerable influence over the Republican party and pursued a well-informed and sustained program to strengthen it. Arguably, he was the most constructive and consistent intervener in party organizational matters of any president after Franklin D. Roosevelt.[32]

Cotter noted that Eisenhower, in order to win his party's presidential nomination, had to overcome the party's activities and organizational leadership, which were committed to "Mr. Republican" Robert A. Taft, by using an outsider's strategy that employed a non-party group—"Citizens for Eisenhower."[33] Once in office, Eisenhower began the revitalization of the Republican Party from the top down, starting with the party chairman and moving on to the organization and staffing of the Republican National Committee (RNC) because he felt that "the party, at the national level, was the president's party,"[34] in order to broaden and enhance the RNC's relationship to presidential administrative power. Eisenhower was a pragmatic politician who felt it wise to placate Taft supporters and integrate them into the new power structure. After the selection of what he felt was an appropriate chair, and peopling the RNC with Taft supporters, Eisenhower began the integration of the Citizens for Eisenhower movement into the regular RNC. The president as party leader then moved to use the White House's social calendar and private events to lend support and prestige to the RNC. He also used his cabinet meetings and cabinet affairs to help remake and reshape the party.

Finally, there is the matter of "party-building in the states."[35] In this section of his breakthrough article, Cotter emphasized the role, power, and influence of patronage in linking and coordinating the state party organizations with the RNC. However, Cotter noted that a major problem of Eisenhower's party leadership was the rebuilding of the southern Republican Party: "Entering the 1950s as a set of electorally dormant organizations which existed to barter convention delegate votes for the prospect of presidential patronage, the state Republican parties in the South were established as having electoral significance at the presidential level by the time Eisenhower left office."[36] These solutions to the Republican problem in the South "have tipped the scales toward conservatism."[37] Therefore, "the renaissance of the Southern Republican party strengthened the conservative cast of the national party and facilitated the nomination of candidates who promised to turn the nation around."[38] Thus, President Eisenhower remade the southern Republican party, but in a conservative direction.

Presidential party leadership is more than *symbolic* and *ceremonial* in nature. The Eisenhower case study revealed that the president could remake the national aspect of the party organization. State party organizations could be coordinated by patronage. Discipline, however, was another matter. The reforming of the southern Republican Party led to a transformation of the national organization and a new crop of leaders. Hence, the ability to remake the party was both a blessing and a curse: it could be done from the top down, but there were inherent problems at the regional level.

What these academic approaches left unexplored is how presidential party leadership can remake state and local parties beyond the use of elite patronage policies. Such an approach can generate citizen activists, but little more beyond that is mentioned. Elite patronage policies were discussed only in terms of their role in the reinvigoration of state and local units that had been permitted to disintegrate as opposed to prodding them into lockstep with the national party organization.

Since the publication of Cotter's article, Sean Savage has written two books on presidents as party leaders: one on Franklin Roosevelt and the other on Harry Truman. Of how Roosevelt, Johnson's mentor, played his role, Savage wrote:

> The fact that the liberal Democratic Party developed by Roosevelt's party leadership could continue its electoral success and endure as the nation's majority . . . revealed that Roosevelt had not built a fragile, ephemeral personal following that would quickly disintegrate after his death. Instead, his party leadership and party-

> building strategy under the New Deal had transformed the Party into the enduring majority party among the electorate at large, in Congress, and until 1968, in the presidency.[39]

What Savage discerned from his archival research was that Roosevelt's party-building strategy differed from Eisenhower's. Eisenhower had followed a conventional organizational route to remake his party. Roosevelt, however, tried in the 1938 congressional primaries to purge his party of southern conservative Democrats only to see those he had targeted for defeat reelected.[40] His challenge was not a response to his opponents' policy of racial segregation, but came essentially because of their opposition to his New Deal programs.[41] Savage disagreed with much of the literature on the topic that Roosevelt had failed to reform the party apparatus.

> The purge of 1938, therefore, did beneficially contribute to the long-term, liberal transformation of the national party by dramatically publicizing the ideological-policy differences and conflicts between the liberal and conservative elements of the party.[42]

In short, although Roosevelt's organizational attempt did not remake the party, his "ideology, domestic policy politics and the policy interests of its major voting blocs and interest groups" did.[43] In Savage's view, his partial remaking of his party took a different route than Eisenhower's.

Regarding Truman's party leadership role, Savage wrote that he "maintained the programmatic, ideological and coalitional foundation of the expanded Democratic party and liberal identity that Franklin D. Roosevelt had established . . . through defiant rhetoric toward conservatives in both parties and divisive policy behavior that included vetoing the Taft-Hartley Act and initiating the desegregation of the military."[44] Savage concluded with the observation that "while Truman's greatest strengths and accomplishments as a party leader were his efforts for what he perceived to be his party's long-term ideological, programmatic, and electoral welfare, his greatest weaknesses and mistakes often occurred when his ethos as a party regular dominated his choice of methods."[45] In fact, Truman's party leadership was essentially that of a party regular. He was accepting "of machine politics, staunch loyalty to controversial appointees, straight ticket voting, indifference to rhetorical style, and rejection of presidential primaries as 'eyewash.'"[46] Truman's party leadership was different from that of both Eisenhower and Franklin Roosevelt. He proceeded as any party regular would have except in one fashion—dealing with the conservative southern Democrats. Truman's civil rights programs and policies led to a southern revolt, and eventually he attempted to purge the party of this group, as Roosevelt had done in 1938. Although Savage rejected the criticism of the Roosevelt purge as a failure, his work shows Truman as unsuccessful.[47]

Taken together, Savage's works showed that presidential party leadership can proceed along different lines and does not have to be singularly organizational in nature and come solely from the top down. More important, it revealed that these different approaches led to different degrees of party rebuilding. Roosevelt's approach remade the Democratic Party, and Truman attempted to further this work.

Appearing after the first book by Savage was one on presidential party leadership that covered every president from Franklin Roosevelt to Bill Clinton.[48] Sidney Milkis's book *rejected* all of the preceding theses about the titular party leader concept by Goldman, Cotter, and Savage, and promoted the interpretations of the "new institutional school" of American politics as led by Theodore Lowi. This "school" argued, and Milkis accepted without criticism, that Roosevelt's New Deal policies led to an administrative state that greatly centralized power in the White House and created a new and very strong national-based chief executive, in effect bypassing and subordinating the power of political parties. This made party politics unnecessary, converting partisans into a personal following. Milkis felt that Roosevelt had seriously damaged his own political party.

> The acceptance of a modern concept of presidential power both changed party politics and made them less important in the scheme of things. The elevation of the presidency and administrative agencies to a position of central importance recast parties, so that they were less focused on patronage and local government and more attuned to national politics and programmatic concerns. At the same time, parties were more likely to be defined by presidential politics and governance, thus losing their identity as collective organizations with a past and a future.[49]

Milkis argued that "Roosevelt's party leadership tended towards the development of party administration that would replace party politics with administration. Because the purge and its aftermath confirmed the limits of presidential party leadership," the results of the 1938 election encouraged the Roosevelt administration to intensify its efforts to establish a modern executive that would be released from the constraints of party politics.[50] In Milkis's view, Roosevelt's actions have led every president since to follow his model, and thus even latter day presidents have undermined their own political parties.

Such a thesis clearly breaks with Cotter, Savage, and others who have argued that presidents can strengthen their party organizations. Yet, surprisingly, it fits fairly well into the titular party leader concept that the president is not a "real" party leader. Basically one is left at this point with the need to make a choice between the old concept and this new interpretation. But instead of making a choice, one could ask: What do these theories have to say about President Johnson?

Presidential Party Leadership: The LBJ Literature

We now turn to the scholarship on President Lyndon B. Johnson. Roger Brown and David Welborn studied two of the three southern native-son presidents, Johnson and Carter, and offered a collective portrait on two dimensions of their relationships with the Democratic Party: (1) their performance of the party leadership role, and (2) their party partisanship. They found that of the five presidents between 1961 and 1980 (Kennedy, Johnson, Nixon, Ford, and Carter), only Johnson and Carter were weak in these two areas.[51]

Of Johnson in particular, Brown and Welborn declared, "Johnson avoided a close relationship with the national party organization, because he saw it as a useless and extraneous expense and believed the excessive partisanship it elicited to be 'the enemy, not the servant, of responsible government.'" However, in regard to party partisanship, they noted that, from their evidence, LBJ as a president was "nonpartisan": "Even during one of his numerous outpouring of congratulations to the Democrats of the 89th Congress for its prolific passage of Great Society programs, Johnson chose to temper the partisan atmosphere with these remarks. 'For it is not as Democrats, and it is not as partisans, and it is not as members of factions that we shall prove ourselves worthy of the public's trust, but it is only as free men and only as Americans first.'" The authors concluded, "whereas the Johnson view might be described in terms of the irrelevancy of party, the Carter view is tinged with distrust of party as an entrenched political structure."[52] How did this happen, then, when both "Johnson and Carter came out of political environments dominated by a single party"?[53] As for Johnson, the authors provided as their evidence a quote from his memoirs that the "principal need of the times" was consensus building, which "became the dominating theme of this administration." According to President Johnson, the idea of consensus meant:

> First, deciding what needed to be done regardless of the political implication and, second, convincing a majority of the Congress and the American people of the necessity for doing those things.
>
> I never questioned the capacity or the sincerity, or the ability of a man because he belonged to a different political party.[54]

In Brown and Welborn's view, this need caused Johnson to be a weak party leader.

Sidney Milkis, in his book on presidents and parties, offered another reason for the failure of Johnson's party leadership. He began with the observation that John Kennedy and Lyndon Johnson continued the practices that separated presidents from their parties and contributed to the further "decline of the traditional party apparatus." This decline accelerated under the administration of Lyndon Johnson. Milkis continued, "Johnson had learned from FDR that the full splendor of modern executive leadership required looking beyond the boundaries of party politics, even while promising vigorous and assertive party leadership . . . Roosevelt believed that party leadership should be deemphasized but not abandoned, but Johnson, after 1964, seemed neither to appreciate nor to understand that sort of subtlety."[55] Thus, while LBJ's party leadership was based on that of his mentor FDR and the New Deal, his leadership broke with that tradition and took it much farther.

> Whereas the Roosevelt presidency displaced party politics by circumventing the regular party machinery and emphasizing "nonpartisan" executive administration, the Johnson Administration carried out a much more direct assault on the Democratic organization. For example, the Johnson Administration undertook a ruthless attack on the Democratic National Committee beginning in late 1965, slashing its budget to the bone and eliminating the voter registration division. The president also ignored the pleas of several advisors to replace the uninspired leadership of John Bailey as DNC [Democratic National Committee] chairman. Instead, he humiliated Bailey, refusing to replace him, while turning control of the scaled-back committee activities over to the top political liaison in the White House, W. Marvin Watson.[56]

Milkis concluded, "LBJ's disavowal of party leadership not only threatened the party system, but summoned up a challenge to the modern presidency as well."[57] In the end, the legacy of LBJ's party leadership "jeopardize[d] the already difficult task of electing a Democratic president,"[58] and engendered "a series of reforms that further eroded the link between presidents and their parties."[59] And, one could easily add, it led to the Democratic Party's inability to elect their recent presidential candidates as well. For Milkis, LBJ's Democratic Party leadership was not simply a failure; it was a disaster for the president and the party system itself.

Party scholar Harold Bass Jr. also visited the question of LBJ's party leadership, but in a unique and promising fashion. His case study of LBJ "sought to explore the potential linkage between presidential leadership and party reform . . . [and] considered an instance where a national party convention both nominated an incumbent president and enacted a reform in its rules governing presidential nominations."[60]

Bass's specific focus was the seating challenge of the Mississippi Freedom Democratic Party (MFDP) at the 1964 Democratic National Convention and President Johnson's response to it.[61] The precedent for this effort was the actions of African American Republicans in the South, beginning in 1889, who formed a satellite political party dubbed the "Black and Tan" or the "Lily-Black-Republican" organization.[62] In 1944 the South Carolina Progressive Democratic Party (SCPDP) launched an African American Democratic challenge to the white-dominated state Democratic Party organization, a challenge that served as a model for the fledgling MFDP.

Due to racial discrimination in Mississippi, which expressed itself politically through a local Democratic Party doctrine of white supremacy, African Americans held rival county conventions and at the state level elected a delegation to go to the 1964 National Convention and challenge the regular party's all-white delegation and its governing political philosophy.[63] This challenge was directed to the convention's Credentials Committee, which resolved disputes such as the presence of two or more rival delegates from the same state.

Using a mixture of legal pressure, lobbying pressure, moral persuasion, and media tactics, the MFDP "sought to demonstrate that the Mississippi Democratic party was unwilling to allow blacks to participate in its [state electoral processes], and that it was wrong in doing so. Further, they saw the state party as representative of the large white society in the state, refusing to recognize civil rights for blacks." Party officials and leaders "assumed a predominately legalistic perspective in their attempts to address the controversy. . . . [while] . . . the perspective of the White House was political. . . . Early on, party officials made clear their desires to act in accordance with the wishes of President Johnson."[64] The president met with Senator Hubert Humphrey and permitted him to work out the details of a reform solution. First, the MFDP delegates would be received "as honored guests of the convention," and two Freedom Party representatives would be designated "as special delegates-at-large" and seated.[65] Second, Senator Humphrey would persuade civil rights leaders such as Martin Luther King Jr. to try to convince the MFDP delegates to accept this political compromise to a moral and legal dilemma. The profoundly moving speech of MFDP delegate Fannie Lou Hamer to the National Convention stiffened the resolve of the delegates and their allies; the compromise was rejected, despite pleas from leaders such as King and others. The regular all-white delegation also rejected the Humphrey compromise and walked out of the convention.

However, as a result of this compromise, a special committee was created to see that the problem did not occur in the future. Bass tells us, "Johnson proved vigorous, assertive, and thorough in his exercise of presidential party leadership in this instance. His performance reinforced a fundamental feature of the modern presidency: presidential reliance on White House aides to convey presidential directives to party organizational officials. Further, it demonstrates how modern communications technology, especially the telephone, enables a president to exercise close personal supervision over party affairs from afar."[66] Thus, from Bass's case study, one sees presidential success at least in terms of reform, instead of complete failure. But even Bass qualified his findings of success in terms of one aspect of LBJ's party leadership: "from the party organization's perspective, such domineering exercise of presidential leadership serves to diminish its autonomy and status; and over time it can generate ill will and hostility between the White House and the national party organization."[67] Bass offers no supporting evidence for this contention, and he is historically and factually inaccurate in the article when he writes that "the reform should be seen as the culmination of a trend within the party since 1948, when Hubert Humphrey succeeded in persuading the convention delegates to adopt a landmark civil rights plank, occasioning the departure of several southern delegations."[68]

In 1944, the Democratic National Committee (DNC) leadership had used Congressman William Dawson and civil rights attorney Thurgood Marshall to turn away the South Carolina Progressive Democratic Party delegation before it even reached the door of the convention hall by offering a political compromise. When the SCPDP returned in 1948, they were once again rebuffed. In the history and political science books, including Bass's, the SCPDP's legacy was overshadowed by Humphrey's 1964 triumph.

One finds in the overview literature on presidential party leadership only limited commentary on LBJ's party role. Both the major and the minor literature extol one position: *LBJ was a failure as a party leader.*

> Johnson's talents and attention were mainly in the congressional arena to the neglect of the electoral. From a one-party state, Texas, where political struggles were factional rather than interparty, Johnson was less devoted to party images. . . . As a consequence, he gave little support to the national committee, and in fact cut its budget. His campaigns and leadership were more personal than partisan.[69]

Other observers took the point to its seemingly logical conclusion and declared that his failure as a party leader led to his failure to be reelected in 1968.[70]

But none of this literature arose from the academic study of the "titular leadership" concept. The "failure" literature was rooted in the journalistic coverage of the Johnson White House and its relationship with the Democratic National Committee. Starting shortly after his 1964 landslide election, national newspapers and news magazines began, along with the various nationally syndicated columnists, to note that the president was letting the DNC slide into shambles and that this spelled disaster. Initially these critics used the severe staff reductions demanded by the president as a point of departure and began a drumbeat about eminent party collapse. Then, when the party lost seats in the 1966 midterm congressional elections, the media blamed the losses on President Johnson's refusal to keep the DNC in first-class organizational health, providing proof that the president was letting the DNC stagnate. The media continued this drumbeat until, in March 1968, President Johnson withdrew from the presidential primaries. All of the election postmortems pointed out that the president had let the Democratic Party organization languish, and that this led to his own non-reelection chances. His party leadership had failed at both the congressional and the presidential levels. Herein lie the roots of the scholarly literature, which would emerge in the seventies, eighties, and nineties.

After the Democratic Party's defeat in the 1966 midterm election,

Washington Post reporters Rowland Evans and Robert Novak opened the "party failure" door:

> Not even the angry slap at President Johnson by the Democratic Governors last week seems destined to force the political reform of the President's party so badly needed both within the White House and the Democratic National Committee. . . .
>
> "The Democratic party hasn't been in such bad shape for 30 years" confides an old pro with intimate connections to the President and no sympathy whatsoever for the anti-Johnson recriminations now coming so boldly from the politicians. Why, then is it unlikely that the President will take the necessary steps to rejuvenate his party . . . [because] . . . Mr. Johnson apparently does not want to give the committee an independent power of its own.[71]

However, as table 2.1 reveals, even before LBJ's landslide victory in 1964, journalistic articles were appearing that suggested that he was less than forthright about his leadership efforts to advance his party's internal and electoral strength.

Articles written in 1965 described LBJ as courting one segment of the Democratic Party coalition over another, offering the impression that he was swapping the African American voter for the traditional southern white voter. The implication was that this was poor party decision making and a risky venture for the Democratic Party. LBJ was gambling with the Democratic Party's future.

Within a year, particularly after the party's huge loss of midterm seats, the old criticism of LBJ aligning himself too closely with African American Democrats returned with a new addition—southern white Democrats were now becoming vocal and trying to distance themselves from Johnson. Journalists were again raising party leadership failure, in a slightly different guise. By now the party leadership failure thesis had taken hold.[72]

By 1968, even conservative journalists such as James Kirkpatrick were pointing out how LBJ had failed as a Democratic Party leader. According to Kirkpatrick, LBJ's politics of equality had driven the southern statesmen out of the party, spelling the downfall of the Democratic Party in the South.

With such extensive coverage of Johnson's party failures appearing in the national media, it was only a short time before the same conclusions, simply using different evidence, arose in the scholarly literature. Political scientists and historians used archival data, documents, letters and mem-

TABLE 2.1. The Depiction of LBJ as a Party Leader Failure by Journalists and Newspapers: 1964–1968

Year	Newspapers	Critical Themes in LBJ's Party Leadership Failures	Journalists
July 30, 1964	*Washington Post*	LBJ 1964 Campaign called poorly organized	Evans and Novak
August 11, 1964	*Washington Evening Star*	LBJ is not in contact with DNC	D. Fleeson
August 25, 1964	*The Oregonian*	LBJ as Traitor to Southern Democrats	H. Lundy
March 20, 1965	*Washington Post*	LBJ breaks with Southern Democrats	D. Pearson
April 22, 1965	*New York Times*	DNC holds meeting with Southern Negro Democrats	—[a]
September 25, 1965	*Washington Evening Star*	LBJ gives Negro voters registration to Justice Department, not DNC	—[a]
September 16, 1966	*Washington Evening Star*	LBJ slights Southern Democratic Governors	Paul Hope
November 13, 1966	*Chicago Sun-Times*	LBJ failed to rebuild DNC and Democratic Party	Andrew Glass
November 13, 1966	*Washington Post*	LBJ's Party loses the Midterm Elections	Andrew Glass
November 14, 1966	*Washington Evening Star*	LBJ failed to build National Political Organization	Richard Wilson
November 22, 1966	*Philadelphia Inquirer*	LBJ refuses to communicate with DNC	Ruth Montgomery
November 28, 1966	*Christian Science Monitor*	LBJ seeks New Party Chairman	G. Sperling
December 13, 1966	*Washington Evening Star*	LBJ criticized by State Democrats	Paul Leubsdorf
December 13, 1966	*Washington Post*	LBJ has distanced himself from DNC	—[a]
December 14, 1966	*Baltimore Sun*	LBJ unconcerned with DNC	James Klebba
December 21, 1966	*Washington Post*	LBJ's party leadership lost the Midterm Elections	Evans and Novak
June 1, 1967	*Harrisburg Patriot*	LBJ to woo Negro Democrats	—[a]
June 4, 1967	*Baltimore News-American*	LBJ urged by southerners to stay out of Dixie	Ruth Montgomery
August 25, 1968	*New York Times*	LBJ created disunity in his party	William Shannon
August 27, 1968	*Washington Evening Star*	LBJ drive southern statesmen out of Democratic Party	James Kirkpatrick
August 28, 1968	*Baltimore News-American*	LBJ failure to attend 1968 Democratic Convention is good thing	Bob Considine
August 30, 1968	*Washington Post*	LBJ's actions ruined the Democratic Party	Daniel Broder
September 3, 1968	*Chicago Daily News*	LBJ revolutionized the Party in the wrong direction	Hoke Norris

Source: Adapted from newspaper clippings in various files at the Lyndon B. Johnson Presidential Library in Austin, Texas.

[a]These newspaper articles had no author, which indicate that they were written by the editors.

oranda, and the memoirs of White House staff and both Democratic and Republic Party leaders to describe the relationship between the president and the Democratic National Committee. Added to this archival data, particularly when it was spotty or incomplete, were interviews with party officials and appointees as well as with White House staffers who had party liaison duties during Johnson's presidency. This combined data usually offered a fairly precise portrait of the president as party leader. More important, a great many newspaper clippings extolling LBJ's party leadership failure were now in the files at the Lyndon Baines Johnson Presidential Library. Scholars who used this material were bound to be informed about this perspective, if not influenced in this direction.

Harold Bass initially took the lead in this work. He was both thoughtful in delineating different aspects of this relationship and innovative in his scope. He explored the nature of Democratic Party reform,[73] party leadership transfers,[74] and its national organizations.[75] He was followed by Savage, Goldman, and particularly Milkis, who is unique among this group in that he consistently advanced the proposition that beginning with FDR and his centralized and administrative state created by the New Deal, *all* presidents have become, and will be in the future, party leader failures.[76] In addition to these analyses, there is the less extensive but nevertheless insightful and notable works of Cotter, Robert Harmel, Brown and Welborn, and Lester Seligman.[77] All of these and a few others came to one conclusion: Johnson failed as a party leader.

Yet neither the journalists nor the academics adjusted their remarks about LBJ's party leadership in light of the methodological limitations inherent in the use of archival and interview data. To be sure, the official record can provide a nearly, if not completely, precise description of events. But this approach can be one-dimensional in nature, scope, and ultimately in significance. It provides a perspective on the president's party leadership essentially from the standpoint of his relationship to the national organization, enabling one to see both formal and informal presidential power. Archival data limit one's perspective on the other functional dimensions of the party, such as the party-in-the-electorate and the party in terms of public policy. In these cases an archival and interview approach is too narrowly focused.

Parties are dynamic not static organizations. They are diverse political entities, which official documents cannot alone capture. Few of those writing a description of LBJ as a party leader are forthcoming about their methodological limitations. It is simply not enough to say that the official documents tell the entire story. They simply cannot.

Moreover, none of the subsequent research on single or multiple presidents has linked its finding with the original "titular" concept that launched this research activity. Nor have the findings about LBJ led to any restatement of this concept. In the main, the research and early categorizations have basically remained separated and unconnected. It is as if these findings tell us nothing at all. Slowly, as noted earlier, the concept is being dropped from textbooks. This raises the question as to how useful this concept was in the first place. Now it appears we will never know.

A leading political scientist, Peter Odegard, wrote about the phenomenon before Rossiter suggested that such a role and function would be difficult to characterize in purely organizational and formal power terms:

> Even after his election the relations between a President and his party are largely informal, irregular, and tenuous. As for the party in opposition, we indulge in the fiction that the defeated candidate for the Presidency is the party leader. . . . Even the President's influence as party leader is vitiated by the generally loose character of party organization in this country. . . .
>
> Presidential efforts to enforce party discipline under existing conditions have never been conspicuously successful. Indeed, there are no clear standards by which to measure party loyalty in the American political system.[78]

Historian Gary Dean Best found similar problems in a more recent attempt to apply the concept to a case study of President Herbert Hoover. His study not only supported Odegard's observations but illuminated other debilitating variables: "For Herbert Hoover, the transition to titular leader from President was difficult."[79] The difficulty, Best discovered, emanated from Hoover's own party. "Many Republicans, in and out of Congress, considered it 'good politics' to work with the Democrats to promote the Roosevelt program. This, in fact, appeared to be the view even of GOP chairman Everett Sanders."[80] This intraparty opposition resisted Hoover's efforts as titular leader to criticize the Democrats and their New Deal policies, forcing him to become a "silent titular leader of the Republican Party,"[81] a role he personally preferred. The end result was the lack of any organizational power or mechanism to make his titular leadership effective. This illuminated the importance of both *individual* motivation on the part of the president and *organizational* motivation needed to make the titular concept work.

Taking this array of estimations of presidential party leadership into account, the case studies of presidential relationships with national committees that draw upon official documents and interviews can hope to give us only a limited portrayal of any president as party leader. The problem, then and especially now, is at the level of conceptualization.

Titular Leadership, Presidential Party Leadership, and LBJ as a Native-Son Presidential Candidate

At this point, we have seen that, first, the various models of presidential party leadership have not clarified the initial concept with their one-dimensional methodology, and, second, that they have dismissed LBJ from even remotely being considered as a party leader, describing him as anything but. The question must be raised as to how to address the methodological problem inherent in an archival and interview data approach. Surprisingly, the answers come from one of the promoters of LBJ as a party leader failure and users of the archival data approach. Brown and Welborn were not only quite critical of the one-dimensional nature of their approach but stood alone in pointing out its limitations. In a footnote to their study they declared:

> There is an aspect of party leadership in the Johnson case that is not treated here but which suggest a dimension of the phenomenon that is of vital importance and deserves extensive attention: party leadership through policy-making. Johnson embodied it, pushing the enactment of a Democratic program and one responsive to partisan Democratic views and interest.[82]

Brown and Welborn alone among scholars and journalists made this telling point and in so doing demonstrated that presidential party leadership is at least multidimensional; no one-dimensional portrait can suffice. LBJ may have failed to revitalize the morbid DNC, but there is still his party leadership role as seen through his policy making for the Great Society.

For their evidence, Brown and Welborn drew upon a thoughtful work by James L. Sundquist, *Politics and Policy: The Eisenhower, Kennedy, and Johnson Years.*[83] In this seminal work, Sundquist demonstrated that beginning in 1953 and continuing through 1966 the Democratic Party leadership had developed a public policy agenda in a systematic manner. Despite the fact that the Republican Eisenhower administration was in control of the presidency and that the Democratic leadership in Congress—

House Speaker Sam Rayburn and Senate minority leader LBJ—had decided to work with and alongside of the Republican president, the Democratic Party had created the Democratic Advisory Council. The congressional wing of the party, led by Rayburn and Johnson, had a broad-based policy agenda that would effectively define the Democrats as a distinctive opposition.[84] The Democratic Advisory Council policy agenda, combined with the Rayburn-Johnson policy agenda, allowed for the Democrats to be distinctive in image and public policy in spite of working alongside a Republican president.

In 1954, in the midst of the Eisenhower era, the Democratic majority in both houses began to pass this new and very distinctive legislation. Using public opinion data, Sundquist revealed that even the public saw these two parties as unique and differently focused in terms of public policy. And here, Johnson was moving his party on a unique path. In 1957, Senator Johnson pushed through the Civil Rights Bill. Johnson's party leadership in terms of public policy was gradually taking shape, despite criticism from DNC chairman Paul Butler that Johnson and Rayburn seemed to be closely allied with the Republican president and his agenda. LBJ's retort was that working for consensus was vital.[85]

Sundquist then added the notion of party activists to his theory about presidential party leadership via public policy: "[A]ctivists and conservatives were found within each party, but throughout the period (1952–1966), the activists dominated the Democratic Party and the conservatives, the Republican Party. In the case of the Democrats, the activists control became increasingly pronounced during the fourteen-year span." More important, Sundquist showed that in the same period, "the Democrats had an activist program on domestic issues inherited from twenty years of the Franklin Roosevelt and Truman administrations." In fact, President Truman had added to the FDR legacy with an activist program of his own that included "aid to education, national health insurance, . . . and . . . a comprehensive civil rights program."[86] LBJ's 1957 and 1960 civil rights bills added to this activist legacy.

Kennedy methodically sent forward to Congress most of the program measures to which his party was committed. "Although Kennedy had set forth these goals with a style that attracted the admiration of many Americans, his endeavor to pass legislation that would materialize these goals had been largely obstructed by the congressional opponents of his programs." However, Democratic program proposals initiated under Kennedy became unblocked in 1963 and 1964 by a Congress substantially the same in makeup as the one that had blocked that program two years earlier. The difference was the accession of President Johnson and his use of remarkable legislative skills.[87]

By the time Johnson finished his run, with a legislative accomplishment that was immeasurable for its long-term impact on American society, the Democratic Party had a new and distinct party image. He had given it an extensive "activist approach to public policies—open-minded, innovative, . . . and . . . willing to employ the powers of government." The Democratic-controlled Congress moved "in bold and concrete terms—to outlaw racial discrimination in many of its forms, to improve educational opportunity at every level, to eradicate poverty, to assure health care for old people, to create jobs for the unemployed, to cleanse the rivers and the air and protect and beautify man's outdoor environment."[88] FDR had similarly used public policies in the New Deal to remake the Democratic Party. His lone exception to the Johnson administration's legacy was the lack of civil rights legislation.

But, if civil rights had been dangerous then, Sundquist noted in the sixties, "the political danger of the civil rights issue had been apparent for some time,"[89] and the urban race riots contributed to the negative mood of the country. LBJ had remade the Democratic Party, not only in terms of major social, economic, and cultural issues, but he also had added racial equality. The responses of the Republicans, third parties, and the South in general also remade the Democratic Party, which further remade the American political party process.

The southern leader George Wallace reacted first by reaching outside of the South and building an electoral base in the rest of the country via the Democratic primaries.[90] Four years later, he launched the American Independent Party, which became the first third party to appear on the ballot in all fifty states.

Similarly, Republican presidential candidate Barry Goldwater attacked LBJ's Civil Rights Bill and his activist government and set the stage for the Republican electorate comeback in national, congressional, state, and local politics.[91] A new Republican Party was born. Its rise was driven by Goldwater, Wallace, and later Ronald Reagan as a reaction to the LBJ-remade Democrats.

After a string of losses at the presidential level, the Democratic Party of LBJ became the "New Democrats" under William Jefferson Clinton in 1992 and 1996. As the 2004 election got under way, however, the New Democrats were searching for a new presence, given the loss in 2000 of their next southern native son, Vice President Al Gore of Tennessee, to a southern Republican native son, Governor George W. Bush of Texas. But all of this would shift back when the Democratic Party nominated their first African American, Senator Barack Hussein Obama II, and he won the 2008 presidential election with issues and public policies that led to his own redefinition of the party as the home of minorities and liberal concerns such as health care. Obama provided the continuance of the "New Democrats," initially launched by LBJ, and advanced by Clinton and Gore.

The Missing Political Party Perspective: LBJ as State Party Leader

Unlike those who followed him into the presidency from the South, LBJ not only had served in Congress, he also had served on the state level as an astute, cagey, and successful, if not remarkable, state Democratic Party leader. While students of Texas politics never failed to point this out, few bothered to relate this to his national party leadership or to reconsider the dominant titular party leadership concept. This oversight was indeed uninformative. Ultimately, it meant that the party leadership concept would stagnate and remain basically one-dimensional.

Most of the literature on subnational party leadership tends to dwell on governors or longtime state party bosses as the dominant figures in state party leadership.[92] In fact, despite the voluminous and ever growing literature on Congress, there are few studies on congressional leaders dominating their state political parties. And few did it as well as LBJ.

For instance, if one compares Johnson's state party leadership with that of Carter and Clinton, both of whom served as governors—in Clinton's case, for five terms—they simply do not equal the accomplishments of LBJ in terms of how he assisted and influenced the fortunes of his national party. Not only did LBJ have notable successes with the FDR wins, one Truman victory, one Kennedy victory, and one personal victory against two losses, he even carried the state of Texas for his vice president Hubert Humphrey in 1968 after he had stepped into the political shadows. Carter could not carry Georgia for his vice president, Walter Mondale, in 1984, even though he did help Mondale win the Democratic presidential primaries there.[93] And Clinton could not carry Arkansas for his vice president, Al Gore, in the 2000 election.

By dropping the state political party variable from their analyses, electoral scholars develop inadequate explanations of what occurred in a particular presidential election. Combining the omission of the party variable with that of the native-son state party leader increases the explanatory difficulty and ensures a faulty conclusion about the electorate's choices. The loss of two crucial independent variables significantly reduces the resulting description of what happened in current and past elections.

As Walton has noted in each of his previous books on southern native-son presidents, LBJ, Carter, and Clinton are linked not only by their southern origins and their Democratic partisanship but also by LBJ's remaking of the Democratic Party, which led them, particularly President Clinton and his southern Vice President Gore, to reposition the Party as the "New Democrats," with mixed success. Carter apparently never understood the remade party or the process of reimagining it. Presidential candidate Obama understood it even at the primary level with his description of "change," enabling him to defeat in the presidential primaries and caucuses the most formidable presidential candidate partnership that the party has seen in recent years, former first lady and senator Hillary Clinton and her presidential husband, William Jefferson Clinton. Candidate Obama's "hope and change" seemed much more visionary than Hillary Clinton's experience plus change. She lost.

In order to explore LBJ's unique role as state party leader, we offer in table 2.2 empirical evidence of his part in the factional infighting that took place in Texas's one-party system over the seven presidential elections that occurred during LBJ's years as a politician. As a congressman, he intervened eight times in intraparty rivalries when state party leaders sought to have the state electoral support go to someone other than the incumbent president or party nominee. LBJ's two losses in 1952 and 1956 in getting Texas to support the Democratic presidential candidate were due in part to his less-than-enthusiastic support for the party's nominee, and not so much because of his leadership strength.

O. Douglas Weeks described the political party context in Texas just before LBJ entered the Democratic Party ranks: "A new era of politics began in Texas near the turn of the century. Rather suddenly the Democratic Party found itself without rivals. The minor parties were gone. The minority Republican Party became less and less a factor in state politics, and its presidential vote declined after 1900."[94] This led in Weeks's view to "the complete dominance of the Democratic Party and the full development of a one-party system" in the state. But having given us this portrait of Texas party politics, Weeks went on to state that "the one-party political system of Texas had been under a growing strain since the advent of the New Deal in the early 1930's." When the national leaders of the Democratic Party moved left of center in the economic crisis of the Depression, "a much more definite liberal-versus-conservative factionalism tended to develop within the party in . . . Texas which could less ade-

TABLE 2.2. The Years of Factional Revolts in the Texas Democratic Party: LBJ's Responses and Party Outcomes

Year	Names, Source, and Efforts of Factional Rivalry	LBJ Response	Party Outcome
1940	Vice President James Garner quits as FDR's vice president over a third term and announces for president, then help create "Democrats for Willkie"	LBJ opposes	FDR wins state
1944	"The Texas Regulars" form as a right wing Anti-Roosevelt New Deal Party and 4th term party. They mount a campaign to capture control of the state party. They also set up and support an opposition candidate to LBJ.	LBJ opposes	FDR wins state
1948	"The Dixiecrats" new version of the Texas Regulars. Achieves a statewide referendum in 1949 on the abolition of the poll tax in state and win.	LBJ opposes	Truman wins state
1952	"The Shivercrats" Governor Allen Shivers, a Democrat, coalesces with the Texas Regulars, Dixiecrats, and organizes the state for Eisenhower with cross-filing legislation The "Loyal Democrats of Texas" (LDT) opposition.	LBJ limited opposition	Stevenson loses state
1956	"The Shivercrats" continued to organize for Eisenhower (1) LBJ opposes him by running for the State Delegation Chairmanship, (2) State's Favorite Son, and (3) offers for President. Other Democrats form the Democratic Organizing Committee that eventually becomes the Democratic Advisory Council (DAC).	LBJ opposes	Stevenson loses state
1960	"The Shivercrats" organized Democrats-for-Nation. "Democrats of Texas" organizes and becomes "Democrats of Texas Clubs" (DOTC) and opposes LBJ nomination for vice president.	LBJ opposes	Kennedy wins state
1964	Party factionalism significantly abated because LBJ's former campaign manager, worker, and personal friend, John Connally, is governor.	LBJ supports	Johnson wins state
1968	Party leaders split over supporting either Nixon or Wallace because of national party support of civil rights.	LBJ opposes	Humphrey wins state

Source: Adapted from George Norris Green, *The Establishment in Texas Politics: The Primitive Years 1938–1957* (Norman: University of Oklahoma Press, 1979), 30, 107–19, 171–99; James Soukup, Clifton McCleskey, Harry Holloway, *Party and Factional Division in Texas* (Austin: University of Texas Press, 1964), 5, 8, 13 and 92; O. Douglas Weeks, "Texas: Land of Conservative Expansiveness," in Williams C. Havard, ed. *The Changing Politics of the South* (Baton Rouge: Louisiana State University Press, 1972), 213, 217–19, and 230.

quately be contained within the shell of a single party. Thus splits in the party became more frequent and more vital in presidential, congressional, and statewide elections." These factional splits began to occur in 1936.[95] LBJ arrived upon the state party political scene with his 1937 election to Congress, as table 2.2 shows, and rose to the occasion. Having won his seat as a New Dealer, Johnson opposed James Garner's presidential effort and the "Democrats for Willkie," and kept the Texas party behind FDR's third term bid in 1940. The state delivered its popular votes and electoral votes for FDR, despite Vice President Garner's long political career in the state.

In 1944, when conservative Democrats formed a party calling itself the "Texas Regulars," because of their opposition to a fourth term for FDR, and got a set of electors onto the state ballot, LBJ once again opposed them. They responded by running Buck Taylor against him in the congressional elections, the first opponent LBJ had faced since his initial election. LBJ's friend John Connally said, "They ran a mean campaign against Lyndon in 1944. . . . The only reason they ran him was to try to cut Lyndon up. They knew that he wouldn't win, but they wanted to try to destroy Lyndon." LBJ's biographer Merle Miller observed, "The campaign . . . was unusually dirty even for Texas. . . . Lyndon carried nine of the ten counties in his district, winning easily in the primaries, which left him free to campaign along with the other Roosevelt stalwarts . . . for the president's reelection to a fourth term."[96] Both LBJ and FDR were reelected in 1944, although FDR did not live to complete his term.

After their loss, the Texas Regulars reconstituted themselves, joining with other conservative Democrats and die-hard segregationists to form the States' Rights Democratic Party (more commonly known as the Dixiecrats) in 1948. LBJ backed the party's loyalist faction that pledged itself to Truman and they fought off the Dixiecrat challenge. In this election, LBJ won a seat in the U.S. Senate, Truman was reelected, and the state party stayed in the loyalist camp. LBJ's party leadership role had proved successful for three presidential elections.

However, in the Eisenhower era, the Democratic governor of Texas simply outmaneuvered the LBJ forces, and the Democratic presidential nominee Adlai Stevenson lost in the state in 1952. In 1956, however, the LBJ loyalist forces were ready, and they managed to secure the Democratic Party pledge for Stevenson. Johnson's state leadership, while organizationally successful, was electorally inadequate. Eisenhower carried the state, and Stevenson lost by a larger margin than he had in 1952.

Up to this point, LBJ's leadership of the Texas Democratic Party from his seat in Congress had beaten off five conservative right-wing challenges and had been electorally successful in three. In 1960, however, the challenge came from the left. "From 1958 to 1960 Mrs. Frankie Randolph's Democrats of Texas (DOT) attempted to weld diverse elements into a statewide network, but failed because many Liberals feared being 'labelled' and wished to form broader alliances with moderate groups." The statewide network referred to liberal groups, organized labor, Negro and Latin American minorities, and assorted intellectuals.[97] In fact, during their struggle with the LBJ-led loyalists, the DOT was forced to change their name to the Democrats of Texas Clubs.[98] Next, "Mrs. Randolph's supporters held fast for Adlai Stevenson and bitterly fought Johnson's bid for Texas support in his efforts to attain the Democratic presidential nomination" for himself.[99] But "[w]hen organized labor refused to join the fight against him, [along with African Americans] . . . the DOT suffered irreparable damage."[100] Eventually these groups "contended that it was futile to fight Johnson, and that 'tactical' cooperation with Johnson moderates might prevent conservative control of the state Democratic convention."[101] During the battle at the state Democratic Convention against the liberal challenge to his party leadership, Johnson put down this liberal uprising: "[H]e ordered Texas congressmen and their aides to determine which delegates to the party's state convention were flirting with the liberals, and these delegates, . . . were confronted by their 'banker, preacher, lawyer, congressman, brother, and threatened unless they got back in the fold.'" When Judge Woodrow Bean of El Paso could not deliver his promised delegation support to LBJ, who had made him a judge, Johnson "had the convention's credentials committee decertify Bean's entire delegation."[102] The end result was that Mrs. Randolph was ousted from her position as national Democratic committeewoman, and Texas gave the Democratic Party its electoral votes. John F. Kennedy and his running mate Lyndon B. Johnson won the 1960 presidential election.

By 1960, LBJ's longtime aide, associate, and former campaign manager John Connally was now governor, and factionalism was significantly abated in the state Democratic Convention. In 1972 Weeks observed, "To a large extent this faction, formerly led so ably by Lyndon Johnson and later by John Connally, has been responsible for keeping the Democratic Party in Texas to the right of center or in the moderate center."[103] Overall, LBJ's state party leadership, as table 2.2 demonstrates, gave him success in six out of eight presidential elections, and it enabled the Democratic Party to dominate state politics long after his departure from the political scene. It is one of his great legacies. At the state level, LBJ learned to fight off both right-wing and left-wing challenges and to keep the Democratic Party defined as a conservative party in Texas politics. But the same man would remake the Democratic Party on the national level into one with a liberal image, through his own poverty and civil rights policies. It was his state leadership role that thrust him into a national position and then into a national party leadership role. We argue that there is a linkage, a learning curve.

Figure 2.1 demonstrates this relationship and what it taught LBJ for his rise to the next level of party leadership. Here we focus on four major variables. First is the state variable, reflected here in Texas's one-party system, the Democratic Party. The endless power struggles and factional fights within the party required clever political maneuvering and coalition making in order to successfully reshape and remake the party. Second is the southern regional variable, reflecting the efforts of the South to have the Democratic and Republican Parties adopt a policy of nonintervention in the southern system of racial segregation and white supremacy. This required Johnson to be adept at convention politics, presidential nomination politics, platform politics, and regional bloc voting. The third variable is the Democratic National Committee, reflected in LBJ's personal party leadership as it showed in his campaign fund-raising. For additional insights on this third variable, one needs to look at both LBJ and the 1940 congressional election.

With three weeks to go before the 1940 general election, "[t]he Democratic Congressional Campaign Committee was in a state of near-collapse. . . . Sam Rayburn . . . and Democratic Floor Leader John W. McCormack of Massachusetts went to Roosevelt and told him bluntly that something had to be done, and at once. The President asked for suggestions."[104] He was given one: "that Lyndon Johnson be put in charge of the campaign committee. . . . The next morning Johnson was in charge. He had a secluded office and no official title. His only instructions were to elect Democrats to Congress."[105]

"In 1938, the Democrats had lost eighty-two seats in the House, . . . but polls early in 1940 showed that about sixty additional Democrats could expect to lose their seats in 1940. And the campaign financial picture added to the gloom."[106] LBJ biographer Robert Caro wrote that despite the dire prospects the party faced, "Lyndon Johnson knew how to solve the problem. He himself could provide the party with substantial funds, and he could provide them fast."[107] And he had to, given that only three weeks were left before the election.

Johnson came through for the Democrats. "The Democrats came out of the election stronger than ever. Instead of capturing the House, the Republicans actually lost six seats. "Johnson had been responsible for ac-

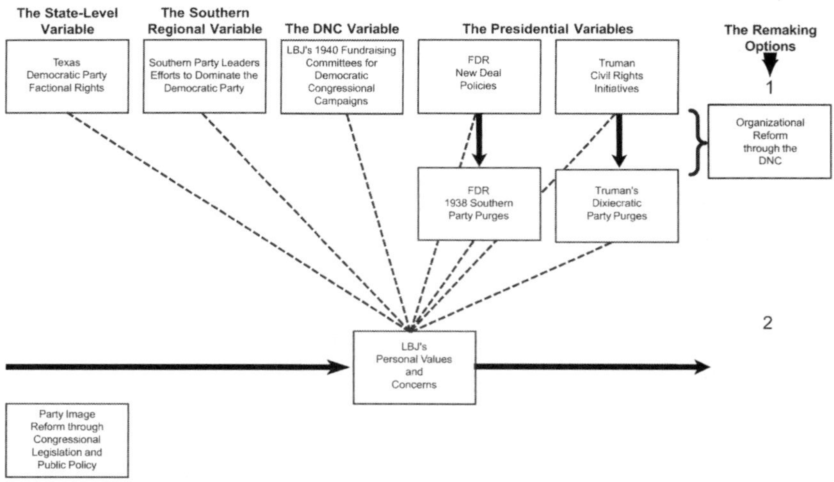

Fig. 2.1. The Independent Variables in LBJ's Party Leadership Learning Curve: The Political Options to Remake the Democratic Party

tively assisting more than 150 candidates for Congress."[108] No party leader had ever seen anything like it. "Lyndon Johnson's work with Democratic congressional candidates had in effect added a new factor to the equation of American politics. . . . The scale of money he raised for congressional races was unusually large for his party; his involvement in other aspects of congressional races . . . was unprecedentedly active."[109]

From this unique experience, LBJ learned that he could bypass the DNC and the leadership of the Democratic Congressional Campaign Committee , and personally accomplish more than the two of them combined. At this point, he had been in Washington for only three years, and he had proved more effective than the entire Democratic national apparatus. Here was a new party leader without formal organizational position or authority. This experience had taught him a new lesson in party leadership politics.

The fourth variable in LBJ's rise to party leadership is the example set by others. FDR used a host of New Deal policies to redefine and remake the Democratic Party's economic image. Truman used civil rights initiatives to redefine and remake the Party's social image. When there were party revolts and objections to FDR's Court packing plan, FDR attempted to purge the party of these nonsupporters by opposing them in various state congressional elections. The result was mixed, and this party organizational reform effort fizzled.[110] Similarly, Truman's civil rights initiatives set into motion the Dixiecrat revolt. When Truman tried to purge the party of this element, his effort also failed.[111] LBJ was aware of both and learned that the DNC could not always effectuate much-needed reform. The party system's decentralized structure did not give the DNC enough power to deal with entrenched grassroots personalities and electoral party officials no matter how obnoxious. However, LBJ did see that FDR's economic policies and Truman's civil rights policies did remake the Democratic Party. Congressional policies do force a party renewal.

The final variable in figure 2.1 is the personal values and interests of LBJ himself for his political career. Earlier in his career, as a teacher, he had learned from Latino children about their needs and from African Americans about their second-class citizenship. He merged these personal concerns with his experiences with the other variables as he made his party leadership choices.

LBJ learned that there were two major choices for presidential party leadership: (1) organizational reform through the DNC, and (2) public policies that reform the party through congressional legislation. His choice was in effect made for him, as Doris Kearns (Goodwin) tells us in her very perceptive biography. When Johnson entered the Senate, "there was no external party influence either on the current leadership or on the process of selection, as there might have been under a strong Democratic President and a united Democratic Party."[112] LBJ did not need the party to attain either his personal leadership goals or the type of public policies he desired. He had learned to maneuver within the party and the legislative branch.

What is ultimately shown in figure 2.1 is that LBJ mediated all of the major variables through his own personal values and chose to reform the Democratic Party through congressional legislation. The social and economic issues of his Great Society program remade the Democratic Party. Even his party reform efforts, which were drawn into national convention politics by the Mississippi Freedom Democratic Party[113] and later the National Democratic Party of Alabama, were resolved using what he had learned. His response was to acknowledge the presence of the MFDP, provide it with symbolic representation, and then play to the strength of the party, the party regulars, and maybe party loyalists, but surely to their past experiences and activism.[114] The party regulars were the battle-worn foot soldiers. Moral sentiment did not dissuade him from understanding and appreciating the role of power and experience in factional rivalries.[115]

But this was more than just LBJ's choice of strategy. Once he made his choice and set it into motion, LBJ's remaking of the Democratic Party also remade the American political process and the subsequent battles that would take place in this new terrain. Edward Carmines and James Stimson tell us that the "anti-civil rights forces . . . had been deserted by the national Democratic party."[116] They add, "In sum, Johnson could have tread softly on racial issues after 1964 in an effort to bring white southerners back into the Democratic fold. That he chose to do just the opposite further solidified the Democratic Party's relationship with blacks but strained even more the party's now extremely tenuous ties to the white South. . . . [T]he post-1964 Democratic party showed not the slightest remorse concerning its past support for civil rights and indicated no hesitation about present and future support."[117] Clearly, these authors put the onus on the Democrats, not the white South. It was the white South that had been abandoned by the Democrats. It was the tender feelings of these racist segregationists that were not appeased. Conversely, it was the inequality and white supremacy of the South that were not tolerated. Carmines and Stimson made it very clear that despite the white South's long hegemony over the nation's principles about liberty and equality, the Democratic Party should not have run roughshod over them. Omitted from their discussion were the years of suffering and violence sustained by the African American community. For Carmines and Stimson, in an ordering of values, the white South was privileged. They summarized their empirical but flawed argument thusly:

> The Democratic nominees who succeeded Johnson, moreover, kept the party on the racial left by adopting tough pro-civil rights stands on a variety of racial issues. The Republican party, by contrast having moved to the racial right in 1964, more or less stayed there after 1964.[118]

Nothing could have been further from the truth. In 1992 Clinton came along and, with the Democratic Leadership Council, repositioned the Democratic Party back to the right through his image of the New Democrat. Then in 2000 George W. Bush of Texas began to reposition the Republican Party back to slightly right of center. The problem here is not that Carmines and Stimson could not see either Clinton or Bush from where they stood (and they could not); they did not even make it possible for them to be seen, for they never recognized the function of the native-son variable nor its southern variant. Although Clinton and George W. Bush were not yet on the political horizon, the brilliant scholarly work of Michael Lewis-Beck, Tom Rice, and Steven Rosenstone appeared in 1983, and that of Harold Gosnell and V. O. Key Jr. even earlier. Beyond the theoretical level, the original New Democrat, Senator Al Gore, appeared in the presidential primaries of 1988, and Governor Clinton was in the wings in Arkansas. Also visible were the early efforts of the Democratic Leadership Council, which was formed after Mondale lost in 1984.[119] Previously, there was Carter in 1976 and 1980.[120] All the indicators were there to consider, but they made no such consideration.

In fact, Carmines and Stimson are symptomatic of the discipline itself, with an overreliance on survey data to explain electoral outcomes, which preelection polls are not really designed to do. A dependency upon polls and surveys drives psychological concepts that explain, if at all, only at the individual level. This is not enough to discern the impact of the southern native-son concept, nor its powerful role and function in the political party system. One southerner, LBJ, in his remaking of the Democratic Party, would reshape the Republican Party as well, due to its reaction to LBJ's Democrats. This made the ensuing political party battle for the last quarter of the twentieth century play itself out around the party legacy of a southern native-son president, LBJ. In the 2000 presidential election, both Al Gore and George W. Bush were responding to this legacy. And by 2009, President Obama used some of FDR's and LBJ'S legacies to respond to the nation's new economic crises and the huge unemployment that it had created.

In the end, to argue that LBJ's party leadership was a failure is a poor conceptualization that refuses to acknowledge that party policy and party leadership are intertwined. Similarly, such an argument refuses to acknowledge that Johnson's party leadership did shape the party leadership roles and functions of his southern native-son successors, Presidents Carter and Clinton. It also ignores the problems that party nominees Humphrey in 1968, McGovern in 1972, Mondale in 1984, and Dukakis in 1988 had in trying to overcome the party image, which they had inherited from LBJ. Moreover, to overlook LBJ's remaking of the party is to overlook the subsequent attempts to do so in the 1992, 1996, and 2000 elections by the New Democrats in their efforts to move the party to the center and toward a public philosophy of moderation, leaving the Republicans to exude extremism. And to overlook LBJ's party leadership legacy is to be blindsided and to lack vision about the future nominations of Senator Obama and Governor Clinton, as well as the minority-majority coalition that won the 2008 and 2012 presidential election.

Finally, as was noted in Walton's book on Clinton, the missing political party perspective requires a conceptualization of LBJ's party leadership so that it is not defined purely in organizational terms but in public policy terms as well. This oversight has crippled the intellectual imagination and the understanding of the role and function of the native-son variable in fixing voting preferences and behavior, as well as breaking up the solid Democratic South. LBJ, as a southern native-son president, remodeled his political party not only for his region, over their strong opposition and dismay, but for his nation as well. And in so doing he redefined the party leadership of southern native-son presidents and presidential candidates for the future. This led to a remaking of the Democratic Party and the entire American political process.

★ Part I

Epistemology and the Native-Son Candidate

To expand the discipline's knowledge base as to how the native-son candidate shapes and influences electoral choice, it is essential that one undertake an analysis of it in Texas. Unlike Arkansas and Georgia, Texas has generated successful and unsuccessful presidential nominees from both the Democratic and Republican Parties, and it has offered a number of third-party candidates as well. Thus, Texas, due to its sheer size and large number of electoral votes, provides more examples than nearly any other state for empirically testing the influence and impact of this factor on voting behavior.

Texas is a unique political context for this variable in another way. LBJ became the first southerner since the Civil War to break through the "glass ceiling" set by the national parties for southern candidates. Before LBJ, southerners could only hope to attain the vice presidency; because of their regional political culture that embraced the values of white supremacy and segregation, they were never permitted to attain their party's nomination as a presidential candidate. In 1964, LBJ won the presidency on his own and set the stage for additional Democratic candidates, notably Carter, Clinton, and Gore.

Indirectly, LBJ's political breakthrough made it possible for Republican southern native-son candidates as well, notably George H. W. Bush, George W. Bush, and other regional hopefuls who are currently waiting in the wings. Both Bushes, like LBJ, came from Texas, and therefore carried the possibility of capturing a large number of electoral votes simply by winning their home state, and like LBJ possibly some, if not all, of the votes of the entire bloc of southern states of the old Confederacy.

To ensure that the intellectual insights, which were derived from Walton's case studies of Arkansas and Georgia, bear further theoretical fruits, chapter 3 delineates the concept of the native-son variable from the theory of localism, that is, "friends-and-neighbors" voting. The pioneering work on the topic by Michael Lewis-Beck and Tom Rice allows us to see these two related variables as the same political phenomenon. Again Texas is unique in that, as Key found in his 1949 classic, localism as an independent variable shaping voting behavior did not exist in Texas, although it was found in Arkansas and Georgia. Thus, chapter 3 separates these two variables and notes empirically what this means for LBJ's electoral efforts and for the theory of the native-son candidate in general.

Chapter 4 explores for the first time the methodological techniques employed in the long search to undercover localism in all regions of the country and within states in the South such as Alabama and Mississippi, as well as in statewide elections, such as for U.S. senator and governor. This chapter offers a comprehensive and systematic analysis of these methodological tests and the findings from them.

Next, chapter 5 offers its own methodology for analyzing the native-son variable and how it relates to the two other case studies and the localism variable as well. In addition, this chapter addresses the question of ecological inference that some readers might want to raise. Of this unique problem, Gary King has written, "Ecological inferences are required in political science research when individual-level surveys are unavailable (for example, local or comparative electoral politics), unreliable (racial politics), insufficient (political geography), or infeasible (political history)." He continued, "scholars began to avoid using aggregate data to address whole classes of important research questions . . . [which] meant that numerous, often historical and geographical, issues were put aside, and many still remain unanswered. What might have become vibrant fields of scholarship withered. . . . The literature's nearly exclusive focus on national surveys with random interviews of isolated individuals means that the geographic component to social science data is often neglected."[1] In LBJ's electoral time frame—1937 to 1964—there were no reliable local and state surveys. And more important, even when these surveys did exist, there were no questions regarding the native-son variable. Thus, the epistemological options were to ignore the matter and leave the variable unexplored or to resort to the use of aggregate election data.

Since King had to rely on aggregate election data, he confronted the ecological inference problem by noting his attempt to "infer discrete individual-level relationships" from election data taken from political units. He explained group political behavior, not individual level behavior; hence the ecological inference problem was not set into motion. The intellectual base of the discipline can expand in terms of which factors shape and influence presidential vote choice at the group level.

Given the South's enormous influence in national politics, academic reluctance to assess it led inevitably to a failure to understand American politics and regional influence in it. In fact, this regional influence held even during midterm congressional elections. J. B. Shannon wrote, "In 1938 . . . the war between the national leader of the Democratic party and state party leaders, focused national attention upon the South's peculiar political system."[2] After an extensive analysis of the 1938 southern Democratic primaries and general elections, Shannon noted what these midterm electoral outcomes held for the president and his New Deal:

> The continuance of the present one-party system in the South operates as a barrier upon the progress of the entire nation since it makes impossible a national cleavage on logical lines. Consequently, it seems to confuse and lessen confidence in democratic processes and encourages the possibility of adopting coercive systems of either the right or left to cut through the impasse.[3]

A failure to analyze the role of sectionalism in American politics in both presidential and congressional politics is a failure in the discipline at the crucial epistemological level. Such, given the rise of southern native-son presidents and presidential candidates, is a grave sin of omission. This study of Texas and LBJ overcomes this epistemological problem.

★ 3

Theory

James Sundquist's empirically based theoretical perspective on presidential party leadership as a function of public policy was not only a significant intellectual breakthrough—it embraced the very essence of good theory building. It demonstrated the necessity of moving beyond one-dimensional explorations and limited methodological approaches. Sundquist's work loosened the intellectual inquisition as should any scholarly work in the crafting of a theoretical model.[1]

LBJ's remade Democratic Party significantly realigned the electoral politics of his region, the South. Emerging from a review of his major newspaper obituaries was the "considerable disagreement . . . as to whether LBJ belongs to the Southern conservative or Texas conservative tradition, or to the New Deal-Great Society tradition."[2] Edward Chester, professor of history, noted that "[d]uring the 1965–6 session he engineered the passage of more domestic legislation during a two year period than any other President in history."[3] Much of this public policy, particularly the civil rights and voting rights policies, drew the animosity of the South. "Many Southerners disliked Johnson because of what they perceived as his abandonment of conservatism as chief executive; to the Richmond *News Leader,* 'He was a brilliant practitioner of liberalism, the most successful ever.'"[4] To other southern newspaper "commentators . . . such as the Norfolk, Virginia *Ledger-Star*, Johnson was little more than a political opportunist who shifted his ideology as circumstances dictated to get elected and stay in office: 'He bespoke no firm principles of government, neither of conservative or liberal (or mixed) proclivities, for though there was something of New Dealish liberalism about his approach, much of what he attempted weighed out as merely a yen to be all things to all men.'"[5]

As these reflections indicate, LBJ's remade Democratic Party seriously altered public opinion about him and his party in the region. This public opinion expressed itself in an electoral realignment of white southern Democrats with the American Independent Party and the Republican Party of Nixon, Reagan, and Bush, changing the political context for southern native-son presidential candidates. But perhaps most important, this is the critical place to commence with theory building about this variable that shaped voter preferences as well as electoral behavior.

The Roots of Theory: V. O. Key Jr.'s Voting Behavior Model

If LBJ's public service is ground zero for theory building about the southern native-son presidential candidate in particular and the native-son candidate in general, then Key's concept of friends-and-neighbors voting behavior is a major point of departure because it envisions the party-in-the-electorate aspect of the American voter. At the basic theoretical level, the friends-and-neighbors voting model establishes the nature of the relationship between the hometown boy and the voters in his community. It also permits an empirical reading of this relationship.

Key reconceptualized the native-son variable of his teacher and mentor, Harold Gosnell, to fit southern local politics. He defined it as "candidates for state office tend to poll overwhelming majorities in their Home counties and to draw heavy support in adjacent counties."[6] It was this feature that Key discerned in the majority of southern states, which he dubbed "localism." In a one-party region, where there was an absence of competition, Key found that "an important place must be assigned to localism. A local potentate or a leading citizen of a county who takes a notion that he wants to be governor polls an extremely heavy vote in his own bailiwick."[7] Key's analysis of southern politics in Alabama noted:

> A candidate for governor normally carries his own county by a huge majority, and the harshest criticism that can be made of a politician is that he cannot win in his own beat or precinct. If his friends and neighbors who know him do not support him, why should those without this advantage trust a candidate?
>
> The controlling factors in voting were local pride and paternalism, reinforced perhaps by county machines and by the candidates' personal followings.
>
> The battle of state politics is not a battle between large factions.

> It is rather a struggle of individuals—perhaps with the support of their county organizations—to build a state-wide following on the foundation of local support. This localism appears most clearly in the so-called "first primary."[8]

Key found six of the eleven states of the old Confederacy exhibited clear-cut characteristics of localism, while the others had none. Thus, other factors must form the basis of local voting behavior there. As Key saw it, these other factors were economic or social in nature and could be set into motion by some crisis that emanated from a candidate's appeal or by a social or economic dislocation set into motion by a governmental or economic crisis.[9]

Moreover, Key adds that party context, in terms of the diversity of factors in each of the states, indicates the lack of commonality. A one-party system is not synonymous with localism, nor does it breed a uniform local voting pattern. Other variables in different geographical systems provide the roots for local voting behavior. This is where Key left the matter but others moved the concept further.

However, before Key closes his initial formulation of the concept of localism as an explanation of voting behavior in the South, he comments on its existence in Texas politics (see table 3.1). Thus, given our interest in LBJ, as well as the fact that localism was a factor in Georgia and Arkansas politics, Key's insight here is central. On Texas and localism Key is reflective:

> Most types of analysis applied in earlier chapters to the politics of other states yield little when used on the Texas voting statistics. The friends-and-neighbors pattern, for example, turns up, especially in the vote of weak candidates. In so large a state, however, a few friends and neighbors make little difference in the outcome. Nor do local followings seem to grow into sectional or regional groupings as happens in other states.[10]

Thus, for the ensuing analysis on LBJ, localism might have played a role in his electoral and party politics but not as it was understood in Key's initial formulation. It might be useful, then, to take a look at other supportive variables in LBJ's political context. The identification of these other variables will be quite useful in developing a full understanding of how native-son candidates can emerge without the benefit of friends-and-neighbors voting support. This also can aid in the development of a comprehensive theory about the native-son variable in American politics.

LBJ as a Native Son and the Political Party Perspective

Localism might not have been a voting determinant in the Texas political process. The African American population was limited to and isolated in East Texas. The Texas Democratic Party, like those in Arkansas and Georgia, did commit itself to the regional thrust by the southern states to capture the national party and limit its sporadic efforts to change the segregation politics of the region. Texas Democrats might not have produced outstanding racial demagogues like the other southern states, taken the lead in the "unpledged electors movement," or for that matter given rise to leaders of third party movements; but they did lead the constitutional fight for white primaries that lasted for nearly three decades, implemented a poll tax and fought against its removal, and opposed the expansion of the African American electorate.[11] The Texas Democrats had one factor in common with their southern partisan counterparts: opposition to federal intervention on behalf of African American constitutional rights. LBJ came to political maturity in a party system that clearly proscribed the state Democratic Party role vis-à-vis the national Democratic Party, unlike the party systems that gave Carter and Clinton power. Nevertheless, Carter and Clinton saw and felt the legacy of their party's past; they also saw and felt the remade Democratic Party of LBJ.

The Democratic Party of Texas had in LBJ's time sponsored a state law that urged the chairman of the Democratic National Committee not to permit duly elected African American delegates from other states to attend the party's national presidential convention.[12] This state law sought to segregate the Democratic National Convention. When this effort

TABLE 3.1. The Southern States with Localism (Friends-and-Neighbors Voting) and the Types of One-Party Factionalism

Southern States Exhibiting Localism[a]	Factional Typology
Arkansas	Multifactionalism
Alabama	Multifactionalism
Florida	Multifactionalism
Georgia	Bifactionalism
Mississippi	Multifactionalism
South Carolina	Multifactionalism

Source: Adapted from V.O. Key Jr., *Southern Politics in States and Nations: A New Edition* (Knoxville: University of Tennessee Press, 1977), 19–277.

[a]Southern States without Localism = Louisiana, North Carolina, Tennessee, Texas, and Virginia.

proved ineffective, the party split in 1944, and one segment organized itself into a third party called the Texas Regulars. Ostensibly the Texas Regulars were opposed to a fourth term for FDR, but they also "adopted a resolution condemning Supreme Court decisions in the white-primary cases and alleged efforts to break down segregation."[13] The leader of the Texas Regulars, Merritt Gibson, later became the national campaign director for the Dixiecrats. Thus began a revolt using third party tactics to maintain constitutional inequality in the state of Texas.

Table 3.2 reveals the use of third-party voting as a protest to the national Democratic Party and its leadership for supporting the constitutional rights of equality for African Americans. In the forties, about 10 percent of the state electorate was willing to engage in this type of ideological voting behavior. Its decline in the LBJ presidential years 1960 and 1964 was indeed substantial, but it continued nevertheless and rose again in 1968. Since 1968 the protest voters have moved into the Republican Party, which has become the main protestor against Democratic Party action.

Long before Goldwater's 1964 presidential race, which permitted disgruntled southern Democrats to join the Republican Party, Texas Democratic governor Allan Shivers led a successful revolt in 1952 to pass a cross-filing law where the voters of both parties were permitted to vote for

TABLE 3.2. The Vote and Percentage for Conservative Third Parties in Texas: 1944–96

Year	Total Votes	Percentage	Third Parties
1944	135,694	11.8	Texas Regulars
1948	113,920	9.1	Dixiecrats
1952	1,563	0.001	Constitution
1960	18,162	0.1	Constitution
1964	5,060	0.002	Constitution
1968	584,269	19.0	American Independent
1976	41	*	American Independent
1992	359	*	U.S. Taxpayers
	217	*	Natural Law
	169	*	Economic Recovery
total	745		
1996	7,472	0.001	U.S. Taxpayers
	4,422	0.001	Natural Law
total	11,894		

Source: Adapted from Congressional Quarterly, *Guide to U.S. Elections*, 3rd ed. (Washington, DC: Congressional Quarterly, 1944), 456–68; 473–78. See also Richard Scammon, Alice McGillivray and Rhodes Cook (compilers), *American Votes 22* (Washington, DC: Congressional Quarterly, 1998), 482 (for 1996 data).

*indicates that the party's percentage of the state vote is less than one hundredth of one percent.

him and others in the primary election. Shivers ran as both a Democrat and a Republican and urged his former Democratic voters to back Eisenhower in the presidential election.[14] It worked, and the Republicans captured Texas's electoral votes in 1952 and again in 1956. Democrats, with a native son on the ticket, recaptured the state in 1960 and 1964.

Figure 3.1 summarizes the key variables at the national, regional, and state levels that shaped the creation of LBJ's presidential party strategy. These variables were identified from numerous biographies and from the host of articles on presidential party leadership and the endless party upheavals that occurred during LBJ's time in public life (1937–68). Several early analysts mentioned LBJ's knowledge of FDR's purge attempts[15] or his dislike of Paul Butler's creation of the Democratic Advisory Council[16] as variables that may have influenced his own party leadership. LBJ was quite aware of the previous Democratic presidents' efforts to reform the Democratic Party by purging specific elements. FDR was trying to purge ideological conservatives, which included southerners and individuals from LBJ's own region. President Truman sought to purge racial conservatives and dealt with questions of party loyalty when it involved southerners rebelling over racial issues.[17]

Other national-level actions came from the DNC chair, Paul Butler, who wanted to shape the party's policy goals when it was the out party but had a congressional base. He wanted the party to take a stronger civil rights position, which would have angered southern congressional leaders and their constituencies. But if these southern legislators would not budge on the issue, pressures to make them do so would have to come from somewhere. The national party apparatus became the needed source of political power.

Beyond these national-level variables stood the southern regional ones. Since 1880, when the South began voting in presidential elections as a solid bloc for the Democratic Party, it had begun a process of trying to reform the national Democratic Party in its own image and to get it to support segregation and white supremacy. It had developed several well-honed political tactics to secure its position. This was the case when LBJ came to electoral power in 1937. Hence, in figure 3.1 we can see some of the major techniques it used to control the national party and its apparatus. Since 1936, when FDR had done away with the two-thirds rule, southerners had fought vigorously to get it restored.[18] At each successive national convention, they sought to have the delegates nominate either a southerner or an individual, such as Adlai Stevenson, who was supportive of the South and would permit their policies of segregation and white supremacy to remain intact.

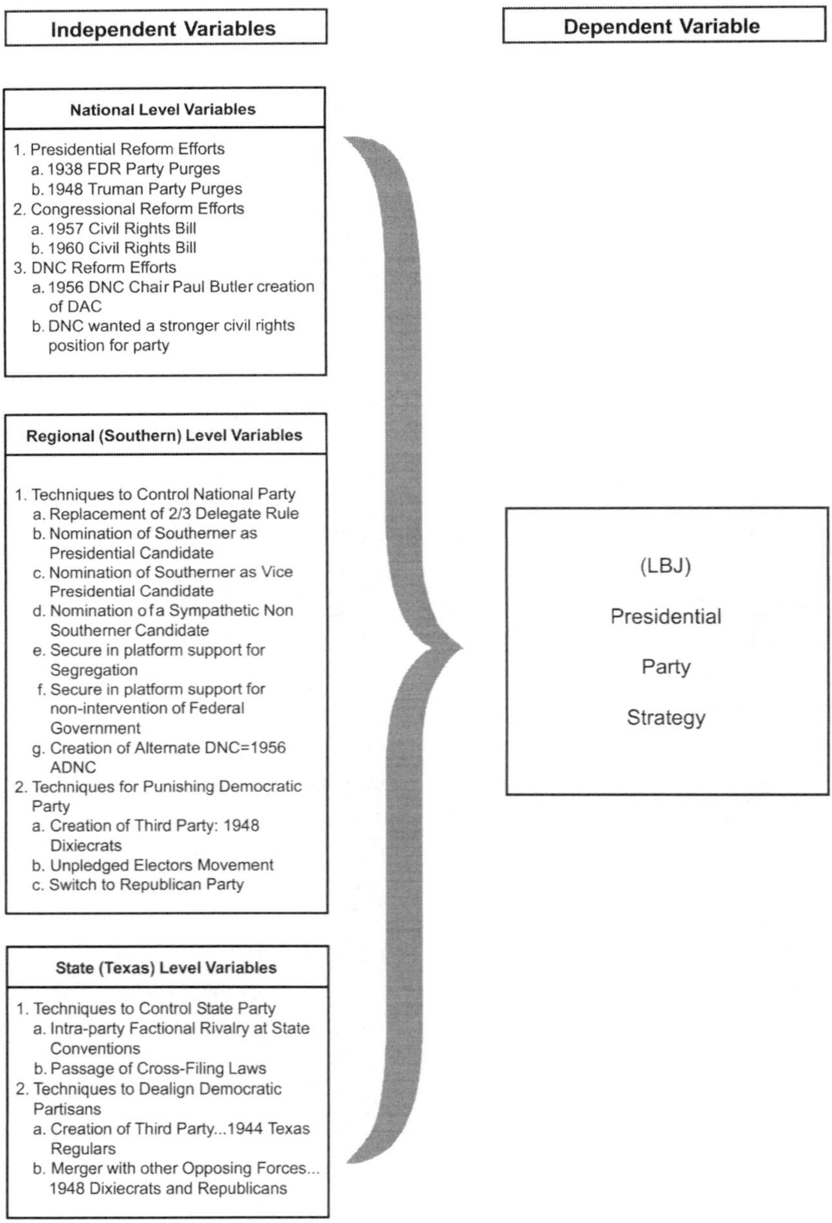

Fig. 3.1. The Independent Contextual Variables Influential in Shaping Presidential Party Strategy

At the national convention, southerners wanted nothing in the party's platform opposing segregation nor anything that might cause federal interference in southern inequality practices, such as antilynching and anti–poll tax legislation. Finally, when the South could not get cooperation from the DNC, it formed parallel organizations, such as the American Democratic National Committee.[19] All of these tactics were used in an attempt to shift control of the national organization, its apparatus, and its nominee toward the South.

The South as a region had a number of techniques for punishing the national Democratic Party for not following its lead and supporting its wishes. The South created several different third parties, the best known of which was the 1948 Dixiecrats. Next was the unpledged electors' movement, in which the Democratic electors in presidential elections were not required to cast their votes for the party's nominee who had won the state. Another tactic was realignment with the Republican Party. These regional-level tactics were designed to capture or control the national Democratic Party. At the state level the thrust was basically the same. Numerous factional groups, particularly conservative ones, tried to capture control of the state apparatus and depose the followers of FDR, Truman, and Kennedy.

Overall, these three types of independent variables—national, regional, and state factors—shaped LBJ's presidential party behavior and motivated him to remake the Democratic Party via public policies instead of organizational reforms, ensuring that this particular remaking would prove successful. By the time LBJ left office, his party leadership had merged economic and racial liberalism. And it was to this remade party that Carter, Clinton, Gore, and Obama would react during their presidential election efforts. It was also to this remade party that the Republican Party and third parties would react.

Unmentioned in this discussion of independent variables is the race variable. Although not listed separately at any level, it is quite prevalent at all three levels. Unlike the other variables, however, race is so interwoven that it would be difficult to set it out alone. Nevertheless, it is a controlling variable.

Linkage: The Friends-and-Neighbors Voting Model and the Native-Son Theoretical Foundation

Jimmy Carter in his initial statewide race in 1966 failed to receive friends-and-neighbors support.[20] Bill Clinton lost in the 1974 general election for

Arkansas's third congressional seat in Garland County, where he and his family had lived since shortly after his birth. In 1976 he ran for state attorney general and won, but his home county gave him fewer votes than it had in the 1974 election. Afterward, the hometown voter support stabilized and continued to support Clinton in all future elections. From this we see that the friends-and-neighbors vote is not always continuous and does not always remain a local force in subsequent statewide elections. Even after Carter and Clinton each became president, their hometown votes fluctuated.

Building upon all of the theorists who have studied the native-son presidential candidate and linking them together for the first time, we can begin to formulate a theory from the resultant composite portrait.[21] As the unique contextual features of LBJ's Texas political environment become clear, it is necessary to revisit Key's original friends-and-neighbors local voting behavior model. Friends-and-neighbors voting can be replaced with issue politics—economic issues in this instance—and give rise to a southern native-son presidential candidate. This model does not appear in all regions of the country; other dependent contextual forces are involved. LBJ arose initially without either of these factors.

Key wrote in the 1940s. Yet the data on Carter, Clinton, and Gore demonstrate that this local voting model can appear and disappear at the presidential level. As recent research on New England reveals, Rhode Island exemplified none of the characteristics of the model in the fifties, but they appeared before the nineties faded.[22] Thus, here is a variable that is not only contextually determined but one that is also dynamic. It is both continuous and discontinuous.

One can conclude by saying that an emerging native-son presidential candidate can rise via (1) friends-and-neighbors voting or, if it is missing, via (2) bosses and machines, (3) issue politics, (4) personality politics, (5) organizational politics, or (6) partisanship. Hence, the diagram in figure 3.2 describes the theoretical insights that the friends-and-neighbors voting model could impart to the theoretical formulations taking shape in regard to the native-son presidential candidate, southern or otherwise. There is a linkage here at both the analytical level and the empirical one. A study of LBJ as a southern native-son presidential candidate offers rich theory building possibilities on localism and party leadership

Moreover, LBJ's electoral journey to the presidency was a pivotal one. Not only was his the foundational starting point for theory formulation about the native-son presidential candidate, but also about party leadership, as his vice president, Hubert Humphrey, tried to succeed him, as did

Carter's vice president, Walter Mondale, and Clinton's vice president, Al Gore. Using Mondale as a point of departure, it has been possible to discern how Gosnell's original concept could be expanded.[23] LBJ's vice president, Hubert Humphrey, offers us not only original insights but formidable comparative insights, given that both Humphrey and Mondale were from Minnesota and both in southern eyes were Democratic liberals. Even after LBJ's departure from national politics, Texas put Senator Lloyd Bentsen into play in 1988 as another potential southern native son when Democratic nominee Michael Dukakis selected him as his vice-presidential candidate. The effort failed, but the theory acquired another data point in LBJ's Texas. Finally, in Carter's reelection failure to Republican nominee Ronald Reagan, another Texas native son, George H. W. Bush, helped realign presidential politics in the state as the vice-presidential candidate in 1980 and 1984 and moved to capture the presidency himself in 1988. Bush faced the paradoxical situation, which Gosnell noted, of two native sons from the same state. In 2000 Clinton's vice president, Al Gore, lost to another southern native son, Governor George W. Bush of Texas. LBJ gives us a window on all of this.

★ 4

Literature

Testing for the Localism Variable in the Non-South

In his now classic *Southern Politics*, V. O. Key Jr. developed an empirically based regional concept of Gosnell's theoretical-based national concept of friends-and-neighbors voting. Numerous scholars have tested for the existence of this variable not only in other regions of the nation but in the recent South as well. However, this fragmented literature has not been drawn together and developed into a composite portrait.

This chapter provides a systematic analysis of this literature and produces a composite portrait of the friends-and-neighbors voting variable, and creates both insight into Johnson and a greater understanding of the linkage between regions and into the concepts of localism and the native-son candidate. Therefore, it is essential that we explore the literature of those who revisited Key's initial formulation in analyzing both southern and no southern electoral political behavior to get some clues about this linkage.

Beyond the Friends-and-Neighbors Concept

Test Cases in Southern Politics

Electoral politics in Mississippi became a test case for the concept of localism. Raymond Tatalovich did a three-decade analysis (1943–73) of the

Democratic Party's vote in the state for elections at every level.[1] Since he wanted to refine Key's initial definitions, Tatalovich operationalized "adjacent counties" to mean those counties near the candidate's home county. Hence, in his analysis of Mississippi's 82 counties, "the inter-county distances had to be calculated for every different county of residence encountered," which he measured by "correlating the percentage of each county's total vote going to a candidate against the distance of each county from that candidate's county of residence." He then removed from his data set "those candidates given extremely marginal or virtually unanimous support."[2]

Tatalovich's data analysis was guided by the hypotheses that flowed from the logic of Key's argument that candidates were likely to receive overwhelming amount of support from their home and surrounding districts. Generally speaking, he found:

> Overall, three-fifths of all elections studied confirmed "friends and neighbors" voting, and this phenomenon was not limited to only a few persons. Thirty-seven different individuals experienced "friends and neighbors" at some election in their careers, whereas only seven individuals never exhibited this electoral base. And "friends and neighbors" voting was found throughout the major regions of Mississippi's political culture.[3]

Of particular interest for national elections was his finding that the twenty Democratic candidates for the U.S. Senate received 65 percent of their votes from friends and neighbors who voted on their behalf.[4]

Subsequent related work on voting behavior in Mississippi has not explored the impact of this variable on electoral outcomes.[5] However, one study did indicate that Lyndon Johnson's leadership of the Democratic Party resulted in the white electorate's partisan realignment in the state's presidential elections. In this instance, localism was shaped by national issues and a national candidate from the region, demonstrating that localism was being reshaped by outside forces on behalf of African Americans.[6] Although the two articles do not say it, when read together they clearly indicate that the realignment of whites occurred because of the changed localism in favor of African Americans. This was a clue to the factor motivating localism in southern states.

In Alabama, Earl Black and Merle Black analyzed the nature, scope, and significance of the friends-and-neighbors vote for George Wallace over eight of his statewide elections and his wife's 1970 gubernatorial campaign.[7] Here, friends-and-neighbors voting was part of five independent variables, which they used to explain the Wallace vote in Alabama. This study also gave a different meaning to Key's term "adjacent counties," which the Blacks interpreted to mean the isolation of "seven geographically contiguous counties in southeastern Alabama, including [Wallace's] home county of Barbour."[8] They operationally defined a friends-and-neighbors county as one in which Wallace received at least 45 percent of the vote in his first primary in 1958 and in which he continued to obtain in each subsequent election a percentage of the vote exceeding his share of the total state vote. After their multiple regression analysis of the seven-county data over eight elections covering 12 years, the Blacks stated that "several generalizations appear in order":

> Note first the continuing importance of the friends-and-neighbors indicator. While the proportion of the variance explained by this variable has substantially declined, the data provide evidence for the persistence of a strong degree of localism in the politics of this one-party state. In this case, a group of seven southeastern Alabama counties has continued to give Wallace a measure of support beyond what would be expected on the basis of their racial and occupational structure.[9]

Figure 4.1 reveals the amount of variance explained by the friends-and-neighbors vote in each of Wallace's eight elections. Clearly, there is a rapid decline in its influence over time. Part of the decline can be explained by the fact the friends-and-neighbors vote is always higher in the first primary than in the runoff primary.[10] The decline in 1966 can be accounted for by the 1965 Voting Rights Act, which increased African American voting and reduced the impact of the white friends-and-neighbors voting. African Americans were not voting for this alleged friend and neighbor.[11]

In 1970, Lurleen Wallace's candidacy effectuated a different kind of voter support and party coalition. While similar, it was not quite the same as that of her husband; hence the quantitative assessments are lower. The Blacks did not note this critical fact.[12] Nevertheless, one can conclude from this study that the friends-and neighbors vote was a powerful factor under certain circumstances in Alabama.

In an earlier study of the voting behavior of the electorate in Alabama, Walter Dean Burnham said, "It would require no small external force acting upon a Southern political community to break down these powerful defenses of local one-partyism."[13] However, he found in the 1962 Senate election that the friends-and-neighbors phenomenon had almost totally

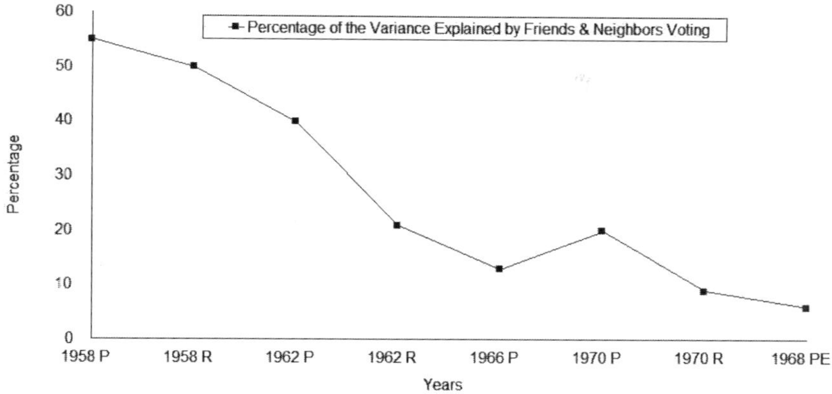

Fig. 4.1. The Percentage of the Wallace Vote in Alabama Explained by "Friends-and-Neighbors" Voting
(Key: P = Primary Election; R = Run-Off Election; PE = Presidential Election. Data from Earl Black and Merle Black, "The Wallace Vote in Alabama: A Multiple Regression Analysis," *Journal of Politics* 35, no. 3 (1973), table 1, p. 734.)

disappeared.[14] Democratic senator Lester Hill sought a fifth reelection. Burnham found that "Senator Hill fared very badly in the counties of his old Second Congressional District; indeed, these counties formed part of the epicenter of the Republican earthquake. If he held Republican gains over 1960 in his home county of Montgomery to a modest 4.3%, Hill still lost it heavily, receiving only 42.0% of its vote."[15]

What caused the disappearance of friends-and-neighbors voting in this election? According to Burnham, it was the Democratic Party's embrace of African American equality and the Republican Party's pledge to make "the preservation of local control over racial relationships" their central focus.[16] The Alabama white electorate's "perceptions of the Kennedy Administration's racial policies . . . [made] the G.O.P. become rather suddenly visible as a meaningful political alternative. It was a weapon which could be punitively employed by aroused white voters against the President and the national Democratic Party."[17] Thus, it made no difference that "only twice had Hill been opposed by Republicans during this entire period of nearly forty years, and even this opposition had been nominal."[18] In the 1962 election, friends-and-neighbors voting made no difference, only race. The Republican Party took a conservative states' rights position on this enduring issue and the long-standing friends-and-neighbors vote simply vanished.

Collectively, these related studies on friends-and-neighbors voting in Mississippi and Alabama effectively demonstrate that there is a limitation to its influence in those states where it exists. But more important, for our purpose, these studies indicate that the national Democratic Party's intervention to ensure the constitutional rights of African Americans caused a massive restructuring of this determinant of local voting behavior. Furthermore, it made the leadership of the Democratic Party electorally responsible for this intervention, making the Republican Party the beneficiary. Two years before the arrival of Wallace and Goldwater on the national scene, Burnham saw the rising tide of party realignment in the 1962 Alabama senatorial election.[19]

The insight gained here is that the race variable had priority in shaping local and regional voting behavior over other important variables operating in the southern political context. Race was central, and it was regionwide, unlike the friends-and-neighbors variable. Race could introduce into an otherwise issueless environment a consciousness that could sweep aside long-standing concerns. The race variable could and most probably would be introduced from the outside—by the federal government via the Democratic Party.

The Test Cases in the West

Books on regional politics in the Rocky Mountain West, Far West, and the Southwest are much different from the books on the southern, eastern, border, and midwestern states. The former tend to be edited volumes rather than single-subject monographs. Although these western regional studies took Key's work as their point of departure when that was possible, they use different organizational and methodological approaches and tend not to have the native-son and localism variables as centerpieces of their analyses and political interpretations.[20] This is also true of the analyses of the states that are two-party states.

Of the four books on the western section of the country, three used aggregate election and Census data to form the empirical bases of their findings. Alfred DeGrazia's *The Western Public* used a 1952 survey of the national electorate. The author revealed in a footnote that "very few of the comparisons made in this book are statistically significant at the .05 level, owing to the small size of the sample."[21] The results were reported anyway, although they lack any precision or predictive ability, making this book less empirically reliable than the edited volumes.

The first book to appear, *Rocky Mountain Politics* in 1940, covered eight western states. It preceded the works by Gosnell and Key, and so the concepts of native son and localism had not yet been published, although some of the individual state chapters made mention of these variables. Frank Jonas's chapter described a case of localism in a Utah election: "a candidate hailing from a leading county can swing the vote in his favor."[22]

In Wyoming, Henry Peterson found that "Wyoming for many years was dominated by family dynasties such as the Careys and the Warrens. These families were able to influence many voters,"[23] another example of localism. This article pointed out party factionalism in the state, the existence of which enabled localism to emerge.[24]

New Mexico's party system was like the one in Wyoming in that it was beset with factionalism. Thomas Donnelly described the bifactional nature of New Mexico party politics thusly: "John J. Dempsey, lone congressman of the state, now serving his third consecutive term in the House of Representatives, is the leader of a second faction of the Democratic party and has a strong personal organization of his own. . . . Senator Dennis Chavez, a native, is the leader of the Spanish-American wing of the Democratic party."[25] However, despite noting this bifactionalism, the author did not link it to any localism in state politics.

In the chapter on Arizona we found evidence of machine politics and party factionalism in the one-party system, but once again no linking of these forces and localism in state voting.[26]

In sum, only three of the eight states described in this pioneering regional volume showed any traces of the political context factors that shaped localism and native-son politics. None of these three authors made any connection with each other's analyses or in their overview assessments. This volume provided some interesting insights about this region's politics but nothing very conclusive about other sectional variables.

One of the contributors to this volume, Frank Jonas, later edited a second volume in which he acknowledged his debt to Key and others working in sectional politics. His 13-state compendium included six of the states that had appeared in Donnelly's work. In the overview chapter, Jonas hinted at the existence of the native-son variable in the region's politics: "For the 1960 results, one may advance the hypothesis that reasons in addition to Kennedy's Catholicism can be suggested to account for Nixon's acceptance in the West. . . . Analysts should not overlook the fact that Nixon was from the West."[27] Nevertheless, in his new chapter on Utah, Jonas found no additional traces of the localism and native-son variables.

The author of the chapter on California, Totton James Anderson, did suggest that localism existed there by noting that "successful candidates build 'incumbent empires' and declare their independence of any party control."[28] However, he did not follow up on these observations.

Hugh Bone, in analyzing the electoral politics in the state of Washington, finds an environment similar to that found by Anderson in California: "Many candidates built their own organization and raise the major portion of their own funds. . . . Personal politics is undoubtedly important elsewhere but more careers are probably based on it in Washington than in any other state."[29] Although personalism and personal political organizations are features of localism and native-son politics, Bone forges no linkage of them here. But before closing his analysis, Bone notes that ethnic enclosures in the state did support localism: "Party leaders and candidate have found the large Scandinavian vote highly independent but a Scandinavian name appears to be a real asset to a candidate."[30] Racially this was also true, for in the largest concentration of African Americans, in the 37th District, "the district has elected one Negro member to the state House of Representatives."[31] Thus, here localism is ethnically and racially based. Some scholars who have found this phenomenon in the East and Midwest call it the persistence of ethnic voting.[32] Yet Bone closes his chapter without connecting these factors to either of the two variables under analysis here.

Charles Beall in his chapter on Wyoming found that "the Wyoming voter is perhaps more independent than the average American voter and more interested in the personality of the candidate than the party label; yet most voting habits parallel those found elsewhere."[33] However, he revealed that localism here was based upon religious affiliation: "A Mormon candidate . . . would find . . . in many communities in the western part of the state his religious affiliation would be of real political advantage, since Mormons tend to vote for Mormons."[34] But that was where Beall left the matter. He offered no empirical data or evidence of trends based on such data to support his claim. It remained merely an observation.

Although only hints and simple observations emerge from the aggregate election-based studies of regional politics in the West, the book using survey data had a chapter devoted to "Native Sons." There he found that "when asked for remarks for or against the Republican candidate for vice-president, Richard Nixon, the Westerners mentioned more positive things. About 13% more people reacted positively to Nixon in the West than in the Northeast or Midwest . . . of course, the factor at work here was Nixon's Western origin. The West was hence more attentive to him; he received more favorable comments for being a native-son."[35] However, we must caution the reader here that these statistical findings did not reach a level of significance.

Beyond the books on the West described above, W. Eugene Hollon's work on the Southwest found nothing about the localism and native-son variables at all, even at the level of observation.[36] One of the states covered in this volume was Texas; and as in Key's classic it did not show any pattern of localism, nor did the author note LBJ's role in helping Kennedy carry the state. In two of the other three states covered by this volume, New Mexico and Arizona, no trace of localism was found, even though earlier volumes had found a few traces of it.

Taking all of these volumes on the western section of the country collectively, one finds only scattered references to localism, and none of these observations are fully developed. They are simply offered as insights. However, the exception in terms of the native-son variable is California. This is hinted at in one study where a further systematic analysis of it was made.

Political scientists Eugene Lee and William Buchanan extracted the friends-and-neighbors concept and imported it to their analysis of the 1960 California presidential election: "California gave 50.3 percent of its two-party vote to Richard M. Nixon, just four-tenths of one per cent more than the nation, but enough to switch the state's electoral vote into the Republican column."[37] Using this as a test case, the authors discussed the impact of friends-and-neighbors voting by arguing, "It is assumed that presidential candidates are chosen from populous, doubtful states so that the extra fillip of pride in a 'local boy' will win a few votes that a more remote candidate could not obtain. Nixon carried California by so narrow a margin that the soundness of the GOP's strategy must be admired. . . . A rough estimate of what he added to the Republican ticket may be secured by noting the percentage difference between the national and state vote for president. The state vote should be higher when a Californian is on the ticket."[38] Table 4.1 demonstrates this in empirical terms. Although Nixon's pulling power as a native son was not extremely strong as a California native son, it did help the Republican Party carry the state in 1960 and turned the Kennedy-Johnson victory into a wafer-thin one.

Insights from this case suggest that nationally prominent native sons—in this case Nixon had been a vice president, a senator, and a member of the House of Representatives—do not always have the same influence upon the home-state electorate as other candidates. Lee and Buchanan find that specific characteristics of the candidate's personality and performance in office could have an impact as well. This can be seen in the drop in state support for Hoover between the 1928 and the 1932 elections. But what doesn't show up in this analysis is the Democratic Party's support of constitutional equality for African Americans and how that influenced friends-and-neighbors voting behavior in the state.

The Test Case in New England

Duane Lockard imported Key's friends-and-neighbors concept to his analysis of the six states in the New England area,[39] reporting on the phenomenon in four of these six states. Of Vermont, Lockard wrote the following: "Since Vermont is the most one-party-dominated state north of the Mason Dixon line, it is interesting to compare the operations of Vermont's Republican party with the tactics of the Democratic party in the Southern states." Lockard noted that Key characterized one-party politics in the South as "a tendency to emphasize personalities instead of issues in running for office."[40] Lockard added:

> In the Southern multifactional states, according to Key, localism plays an important role in deciding primary elections. Where personality is emphasized above policy, the contacts of the candidate with the people take on an exaggerated importance. Since his connections are greatest in his own home area the candidate is likely to pull a very strong local vote.[41]

At this point, Lockard raised the central question, "How important is localism or 'friends and neighbors' [voting] in Vermont?" He answered by

TABLE 4.1. The California Vote Percentage Difference from U.S. Vote Percentage for President with a Native-Son on Ticket: 1928–60

Year	California on the Ticket	No Californian on the Ticket
1928	+4.6% (Hoover)	
1932	−2.1% (Hoover)	
1936		−5.4%
1940		−3.1%
1944		−3.0%
1948	+2.1% (Warren)	
1952	+1.5% (Nixon)	
1956	−2.4% (Nixon)	
1960	+0.4% (Nixon)	

Source: Eugene Lee and William Buchanan, "The 1960 Election in California," *Western Political Quarterly* 14 (March 1961): 314, table 1.

saying, "It has some effect, to be sure, but nothing like the patterns of the multifactional parties in the South. Localism showed up in the Home counties of most candidates in recent elections, but equally or more important was the bifactional division in the party." In short, the "'friends and neighbors' pull was reinforced by factional pulls—that is, the candidate was from the area in which his faction had its greatest strength."[42] Overall, the friends-and-neighbors variable was of limited scope in Vermont, and race did not influence or affect it.[43]

Over in New Hampshire, "localism has some effect on New Hampshire Republican primaries, although in recent factional battles the degree of exaggeration of local pluralities has not been really excessive. . . . There is little if any tendency toward geographic alignment."[44] But this is not the historical pattern in Maine, where at least in "gubernatorial and senatorial contests . . . in most primaries the 'friends and neighbors' pull for local candidates is present to a remarkable extent." This leads Lockard to conclude, "Even though it is not always present to an extreme degree, the 'friends and neighbors' attraction is far greater in Maine politics than in Vermont or New Hampshire."[45]

Finally, in Massachusetts, "the analysis of the 1950 gubernatorial primary does not indicate that the 'friends and neighbors' factor was decisive by any means, although it apparently has some minor influence."[46] Another statewide candidate, Clarence Barnes, had a "locally restricted following. . . . He led in his own county and the Cape Cod, Martha's Vineyard, and Nantucket regions." Nevertheless, Lockard discerned that the friends-and-neighbors explanation did not fit the facts. "Other more persuasive forces were decisive." Of these, he argued that "the blessings of the organization . . . were more crucial than residence."[47]

To be sure, these four New England states had varying degrees of friends-and-neighbors voting behavior, but such behavior was not undercut by the race variable. Differing patterns of an in-state party factionalism tended to determine the nature, scope, and significance of these variables.[48]

Lockard conducted his study in the fifties. Robert Speel, writing more recently about New England state politics, noted that the friends-and-neighbors syndrome continued into the 1990s in Vermont and to some extent in Rhode Island.[49]

The Test Case in the Midwest

We now move to the Midwest and the politics of the six states that comprise the region: Michigan, Wisconsin, Minnesota, Ohio, Indiana, and Illinois. There is no need to pursue the friends-and-neighbors concept there because this is a competitive two-party region and, essentially, the friends-and-neighbors concept arises out of one-party, issueless politics. Nothing of the sort exists in the Midwest.[50]

John Fenton, one of Key's students, produced two regional studies: one on the border states and one on the Midwest.[51] Both employed the statistical techniques and methods used by Key in *Southern Politics*, yet Fenton was unable to locate any friends-and-neighbors voting patterns. Such voting behavior was not a political base for entrance into electoral office. According to Fenton, "three of the states (Michigan, Wisconsin, and Minnesota) were rather widely represented as possessing programmatic or issue-oriented parties; and the other three states (Ohio, Indiana, and Illinois) were equally widely advertised as states with 'traditional' or job-oriented parties."[52] Since the two-party system was the norm and not the exception, the friends-and-neighbors variable was of little consequence.

But the race variable was an important factor in the Midwest, particularly in the large urban centers. It made its presence felt in Democratic Party circles especially because of the large number of Blacks in the auto industry workforce in Detroit. Along with labor leaders and statewide politicians, the Michigan Democratic Party began to have an impact on the national Democratic organization, especially the "liberal wing of the party rather than the labor wing."[53]

In other states in the region such as Indiana, African Americans didn't organize into a strong labor coalition that influenced the Democratic Party in a liberal direction. "The influx of immigrants and Negroes into the Democratic party frightened native whites out of the party."[54] This led to a job-oriented party that emphasized employment and unemployment concerns, giving the workingman's orientation of the Democrats a major advantage. These types of issues removed friends-and-neighbors voting to a minor place in Midwest politics. The presence of the race variable did have an impact, particularly during the 1964 presidential race.

Many of the midwestern states had been settled by southerners, who had pro-Confederate sympathies that were expressed through the Copperhead movement during the Civil War.[55] In fact, a significant portion of the Copperhead movement leadership, notably Clement L. Vallandigham of Ohio, had come from this midwestern region. Therefore, when George Wallace went north in the 1964 Democratic primaries, his greatest support was found in several of the states of the Midwest.[56] Race here had created an electoral cleavage in the Democratic electorate. Thus, LBJ as a southern native son, even in the absence of a friends-and-neighbors voting pattern and in an area where a southern regional consciousness had existed since the Civil War, would lose Democratic Party support.

The Test Case in the Border States

In the border states—Maryland, West Virginia, Kentucky, and Missouri—Fenton found that the poverty of the region shaped the behavior of the political parties and the electorate in unusual and significant ways. Geography as a determinant of voting behavior was not as dominant here as were economic forces. Party organization thus became critical because it was needed to manage and manipulate the vote via patronage and contracts in the low-income counties and in the growing urban centers of these states. He found that "the Democratic 'organization' . . . controls a body of votes in Democratic primaries which is relatively independent of the social and economic groupings of the party. This vote is derived primarily from the rural low income counties of the state."[57] This, then, rather than the friends-and-neighbors vote, was the road to political emergence and electoral victory in the region.

In the border states, powerful individual leaders, political machines in West Virginia and Missouri, tightly knit political organizations, and the adroit use of political patronage and contracts foreclosed the possibility that a native-son presidential candidate could emerge to attain elective office solely on the support of his friends-and-neighbors voting. Local geography played little role here in launching a native-son presidential candidate.

Fenton's studies demonstrated that the usefulness of this geographical base in shaping voting behavior for the benefit of beginning political candidates was, at least in these time frames, not a factor in sending a native son up the political ladder. Candidates had to rely on other electoral variables that were germane to their political context.

Fenton's two studies completed the regional picture started by Key in the South and advanced by Lockard in New England. A comparative regional understanding of this electoral phenomenon was possible across the entire country, and a composite picture could be made. Yet, since that time, more recent studies of the concept in statewide and local landslides have emerged.

The Test Case in Statewide Elections

Tom Rice and his associate Alisa Macht, pioneers in testing the impact of the friends-and-neighbors variable, decided to explore the possibility that it plays a role in electoral behavior at the subpresidential level.[58] In a follow-up and extension of their initial research, they analyzed "gubernatorial and senatorial general elections in 46 states over the 1976 to 1982 period . . . A candidate's 'hometown' was considered his or her home county.

Home county information was obtained by contacting the Secretary of State's Office or Election Office in each state."[59] They found that "localism was evident in over two-thirds of the cases, with the average gubernatorial or senatorial candidate polling a home county advantage of 3.66 percentage points. While this advantage is far from overwhelming, it can be important in determining election outcomes."[60] Democratic candidates received a larger friends-and-neighbors vote than did Republican candidates, and "nonincumbents poll better at home than incumbents."[61]

This study moves research beyond a regional analysis by exploring specific types of elections that transcend particular regions. In major statewide races for U.S. Senate seats and for governor, the friends-and-neighbors variable helps to shape and influence voting behavior, at least at the collective level. We now know that voting behavior in presidential, senatorial, and gubernatorial elections is determined in part by geographical closeness, just as much as candidates, issues, and parties influence electoral behavior. Geography influences behavior because issues can become regional issues—especially economic issues.

These findings provide a clue to the study of LBJ's senatorial and presidential races. Unfortunately, the Rice and Macht article does not include Texas, because the secretary of state failed to send any data.[62] Hence, the article is only suggestive. However, the nonexistence of this variable is also significant because we can see what other variables are operative. In addition, Rice and Macht do not test for localism, which means that their findings about subnational elections must be taken as no more than a potential help in examining Texas's voting behavior.

A recent article extends the findings of the Rice and Macht analysis of general elections by focusing upon primary elections at the gubernatorial and senatorial levels. Matthew Potoski used a sample, 88 contests, that occurred between 1988 and 1992 from 35 states. In this sample, "a total of 197 candidates, 109 senatorial and 88 gubernatorial . . . [races] . . . were analyzed."[63] This type of coverage makes this study the largest one ever conducted on this variable in primary elections.

His findings "confirmed the existence of localism in statewide primary [elections . . . and noted that] on average, candidates received 12.08 percentage points more of the vote in their home county than in the rest of the state." And more important, he found that "candidates in the Deep South poll better in their home counties than do candidates in the rest of the nation in theirs."[64] These findings were quite suggestive about Johnson's senate races in Texas.

Finally, only the analysis of Bill Clinton provides any insights into the possibility that friends-and-neighbors voting might exist in House of Representative races.[65] Clinton's initial races in Arkansas suggest that it might be found in LBJ's congressional races, at least at a smaller level of influence.

Taken together, these works suggest that there might be some degrees of localism in LBJ's congressional and senatorial races, just a different type.

The Test Case for Local Landslides

In his third article on friends-and-neighbors voting, Rice sought to find those variables that determine why people are more likely to vote for their hometown candidates. Rice and Macht treated the large hometown vote for native sons as local landslides and sought to determine whether "a hometown edge can be the result of mobilizing nonvoters or converting voters usually loyal to another party. Of course, a hometown advantage could well be the product of both these forces."[66] Using 1982 gubernatorial election data, Rice and Macht discovered that local landslides were indeed a result of both mobilization and conversion. Voter turnout increased in most of the candidates' home counties, evidence that new voters were mobilized in support of the hometown candidate. In most cases, however, the hometown advantage was quite large, suggesting that part of it was due to traditional voters' converting to cast ballots for the local politician.[67] Thus, the hometown candidate reached across party lines and drew old voters as well as activating new voters. Friends-and-neighbors voting were truly pervasive across the entire electorate, irrespective of previous partisan attachment or voting status.

As for southern native-son presidential candidates, Rice and Macht found that "[i]n each of Carter's four races for the governorship, he enlarged and broadened his base of support until it became unbeatable."[68] There were both similarities and differences with the Clinton electoral coalition in Arkansas, the central difference being that Clinton made six runs for the governorship in Arkansas, losing only on his second effort, whereas Carter served only one term. Clinton's "initial gubernatorial coalition did not sustain itself into his second race for governor. . . . The rebuilt election coalition of 1980 not only lasted but grew over the next series of elections and sustained itself until Clinton moved on to his next electoral plateau," the presidency.[69] Into each of these coalitions, Clinton attracted both new and old voters.

The suggestion here is that, despite the fact that he never ran for a state office, LBJ's local landslides for the House of Representatives, Senate, vice presidency, and presidency came from both new voters and old voters.

The Carter and Clinton cases should sensitize the researcher to these possibilities. Such findings are of invaluable assistance in helping to shape a full theory of the native-son presidential candidate.

It must be said here that recent scholarly work tells us that the friends-and-neighbors vote is dynamic, not static. It is a growing and evolving vote. New friends-and-neighbors voters can be added, and old friends-and-neighbors voters can drop out and disappear. These new voters can come from the mobilization of old voters as well as from converted voters. Thus, in probing LBJ's electoral coalition, one should explore these possibilities.

The Friends-and-Neighbors Voting Behavior Model: Theoretical Suggestions for LBJ

Since theory building about the southern native-son presidential candidate is the purpose of this volume and LBJ is the case study under analysis, a composite portrait drawn from the insights gained from the friends-and-neighbors voting behavior literature is the obvious place to commence. Localism prevailed in Georgia and Arkansas, but it did not exist in Texas. It was not something that LBJ could count on to help him to emerge as a native-son politician in the state. There had to be another route; hence our concern here is with the other electoral routes and their relationship, if any, to friends-and-neighbors voting. Thus, the approach to LBJ's rise as a native son has to differ from the earlier approaches to Carter and Clinton.

In our theoretical formulation, we need to know the location of African Americans in this friends-and-neighbors voting equation. Key was silent on this matter, since at the time African Americans could hardly vote in influential numbers. By the Carter and Clinton eras, however, the Voting Rights Act had made this possible, and these native sons could benefit from the support of these new friends and neighbors.

To explore the different regional manifestations of the friends-and-neighbors voting behavior model, a composite of findings from the literature review must be attempted. Figure 4.2 depicts the original subsequent theorists, the regions under analysis, the localism voting model, and the broad-based findings that are relevant to LBJ as a southern native-son presidential candidate and, more generally, to the theoretical formation about this variable itself. First, the data from the five geographical regions tell us that localism is likely to turn up in essentially one-party states and in the dominant party primaries. Second, where there is an absence of this voting determinant in one-party state primaries, the native-son candidate

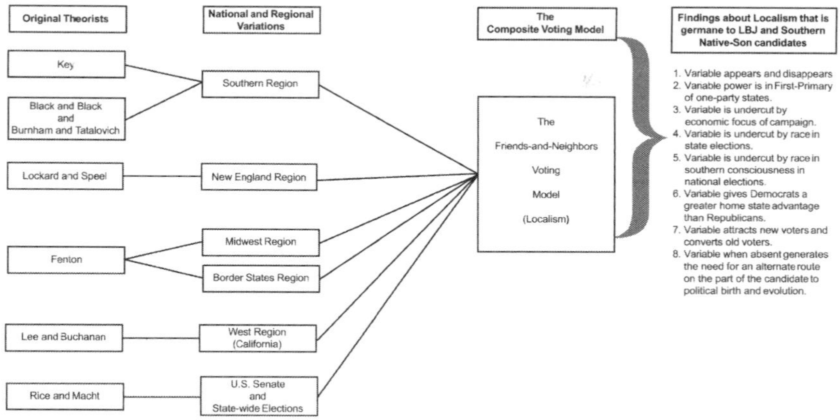

Fig. 4.2. The Findings in the Composite "Friends-and-Neighbors" Voting Behavior Model Germane to the Study of LBJ and Southern Native-Son Presidential Candidates

must find another electoral route to success, such as economic or class variables, organizational variables, and issue variables. It is noteworthy that the friends-and-neighbors variable is not continuous everywhere, and it can occur where it has never been before. Third, racial issues can negate the impact of the friends-and-neighbors voting determinant if they are embedded in the culture and history of the region. And finally, a southern native-son presidential candidate cannot count on sustained southern regional consciousness to electorally support him if he is advancing racial equality.

As a political neophyte, LBJ could not rely on the friends-and-neighbors vote to capture and sustain his initial political career in the House of Representatives, nor could he rely upon the voters who had put his father into the state legislature six times. Yet it helped. Instead, he relied upon economics to get started, and upon a different position on economics to maintain himself in office.

By the time LBJ came to electoral power, the economic forces shaping the Texas political context had led to "the most bitter intra-Democratic fight along New Deal and anti-New Deal lines in the South," according to Key.[70] "This sort of division of the popular vote suggests the hypothesis that voters divide along class lines in accord with their class interests as related to liberal and conservative candidates."[71] LBJ ran his initial 1937 campaign for the House of Representative as an FDR New Deal Democrat. Even as he claimed FDR and the New Deal, "he perceived that Texas was drifting to the right and that oil was the name of the game."[72] Initially, therefore, "Johnson and some of the other Texas congressmen could afford to be liberal because the oil, gas, and other corporate interests had not yet fully asserted their political power."[73]

George Norris Green labeled him a "countryside liberal" who by the time of his 1948 Senate race had become a moderate conservative and part of the state's political establishment. Green defined this "countryside liberalism" as "farm-to-market roads, rural electrification, river development, and aid to the aged."[74] One could also add, aid to the African American community.[75] This liberalism involved the use of the federal government to attack problems of rural poverty and economic dislocation. It also involved a legislative effort against African American equality. During his House years, Johnson voted against antilynching bills and four times for the poll tax.

In 1948, when LBJ began his second campaign for the United States Senate, "in Texas the vague outlines of a politics were emerging in which irrelevancies are pushed into the background and people divide broadly along liberal and conservative lines." This modified class politics evolved "not because of an upthrust of the masses that compels men of substance to unite in self-defense, but because of the personal insecurity of men suddenly made rich who are fearful lest they lose their wealth."[76] As Key saw it, "[t]he Lone Star State is concerned about money and how to make it, about oil and sulfur and gas, about cattle and dust storms and irrigation, about cotton and banking and Mexicans."[77] And such concerns fostered by 1948 an ideological conservatism in the Democratic Party. LBJ, who had started out as a New Deal economic liberal, became an economic conservative in line with the changing political preferences of his constituency.

Therefore, in an electorate devoid of a tendency toward friends-and-neighbors voting, LBJ used economic issues, class politics, and ideological leanings to rise to office, and then moderated his stands on the economic issues to maintain himself in office. Merle Miller, one of his biographers, wrote, "Nationally, Lyndon voted with Roosevelt. Democrats, always. But concerning Texas, he had, sometimes, to be careful"—for there was the matter of the race variable as well as the changing ideology in the state.

In terms of his legislative voting in the House of Representative, LBJ voted with the southern bloc against African American constitutional equality, but in passing out economic resources and federal support he distributed to the African American community a reasonable share. Once in the Senate, particularly after the 1948 election, LBJ rhetorically came out against the constitutional rights of African Americans, a stance he had avoided in the House years.[78] However, he still saw to it that some economic benefits from the federal government flowed into the African American community.[79] Later, in 1957 and 1960, he would spearhead the first civil rights bills of the century. LBJ represented his constituency on issues, particularly economic and racial, that were important to them. But on personal and conscience issues, he broke with the regional tradition, his regional culture, and his political mentors to embrace and disavow the southern Democratic Party tradition.

Finally, LBJ as a native-son candidate would embrace and include African American voters in his economic coalition of the "have-nots." In a sense, African American voters became his friends-and-neighbors voters beginning with his initial campaign in 1937, long before the 1965 Voting Rights Act, and never deserted him.[80] Even in 1948, when he denounced their drive for constitutional equality, they protested to his face during a visit to his senatorial office, but they continued to support him––not only because of his past efforts but also because he was one of their few elected supporters in office (in other words, because they had few alternatives).[81]

In sum, LBJ as a native-son candidate bypassed traditional localism by creating an economic following instead of a geographic one and became quite creative in dealing with the race variable in his local contextual setting. LBJ's friends-and-neighbors voters, if they can be called that, were economically based and contained both liberals and conservatives, Blacks and whites. This was unique, when one sees it in light of the other native sons, Carter, Clinton, and Garner, as well as with the initial African American president, Obama.

★ 5

Methodology

A pioneer in so many ways, LBJ's electoral trek provides a wealth of quantitative data for some striking empirical evidence on this variable. True, there are similarities between the recent southern native-son presidential candidates; yet there are also notable differences.

Although Carter had a total of 12 elections en route to the presidency, LBJ and Clinton had 21 each. Nevertheless, the story is not in the totals nor in the differences but in the rank order itself. LBJ was the first southerner since the Civil War to capture the presidency. Thus, his initial presidential election data will tell us something about the electoral response of the nonsoutherner to a southern president, just as President Obama's electoral trek will tell us about the electoral response of southerners to nonsoutherners. Next, LBJ's election data will reveal how southern partisanship changed in a remade Democratic Party. Finally, it will reveal how a change in native-son ideological posture is reflected in the party-in-the-electorate.

Green posits that LBJ shifted his ideological stance from a "countryside" liberal to a moderate conservative.[1] From his rise to Congress, James MacGregor Burns described "Lyndon Johnson's voyage from the moderate-conservative wing of the Democratic party to the liberal [wing]"[2] later in his career. As LBJ made this personal quantum leap, he took part of the southern electorate with him, and his electoral coalition reflected this movement.

Embedded in LBJ's election data beyond the theoretical insights into collective voting behavior is the unique election-specific information. They reveal the nature and scope of his support in "special elections," that is, his 1937 House and 1941 Senate contests, and provide trends in Latino (Mexican-American) voting behavior.[3] Of Georgia, Arkansas, Alabama, Tennessee, and Texas, only Texas has had a substantial Latino voting population.[4] LBJ's election data offer reflections on political bossism as an independent variable influencing the electoral outcome of a southern presidential candidate.[5] Although this variable was a factor in both Carter's initial state senate election and Clinton's initial congressional election, political bossism did not have the continuity it had in Texas politics.[6] LBJ's election data brings to light "a dual or simultaneous" election coalition for different offices. A Texas law approved in 1959 permitted LBJ in 1960 to run for vice president and the United States Senate in the same election. He won both. This was predated by a Texas law that permitted Congressman James Nance Garner to run for his House seat and the vice presidency in 1932. He too won both.[7] Finally, LBJ's election data provide a perspective on racial voting, the vote of white segregationists and African Americans in the era of segregation.[8]

Perhaps what is most important about LBJ's election data is his defeat of the century-old efforts of southern Democratic elites to dominate the Democratic Party's course on race. LBJ's election data capture in stark terms a single-handed realignment of the "cleavage axis" in the American party system. James Sundquist's refinement of Key's concept of realignment notes how the party system could be shifted on its axis by the resetting of a new cleavage.[9]

Race was the new cleavage that cut across all elements of the political process: class, ideology, demographics, and partisanship. First, within his own party, LBJ's confrontation with dominant southern party elites eventually altered, with George Wallace's help, the Democratic Party coalition and then the Goldwater-led Republican Party response. And second, in 1968, the revival of a southern third party with a racial strategy came via Wallace's American Independent Party.[10] LBJ's party remaking strategy was quite unique, for it set into motion political changes in the Republican and third party coalitions.

All southerners prior to LBJ who had become vice president sought to maintain an agenda of protecting the region's ideology of white supremacy and segregation. Table 5.1 indicates that the Democratic Party began to explicitly nominate segregationist southerners beginning in 1928. The exception was Senator Estes Kefauver from Tennessee in 1956. These nominations were a political reward to the South for delivering its bloc of electoral votes. But it was LBJ who confronted the region's long-standing efforts to capture the Democratic Party and remake it in its image of moonlight and magnolias, uncles and mammies. It was, in the words of novelist Ralph Ellison, a system of "unjust stability."[11] LBJ began to demolish that party system with the 1957 and 1960 Civil Rights Acts while he was in the Senate and with the 1964 Civil Right Act, the 1965 Voting Rights Act, and the 1968 Civil Rights Act while he was president.

Wallace's attempts to maintain the southern wing's ideological posture in 1964 occurred in eastern and midwestern Democratic primaries and not in the South because the region at that point held so few presidential primaries. This was the crucial weakness of his electoral strategy, and it left southern voters only one main option—an overnight conversion to the Republican Party with its anti–civil rights stance. Of this unique electoral phenomenon, Courtney Brown noted that "in 1964, there were actually two landslides. The first occurred in areas outside of the Deep South, in favor of Johnson, and the second occurred in the Deep South, in favor of Goldwater. A comparison of the two landslides offers an extraordinary chance to begin to discern, in more general terms, differences in the internal structure of landslides."[12] In sum, LBJ's election data permit one to see and probe a "dual landslide" in America's electoral history. This is quite

TABLE 5.1. The Number and Percentage of Southern States Won with a Southern Native-Son Vice Presidential Candidate on the Ticket: 1928–2000

Years	Presidential Candidate	Southern Vice-Presidential Candidates	Number of Southern States Won	Percentage of Southern States Won	Election Outcomes
Non-Native-Son Presidential Candidates					
1928	Al Smith	Joseph T. Robinson	5	46	Lost
1932	Franklin D. Roosevelt	John W. Garner	11	100	Won
1936	Franklin D. Roosevelt	John W. Garner	11	100	Won
1948	Harry Truman	Alben Barkley	7	64	Won
1952	Adlai E. Stevenson	John T. Sparkman	7[a]	64	Lost
1956	Adlai E. Stevenson	Estes Kefauver	6	55	Lost
1960	John F. Kennedy	L.B. Johnson	7[a]	64	Won
1988	Michael S. Dukakis	Lloyd Bentsen	0	0	Lost
Native-Son Presidential Candidates					
1964	L.B. Johnson	—[b]	6	55	Won
1976	James E. Carter	—[b]	10	91	Won
1980	James E. Carter	—[b]	1	9	Lost
1992	William J. Clinton	Al Gore	4	36	Won
2000	Al Gore	—[b]	0	0	Lost

Source: Adapted from Michael Nelson, *Guide to the Presidency* (Washington, DC: Congressional Quarterly, 1989), 1447–51.

[a]Some of these states cast part of their electoral votes for another southerner.

[b]These candidates did not have a southerner native-son vice presidential running mate.

unique. We now turn to the methodological techniques used in the analysis and interpretation of LBJ's election.

Measuring the Friends-and-Neighbors Vote: The Pioneers and Beyond

Having introduced in the Carter volume the president's home county as the measurable unit indicative of the native-son variable,[13] it became possible in the Clinton volume to assess *all* of the different measurable units of the native-son variable and discern how they related to and possibly reinforced each other.[14] Thus, in this volume we can explore the measurable antecedent, the friends-and-neighbors vote, in the emergence of the native-son presidential candidate.

In figure 5.1 we can see the various attempts to analyze friends-and-neighbors voting behavior and how Key's model works outside of the South. Key launched the local voting behavior model in 1949, and Duane Lockhart tested it in New England a decade later. Key used the mean for the candidate, the mean for his opponent who was not a resident of the local area, and the mean for the county. His tabular presentation procedure meant that the reader had to visually see the differences. Eugene Lee and William Buchanan changed this data presentation procedure and instituted a percentage above the mean for the state. This refinement moved the measurement technique from a *visual* one on the part of the reader to a *calculated* one in which the difference between the state mean and the candidate mean was presented as the percentage above the mean of the friends-and-neighbors vote. In addition, they looked at presidential instead of local elections.[15] This was clearly a refinement of Key's technique.

Key's original measurement approach was basically univariate in nature. Yet another refinement to his original technique was the technique of multiple regression (OLS) used by Earl Black and Merle Black in their test case of Alabama.[16] This multivariate procedure permits the researcher to analyze several independent variables simultaneously and determine the relative strength and influence of these variables in relationship to each other. Simply put, the OLS technique rank orders the numerous independent variables whereas the univariate approach uses a single independent variable. The multivariable approach demonstrates the power, influence, and impact of the friends-and-neighbors vote among several variables.

The separate works of Raymond Tatalovich and Robert Speel, a continued refinement, give a time dimension for the variable beyond the years in

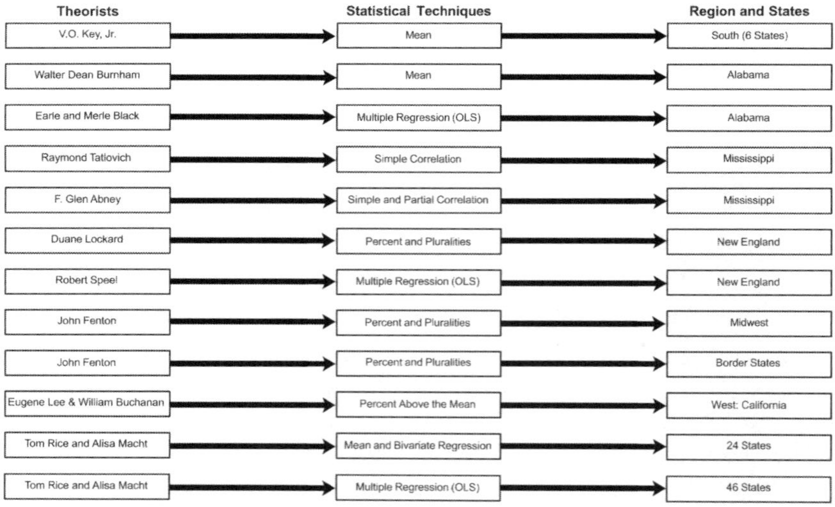

Fig. 5.1. The Theorists and Their Methodological Techniques for Analyzing "Friends-and-Neighbors" Voting Behaviors in Different Regions and States

which Key worked. Their works conclude that the variable is context dependent and that it is a valuable factor in the past and in the present.[17]

Drawing from these three refinements of the friends-and-neighbors vote measurement, one learns that at the univariate level the difference above the mean is a much more efficient data presentation than the visual one, and that the multivariate approach helps measure it with other independent variables. Such an insight can indicate where this local voting behavior determinant did not exist but might surface later in a state like Texas, particularly in congressional districts where casework and constituency service builds a substantial personal following for the congressional incumbent.

David Mayhew's pioneering work on the drive among congressional incumbents to get reelected,[18] followed by Richard Fenno's innovative books, reveal how casework and pork barrel policies build a set of core supporters for the congressperson[19] and suggest that a "potential," although not exactly, friends-and-neighbors vote could emerge. These refined measurements could be quite useful in exploring this variable in the later years of a congressional career such as LBJ's. In the final analysis, the refinements growing out of Key's original concept of "localism" permit one to get beyond some of the features that Key's model did not permit one to see. Thus, a composite portrait of the friends-and-neighbors vote beyond the South provides a richer understanding of the native-son variable and a chance to develop a more comprehensive theory of it.

The Relationship of the Friends-and-Neighbors Vote to the Southern Native-Son Presidential Candidate: The Measurement Linkage

At this point, it is essential once again to remind the reader that Key's concept was based on data from the candidate's home county and surrounding counties. It posits that in a one-party political context where issue voting was unimportant and parties were not competitive, a candidate could launch his political career solely on the basis of the geography, of simply being known by his friends and neighbors. However, Key's model had in mind a candidate for the state governorship, not the presidency. Not everyone who applied his concept of localism stayed within Key's intellectual and definitional parameters. Michael Lewis-Beck and Tom Rice significantly modified it, and in doing so they pioneered the measurement of the relationship between friends-and-neighbors voting and the southern native-son presidential candidate. Lewis-Beck and Rice used a "rolling mean" measurement technique to analyze the impact of the native-son presidential candidate. They went on to say that "the forces of localism are believed to operate in presidential races, as well as in state ones."[20] Here, they acknowledged two different paths, with the implication that they might be connected. The real focus of their article was not upon the friends-and-neighbors vote at the county level as developed by Key; rather, they advanced the entire matter to the state level.

However, to measure the impact of the friends-and-neighbors vote at the state level, Lewis-Beck and Rice moved from a single election mean to a five-election mean (usually called a rolling mean) and took the percentage above it.[21] This gave Lewis-Beck and Rice the data to be able to calculate the home state advantage. Technically speaking, this study is more akin to the spirit of Key's concept rather than the actual letter of the concept, but it did break new ground. Not only did they develop a measurement to determine a president's home state advantage, but they also turned to a multivariate procedure to determine what other independent variables shaped it. They declared, "Besides state population, we expect two other variables to determine, albeit to a lesser extent, a candidate's home state advantage, namely, political party and incumbency."[22] After measuring the impact of these three variables on the home-state advantage, Lewis-Beck and Rice found that "these three variables are statistically significant predictors, and according to the R^2, together account for about one-half of the differences in home state advantage that candidates experience."[23] This was indeed a unique contribution, moving beyond Key's original concept and its measurement.

Lewis-Beck and Rice pointed to localism, as defined from a state level instead of a county level, as having influence in the candidate's presidential efforts. This leads us to the question of whether localism as defined by Key at the county level can link with a native-son presidential candidate's home-state vote. In the context of the powerful findings of Mayhew and Fenno, is it possible that the refined measurement of the percentage above the mean can help us uncover that relationship in empirical terms? LBJ's electoral odyssey might just help us map out this relationship.

LBJ's Native-Son Elections

In reference to Carter and Clinton, Walton found that localism exists within both Georgia and Arkansas. We find as Key did that in LBJ's Texas this was not the case. In Texas, the political context was different, and the electoral route of a new political candidate involved other techniques of voter mobilization. In order to fully understand LBJ's electoral data in light of other southern native-son presidential candidates' rise to power, a comprehensive exploration of the concept outside of these states is crucial. If LBJ's congressional years later set into motion a friends-and-neighbors vote, we not only would know what we are looking for, we would have a set of techniques with which to measure its existence in empirical terms. Texas thus gives us another reference point and a different framework in which to analyze LBJ's election data.

Listed in table 5.2 one will find the types of elections in which LBJ participated from 1937 through 1964: eleven elections for the U.S. House of Representatives, eight elections for the U.S. Senate, and two for the presidency. There is also the delegate vote for LBJ at the 1956, 1960, and 1964 Democratic National Conventions. Texas did not have presidential primaries, such as Georgia and Arkansas had for their native-son presidential candidates. LBJ did not enter any presidential primary elections in 1960 or 1964. Although someone would stand in for him in the 1964 Democratic primaries around the country and in the notable New Hampshire presidential primary in 1968, LBJ himself chose to monitor national convention politics. He began using this convention approach instead of a primary approach in 1956 and continued thereafter in 1960, 1964, and 1968.[24] There is one other feature of note in table 5.2. In 1960, LBJ ran simultaneously for the United States Senate and the vice presidency. LBJ won both elections and later resigned his Senate seat.[25]

Compared with Carter and Clinton, both of whom never served in Congress and came to the presidency via the gubernatorial route, LBJ never held a state office and came through both houses of Congress to the vice presidency and then to the presidency. This is what gives LBJ's electoral data such uniqueness and potential new insights into the friends-and-neighbors voting concept.

Previous southerners who made it to the White House on the Democratic ticket—James Garner, a Texan himself, came from the House to the vice presidency on FDR's ticket, and Kentucky senator Alben Barkley became Truman's vice president—provided LBJ and other southern hopefuls with a political pathway. Others who did not make it to the White House,

TABLE 5.2. The Categories and Types of Elections Contested by Native-Son Lyndon Baines Johnson: 1937–64

	Types of Elections					
Year	Special[a]	Primary	Run-Off	General	Total	Result
Congressional						
1937	X				1	won
1938		X		X	2	won
1940		X		X	2	won
1942		X		X	2	won
1944		X		X	2	won
1946		X		X	2	won
Senatorial						
1941	X				1	lost
1948		X	X	X	3	won
1954		X		X	2	won
1960		X		X	2	won
Presidential						
1960				X	1	
1964				X	1	
Total	2	8	1	10	21	20 won 1 lost

Source: Adapted and calculated from the Secretary of State, *Register of Electoral and Appointed State and County Officials* (Austin: Election Register Texas State Archives, 1838–1964).

[a]Under Texas law, when a senator and/or congressman dies while in office, the governor calls a single special election to fill the vacancy. All candidates of different parties must offer in this special election and whosoever wins goes to the U.S. Congress. There is no run-off and/or other election required.

such as Senators Estes Kefauver of Tennessee, John T. Sparkman of Alabama, Joseph Robinson of Arkansas, and Al Gore Sr. of Tennessee, all followed in the political footsteps of Garner (see table 5.1). But none of these men, save LBJ, ever advanced beyond the vice presidency. Thus, the unique features in LBJ's 21 elections portend much for a theory of the native-son presidential candidate.

LBJ's Election Data: A Demographic Approach

In the present work, as in the Carter and Clinton volumes, the unit of analysis is the county. Georgia has 159 counties, Arkansas 75, and Texas the most of all with 254 counties. In order to permit a comparative analysis both over time and among these states, a demographic categorization of these counties was developed into a rather standard framework: there are the urban counties, followed by town counties, rural counties, the president's home county—which can be his birth county or his county of residence—and finally the Black Belt counties. Those counties with a population of 50,000 and above are placed in the urban category; those with populations ranging from 10,000 to 49,999 are in the town category; and those having populations from 250 to 9,999 are the rural counties. This distinction will not be enough for Texas, however, given the large Latino population in the state and the notoriously corrupt boss counties. The special counties must be expanded beyond the classifications of traditional home and Black Belt counties to include some boss counties and Latino counties.

The basic reason for this county-level demographic approach is that it is the centerpiece of Key's, J. Morgan Kousser's, and Gerald Gaither's works.[26] These major overviews of the Democratic Party in the South supplement Alexander Heard's book on the Republican Party in the region, which also used the county as the unit of analysis.[27] Other works on Texas politics embrace the same demographic technique.[28] Collectively, these works make comparisons possible and offer the opportunity to build a theoretical formulation for the concept of friends-and-neighbors voting behavior. This well-established methodological approach to structuring the county-level data is used in the case of Texas to explore class and elite politics, the ideological politics of the masses, the partisanship of the voters, and the voting behavior of the electorate.

In contrast, journalists at the *Dallas Morning News* employed an ecological approach whereby they divided the state into eight geographical regions and then determined how each of these regions voted in presidential elections:

> Regionalism plays an important role in the state's politics. Texas can be broken into eight geographical regions that have distinct political personalities. Perhaps the greatest division in the state, however, is the so-called I-35 split. The interstate highway in many ways is the state's main street, running through most of the population centers like Dallas, Austin, San Antonio and Laredo, and neatly dividing the population, economic resources into haves and have-nots. More than 80 percent of the population and economic activity in the state takes place along or east of I-35. More than 80 percent of the votes in next statewide electors came from the same area.[29]

As these journalists saw it, there was much to be said for their ecological approach. But the truth of the matter is that sections of I-35 began opening in Texas in 1956, allowing for its consideration as a dividing line in Texas economically and politically in recent time periods. More generally, the ecological approach, as opposed to the demographic county-level analysis, is devoid of a great intellectual tradition and the large number of substantive studies employing the county-level approach.

In using this ecological approach, however, the authors did uncover a unique fact in Texas electoral history. They revealed, "a betting man would look to Reagan County in West Texas to see how sentiment in a presidential election runs. Since the county began holding presidential elections, it has backed the national winner 86 percent of the time, regardless of how the rest of the state voted. Upton and Terrell Counties, also in West Texas, are only a percentage point behind at 85 percent." In addition, "Neither Brooks nor Jim Hogg Counties, both in South Texas, has ever voted Republican [and] . . . [f]orty-two Texas counties have voted 90 percent of the time for Democratic presidential candidates."[30]

As for the Republicans, "Kendall County in West Texas is the champion Republican county, supporting the party's nominee for president 93 percent of the time. . . . Runner-up was Gillespie, also in West Central Texas, with a 66 percent support record for Republicans." Gillespie had been LBJ's resident county since the early fifties. Overall, "ten counties have voted for Republican presidential candidates more than 50 percent of the time." However, "third parties have not fared well in Texas. George Wallace in 1968 carried 21 counties for the best showing." In 1992 and 1996 Texan H. Ross Perot carried three and no counties, respectively. The "champion supporter of third-party presidential nominees is Bandera, voting three times with third party candidates."[31] Bandera County is also in West Central Texas.

The best insight arising from this limited ecological foray into Texas electoral politics is that most of it takes place in east Texas, east of I-35. Such a finding is not as insightful as that emanating from the demographic approach, which has brought forth information on class politics, ideological politics, racial and ethnic politics, and partisan politics. Thus, the latter approach has much to recommend it.

Table 5.3 demonstrates the quantitative pattern that emerges when Texas counties are characterized demographically. There has been a gradual rise in the number of urban counties, which account for one-fifth of the total number of Texas counties; at the same time the number of town counties has steadily declined, although they still comprise about half of the counties in the state. No county in Texas after 1980 had an African American population majority. However, from the 1930s until today the number of Latino counties has grown.[32]

Of the so-called boss counties, Key noted that they had a very strong linkage with the Latino counties:

> To a large extent the politics of the Mexican-American counties is necessarily a matter of negotiation with major and petty bosses.

TABLE 5.3. The Number and Percentage of Texas Counties in the Demographic Categories by Decades

Demographic Categories	1930s	1940s	1950s	1960s
Rural	93 (36.6%)	88 (34.7%)	92 (36.2%)	96 (37.8%)
Town	135 (53.2%)	135 (53.2%)	131 (51.6%)	123 (48.4%)
Urban	18 (7.1%)	23 (9.1%)	23 (9.1%)	27 (10.6%)
Special Categories				
LBJ's Home County[a]	2 (1.0%)	2 (1.0%)	2 (1.0%)	2 (1.0%)
Black-Belt Counties[b]	2 (1.0%)	2 (1.0%)	2 (1.0%)	2 (1.0%)
Boss Counties[c]	2 (1.0%)	2 (1.0%)	2 (1.0%)	2 (1.0%)
Latino Counties[d]	2 (1.0%)	2 (1.0%)	2 (1.0%)	2 (1.0%)
Total Counties	254 (101%)	254 (101%)	254 (101%)	254 (101%)

[a]President Johnson was born in Gillespie County and later his family moved to his boyhood home in Johnson City, which is in Blanco County. In 1952 LBJ moved back into Gillespie County and built his ranch.

[b]The Black-Belt Counties are those in which African Americans make up more than 51% of the population. They are Marion and San Jacinto.

[c]The Boss Counties are those in which the Latino vote has a history of being managed in sundry elections. They are Duval and Zapata.

[d]The Latino Counties are those in which Mexican Americans make up more than 51% of the population. They are Kennedy and Starr.

> There is greater emphasis on the trade, the swap out, and the *quid pro quo* than elsewhere in the state. The politician attempting to appeal over the heads of the local bosses encounters a remarkable degree of personal attachment that he cannot break through with funds or oratory. In negotiating with some *jefes*, an ample supply of campaign funds is no handicap. It also appears that some bosses are fickle, and the candidate who gets there last with the cash or promise of favor sometimes cuts out an opponent who thinks he has already sewed up the vote.[33]

Of all the Latino counties with bosses, Key chose Duval County as his prime example.[34] Given that this county helped LBJ to win the Senate, and that recent research has unearthed another relationship between a Latino boss and LBJ in Zapata County, both counties were included in this category. Yet despite their sharing a very close connection, Key never equated the two things. This book separates the two variables: and that is why this book uses these separate categories instead of a single one, boss counties.[35]

Finally, in his analysis of Texas politics through the mid-forties, Key noted that besides whites, Latinos, and African Americans, Texas had several German counties. He declared, "[t]he so-called German counties of Texas, although they do not bulk large in the politics of the state, constitute an item of southern political curiosa that attracts attention because of the rarity of minority politics in the South. . . . Historically the German counties have inclined toward Republicanism. During the [Civil] War they found themselves out of sympathy with their neighbors who would destroy the union to preserve slavery. The Germans were not slaveholders; they were liberals and revolutionists who took their American democracy literally." In statewide contests, "these [German] counties usually gave more enthusiastic support to the more conservative Democrats."[36]

As with the Latino counties, Key selected Comal out of the seventeen German counties as the best example and analyzed its voting behavior.[37] Yet by the time of the publication of *Southern Politics* in 1949, he indicated that "the German counties of today are not readily identifiable."[38] Hence, table 5.3 does not have a special category for the German counties, but we shall refer to the voting behavior of Comal County in LBJ's elections as it appears relevant.

Overall, with these demographic county categories we will be able to determine the nature of LBJ's electoral coalitions, the persistence of those coalitions, and their importance as he rose from Texas native son to Congress and finally to the presidency. These will permit an analysis of how his sources of support then convert to subsequent southerners such as Carter, Clinton, Bush, and Gore.

In addition to the county-level data, we will use, where the historical record permits, precinct data to explain voting behavior for the native-son candidate, as was done in the Carter volume. Unique to Texas is the existence of collections of some city data, which will permit the analysis of some demographic groups as they supported this native son over time, enriching the county-level data.

Defining the population parameters of the demographic approach and describing the county categorization inherent in the approach leave one essential task: placement of this particular methodological procedure into the disciplinary context of voting behavior studies. Basically speaking, there are two traditions in voting and election studies. First to appear were the studies that analyzed the behavior of electorates, that is, as an aggregation of voters within particular, comparable geopolitical units, such as counties, cities, precincts, and wards. Studies in this tradition select one or more of these political units, acquire official or unofficial election returns from them, and tabulate and analyze these data in various ways so as to identify recurring patterns of voter turnout in single or multiple time periods.[39]

The second and now dominant tradition in the discipline is the focus upon the behavior of individual voters. Instead of focusing on political units such as counties and cities, these studies have as the basic unit of analysis for research the electoral behavior of individuals. Such studies seek to determine the psychological determinants of an individual voter's motivations, "to explain why Americans voted as they did in national elections."[40] In addition, since these individual-focused studies usually rest on preelection political attitudes, they permit researchers to predict how individuals will vote before the election actually takes place.[41] Thus, because of its explanatory and predictive characteristics, this tradition in its sundry variations has gained hegemony over the earlier one, which proved to be less successful in its explanatory and predictive powers.

Given these two traditions, we see that "scholarly studies of electoral behavior depend mainly upon two types of data for their raw materials."[42] The first tradition uses aggregate election data for the chosen political unit, while the second uses survey data or public opinion polls, or both.[43] The election data permit an analysis of segments of the population inherent in these political units, such as "farmers, labor union members, women, youth, ethnic and religious groups,"[44] or, as in the present study, urban, town, rural, African American, Latino, and possible friends-and-neighbors voters. The latter data, surveys and polls, permit an analysis of individual farmers, individual labor union members, and individual Protestant, Catholic, or Jewish voters. These data reduce the macropolitical behavior of the group to the micropolitical behavior of the individual. Each database offers, in the end, its own strengths and explanatory powers.

The strength of the aggregate election return data is inherent in the time dimension that it can give. Angus Campbell, a pioneer in survey-research-based voting behavior, said this of the election return data tradition in voting studies: "[I]n some cases these records have been kept over a long period of time and with great care. Each new election adds a new chapter to this archive of voting statistics. . . . the fact that aggregative data have commonly been systematically reported over a period of many years make possible the analysis of trends and regularities in voting behavior at the various local and national levels over time." In Campbell's view, "aggregative statistics are less subject to errors of one kind or another than are survey data."[45]

Nevertheless, despite these strengths, there has been a widely reported weakness of voting studies based upon aggregate election return data. According to Angus Campbell, "In a widely-cited article of a decade ago, W. S. Robinson demonstrated that 'ecological correlations' (those using aggregate data inclusively) have no necessary relation to or correspondence with 'individual correlations' (those using individual data) about the same populations." Numerous studies over the years "have confirmed Robinson's findings that correlations based on aggregate data cannot be relied upon to produce reliable descriptions or explanations of the behavior of individuals."[46] Simply stated, the voting behavior of political units, no matter how small, cannot be said to be the voting behavior of individuals.[47]

This problem with the earlier voting behavior tradition was called the "ecological fallacy" then and is now referred to as the "cross-level inference problem," which has been defined as "a problem of statistical underidentification, that is . . . data gathered at the macrolevel do not allow us to definitely determine the process at work among the same variables at the micro-level."[48] Some political methodologists have claimed to solve this technical statistical problem, while others have remained more skeptical. When one looks back in time, there is either no survey or polling data or no reliable survey or polling data, or both. Reliable scientific polling did not emerge until about 1936, and survey-based voting data was not collected until the mid- and later 1940s.[49] Therefore, to study voting behavior in America before this period means that all one has available to analyze is aggregate election return data.

Such is the case if one wants to analyze all of LBJ's 21 elections. Joe

Belden's Texas Polls do exist from some of LBJ's elections, but they do not offer enough subsamples of the Texas population to provide reliable estimates.[50] This was also true for Carter and Clinton, particularly for electoral contests below the congressional levels, where there is no or little competition. Hence, the only way to analyze these elections is with aggregate election data.

Second, the way to handle the cross-level inference problem is to not commit it, by acknowledging that this book, like the volumes on Carter and Clinton, is a study of group voting and not of individuals. It simply stays within the strengths of the aggregate election return data.

Finally, to control for the ever-changing dynamic in elections, the demographic framework is reconfigured each decade as the state population shifts. Table 5.3 offers this decade by decade regrouping. This allows comparability with the other studies, as well as with the regional data from election to election.

Theorists and Their Methodological Techniques: A Revisit

It was found in the Carter volume that presidential candidates residing in their birth state did better than those in their adopted states.[51] The measurement for birth and resident counties discerned, at least in the Clinton volume, that there was a difference in the presidential primaries and general elections, where Clinton received greater support in his birth county than in his county of residence. This did not hold in his gubernatorial and attorney general elections, where the reverse was the case.[52] This difference in the findings between the county level and the state level gave new insights about keeping Key's original county-level approach in perspective and not abandoning it as Lewis-Beck and Rice had. Each approach adds useful theoretical information, which must be understood and placed in the overall measurement model.

The friends-and-neighbors vote measurement technique demonstrated that the percentage above the mean is more precise than the older technique of visual presentation of each percentage, and provides insight into the roles that other variables played in launching the career of the native-son presidential candidate. Moreover, this measurement technique can enable us to determine, particularly in congressional elections, whether the friends-and-neighbors vote emerged later in LBJ's electoral evolution.

These are just some intellectual paths that these measurement techniques will provide when examining the native-son presidential candidate. But what about LBJ's vice-presidential running mate? It will be possible to determine how well birth and resident counties turn out on his behalf as well.[53] This technique will likewise be informative about other candidates, such as LBJ's friend and later vice presidential hopeful, Texas senator Lloyd Bentsen.

Last are the insights that these measurements can provide in matters of party realignment, where native sons of the opposite party emerge. How much electoral switching occurred in the birth and residence counties of LBJ when George Bush ran on the Republican ticket? How many friends-and-neighbors voters switched and abandoned the Democratic Party? From the Carter study we know that his cousin Hugh Carter "ran for and won [his] senate seat. . . . [but] the percentage of the total vote which Sumter County provided both Jimmy and Hugh Carter . . . began a slow and steady decline. . . . By 1984, when the Carters were no longer running, the votes and percentage again rose to a new level for a new Democratic candidate."[54]

Carter's home county also provided support to African American candidates who ran statewide, as well as to the occasional Republican candidate who appeared at the statewide and district levels. From 1968 through 1982, in "over five statewide elections with seven candidates, the mean vote in the county comes out to 8 percent" for the African American Democratic candidates.[55] For Republican candidates, this county tended to give them from one-third to one-fourth of its vote.

Clinton's birth and resident counties are just as instructive. As discussed earlier, there was a fluctuation of support in Clinton's resident county at both the Democratic and Republican Party realignment levels. These measurement clues emanate from the county-level approach initially employed by Key.

Given Texas's large number of electoral votes, it has engaged national party leaders and strategists in their efforts to win presidential elections. Texas has been important to both the Republican and Democratic Parties either for the presidential or vice presidential nominees, or both. FDR chose Texan Jack Garner as his vice presidential partner twice. John Kennedy chose Lyndon B. Johnson. Then the party nominated LBJ. Michael Dukakis chose Lloyd Bentsen, while Ronald Reagan chose George Bush. The Republican Party chose George W. Bush. Native-son presidential candidates from Texas offer more for our theoretical formulation regarding the native-son variable than do candidates from Georgia and Arkansas.[56]

From LBJ's electoral data we can move backward in time and explore the data for James Garner in 1932 and 1936. Then we can move forward again to explore Lloyd Bentsen in 1988 and party realignment data since 1980 in general. Recognizing the rich possibilities that these new and old data bring to the theoretical table, the measurement of demographic data is not enough. It is these other measurement techniques that flow from these studies that enable a more comprehensive and systematic treatment of this rich election return data and the further structuring of the theoretical formulation, if these additional measures are allowed to supplement the findings flowing from the demographic approach.

A note can be made here about the missing political party perspective raised in earlier volumes on the subject. The multiple presidential candidacies from Texas clearly denote the importance of this perspective, at least for party leadership and party strategists. They continually find Texas electorally important, and this gives this study some of its comparative thrust over time, as seen in the Lee and Buchanan article on another important electoral state, California. Texas and LBJ indeed offer extensive possibilities, which the merger of older and newer measurement techniques will enable to arise empirically.

★ Part II

The Political Context of a Native-Son Candidate

Lyndon Johnson began his rise to political power in a state with a clear-cut political environment already in place. Texas was a solid one-party state when LBJ announced his run for Congress in 1937, a time when nearly all state and national political figures were Democrats. All other party alternatives were essentially avenues to protest politics and to shadowbox.

At the level of Texas's political culture, the Democratic Party had promulgated white supremacy and its social custom of strict racial segregation. Hence, the prime political issue in every election was the question of race. Every other issue was subordinate to this one whether it was political corruption, poverty, inequality, or governmental service; they all had to stand in the shadow of race. This meant that all elected and appointed public officials as well as the state electorate had to embrace the following: (1) the white primary, (2) voter disenfranchisement, (3) second-class citizenship for African Americans, (4) the denial of public office to members of the African American community, and (5) the denial of constitutional and democratic principles to members of the racial community. For white Texans the circumscription of civil liberties and civil rights was an omnipresent state and community norm. LBJ both acquiesced to and defied the norm, and ultimately he would eliminate it.

Why, one may ask? First, LBJ would discover that within the Democratic Party in his state, there were those—the liberal wing—that opposed the social and political norms. Second, he would find that in Texas's large Latino community, these norms had severe human and economic consequences—consequences he found appalling even before he entered public office. Third, he found that in the large racial community there were serious legal and electoral opposition to these social and political norms and its severe consequences. But even here he found electoral allies to support his national political aspirations.

The Texas political context then is dissimilar to Arkansas and Georgia in its demographic composition, in how segments of its population strategically related to the political process, and in its rising native-son presidential candidate. It is the unique relationship between LBJ and African American and Latino voters and leaders that set Arkansas and Georgia apart from Texas.

First, there was the matter of the significance of the Latino population. This group had the legal right to vote and many resided in Austin, within Johnson's congressional district, and their support was necessary in statewide elections because of the lack of friends-and-neighbors voting. The Latino voters in Texas were both "managed" and independent. Second, equally dissimilar to Arkansas and Georgia was the aggressiveness and the continued assertiveness of the African American electorate in attacking the white primary. It was the African Americans in Texas whose pursuit of legal action led the Supreme Court to abolish it in Texas and in the ten other southern states in the 1944 *Smith vs. Allwright* decision,[1] thereby providing a leadership model of voting-rights activism for African Americans in the other southern states. Third, Texas law did not ban African Americans from participating in special elections.[2] As a result, this group of voters was quite aggressive in helping LBJ in these types of contests. LBJ made use of this segment of the Texas electorate as he rose to political power. Later he would champion their cause of an inclusive democracy.

In interviews with southern politicians and community leaders for V. O. Key's classic *Southern Politics*, Donald Strong interviewed 538 "politicians and political observers" from the eleven states; 55 (10.2 percent) were interviewed in Texas. Three of the interviewees talked about LBJ, and one subject reflected that "Johnson . . . does innumerable constituents personal favors, and they allow him to vote more or less as he pleases."[3] Because of his political and policy leeway, LBJ made modifications to the political context and value system that were embedded in the one-party Democratic political environment of Texas. When he became the Senate majority leader, he was lifted in part out of the confines of that environment and moved from being a southern politician from Texas to a national one with national aspirations and possibilities. The pull of the political context of the South and Texas now had competition from the pull of the North and the needs of the national Democratic Party. The former pulled least.[4]

In this section, we analyze empirically the three dominant demographic groups in the electorate: (1) whites, (2) African Americans, and (3) Latinos. These chapters probe their voting behavior over time and delineate their voting patterns not only in presidential, congressional, and statewide elections but also within their electoral cohorts in urban, town, rural, and home counties. Here we find a comprehensive and systematic analysis of group voting behavior in Texas. We review the electoral parameters in LBJ's political context and analyze the ways in which he used these factors in crafting his own winning electoral coalitions in a state political environment that was devoid of friends-and-neighbors voting.

★ 6

The Texas Electorate

The electoral birth of LBJ began "on February 22, 1937, [when] Texas Congressman James P. Buchanan, age seventy, suffered a fatal heart attack in Washington."[1] Under Texas law, the state's governor is required to call a special election in such a case, with the seat going to the person receiving the highest number of votes. Thus LBJ, who had returned to the state to head up the National Youth Administration, resigned his job and "at twenty-eight, was one of seven candidates who entered [the] special election on April 10, 1937, to fill the seat from the 10th Congressional District left vacant by the death of Representative James P. Buchanan."[2] Since Texas special election law permitted "the leading vote getter on April 10 . . . [to] . . . be the winner, with no necessity for a runoff,"[3] LBJ's victory launched him on his political career. Thus, unlike Carter and Clinton, who launched their presidential careers on the statewide level, LBJ began his in Congress, as did Al Gore and Barack Obama.

Yet Texas, like both Georgia and Arkansas, had been a one-party state since the Civil War and had an electorate that by 1937 had developed a persistent and nearly consistent partisan voting pattern, with three major discernible demographic voting groups: (1) whites, (2) Latinos, and (3) African Americans. There also was a German American group in the electorate, but it was gradually fading by the time of the 1937 special election.

Of these different racial and ethnic groups, there were some legal barriers. Latino (Mexican-Americans) in the state found that "[t]heir social status lies somewhere between the 'whites' and the Negroes."[4] They were permitted to vote, although it was usually managed because of their low economic status. On the other hand, African Americans were simply disenfranchised via the poll tax, the white primary, intimidation, and violence. Interestingly, they somehow continued to vote in the large urban centers of the state and in some rural areas, out of sheer determination and moral fortitude, and on occasion via political bosses and machines. When African Americans did vote, it was in special and general elections. A few even voted in the "white only Democratic primaries,"[5] although it was illegal to do so. These barriers notwithstanding, both Latinos and African Americans participated in the initial election of LBJ to Congress in the 1937 special election. This special election took place in a political and electoral context that had been set in concrete with the Civil War.

As Key found in his classic 1949 study, Texas was a one-party Democratic state like most of the South. With the shifts in Texas's demography, however, there was a shift in partisanship that found parallels only in Florida and Arkansas. Part of the reason for this was the small African American population in Texas and its basic residential grouping in the eastern part of the state. Key writes, "Texas . . . like other southern states . . . is a one-party state because in 1860 a substantial part of its population consisted of Negro slaves. Most of its people then lived in East Texas, and the land to the west was largely undeveloped."[6] Nine decades after the Civil War, the dynamism in Texas—which developed from its rapid population growth, the setting and development of western Texas, and the discovery of its national resources—"weakened the heritage of southern traditionalism, revolutionized the economy, and made Texas more western than southern."[7] But perhaps most importantly the state's development significantly reduced the size of its African American population. Thus, "[i]n 1940 only one Texan in seven was a Negro. White Texans, unlike white Mississippians, have little cause to be obsessed about the Negro."[8] The end result of this dynamism was that the one-party system in Texas persisted even though "its original basis [had] shrunk to minor significance." In Texas, the Democratic Party was supreme, but the "presence of large numbers of Negroes has been influential in determining the lines of political division and often in diverting the attention of the electorate from nonracial issues."[9]

Key described the one-party system in Texas as one concerned with "real" issues in the forties, arguing that "[i]n Texas the vague outlines of a politics are emerging in which irrelevancies are pushed into the background and people divide broadly along liberal and conservative lines." And the dominant issue turned "on the economic policies of the government."[10] Therefore, when LBJ won his congressional post in 1937, the fight in the state's party was along "New Deal and anti-New Deal lines" and was evolving into a politics of class.[11] The Democratic Party was involved in a struggle between the "haves" and the "have-nots."[12] LBJ supported the "have-nots." And this rising class-based politics forced an ideological division onto the state electorate. Hence, "the terms 'liberal' and 'conservative' have real meaning in the Democratic politics of Texas."[13]

There was one more unique characteristic of the one-party Texas Democratic politics in the forties. Key again posited:

> The upshot of the introduction of conservative-liberal debate into Texas politics in recent elections has been the formation of divisions of voters, at least superficially, unlike those elsewhere in the South. A loose, unorganized factionalism exists, somewhat on the order of that of Arkansas or Florida, yet the division of voters takes a form peculiar to Texas.[14]

As Key saw it, Texas's class-based politics, which was expressed by candidates like LBJ who ran as either "liberals" or "conservatives," did not discipline the party in the state. Texas's economically driven one-party system on the eve of the fifties enjoyed "a far more chaotic factional politics" than the five southern states of Virginia, North Carolina, Tennessee, Georgia, and Louisiana. Texas's one-party factionalism was of a "transient nature. Cleavages among voters form and reform from campaign to campaign depending on the issues and candidates involved. In extreme situations, only the most shadowy continuity of faction prevails, either in voter grouping or in the composition of the leadership."[15] Texas had a system that was multifactional in nature where candidates ran as liberal or conservative and the electorate divided along class lines. Yet before he ended his observations on the Texas electorate, Key declared that the "discontinuous and kaleidoscopic quality" of the Democratic Party factions were numbered.[16] Subsequent studies of Texas's electorate have accepted Key's baseline analysis but have noted that dynamism in the state's context has altered this one-party system.

Building upon Key's portrait of the Texas electorate, Alexander Head, writing in 1952 about Republican partisans in the Texas electorate, stated, "There are Republican high points in the South that are explained neither by topography nor by Populist ancestry. Among these are the 'German' counties of south central Texas. . . . The section of Texas most heavily Republican was settled by large numbers of Germans during the Republic and early days of statehood. . . . They disapproved of slaveholding, and . . . became Unionists."[17] After the Civil War, the African American freedmen joined this group.[18] Thus, "in the seventies and eighties and nineties the Republicans Party included politicians and voters of both races."[19] Soon cooperation gave way to intraparty strife and factionalism. In fact, it was African American Republican Party leader Norris Wright Cuney who first coined the term "lily-white Republicans" in 1888–89. "White Republican Clubs" arose in the state that "were founded solely on race prejudice" and sought to "take control of the party functions" from African Americans. This displacement process was slow to push African Americans out of the party; but by the time that Hoover was elected in 1928, the process was complete. This capture of the Republican Party by whites, coupled with the disenfranchisement of the African American electorate and those of the Democratic Party as the party of white supremacy, reduced the Republican Party to presidential Republicans, with the sole exception being the German counties sending a single Republican from Texas to Congress in 1920.[20]

The other ramification was the rise of a Republican boss, R. B. Creager, who from 1928 until he died in 1950 was the party and a staunch supporter of President William Howard Taft's son Robert. As such he warded off with no little skill the attacks of all other would-be leaders and reformers. Heard wrote that Creager's "tight oligarchy for a generation rebuffed all attempts to unseat him."[21] His death created a leadership vacuum and enabled Democratic governor Alan Shivers to lead Democrats for Eisenhower in 1952 and to a lesser extent in 1956 and 1960. When his followers returned to the Democratic fold in 1960, the vacuum reemerged, and the rebirth of the Texas Republican Party came from the rising economic conservative forces in the state.

Following up on the work of Key and Heard, a group of Texas authors focused on the 1962 gubernatorial campaign as a pivotal event. "Republicans in 1962 were priming themselves for serious contention in a number of races, an effort in nonpresidential election years as unusual as it was unpredictable. The element of uncertainty introduced by Republican plans was compounded by the relative anarchy that suddenly emerged in the Democratic Party."[22] The "second Democratic primary of 1962 saw an inexperienced, generally unknown and avowedly liberal candidate come within a hair of winning the Democratic gubernatorial nomination."[23] In addition, in this primary there was a "drop in Negro support of the liberal Democrat" (Don Yarborough). In that election "a group of Negro business and professional people formed another statewide political organization—the United Political Organization—most of whose leaders supported [John] Connally in 1962."[24] These elections "showed the GOP gains to be in large measure by way of solidifying and expanding continuing spheres of influence. . . . The 1962 primaries, by contrast, broke liberal Democratic ranks in North and Central Texas to an extent unknown for several years."[25]

What helped to make 1962 such a watershed year was the election in 1961 of a Republican, John Tower, to the U.S. Senate, taking the seat held by LBJ before he resigned to take the vice presidency. On June 15, 1961, "Tower ushered in a new day in Texas politics. . . . [he was] . . . the first Republican to win a statewide office in Texas since Reconstruction. . . . His victory forever changed politics in the Lone Star State."[26] Thus, "[w]ithout question the Republican effort in the 1962 general election was the strongest since Reconstruction days. . . . Almost all of the local offices filled by Republican were won in 1962."[27] A new Republican revolution had been launched that freed the party from its Reconstruction legacy.

These authors concluded with the observation that "[p]erhaps it is most appropriate to refer to present-day Texas as a 'one and two-thirds party state.' That is, in two out of three respects the Republican Party has a real chance to win elections. . . . The present situation may favor the growth of the Texas GOP as a militantly conservative group. . . . [T]he Texas Republicans now have established more than a beachhead. They have actually opened up two fronts in their political warfare against the Democrats."[28] However, shortly before the book's publication, LBJ had succeeded to the presidency. This led them to forecast the effect of LBJ's rise on Texas party politics and the prospects for the Republican Party in a postscript: "Within the short range, it seems likely that the accession of Johnson to the Presidency will again make Texas safe for the Democratic Party in 1964. . . . It seems probable too that a bid by Governor Connally . . . for a second term will be resisted less strenuously than was his first, both in the Democratic primary and in the general election."[29] They continued, "Thus, the Johnson Administration seems likely to produce but a temporary interruption to the process of political realignment in Texas. . . . But, as the memories of November 22 fade, and as the novelty of a Texan at the head of the national Democratic Party wears off, a revival of [Republican] tendencies . . . will again emerge."[30] This was a surprisingly accurate forecast: LBJ carried the state in 1964 and for his vice president in 1968.

Beginning in the early seventies, on the eve of the 1972 election and shortly thereafter, a spate of books on southern politics appeared.[31] Most attempted to update Key's classic, given the impact of the 1965 Voting Rights Act and its 1970 and 1975 renewals, which produced an increasing wave of African American elected officials across the nation and many African American candidates in the states of the old Confederacy.[32]

Among these books were a large number of edited volumes with contributors writing on a particular state. O. Douglas Weeks, a prolific political scientist who had written a large number of excellent works on his home state of Texas, offered unmatched insights into Republican partisanship in the state. In one of his last works—he died in 1970—he assessed the dynamism in the state's two-party evolution:

> In spite of the stress and upheaval in Texas politics since 1952, the state seemed to come out in the campaign year of 1968 remarkably unchanged. The Republican Party has tried strenuously to become a second major party in Texas and to establish a two-party system, but still the Democrats hold the center of the political stage. . . . Texas in the elections of 1966, 1968, and 1970 went largely back to normal—a one-party state with its politics mainly confined to the factionalism of the Democratic Party.[33]

Weeks found that the Republican Party "has improved its position of competitiveness in presidential, gubernatorial, and United States senatorial elections." The party's growth came not so much as a result of its own efforts as much as it came from immigration from outside of the state and factional in-fighting within the Democratic Party. Weeks found that by 1970 the Texas "Republicans are chiefly a reactionary or very conservative group, but they have by no means won away from the Democrats a large reactionary or conservative faction, which still clings to the latter party."[34] Thus, as the decade of the seventies began, the Republican partisans had increased, and they had a Republican United States senator. Much work remained in order for the party to establish itself in the political culture of Texas.

Ronald Reagan's victory over regional native son Carter in 1980, his reelection in 1984, and the election of his vice president, a native son of Texas, in 1988 gave the party a surge of recruiting energy in the state. The new realignment in the state's electorate led southern white political scientists to evaluate the changes thusly: "Texas is a state undergoing considerable change. Even the casual observer is aware of Texas's move from the status of a somewhat atypical and idiosyncratic 'southern' state to its new position as a prominent member of the fast-developing Sunbelt."[35] They added:

> Since the Eisenhower era, Texans have supported the Republican nominee in every presidential election except for native son Lyndon Johnson in 1964 and Jimmy Carter in 1976. Republican Bill Clements was elected governor in 1978 and again in 1986. . . . The

> strength of the Republicans in statewide contests in Texas has been significant in this past decade. . . . Republicans are increasingly competitive for state and local offices, virtually dominating countrywide offices in areas like Dallas and parts of West Texas.[36]

Despite these movements in the 1980s with a Republican president in the White House, the authors hastened to add, "The election of Governor Bill Clements in 1986 should not, however, be viewed as a signal of new Republican ascendency in Texas politics. Clements won in 1986, but the Republican party did not experience a surge of new identifiers after his election."[37] Therefore, they concluded that "the stage is set for a long struggle between Republican and Democrats for the control of Texas politics."

With the subsequent defeat of adopted son President George H. W. Bush in 1992, another group of southern white political scientists assessed the evolution of Republican partisanship in Texas vis-à-vis traditional Democratic supporters. Reflecting on Key's original portrait, these authors noted, "No single factor, such as race or oil and gas or conservatism or Key's 'modified class politics,' can describe the politics in Texas today. If there is a dominant theme to Texas politics today, it is change. . . . Texas today bears little resemblance to the Texas of five decades ago."[38]

Figure 6.1 examines the variables that these authors described as sweeping the Texas electorate away from its Democratic foundation and toward a realignment with the ever-rising Texas Republican Party. First among the three independent variables is race: "Certainly race has been a major factor in the Republican upsurge in Texas. As the national Democratic Party became identified as the party representing the interests of African Americans and other racial and ethnic minorities, white Texas increasingly considered the Republican Party a viable alternative. . . . [T]he Democratic Party's image . . . accelerated white flight from the ranks of the Democrats."[39]

The second determinant is the power ideology in the state's dynamic political culture. "Ideology," these authors found, "contributed to the emergence of the Republican Party in Texas. The nomination of liberal George McGovern as the Democratic Party's presidential candidate in 1972 . . . hastened the exodus of conservative white Texans to the GOP."[40]

The final variable is population. "Demographic patterns . . . spurred Republican growth in Texas. Texas is a Sun belt state with a steady flux of immigrants from other states. Many of these new Texans came from traditionally Republican states; scholarly research suggests that nearly one-fourth of Texas's Republicans are not native to the state."[41]

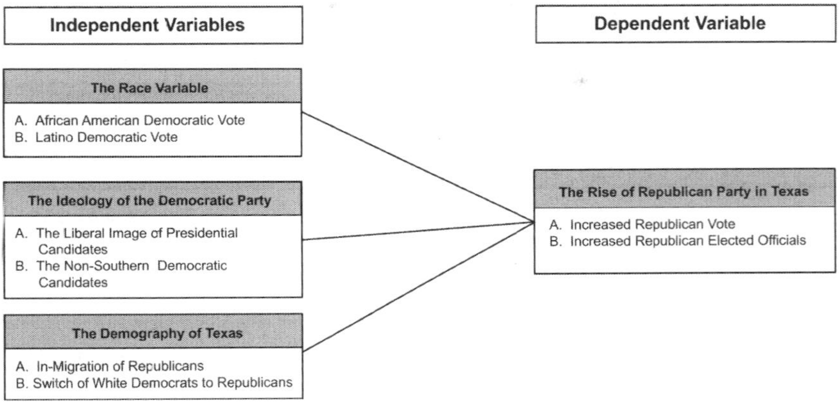

Fig. 6.1. The Independent Variables Leading to a Republican One-Party System in Texas Politics
(Data from James W. Lamare, J. L. Polinard, and Robert D. Wrinkle, "Texas: Lone Star (Wars) State," in *The New Politics of the Old South: An Introduction to Southern Politics*, edited by Charles S. Bullock III and Mark J. Rozell [Lanham, MD: Rowman & Littlefield, 1998], 248–49.)

Drawing upon the power of these three central variables, the authors forecast a partisan future for the state: "[T]he issue no longer is whether Texas is a two-party state; rather it is whether Texas is becoming a one-party state with the Republican Party wearing the crown."[42] Drawing upon electoral data and the victories of the Republican Party in the state, they wrote, "In 1980, a Republican occupied the governor's office, a Republican was the state's senior U.S. Senator, and Ronald Reagan . . . had just been elected president."[43] Then in four years things improved:

> In the 1984 elections Ronald Reagan easily carried Texas, Phil Gramm became the second Republican from Texas elected to the U.S. Senate, and, perhaps more important, Republicans gained seats in both the state senate and the state house. Republicans also made significant inroads in county elections, winning twice as many seats as they had held prior to the election.[44]

They found more Republican trends. "[F]avorite son George Bush in 1988" as head of the party's ticket carried the nation and Texas as well, making it possible for "the GOP upsurge [to] continue throughout the 1980s. . . . The net result: by the 1990s, party identification was virtually identical between the two parties."[45] By 1993, when Kay Bailey Hutchinson won, both of Texas's U.S. senators were Republican. Then former president Bush's son George W. Bush became "the second Republican governor of Texas since Reconstruction."[46] Therefore, they observed, "Forget Dixie: as far as Texas partisan politics is concerned, old times there may soon be forgotten."[47] Texas governor George W. Bush won the Republican Party presidential nomination and was the state native-son presidential candidate in 2000. In that election, he won the state and the presidency.

To summarize these decade-by-decade portraits of the Texas electorate, the Republican Party has become competitive, not in a linear fashion but in a cyclical fashion. Texas has shifted in five decades from a one-party Democratic state to a potentially one-party Republican state with the fading Democratic Party rooted not in the white electorate but in the African American and Latino communities. In the aftermath of the first presidential election of the twenty-first century with a Republican native son again winning the presidency, can the portrait have formed itself into a simple partisan reversal?

The Turnout of the Texas Electorate

The creation of a portrait of the Texas electorate across time is hampered by the nature and scope of the literature. While significant in its own right, the literature's basically decade-by-decade analysis provides a piecemeal continuity. For the most part the literature emphasizes Republican growth and evolution with little focus on the Democrats. It tends to treat partisanship in the Texas electorate as a zero-sum game, where the Republican electorate gains at the expense of the Democrats. This sequenced portrait of the Texas electorate omits several things, particularly the size and turnout of the electorate. Therefore, to provide the empirical parameters of the Texas electorate, it is essential that we begin with its central contextual characteristics, and then move to its partisanship characteristics and the voting behavior of its major demographic groups.

Texas was worse than both Georgia and Arkansas in not having a statewide voter registration system. Because of this, there was no data to preserve. The only criteria one needed to vote was a poll tax receipt. Such a tax was instituted in the Texas Constitution of 1877 but was not made a prerequisite for voting until 1902, where the provision requiring the payment of a poll tax was finally enforced.[48] It is from these poll tax receipts, as voter registration data, that it is possible to estimate voter turnout. We can take these receipts and add in those who are exempted because of age and other reasons, and derive an empirical estimate of those registered to vote in the state. Using that data along with the election return data, we can calculate a measure of voter turnout in the Texas electorate.

Shortly before LBJ became a congressional candidate, political scientist Idella Swisher wrote, "Only Delaware, Maine, Texas and North Dakota have no official state publication containing election returns."[49] "Primary election returns [in Texas] . . . are not available in the office of the secretary of state, but must be obtained from the state executive of each party."[50]

With these provisos in mind, it is possible then to see how the Texas electorate turned out to vote in four presidential and thirty-two gubernatorial elections. And while the data estimated from the *Texas Almanac* are incomplete, they do reveal that beginning in 1880 more than four-fifths of the electorate turned out to vote. But in all three categories—presidential primary, gubernatorial primary, and general election—turnout declined consistently until 1952, when there was a huge upsurge. This was the year in which the Republican and Democratic Parties fused under the leadership of Democratic governor Allan Shivers. The resulting Republican sweep temporarily reversed the voter turnout trend.

Figure 6.2 examines the total votes cast in most of the presidential, senatorial, and congressional elections from 1860 to 1996. In 1872, 1876, and 1880, the voter turnout was greater in the congressional contests than in the presidential ones. From 1884 through 1900 the electorate turnout in those two elections was about the same. Then in 1904, the first election after disenfranchisement, the electorate began a pattern of turning out in greater numbers for the congressional candidates.

Sporadically, from 1876 to 1964 the Texas electorate had one congressional representative elected at large as a result of the state designating newly allocated districts at large in 1870 (these districts did not change status until 1965). In these at-large districts, where numerous candidates ran for the position, the electorate turnouts in many years greatly exceeded the turnout in presidential elections. With the exception of these ten elections, however, more people in Texas voted in presidential than in senatorial elections except in 1924, and more Texans voted in presidential than in congressional elections. In this one-party state, presidential elections bought more people to the polls. Such was not the case in either Georgia or Arkansas, yet the Texas electorate was closer to the model of the Georgia electorate, where every voter generally turned out in congressional elections.[51]

At the presidential level the voter turnout of the Texas electorate began at less than 100,000 before the Civil War and rose steadily to over half a

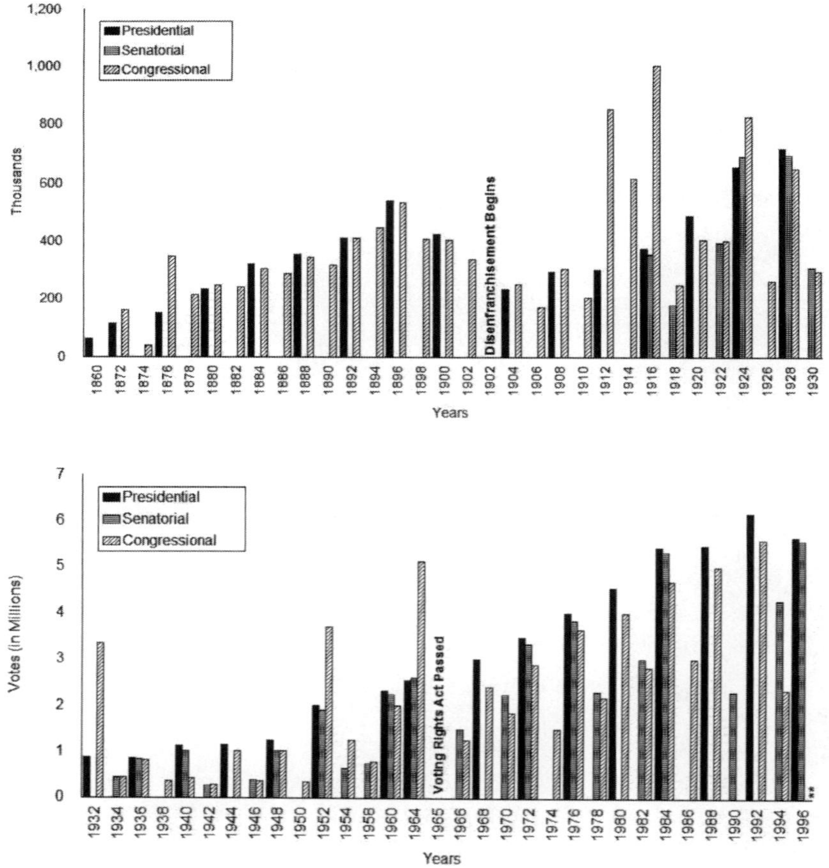

Fig. 6.2. The Total Votes Cast in Texas's Presidential, Congressional, and Senatorial Elections: 1860–1996

(Adapted from Congressional Quarterly, *Guide to U.S. Elections*, 3rd ed. [Washington, DC: Congressional Quarterly, 1994], 435–68, 841–42, 1026–1325; and Richard Scammon, Alice McGillivray, and Rhodes Cook, eds., *America Votes 23* [Washington, DC: Congressional Quarterly, 1998], 465.)

million in 1896. Turnout then declined in 1900 and again in 1904, and did not reach its 1896 level again until 1924. From that point on, voter turnout steadily increased as Texas grew in population, declining only with Clinton's reelection bid in 1996. This trend reversed itself, however, with George W. Bush's presidential bid in 2000. Johnson's 1964 vote total was nearly 300,000 votes greater than that received by John Kennedy in 1960. However, when George H. W. Bush ran in 1988, he received only a 29,839 vote increase over Reagan's 1984 turnout. Thus, Republican and Texan George H. W. Bush did not rally the state's electorate as much as Democrat Lyndon Johnson.

Overall, the turnout of the Texas electorate peaked in 1880 at 88 percent in the presidential election and 80 percent in the gubernatorial general election. After review of the poll tax data, we know the electorate declined precipitously thereafter, with a revival coming in the Eisenhower-dominated fifties. Using actual votes, however, the story is a steady rise with a few exceptions until 2000 when nearly seven million voters turned out for the presidential election. Below the presidential level, the leading structural force in increasing turnout has been the existence of at-large statewide congressional districts in 10 elections. In the 66 elections from 1860 to 2000, these 10 have seen turnout increased by institutional changes in the state's electoral procedures. Another institutional change, the disenfranchisement of the African American electorate, aided in the decline of voter turnout from 1898 until 1922.

With these institutional changes aside, the Texas electorate has turned out in their greatest numbers in presidential, then senatorial, and finally congressional elections. In national elections, the turnout of the Texas electorate has declined over the years, but its sheer voting size has significantly increased, more so since the forties. And LBJ became one of the independent variables affecting the size of that voting turnout in 1964.[52]

Party Voting in Texas Presidential Elections

Shifting from the broad parameters of the Texas electorate to focus specifically on the presidential elections, it is possible to refine our portrait and sharpen the analysis to explore the precise impact of Texas's native son LBJ, as well as that of Democrats James Nance Garner and Lloyd Bentsen, and Republicans George H. W. Bush and his son George W. Bush. Figure 6.2 provides the amount of voter participation in each of Texas's 39 presidential elections from 1848 to 2000 (Texas did not participate in the 1864 and 1868 elections due to the Civil War). Nearly three out of every four voters participated in the initial presidential election in 1848, after the state joined the Union. Then came a decline up until the eve of the Civil War when the issue of slavery increased participation. After the Civil War, the turnout slowly increased until the turn of the century, when informal and then formal disenfranchisement of the African American electorate cut voter participation in half. African Americans' successful struggle to eliminate the white primary in Texas in 1944 pushed up voter participation through 1964, followed by a substantial increase after the 1965 passage of the Voting Rights Act. In this instance, Texas presidential voter participation is similar to that in Arkansas and Georgia.[53]

Substantial structural forces reduced and later increased Texas's participation as racial discrimination was a factor in 30 of Texas's 39 presidential elections. LBJ, Carter, and Clinton led to a resurgence in voter participation in presidential elections. Later, Bush senior and President Obama would do the same.

Knowing the levels of voter participation in Texas presidential elections, one can ask, How did this participation appear in a longitudinal fashion in terms of partisanship, despite the fact that this was a one-party state? Figure 6.3 shows the partisan vote for Democratic and Republican presidential candidates. The Republican Party captured the state in 11 presidential elections and the Democrats won 23, or 70 percent. When the Texas electorate turns out to vote in presidential elections, they usually have turned out to vote for the Democratic Party. In 13 straight elections from 1876 to 1924, the Democratic Party won each one, and again from 1932 until 1948, followed by the Eisenhower landslides of 1952 and 1956, which swept this one-party Democratic state. The influence of native son Lyndon Johnson confronted and reversed the Republicans in 1960, 1964, and 1968. Of the three other successful Democratic presidential candidates following Johnson, only one won Texas: Carter. Clinton did not win Texas at all; neither did Democratic nominee Senator Obama in 2008 nor his 2012 reelection.

In addition to the two major parties, the state's electorate has voted strongly for a variety of third-party presidential candidates. In 1892 and 1912 the combined vote for third parties was higher than the vote for the Republican Party. Table 6.1 shows that left-wing economic parties have done quite well in the state over a substantial period of time. Initially, parties that focused on the economic distress of rural and urban laborers got the electorate's support. In fact, in 1892 the Populist Party and other third parties captured one in every four votes cast by the electorate. In 1912 the Socialists and Progressives together received 17 percent of the vote. However, it was not until the forties with the Texas Regulars and then the Dixiecrats, followed by the American Independent Party (AIP) in 1968, that the right-wing race-based segregationist parties began to show their strength and capture electoral support in state presidential voting. The strongest of these three parties was George Wallace's AIP, which got nearly one out of every five votes in the state. Even in a state with an economic

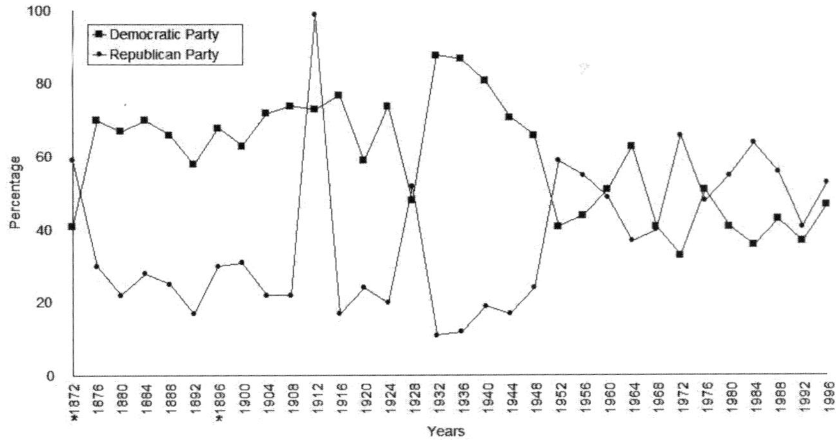

Fig. 6.3. The Major Political Parties Percentage of the Presidential Vote in Texas: 1872–1996
(Adapted from Congressional Quarterly, *Guide to U.S. Elections*, 3rd ed. [Washington, DC: Congressional Quarterly, 1994], 435–68, for data through the 1992 elections; and Richard Scammon, Alice McGillivray, and Rhodes Cook, eds., *America Votes 22* [Washington, DC: Congressional Quarterly, 1998], 465, for data for the 1996 election.)

focus, race can enter into presidential voting behavior as it did in 1944, 1948, and 1968. As the vote for Wallace's AIP shows, race and racial concerns outlasted LBJ's effort to solve them, at least in his own state.

Yet this is not the entire story. Texas is uniquely different in its third parties from Georgia and Arkansas, and more akin to Alabama and South Carolina in that it has generated a native-son third party presidential candidate. In 1992 and again in 1996, Texas billionaire H. Ross Perot launched his own conservative economic party known as the United We Stand America Party. This party's support in the Texas electorate was nearly the same as it was in the other 50 states. Perot captured 19 percent of the national vote in his 1992 run, while in Texas it was 22 percent. The Perot vote did not reach these levels in either Arkansas or Georgia. Even for a third party candidate, the Texas electorate turned out for its native son.

If party voting in Texas has substantially favored the Democratic Party, one can ask a follow-up question: How much did the partisans in the state electorate favor the Democrats? The Democratic Party's winning pluralities reached a high of 77 percent in 1932 and low of 1 percent in 1968. Republican pluralities peaked at 33 percent in 1972 and were at their lowest in 1928 and 1992. Thus, while the Republicans have captured 11 elections, they have not been able to convert as much of the state electorate to their cause as have the Democrats. Support for the Republican Party, even with a native-son candidate at the helm, has never come close to approaching the levels enjoyed by the Democrats. This is as true for Arkansas and Georgia as it has been for Texas, although Arkansas and Georgia have not had Republican presidential nominees.

LBJ in 1964 pushed the Democratic Party plurality to 26 percentage points, while George H. W. Bush pushed the GOP plurality only to 13 percent in 1988 and George W. Bush to 21 percent in 2000. Carter in 1976 pushed the party's pluralities as high as 3 percentage points, which was greater than LBJ's 2 percentage points in 1960 when he was a vice presidential candidate. Bush, as the vice president on the 1980 ticket, received a 14 percentage point plurality, and 28 percent in 1984. Both of Bush's pluralities were much higher when he was the vice presidential candidate than when he was the presidential candidate, which suggests that Reagan had significant pulling power himself, in addition to this native son. The

TABLE 6.1. The Vote Percentage for Significant Third Party Presidential Candidates in Texas: 1880–1996

Year	Vote (%)	Third Party
1880	12	Greenback
1888	8	Union Labor
1892	24	Populist
1900	6	Combined
1904	2	Prohibition
1908	3	Socialists
1912	9	Progressive
1912	8	Socialists
1916	5	Socialists
1920	2	Socialists
1920	16	Combined
1924	7	Progressive
1944	12	Texas Regulars
1948	9	Dixiecrats
1968	19	American Independent Party
1980	3	John Anderson
1992	22	H. Ross Perot
1996	7	H. Ross Perot

Source: Congressional Quarterly, *Guide to U.S. Elections,* 3rd ed. (Washington, DC: Congressional Quarterly, 1994), 438–68, for data through the 1992 elections; Richard Scammon, Alice McGillivray, and Rhodes Cook, eds., *America Votes 22* (Washington, DC: Congressional Quarterly, 1998), 465, for data for the 1996 election.

Democratic Party secured its greatest percentage plurality in 1932 and 1936 when native son James Nance Garner was the vice presidential candidate on the ticket running with Franklin Roosevelt. When Garner abandoned the ticket in 1940 and 1944, the pluralities for the party in the state dropped but remained at well over 50 percent, demonstrating the pulling power of the native-son vice presidential candidate.

Party Voting in Texas Congressional Elections

If party voting in presidential elections in Texas has a Democratic look, then what is the story in congressional voting behavior in the state? To get a more balanced picture of party voting in the state, it is necessary to establish when the Republican Party competed with the Democratic Party for seats in Congress before we explore the data for an empirical rendering. The Republican Party was a minority party in state politics for a very long time simply because it did not put up a candidate for every seat at every congressional election over time, despite the very large numbers of congressional seats in this big state. There have been very few times in the 65 elections where the Republican Party competed in 100 percent of the races. In 1880, the Republican Party put no candidates up for congressional office. Even during the Eisenhower years, particularly 1952, only 5 percent of the congressional candidates were Republicans; and even during the Reagan and Bush years, the party did not field a candidate for every congressional race. The historical mean is 68 percent of the seats being contested by Republican candidates. However, in recent years, the Democratic Party has not put a complete slate of candidates into the field; but this is a very recent phenomenon. For nearly every congressional cycle the Democrats have dominated the competition and therefore the victories.

Having seen that the Democratic Party has been more competitive than the Republican Party for congressional seats, one can move to the matter of voter turnout and participation in congressional elections. Data published by the U.S. Census Bureau beginning with the 1960 election has estimated voter turnout in both presidential and congressional elections for each one of the elections that took place between 1960 and 1996. A comparison of the turnout in the presidential and U.S. House of Representatives elections in the state of Texas reveals that more voters participate in presidential than in congressional elections. But the two times that the turnout was closest, 1964 and 1976, was when southern native sons Johnson and Carter were running. Similarly close results occurred when native-son vice president George Bush was on the ticket in 1980 and 1984; but when he headed the ticket in 1988, participation in congressional elections fell. Thus, the Census Bureau data confirm what the *Texas Almanac* revealed earlier: there is a decrease in turnout between presidential voting and congressional voting in the state's electorate.

Understanding that the Texas electorate does not turn out in great numbers to vote for their congresspersons, we can now study how this affects the state's political parties. A comparative analysis tells us that there is little doubt that the Texas electorate shows a dominant if not overwhelming preference for the Democratic Party. On nearly every occasion from 1872 until 1996, Texas voters sent Democrats to the U.S. House of Representatives in large numbers. Only in recent years has the mean vote for the Republican Party started to catch up with the vote for the Democratic Party.

The vote for congressional Democrats always has been high, but in 1910 it leaped to the 90 percent level, stayed there fairly consistently until the 1950s, and began a decline thereafter. Thus, when LBJ went to Congress in 1937, the mean Democratic vote was between 94 and 99 percent, and it continued at this level though his tenure in Congress. After LBJ, the mean Democratic vote began a relentless descent from which it has yet to recover. None of the subsequent native sons have reversed the continued slide. In contrast, the Reagan-Bush presidencies gave the Republican mean vote for congressional candidates a boost, and it has continued to increase since then.

As in presidential voting, the Texas electorate's one-party voting behavior held at the congressional level as well, until very recently when Republicans captured both Senate seats and a growing number of House seats. One-party voting in Texas is now a diluted reality. Unlike Arkansas but like Georgia, Texas is heading toward a two-party system, at least at the congressional and presidential levels.

Party Voting in Texas Gubernatorial Elections

We have seen that in national election contests Texas had recently started to shift toward a dual partisanship. More and more of the Texas electorate is voting Republican, and more and more Republican candidates are winning in the state and carrying its electoral votes in presidential elections. Much of this, though not all of it, has been a feature of the state's electorate since LBJ departed from the political arena. The 2008 election revealed a tendency toward the Democratic Party. However, the 2012 election stalled this reality.

Starting with the matter of voter turnout, data shown in figure 6.2 indicated that primary elections get greater participation than general elections as far as races for the governor's office are concerned. This is a feature of the one-party South in general and Texas in particular. On this matter the Texas electorate is closer to the Georgia electorate than to Arkansas.[54] In these states, primary elections simply get more voters than the general elections.

Since it was a one-party state, we can analyze the Texas voter turnout using raw vote totals in the Democratic primary, the runoff elections, and for Democratic candidates in the general election. A comprehensive portrait of voter turnout for the Democratic Party in every election is possible, which also will permit an analysis of the turnout specifically when LBJ was on the presidential ticket. This will provide clues to his influence on the mobilization of the electorate for the state ticket. Such an analysis was not possible with Carter since he ran in 1976 and the state gubernatorial elections were in 1974 and 1978. The same pattern was true for Clinton in Arkansas. This provides yet another unique perspective on the native-son candidate variable.

Texas's Democrats turn out in larger numbers for gubernatorial races than they do for runoff and general elections, with a few exceptions. One of the notable exceptions is the 1964 gubernatorial election, when the general election vote for the Democratic candidate exceeded the total vote in the primary. This huge turnout in the general election was not necessary, since the Republican candidate was not particularly competitive. Clearly LBJ's run mobilized the Democrats to go to the polls in his home state.

However, beginning in 1982, when the second Republican governor in the state's history, William Clements, sought reelection, more Democrats turned out and denied him reelection. This year seems to have set a benchmark because thereafter more Democrats voted in general elections than in primaries and runoffs, reversing a long historical pattern. George W. Bush's election and reelection reversed that trend.

Analyzing voter turnout from raw vote totals, the final election data for primaries and general elections for governor demonstrate that on most occasions more Texans have voted in the Democratic primaries than in the general election or in Republican primaries. Rarely did runoff elections, except in 1954, get more voter turnout than did the Democratic primaries. Texas, like Arkansas but unlike Georgia, had two-year gubernatorial terms until 1974, when four-year terms were mandated. In that year voter participation dropped by two million votes. Only in 1982 would it rebound back to that level and begin a steady rise. George W. Bush's initial election in 2000 brought out four million voters, but his reelection bid dropped back to three million votes in 2004. Thus, in recent years, as the system has moved toward two parties, the number of participants has steadily increased; and like Arkansas and Georgia, Texas has now had Republican governors. Not being a participant in the gubernatorial arena, LBJ does not arise as an independent variable on this group of gubernatorial elections, nor do any of his congressional or presidential elections correlate with a significant event that may have shaped an outcome in a gubernatorial election in the state. But this does not eliminate the fact that LBJ was close to several of these Democrats governors.

Using the vote percentages for Democratic, Republican, and third party gubernatorial candidates from 1869 until 1998, this time series shows Democratic gubernatorial candidates have won 53 (91 percent) of the 58 gubernatorial elections. Truly, one party has dominated on the state level as well as in national elections. The first Republican to win the governorship came in 1869, during Reconstruction, and the second did not come for over one hundred years, in 1978. This was followed in rapid succession by Republican victories in 1986, 1994, 1998, 2002, 2006, and 2010.

In 1952, when the Democrats fused with the Republicans, the joint candidate won 100 percent of the vote. But the Democratic Party alone had won 96 percent in 1934 and 1936 and 97 percent in 1938. In contrast, Republicans have received few to no votes on seven occasions from 1896 to 1952. When LBJ ran for vice president in 1960, the Republican candidate for governor got 27 percent of the vote; 36 percent in 1964, when Johnson ran for president; and 43 percent, after he stepped down in 1968.

Minor party candidates have not been without their influence as well. In the 1892 through 1898 elections, third-party gubernatorial candidates received from 25 to 44 percent of the vote. Although they have not attracted double-digit electoral support since 1920, they have continued to participate in state politics. Surprisingly, no race-based third-party gubernatorial candidates have come forth. However, African American and Latino third parties have fielded candidates in recent gubernatorial elections.

Voting at the gubernatorial level in Texas has been a totally Democratic affair until recently. In recent years, Texans have placed a few Republicans in the governor's mansion, but this has occurred long after LBJ departed the political scene.

Party Voting in the Presidential Home Counties

Previous volumes on Carter and Clinton merged and analyzed together their home counties. Carter's home county of Sumter was both his birth and his resident county and could be treated singularly. Clinton had a different birth county and resident county.[55] A time-series analysis of both of Clinton's counties' voting behavior revealed that the Democratic Party had won continually at the national and state levels, enabling one to study these counties via a merger and a summary statistic, the mean, to be used to view their voting behavior in a longitudinal fashion.[56] But this is not the case with LBJ. Like Clinton, LBJ had both a birth county, Gillespie, and a resident county, Blanco; but unlike Clinton he moved back to Gillespie in the early 1950s. A time-series analysis reveals that these two counties differed significantly in their partisanship, so they will have to be separated if we are to understand the nature and scope of party voting there. Moreover, as we have seen in our parameter analysis of the Texas electorate, third-party voting has been significant at both the national and state levels. Hence, major party voting will not capture the total party voting in the state, nor in the candidate's home and resident counties. Our analysis must not only separate the two counties, but it must include third-party voting as well. With these caveats in mind, we can begin our analysis of voting behavior in LBJ's home and resident counties.

First, we will begin with Blanco County, the early-life residence of President Johnson. The Democratic partisanship of the county over time is unmistaken. Of the 32 presidential elections covered, the Democratic Party has won 20 (61 percent), and the Republican Party has won 11 (33 percent), and on at least two occasions a third party has carried the county. The vote in LBJ's home county stayed in the Democratic column throughout his time in office, except in 1952 and 1956, when Eisenhower swept the state. When LBJ ran for president in 1964, the county gave the Democrats 80 percent of its vote, and it remained in the Democratic column in 1968, voting for Humphrey. But that was the last year the county went Democratic. Carter came closest to restoring it to the Democratic fold in 1976 when he captured 47 percent of the county vote. Even so, native son George W. Bush captured only 62 percent of the vote in 1988, not nearly as much as LBJ had. Ross Perot captured 27 percent of the county's vote in 1992.

On the other hand, LBJ's birth and later-life resident county of Gillespie reveals a different electoral history. Voting for the presidency began in a balanced fashion with no party having much of an advantage as Republicans and Democrats won about the same number of times. Over time, however, the Democratic Party has won the county six times, while the Republicans have carried it 25 times and third parties twice, in 1912 and 1924. Basically speaking, this birth county of the president has showed a decidedly Republican tendency, which has been largely unbroken from 1896 to the present. Two exceptions to this trend are the FDR New Deal landslide and Johnson's run for the presidency.[57] However, Johnson failed to carry Gillespie County in 1960 when he was on the Democratic ticket as vice president, although he did improve support for the party from 7 percent in 1956 to 23 percent in 1960, nearly tripling the party vote. Since 1964, Gillespie County has given the Democratic Party about one vote in five. As in Blanco County, neither Johnson nor subsequent southern native-son presidential candidates Carter, Clinton, and Gore have changed the partisanship patterns or the level of partisan support for the Democratic Party in Gillespie County. Thus, only Blanco County tends to approach the voting behavior pattern of Carter's and Clinton's home counties.

Using gubernatorial election data, it is possible to explore party voting in these two presidential home counties at the state level. Overall, Blanco County kept its Democratic partisanship tendencies. Of the 57 gubernatorial elections, the Democratic Party lost LBJ's home county only eight times. Third parties carried the county in 1894 and 1896, and the Republican Party has carried it only six times, all since the 1978 gubernatorial election. LBJ's county of residence has been very stable in its partisanship.

Gillespie County, however, has been rather much more fluid in its partisanship. Of the 57 state elections, the Republicans won the county 29 times and the Democrats 27 times. The Republican partisanship of this county has been much more pronounced in presidential than in gubernatorial elections where, due to the dominance of Democratic gubernatorial leadership, the county has been moderate in its Republican tendencies.

Third parties won both counties in 1920, with the greatest support coming from Gillespie where the third party got 61 percent of the total vote cast. Both counties also went strongly Democratic in 1964, the year that LBJ won the presidency. They split in 1960 when LBJ was the vice presidential nominee. In that year Gillespie backed a Republican gubernatorial candidate.

Again, the party voting behaviors of LBJ's home and resident counties at the state level are different from that of Carter and Clinton. These native sons had their home counties go Democratic. Only Blanco County is close to the political behavior of Carter and Clinton's home counties. LBJ's home counties were split in third-partisan support *and* both currently are trending toward a Republican partisanship, as is Texas in general.

Conclusion

What of the Texas electorate? Turnout in the state tended to be greatest in national elections and then followed by state elections, with a few exceptions. While voter turnout has been declining over time, with occasional rises, the actual number of voters has steadily climbed as the decades have passed. Until the 1970s the electorate tended to vote Democratic at the national and state levels. Texas truly has been with few exceptions a one-party state. The Democratic Party has dominated state politics and rising politicians have embraced the party in order to be elected. Since the 1970s the Republican Party has become competitive with the Democratic Party, and, as of 2015, both U.S. senators, the governor's mansion, and the state senate are completely in Republican hands. As the Democratic Party has recently loosened its political grip on state and national power in Texas, there has been a rise in African American and Latino elected officials. The class-based economic conservatives and the race-based conservatives have shifted the Texas that V. O. Key Jr. saw and captured in the forties to the Republican Party. The baseline portrait of the electorate captured so ably by Key has been in transition in the six decades since.

In this gradual transition of the Texas electorate's partisanship, various candidates have caused surges in Democratic dominance and a decline in the rising Republican electoral tide in the state. This has been true of national and state elections as well as of LBJ's influence on his home and resident counties. Shortly after LBJ's exit from national power, the evolving Republican electoral tide began to erode the Democratic dominance that had been enabled by LBJ and his political allies. The appearance of recent Republican native sons has continued this decline of Democratic dominance and reduced their power, as the once-powerful Democrats did to state Republicans. The Texas electorate still has not created a true competitive two-party system, Democratic and Republican native-son presidential candidates notwithstanding.

★ 7

The African American and Latino Electorates

Political abolitionism came to Texas in an institutionalized manner when the state sent a delegation to the 1860 Republican National Convention in Chicago.[1] There were six men in the delegation: two from Austin, two from Galveston, one from San Antonio, and one from Denton County.[2] Since no invitation had been extended to Texas to send a delegation to this second national convention, the seating of the delegation was immediately challenged before the Credentials Committee of the convention by P. A. Hackleman of Indiana: "I want to hear from the delegates from the State of Texas, to know who appointed them to come here. All the others I shall welcome with open hands. I do want an investigation, so far as Texas is concerned."[3]

Responding to this question was M. S. C. Chandler of Galveston, who declared:

> I cannot believe that you are prepared to stifle the voice of Texas, because there the Republican party is in its infancy; for though it is in its infancy, it is nevertheless a hopeful child. [Loud cheers.] Gentlemen, the foreign population—the Germans—are with us. [Loud cheers.] And there will be an electoral ticket in the field there. We come here with no axes to griend [*sic*]. We have our preferences to be sure, and when the time comes, if we are permitted, we shall express that preference.[4]

Chandler continued his response by saying, "Organize yourselves and train under the Republican banner before you accuse us in Texas of not having a Republican organization. It is unbecoming, it is unmanly, it is anti-Republican. [Cheers.] I hail from Galveston. There is free soil—there is anti-slavery sentiment there, and it will be expressed next fall at the polls, depend upon it. [Loud applause and cheers.] We ask a hearing on the floor of this Convention."[5]

After much discussion of this challenge, the Committee on Credentials voted "to report that Texas be allowed six votes in this Convention" and to seat the delegation as representing the state.[6] The committee's report stated why they had made the decision in favor of Texas:

> It was proved before the committee that the Convention which elected the delegates from Texas—resident delegates who are here in attendance, was a mass Convention; that it was called upon a petition signed by some three hundred of the legal voters of Texas. [Applause.] That call was published in some two of the German papers published in the State; that written notices and advertisements were posted up in various parts of Texas, where there is any number of people in favor of the principles of the Republican party, and the committee were almost unanimously of the opinion that these delegates, elected under these circumstances, were fairly entitled to act as the representatives of the Republican party of the State of Texas. [Prolonged applause.]
>
> The question being on the adoption of the report; it was adopted unanimously amid great cheering.[7]

With this favorable report, Texas joined Virginia as the only *two* states from the forthcoming confederacy to be in attendance at the 1860 Republican National Convention.[8] After having gained a right to be seated, the Texas delegation placed one delegate on each of the following committees: Committee on Permanent Organization, Committee on Credentials, and Committee on Business. Before the Convention closed, one delegate became one of the vice presidents of the convention and another became one of the secretaries of the Convention.[9]

Table 7.1 shows the balloting for the presidential and vice presidential nominees by the Texas delegation. In its initial presidential balloting, the delegation had a majority for William Seward of New York, which increased to a unanimous vote on the second and third ballots. However, on the fourth balloting, the Texas delegation changed its six votes to Abraham Lincoln. Lincoln had come in second in the first balloting, and gained additional votes by the second balloting but stayed in second place; but by the third balloting, he had attained first place with 231 ½ of the 465 votes cast, nearly 50 percent of the total. With each balloting the Convention was increasingly turning to him as the nominee, but it was only after he had emerged as the favorite that the Texas delegation shifted to support him.

As to the vice presidential balloting, a similar pattern prevailed. In the critical ballot, Texas was the only state to give Sam Houston any votes. Then on the second balloting they switched to a regional favorite, Cassius M. Clay of Kentucky, who had led on the first balloting. On this second balloting, Senator Hannibal Hamlin of Maine captured 357 (78 percent) of the 456 votes. Although the Texas delegation did not support the winners until they had become a sure thing, they did support candidates that carried some of the spirit of political abolitionism, even if only in a limited manner. The Texas Republicans, led by German Americans, had shown that they embraced antislavery efforts, at least on the national level.

No one from Texas showed up at the 1864 National Republican Convention;[10] the foundation for this activity had been laid at the 1860 convention. There they proved that this small region could coalesce with "the German Republicans of the Northern States" and fight against prejudice and stand for rights.[11] These groups stood for, in their words, "the constitutional rights" of people. In 1860 German Americans in Texas had linked

TABLE 7.1. The Votes of the Texas Delegation at the 1860 Republican National Convention for Presidential and Vice-Presidential Nominees

Ballot	Major Nominees		Minor Nominees
	Presidential Candidates		
	William Seward	Edward Bates	10 other candidates
First Ballot	4	2	0
Second Ballot	6	0	0
Third Ballot[a]	6	0	0
	Vice Presidential Candidates		
	Houston	Cassicus Clay	7 other candidates
First Ballot	6	0	0
Second Ballot[b]	0	6	0

Source: Adapted from Charles Johnson, *Proceeding of the First Three Republican National Conventions of 1856, 1860, and 1864* (Minneapolis: Harrison and Smith Printers, 1893), 149, 152, 153, 160, 161, and 162.

[a]During the fourth balloting, Texas switched its 6 votes to Abraham Lincoln.

[b]During the second balloting, Texas switched its 6 votes to Hannibal Hamlin.

the liberation of African Americans with the Republican Party. This linkage occurred long before African Americans themselves could make it.[12]

The Rise of the African American Electorate: On the Wings of the Republican Party

Although Texas Republicans did not predate the rise of the African American voter, the post–Civil War flowering of the party occurred with the grassroots enfranchisement of the African American voter. Previously, African American voting had been a hit-and-miss proposition. In the years of Spanish rule, "although free blacks could not hold government jobs, they were able to pursue any profession, marry whom they wished, and enjoy the freedoms of any Spanish citizen. . . . Even so, slavery existed in Spanish Texas."[13]

However, "Spanish rule ended with the Mexican revolution of 1821, and for the next fifteen years Mexico determined racial policy in Texas. Blacks had considerable social, occupational, and political latitude when Texas was under the Mexican flag. Blacks could hold political office under Mexican law, and slavery was legally banned."[14] There was a major drawback to Mexican rule of Texas, however:

> Mexico . . . realizing that prohibiting slavery absolutely would inhibit both the coming of Anglo settlers and the economic growth of Texas, failed to enforce the ban. Also, incoming Anglos from the slave-holding Southern states circumvented the anti-slavery law by freeing their slaves on the east bank of the Sabine and 'indenturing' them on the west bank."[15]

Hence, African Americans living in Texas during the years of Mexican rule had legal rights on paper, but these rights were hardly "real" rights in everyday life, given the customs and the political context of the state and the habits of incoming slaveholders from neighboring states. But this was just a harbinger of things to come.

Despite the fact that "freedmen and slaves fought alongside their fellow Texians for independence . . . [t]he situation for blacks changed drastically under the Anglo government of the Texas Republic."

> The Constitution of the Republic of Texas ("General Provisions," Section 9) recognized the legality of slavery and prohibited freed-

men from remaining in the country without congressional approval. Although most free blacks who had settled in Texas before the revolution were allowed to stay on, the spirit of this dramatic legislation became the same spirit that rushed the state into secession and the Civil War in 1861.[16]

From the time that Texas entered the United States in 1845 until the Civil War began in 1861, Article III of the new state constitution "granted the right to vote to 'all free male persons over the age of twenty-one years, except Indians not taxed, Africans and descendants of Africans.'"[17] This meant that unlike North Carolina and Tennessee, which permitted "free men of color" to vote, the state of Texas,[18] like Arkansas and Georgia, refused to extend suffrage rights to this group of individuals. Georgia eventually extended it, but extant records reveal that no one took advantage of this particular suffrage right.[19]

Table 7.2 reveals the number of such persons in Texas over this time frame, both statewide and in the six counties selected for detailed analysis. Notable here is the presence of "free men of color" both in the state and in the Latino counties.[20] Yet their presence did not permit these individuals to participate in the politics of the state. One can surmise that, although

TABLE 7.2. The Number and Percentage of Slaves and Free Persons in Texas and the Demographic Categories: 1850–60

Year	Total Population	White Population	Slave Population	Free Black Population
A. State				
1850	212,592	154,634 (73%)	56,161 (26%)	397 (.002%)
1860	604,215	228,797 (38%)	152,566 (25%)	355 (.001%)
B. 1850 Demographic Categories				
Home Counties[a]	1,240	1,235 (100%)	5 (.004%)	0
Other Counties	—[b]	—[b]	—[a]	—[a]
C. 1860 Demographic Categories				
Home Counties[c]	4,017	3,886 (97%)	131 (3%)	0
Black-Belt Counties[d]	3,977	1,960 (49%)	2,017 (51%)	0
Boss Counties[d]	1,248	1,248 (100%)	0	0
Latino Counties[d]	2,406	2,396 (100%)	6 (.003%)	4 (.002%)

Source: Adapted from the Bureau of Census, *The Seventh Census of the United States 1850* (New York: Arno Press, 1976), 503; and Bureau of Census, *Population of the United States in 1860* (Washington, DC: Government Printing Office, 1864), 484–86.

[a]Only Gillespie County existed in 1850.

[b]None of the other counties in the different demographic categories existed in 1850.

[c]These are the combined totals for the two counties in this demographic category.

[d]Only one county in each of these demographic categories existed in 1860.

Texas's Spanish and Mexican heritage provided wider political latitude to African Americans, when the Anglos acquired power they eliminated this culturally based privilege. Despite this heritage, and the German-based political abolitionism and Republican Party alignment, the African American electorate was a nonparticipant in state and national politics. However, after the Civil War, all of this would change.

"The Emancipation Proclamation was delivered to Texas by General Gordon Granger on June 19, 1865—'Juneteenth,' and an already traumatized South changed for blacks and whites alike."[21] The Republican Party, nationally and locally, became the political vehicle for that change. In Texas, "on July 4, 1867, Unionists, Radicals and Freedmen converged in Houston and held the first state Republican convention" after the Civil War. Before this organizing convention, "in Texas, as in the other southern states, the Loyal League aligned Blacks and the Black vote with the fledging Republican Party."[22] Walton cites Paul Casdorph as stating that in Texas the "Radicals through the League lost little time in enlisting the colored voters on their side."[23] With its post–Civil War activities, the Republican Party had arrived in the state for the second time, and a new group was about to enter state politics. The party's first political actions came on "July 19th, fifteen days after the convention, [when] the Second Reconstruction Act was passed by Congress and a call went out in Texas for a constitutional convention to be held in February, 1868."[24] A Republican-led Congress wrote the Second Reconstruction Act.

With a state constitutional convention announced, an electorate had to be established through registration. On March 2, 1867, the U.S. Congress had passed a law placing the South, including Texas, under "the military authority of the United States." The states of Texas and Louisiana "constituted the Fifth Military District, which was placed under the command of Major-General Philip H. Sheridan." Since "General Sheridan's headquarters were at New Orleans, . . . Texas was more particularly consigned to General Charles Griffin. . . . In April, General Griffin issued an order for the registration of the voters of the state, which differs in no material part from that issued by General Sheridan for the guidance and instruction of registration in Louisiana. The registration was completed near the close of the year. . . . The number of registered voters in the state was 104,259."[25] Since this registration was recorded by race, it is from this data that we can get a portrait of the initial African American electorate in the state.

However, there is one problem with the data source. The racial voter registration data was given in *The American Annual Cyclopaedia* by counties for Arkansas, but this was not true for either Georgia or Texas, or for three other southern states, Tennessee, Louisiana, and Virginia.[26] Nor was this vital data given in the 1868 volume of the *Cyclopaedia,* although it did reveal that after the registration process had been completed in Texas, "the whole number of white citizens in the state registered under the operation of the Reconstruction acts was 56,678. The number of colored persons registered was 47,581, making the whole number of registered voters 104,259."[27]

With the state's electorate registered, a vote on calling a state constitutional convention could then be undertaken. There was a turnout of 52.2 percent, with 43,142 for the drafting of a state constitution and 11,246 against it.[28] But before the state constitutional convention could be held, white conservatives held their own convention in Houston and declared their opposition to a new state constitution that would give African Americans the right to vote. The conservative convention resolved that "while we are unalterably opposed to Negro supremacy (i.e., Negro voting) we are in favor of securing to them the full protection of all their rights of person, and of property, under just laws bearing equally on all."[29] This convention wanted the 90 delegates to the state convention—nine of whom were African American—to know the wishes of the white community. Their effort failed because the Republican Party had the majority of the delegates; once completed, Section I of the new state constitution gave African Americans the right to vote in state and local elections. However, on July 20, 1868, the U.S. Congress passed a law prohibiting Texas or any of the southern states from taking part in the presidential election of 1868.[30] By 1872 Texas had been readmitted to the Union and the state's electorate could participate in presidential as well as state politics.

The Initial African American Voter in Texas: April 1867

What did the initial African American electorate look like after federal registration in 1867 created a new state electorate? The difficulty here lies in the failure of the *Annual Cyclopaedia* to include the voter registration data. However, on December 5, 1867, the U.S. Senate passed a resolution requiring the General of the Army to undertake a count of

> the number of white and colored voters registered in each of the states subject to the reconstruction acts of Congress. . . . [As well as] the number of white and colored voters voting for and against the calling of a convention, the number of white and colored voters

> who failed to vote either for or against the calling of a Convention, and as far as practicable, the number of white and colored persons disfranchised and rendered incompetent by the reconstruction acts to vote for a convention, and the number of white persons entitled to be registered but who did not apply for registration.[31]

General U. S. Grant sent this requested data to the president of the U.S. Senate in a letter on May 7, 1868. This letter, known as Senate Executive Document Number 53, is available at the National Archives. It gives racial voting data for all of the states of the old Confederacy except Tennessee, listing the numbers (1) registered, (2) voting for a convention, (3) voting against a convention, and (4) those failing to vote.[32] It is the most comprehensive and systematic data on the initial African American voters in existence. There is only one drawback: this racial electoral data is given in the aggregate for each state. Only for Texas is this data broken down by county, and only for 16 of the 128 counties were voter registration data provided.[33] For a county-level breakdown of voters in each state by race, one must turn to *The American Annual Cyclopaedia, 1867*, for some of the states.

Using the extant data from Senate Executive Document Number 53, table 7.3 displays data on the numbers of African American and white voters in the states of Georgia, Texas, and Arkansas in 1867. Here we can see that both Georgia and Texas had enough registered African Americans to give them a near majority. Arkansas had the fewest number of voters overall, as well as the smallest proportion of African American voters, 34.9 percent. White voters in Arkansas had a clear-cut two-thirds (67.1 percent) majority. Here, whites had, in actual numbers, 20,024 more registered voters than African Americans. In sum, whites had nearly double

TABLE 7.3. The Number and Percentage of African American and White Registered Voters in Arkansas, Georgia and Texas: 1867

State	African American Voters	White Voters	Total Registered Voters in Each State	Differences
Georgia	95,164 (49.7%)	96,333 (50.3%)	191,501	1,169
Texas	49,497 (45.4%)	59,633 (54.6%)	109,130	10,136
Arkansas	23,146 (34.9%)	43,170 (65.1%)	66,316	20,024

Source: Adapted from U.S. Senate, Executive Document No. 53, "Letter of the General of the Army of the United States: communicating in compliance with a resolution of the Senate of December 5, 1867, a statement of the number of white and colored voters registered in each of the states subject to the reconstruction acts of Congress, with other statistics relative to the same subject," 40th Cong., 2nd sess. (Washington, DC: Government Printing Office, 1868): for Arkansas, 10; Georgia, 6–7; and Texas, 11–12.

the number of registered voters that African Americans had. Overall, Georgia and Texas, in 1867, had significant numbers of registered voters.

Table 7.4 indicates how these new members of the Texas electorate voted. Some 82.6 percent of African American voted to hold a state constitutional convention while only 17.4 percent of the whites did so, demonstrating that African Americans wanted a new state government. While 51.4 percent of the state's voters turned out in this election, a racial breakdown reveals that 76.3 percent of the African American voters turned out, while only 30.8 percent of the white voters did.[34] Given a nearly even division of black and white votes, this huge difference in turnout meant that nearly 80 percent of the voters were in favor of a new state constitution. This is major political participation even by today's standards. In the final analysis, without the African American voters the convention would not have taken place.

African American voters in 1867 in Texas, Georgia, and Arkansas were registered in large numbers and in large percentages. Given such significant numbers, they were able to determine, particularly in Texas and Georgia, the organization of new state constitutions, which would provide their citizenship rights in the post–Civil War era. In table 7.5 one can see the nature and scope of the African American electorate.

Map 7.1 shows us the precise areas of Texas where the African American voters resided. They were concentrated within East Texas, particularly in a few counties in that area. This had been the area of Texas more suitable to farming, cotton, and other agricultural pursuits.[35] African Americans thus were able to use their narrow electoral base to put African

TABLE 7.4. The Number and Percentage of African Americans and Whites Voting for and against a Texas Constitutional Convention to Draft a New State Constitution: 1867

	For a State Constitutional Convention		Against a State Constitutional Convention		
Race	Vote	(%)	Vote	(%)	Turnout (%)
African Americans	36,932	82.6	818	7.2	76.3
Whites	7,757	17.4	10,622	92.9	30.8
Total	44,689	100.0	11,440	100.1	

Source: Adapted from U.S. Senate, Executive Document No. 53, "Letter of the General of the Army of the United States: communicating in compliance with a resolution of the Senate of December 5, 1867, a statement of the number of white and colored voters registered in each of the states subject to the reconstruction acts of Congress, with other statutes relative to the same subject," 40th Cong., 2nd sess. (Washington, DC: Government Printing Office, 1968), 12.

Map 7.1. The Counties with African American and White Voting Majorities: 1867

Americans in office at the state and local level, rather than at the congressional level.[36]

The Electoral Revolt of the African American Electorate: The 1920 Election

Beyond the U.S. Senate and state archival electoral data discussed above, there is state archival data on African American voters in the 1920 Texas presidential and gubernatorial elections.[37] It is to that data that we now turn to order to explore the empirical characteristics of this electorate. If our use of political archeology has helped us to precisely fix the number and geographical location of the African American electorate in Texas at

TABLE 7.5. The Percentage and Number of African American and White Voters in Texas: 1867

County	African American Voters (%)	African American Voters *N*	White Voters (%)	White Voters *N*	Total
Wharton	82.9	861	17.1	177	1,038
Brazoria	82.3	1,351	17.7	291	1,642
Fort Bend	80.6	1,418	19.4	341	1,759
Matagorda	74.1	563	25.9	197	760
Harrison	71.6	2,822	28.4	1,119	3,941
Walker	66.6	1,499	33.4	753	2,252
Marion	63.0	732	37.0	429	1,161
Washington	62.5	2,896	37.5	1,740	4,636
Robertson	61.5	1,254	38.5	784	2,038
Brazos	58.9	1,236	41.0	861	2,097
Bowie	55.5	489	44.5	392	881
Polk	54.7	899	45.3	746	1,645
Freestone	53.5	1,053	46.5	916	1,969
Harris	53.4	2,107	46.6	1,838	3,945
Colorado	52.9	1,469	47.1	1,306	2,775
Austin	52.5	1,421	47.5	1,284	2,705
Smith	50.3	1,453	49.7	1,436	2,889
Houston	50.2	1,046	49.8	1,039	2,085
Travis	49.5	1,098	50.5	1,118	2,216
Jackson	49.5	271	50.5	276	547
San Augustine	48.1	399	51.9	430	829
Anderson	47.6	989	52.4	1,088	2,077
Rusk	47.3	1,445	52.7	1,612	3,057
Bastrop	46.6	952	53.4	1,091	2,043
McLennan	46.2	1,192	53.8	1,314	2,443
Victoria	45.2	441	54.8	535	976
Leon	44.9	752	55.1	921	1,673
Jasper	44.3	351	55.7	442	793
Burleson	44.2	652	55.8	823	1,475
Red River	44.0	987	56.0	1,256	2,243
Tyler	43.8	258	56.2	331	589
Navarro	43.2	524	56.8	690	1,214
Liberty	43.1	391	56.9	516	907
Newton	42.7	199	57.3	267	466
Caldwell	42.0	470	58.0	648	1,118
Galveston	41.3	1,427	58.7	2,029	3,456
Madison	41.2	284	58.8	406	690
Gonzales	39.9	775	60.1	1,116	1,941
Fayette	39.7	1,235	60.3	1,876	3,111
Davis	38.0	740	62.0	1,206	1,946
Panola	37.8	608	62.2	1,002	1,610
Chambers	37.7	121	62.3	200	321
Guadalupe	36.4	543	63.6	950	1,943
Shelby	35.9	404	64.1	721	1,125
Nacogdoches	35.6	573	64.4	1,038	1,611

TABLE 7.5.—*continued*

	African American Voters		White Voters		
County	(%)	*N*	(%)	*N*	**Total**
Dewitt	35.5	385	64.5	700	1,085
Upshur	35.0	803	65.0	1,489	2,292
Jefferson	34.4	123	65.7	236	359
Milan	33.9	539	66.1	1,050	1,589
Calhoun	32.6	196	67.4	406	602
Limestone	31.8	392	68.2	842	1,234
Lamar	30.9	857	69.1	1,912	2,769
Hays	30.5	203	69.5	463	666
Cherokee	30.0	805	70.0	1,883	2,688
Lavaca	29.1	464	70.9	1,128	1,592
Ellis	28.6	401	71.4	1,002	1,403
Titus	28.2	540	71.8	1,372	1,912
Henderson	27.9	306	72.1	791	1,097
Goliad	26.3	173	73.7	485	658
Wood	25.4	276	74.6	810	1,086
Trinty	25.0	212	75.0	637	849
Total[a]	61.0	49,352 (47.4%)		54,817 (52.6%)	104,142
Grand Total[b]	120/125	54,698 (37%)		93,075 (63%)	147,764

Source: Adapted from Donaly E. Brice and John C. Barron, eds., *An Index to the 1867 Voters' Registration of Texas* (Bowie, MD: Heritage Books, 2000). This CD-ROM was made from the original files in the Texas Secretary of State Record Group presently housed in Texas State Archives. For a description of this record group files, see Jean Carefoot, *Guide to Genealogical Resources in the Texas State Archives* (Austin: Archives Division Texas State Library, 1984), 95–96. Sterling Chung of the University of Michigan prepared computer work and calculations from the CD-ROM and statistical calculations were prepared by Alethea Predeoux of Spelman College during the summer of 2003.

[a]In 1867 in Texas, there were 126 organized counties with people in 125 of them. African American registered voters were in 120 of these 125 counties. However, for this table we have reported only those counties where African Americans were at least 25% of the total registered voters.

[b]Grand Total = the totals for 120 counties for African Americans and the totals for 125 counties for whites.

the dawn of its emergence, further reliance on this technique will provide a portrait of this electorate at a different moment in time: 1920. The African American electorate revolted in Arkansas and Virginia at the senatorial level in 1920, at the gubernatorial level in Virginia in 1921, and in other southern states at other electoral moments through the 1956 presidential election.[38]

The Texas Republican Party was formed prior to the Civil War under the leadership of German immigrants. After the war, however, Texas became the birthplace of racial factionalism in the Republican Party. The post–Civil War party was a fusion of "Unionists, Radicals and Freedman" on July 4, 1867, when the "first state Republican convention" convened in Houston. "'This convention came about as a result of several mass meetings held throughout the state' by the Union Loyal League, during the first half of 1867. In Texas, as in the other southern states, the Loyal League aligned Blacks and the Black vote with the fledgling Republican Party."[39]

At the initial organizing Republican Convention in Houston, the participants and attendees were "overwhelmingly African in composition; the white delegates did not exceed twenty in number, while the colored numbered about one hundred and fifty."[40]

At the 1867 State Constitutional Convention, a legal issue caused an ideological split in the ranks of the newly formed Republican Party: "This split occurred over the so-called *ab initio* question, which asserted 'that all laws passed in Texas during the Confederate regime were null and void from the very beginning.'"[41] This issue engendered strong feeling and great dissension particularly "when the party members failed to write the *ab initio* doctrine into the state constitution and state party platform."[42] This failure occasioned a schism:

> [A] section of the Republican party under the leadership of two whites—E. J. Davis and J. P. Newcomb—bolted the party. It was at this point that the Texas Republican party became solidly divided into two district factions: the Radical wing led by Davis and Newcomb, the other considered the Conservative element in the party. Most Blacks supported the Davis-led wing.[43]

Here was born, almost simultaneously with the formation of the Republican Party, an ideological rift based on the legality of the actions of Civil War Confederates. Some whites in the Republican Party ranks did not want to hold the Confederates responsible for their legislative action. Although President Grant met with the two groups at the White House and sought to reconcile them, the legality of the Confederates' action would not subside and each group went its own way in the 1869 state election. In that election, the Radicals or liberal wing's gubernatorial candidate E. J. Davis won over the Conservative candidate, A. J. Hamilton, and they "captured control of both houses of the state legislature." Eleven Black Republicans were elected in the party's landslide victory.[44]

Having lost in their initial electoral struggle, the conservative wing refused to merge with the liberal (and African American) wing. Thus, when the national Republican Party itself split in 1872 into the regular party and the liberal Republican party, the state factions chose sides: "The Conservative wing strongly supporting the new Liberal party movement," while the regular party had the backing of the liberal African American wing.[45] "The Democrats captured both houses of the state legislature in 1872. Since the governor was elected for four years, however, Davis didn't lose this seat to a Democratic candidate until 1874. That was the year when the Democrats supposedly restored home rule."[46] And this was the last year that Republicans had influence at the state level: "It was more than 100 years between the time the first Republican governor, E. J. Davis, left office in 1874 near the end of Reconstruction and the second one, William P. (Bill) Clements, Jr., took the oath as Texas' chief executive in 1979."[47]

Davis's defeat for reelection as governor did not remove him from his leadership role as head of the Radical wing of the party nor did it keep him from attempting to regain the governorship. However, "by 1880 the Republican party in Texas, which was rapidly losing its potency in the state, began to play primarily national convention politics and to support the proper [potential winners] for the Presidency so that state patronage would be restored to them."[48] Simultaneously the conservative wing of the Republican Party was shifting its alignment. "By 1876 the Conservative wing had coalesced with the Democrats and what little support the Republicans got in 1876 came from the area of high concentration in East Texas."[49] The Conservative wing was left with only a small contingent of very ambitious white officeholders and few if any white voters. This, then, left the liberal wing with large numbers of African American officeholders and a few white leaders such as Davis. The exodus of the Conservative wing left a major vacuum in the party leadership ranks and electorate that African Americans filled simply by default.

In 1883, former governor Davis died and a Black man, Norris Wright Cuney, emerged as the new state party leader.[50] Cuney was a grassroots activist and organizer for the Union League, and a colleague of George T. Ruby, the leading African American Republican and officeholder in the initial years of Black Reconstruction. "In 1870 Cuney received his first governmental appointment, as the assistant sergeant-at-arms in the state legislature, in gratitude for successfully galvanizing black Texas to elect Edmond J. Davis as governor. A year later he returned home and became president of a newly organized Union League Chapter." Within a decade he was elected as an alderman in Galveston.[51] In addition, "from 1872 until 1896 he was a delegate to every national convention of his party, which increased both his stature in the state and his visibility in the nation."[52] At the 1884 Republican National Convention, he was elected to the vice presidency of the convention. These achievements earned him the enmity of white Republicans and a "protracted struggle . . . [with them] . . . between 1893 and 1896," the year of his downfall."[53] There is more.

In 1884, the year in which Cuney ascended to the vice presidency of the Republican National Convention, "his ability to deliver the votes of his delegation to James G. Blaine, the eventual nominee for president, made him the undisputed party man of the state."[54] In 1888, Cuney was elected as Texas's national committeeman. This led him to even more success in Republican national politics:

> At the national convention in 1888, he campaigned for Benjamin Harrison. . . . Harrison's ensuing election to the presidency resulted in Cuney's most eminent appointment, collector of customs at Galveston, then the most important federal assignment ever bestowed on a black Southerner. The collectorship granted him the power to dole out federal patronage and largesse to Texans—eagerly solicited by blacks and whites alike. He served in this position from 1889 until 1893, when Harrison was defeated.[55]

White challengers to Cuney's power arose immediately. When former Texas governor and now senator Richard Coke "was asked if he would oppose [Cuney's] confirmation as Collector, he replied: 'No, Sir, Cuney is President Harrison's appointee and on him rests the responsibility for the appointment. There is no objection to Cuney, save his color.'"[56] But that was just the point. If a Democratic senator could make it, other whites within his own party would not only say it but also lead numerous challenges to Cuney's leadership. White Republicans challenged Cuney at every state and national Republican Convention until his death in 1898.

To sustain their opposition to Cuney and the long-term African American presence in the state Republican Party, whites began in 1888 to organize "white Republican clubs" throughout the state in hopes of "the building up of a white man's Republican party."[57] Club members tried at every instance to split the African American Republican group. When that failed, they picked up the gun, as occurred in Fort Bend County where the Jaybirds (Democratic Party) fought with the Woodpecker (African American Republican) group.[58] At the 1892 Republican State Convention, Cuney's faction elected seven of the eight delegates at-large to the National Convention at Minneapolis, who were instructed to vote for Benjamin Harrison. The reaction was predictable:

> The "Lily White" leaders took a back seat and some of them left the hall, swearing that they would no longer affiliate with the party. A long struggle had been made to get control of the regular Republican party organization in Texas, but they were at last forced to give up the fight.
>
> On March 10th, after the adjournment of the regular convention, James P. Newcomb, leader of the "Lily White" faction, called a mass convention of his followers to meet in Dallas on April 12th, for the purpose of nominating a State ticket and of selecting delegates to the National Convention, in opposition to the delegates just selected by the regular organization.
>
> It was the first white Republican Convention ever held in the State of Texas.[59]

At that organizing convention, the leadership of the "lily-whites" made the clarion call to the whites of the state by declaring that they consider

> the new departure we have taken as a representative body of white Republicans of Texas. We feel justified in assuming that the Republican party has no organization such as is recognized as requisite to constitute a political party—therefore the necessity has arisen for the organization of the Republican party of Texas, independent of its past history, and upon the further recognition of the fact that only upon the intelligence and manhood of the white American citizens, can any party in this country hope for growth and success.
>
> We call upon the white Republicans of the State, and those in sympathy with the principles and policies of the Republican Party, to come to our aid and give us their assistance in building up Republicanism in Texas. We call upon the white Republicans of the State to organize and come to the support of our standard bearers in the coming State election.[60]

With this clear-cut, raced-based declaration, the ideological split in the party between liberals (Radicals) and conservatives that had been present since day one had now transformed itself into a race-based split—"black and tan" versus "lily-white" Republicans. This factional rivalry would spread out beyond state and local politics and appear every four years at the Republican national conventions. Cuney's political astuteness kept him the victor until President Harrison was defeated by Grover Cleveland in 1892. When President Harrison left office, all the prestige and power that Cuney had gathered came to an end; his influence faded, and that of his "black and tans" or the regular Republican Party faded with him.

Even when the Republicans recaptured the White House in 1896 with William McKinley, Cuney's comeback was thwarted. Because Cuney supported "William B. Allison for the presidency at the national convention, while the Lily-whites supported McKinley,"[61] McKinley's campaign manager, Mark Hanna, who had made several overtures to Cuney to support his man personally, saw to it that Cuney was forced out of his state party chairmanship and the patronage that it carried. The Cuney era had come to an end.

After Cuney's death in 1898, "W. M. 'Gooseneck' McDonald became leader of the Black and Tan Republican Party in the state. . . . In 1912, the Lily-White Republicans became the National Progressive Party, which excluded [southern] Blacks and was sanctioned by Theodore Roosevelt. The Black and Tans continued to support the regular Republican candidate, Taft, and the rivalry between the Black and Tan and the Lily-White parties went into [a short] abeyance."[62] However, when the rivalry was rekindled in 1920, the Black and Tans staged an electoral revolt against the Lily-Whites, launching a two-pronged effort to demonstrate their electoral power in the state. They offered a separate ticket of presidential electors, as well as a separate ticket of state candidates for all of the major offices. In both the presidential and gubernatorial elections, the African American Republican revolt captured over 5 percent of the total vote, and in both elections the Black and Tans came in fourth in a five-party race, outperforming the Socialist Party (see table 7.6).

The Black and Tans' electoral revolt was not equal to the Republican turnout at either the state or national level. However, had the Democrats not passed an amendment to the Texas state constitution in 1902 that established "the poll tax as a prerequisite for voting,"[63] the size of the African American electorate would have been much larger and surely could have helped the Republican Party to be more competitive in the state.

Table 7.7 offers even more evidence on this point. In the 1920 election, the Black and Tans offered candidates for all the major state offices except two. The mean vote for these candidates was 7.5 percent of the total vote cast. Clearly the electoral revolt mounted by the Black and Tan Republicans was a careful and broadly based response. Despite their best efforts, however, given the obstacles placed before the African American electorate, this revolt was ignored by both the Lily-White state leadership and the leadership of the national Republican Party. Neither group saw the possibilities and therefore did not step in after this brave and innovative electoral demonstration. Racial prejudices stymied any effort to embrace and integrate them.

The national party refused to seat the Black and Tan Texas delegation in 1924 at the national convention. Then, "the Credential Committee at the 1928 convention voted to seat the Lily-White group led by R. B. Creager, thereafter Creager ruled unchallenged. Black and Tan Republicanism came to an end in Texas in 1928."[64]

TABLE 7.6. The Vote and Percentage for the Black and Tan Republicans in the 1920 Presidential and Gubernatorial Elections

Candidate	Party	Vote	(%)
Presidential			
James M. Cox	Democratic	287,920	59.2
Warren G. Harding	Republican	114,658	23.6
James E. Ferguson	American	48,098	9.9
several electors	Black and Tans	27,309	5.6
Eugene B. Debs	Socialist	8,124	1.7
Total		486,109	100.0
Gubernatorial			
Pat Neff	Democratic	289,188	60.0
J.G. Culberton	Republican	90,217	18.7
T.H. McGregor	American	69,380	14.4
H. Capers	Black and Tans	26,091	5.4
L.L. Rhodes	Socialist	6,796	1.4
Total		481,672	99.9

Source: For the presidential vote, see Alice McGillivray and Richard Scammon, eds., *America at the Polls, 1920–1956* (Washington, DC: Congressional Quarterly, 1999), 781–82; for the gubernatorial vote, see Mike Kingston, Sam Attlesey, and Mary Crawford, eds., *The Texas Almanac's Political History of Texas* (Austin: Eakin Press, 1992), 284–87.

TABLE 7.7. The Total Vote and Percentage for the Black and Tan Republican Statewide Candidates in 1920

Candidate	State Position	Vote	Total Votes Cast (%)
S.E. Stars	Lt. Governor	26,404	5.5
Andrea McCampbell	Comptroller	27,041	5.6
C.T. Cimbri	Treasurer	26,640	5.5
L.L. Boyd	Commissioner of General Land Office	26,308	5.4
George Burkitt Jr.	Attorney General	26,910	5.5
Jesse Washington	Superintendent of Public Instruction	26,897	5.6
Mean		26,700	5.5

Source: Adapted from the Texas Secretary of State, "Register of Elected and Appointed State and County Officials, 1920–1922 Election Returns," November 2, 1920, A13–A18, 2–7, and 1–9, in *Election Registers, 1938–1972* (Austin: State Archives, 1838–2000), microfilmed copy.

After the 1928 national convention, President Hoover, who had used both the Lily-Whites and the Black and Tans to secure the nomination for himself, capitulated to the Lily-Whites by attempting to remove all the remaining African American state Republican chairs in the South. The exception was Perry Howard, who remained the chair of the Mississippi party until 1960.[65] "In Texas, . . . the Black Republican leader quit and openly declared himself for Al Smith, the Democratic candidate."[66]

With Black and Tan Republicanism dead, the African American electorate in Texas moved on to other political parties. The New Deal of FDR captured their attention and national voter support at least by the 1936 election.[67] In Texas, the New Deal could not be embraced locally nor could it be used for political leverage since so much of the state's politics was antiblack. The African American electorate needed a party player who was a party dissident. The rising LBJ was just such a partisan.

The African American Electorate and LBJ's Role in Partisan Realignment

It was the leader of the state's Black and Tan Republicans, W. M. McDonald, who moved this group toward the Democratic Party. His short-lived victories in Republican National Convention politics had led to little state political power for the group, especially during 1912–20 when the Democrats under Woodrow Wilson held the presidency. Hence, there was little state patronage for McDonald to disperse to use as a tool to mobilize African Americans. When he backed General Leonard Wood, instead of Warren C. Harding, in 1920, his fate was sealed, and it ensured the rise of the Lily-Whites lead by R. B. Creager. Therefore, African American Republicans ran their own statewide ticket in 1920 and backed Democrat Miriam Ferguson for governor in 1924.[68] From then on, the statewide Democrats captured McDonald's attention.

On the national level, McDonald moved in 1924 to support Progressive Party candidate Robert LaFollette. Then in 1928, "as did many other prominent black leaders throughout the nation . . . McDonald actively campaigned for Democrat Al Smith rather than Republican Herbert Hoover."[69] Having switched to the Democratic presidential nominee in 1928, McDonald continued his allegiance in 1932 and again in 1936 by supporting Franklin D. Roosevelt. In fact, "he boasted that he had been responsible for bringing blacks to the Democratic side."[70] In short, McDonald led the active Black and Tan Republicans first to state Democratic candidates and later to national Democratic candidates. Inside the Democratic Party, leaders such as L. A. Nixon of the famous white primary case and Heman Sweatt of the crusade for legal rights continued to keep African American voters in the party.[71] All that was needed, now, was a white Democrat in the state moving as a catalyst to help these African American political innovators to merge with him. LBJ became the force for this conversion, and his 1937 election became the moment in Texas history for this African American–white Democrat alignment.

In 1935 Johnson became the Texas director of the National Youth Administration (NYA) and in that post began to attract major attention for himself and the Democratic Party from the African American community. It all started when Johnson, soon after assuming his duties, "quietly called a meeting of local Negro leaders in the basement of the Austin Negro Methodist church and announced that he would, of course, be including Negro youths in his job program."[72]

> With their help he formed a Negro Advisory Committee separate from its white counterpart. He regularly consulted with the presidents of Texas Negro colleges—there weren't many—on how their students might best participate, and when he established his Freshman College Center Program throughout the state, fifteen of the centers were in Negro colleges.
>
> [T]he Negro kids in their own colleges—he'd do everything in the world for them. Which in Texas, 1936, wasn't a small thing.[73]

In the two years that LBJ served in this post, he gained not only a statewide reputation among the African American community, he also gained one among the national African American civil rights leadership.[74] Nevertheless, this reputation of fair dealing with African Americans was not without criticism. Historian Monroe Billington wrote, "Johnson's was a paternalistic administration committed to the status quo in regard to race-relations."[75] Billington arrived at this evaluation by analyzing the documents in the Lyndon Baines Johnson Presidential Library. He found that "the NYA files contain no information that Johnson discriminated against black youth, no comments of disparagement; nothing negative. To be sure, be operated a segregated administration . . . Johnson did not consciously discriminate against black youths, but he did not appoint blacks to paid supervisory capacities, and he was interested only in helping black youths economically, not in altering traditional social patterns."[76]

For this failure, he was criticized by Mary McLeod Bethune, the national director of the NYA's division of Negro activities, as well as by the members of his own Negro Advisory Committee. LBJ responded by declaring that a definite set of customs existed "which cannot be up-set over night . . . [and] . . . up-set a custom so deeply rooted, by any act which would be shockingly against procedure."[77] This explanation was a bit disingenuous, for in many of the New Deal federal programs in the South, African American supervisors were hired to oversee the African American contingent. This was inherent in the very nature of the policy of separate but equal. Numerous whites, like LBJ, merely overlooked this policy and placed only whites in supervisory positions. These criticisms notwithstanding, LBJ's reputation as a fair-minded individual grew in the community and among the electorate. As a consequence, the African American electorate found at the state level a political dissident and potential avenue into the New Deal Texas Democratic Party. They also found a Democrat for whom they could vote on the local level. This political event provides us with another opportunity to trace the African American electorate in state politics.

In March 1937, a special election was held to fill the vacancy caused by the sudden death of Congressman James Buchanan. LBJ was among the 10 Democrats who declared themselves for the seat. In Texas, despite the fact that state law banned African Americans from voting in the all-white primary elections, nothing kept them from voting in special elections. As soon as LBJ put his political hat into the race, the African American electorate went into the Democratic Party to support him. Although the archival data do not provide precise voting statistics, it is possible to estimate the African American vote in this election (see chapter 6). Suffice it to say here that, simply put, the 1937 election became a catalyst for shifting the African American Republican voters—the Black and Tans—to the state Democratic Party.

The African American Electorate and Voter Registration in Texas

Having discerned that there is a nonlinear aspect to African American voting behavior in Texas, we now turn our attention to one of these factors, the poll tax. In Texas, as in Arkansas, there was no formal system of voter registration. "Texas is one of the three states that have no system of personal registration. Poll tax payment is the closest approximation to such registration or listing of the qualified voters."[78] There was a temporal as well as an economic feature in the poll tax that affected the African American electorate. In Texas,

> Poll taxes must be paid by January 31. Texas primaries occur in July and August; general elections, of course, are in November. Thus, the period of time between qualifying one's self to vote and voting is considerably longer than under the average registration system. The Texas poll tax is a crude equivalent of a registration system.[79]

Unexpected special elections in nonelection years tended to catch those who did not pay their poll tax each January, as V. O. Key explained: "When the tax is due six months or more in advance of a campaign, before the candidates have announced and before political interest is aroused, the natural result is a smaller degree of payment than would occur if collection continued until a shorter time before the voting."[80] Hence the temporal impact of the poll tax on the African American electorate reduced participation.

As to the economic impact, Key found that "[o]n the average, the counties with higher proportions of Negro population have lower tax-payment rates than do the predominantly white counties. The differences that emerge from the contrast, however, probably cannot be attributed solely to variations in Negro population."[81] This study found that, as the African American county population increased, the rate of poll tax payments decreased. Where there are fewer African Americans, there are greater poll tax payment rates. Moreover, in the rural areas of Texas with the same proportion of African Americans as similar urban areas, the rural areas show greater payment. The reverse was found in Arkansas, where African Americans in the cities out-paid and out-registered the rural residents at least until 1964.[82] In this case of poll tax payments, the political context mattered.

One other factor helped to soften the economic impact of the poll tax. Political machines, African American political bosses, and civic-minded leaders often paid the poll tax for many in the African American electorate. The leading African American political leader in the state, William McDonald, "apparently used fraternal funds to pay poll taxes for blacks who could not afford to pay their own." He used "every possible means, even if it meant depleting the treasury of some local lodge, he saw to it that poll taxes were paid and that members of his race voted."[83] McDonald during his political life belonged to the "three older, larger, and more prominent . . . fraternities . . . : the Knights of Pythias, the Odd Fellows, and the Prince Hall Free and Accepted Masons,"[84] as well as smaller ones such as the Seven Stars and the women affiliated with Masons, Heroines of Jericho.[85]

San Antonio's African American political boss, Valmo Bellinger, played a similar role in that county.

> At poll tax payment time, he would have $3,000 or $4,000 which probably had come from white candidates who were interested in securing his aid. Bellinger would round up a sufficiently large number of Negroes and give them money to pay the tax. After having done so, they would turn their receipts over to Bellinger who would hold them until election day. On election day, the receipts would be distributed to individuals whom Bellinger regarded as reliable. Hence, he "owned" the receipts.[86]

However, these reports failed to present a balanced picture of poll tax paying in the African American community and tended to dwell upon the corrupt operations. Many individuals did pay their own poll taxes.

We now turn to an exploration of how the African American electorate that was registered to vote in Texas before, during, and after LBJ became an electoral force in state politics. Key in his classic *Southern Politics* advanced the thesis that the sheer size of the African American population determined the nature and scope of voter registration in the southern states.[87] Before Key, Ralph Bunche had advanced the same thesis in the memoranda that he prepared , in 1939–40, for Gunnar Myrdal's *An American Dilemma*.[88] Both scholars noted that the larger the African American population in an area, the smaller the number that will be registered to vote under a segregated system. The reverse is also true, that is, the smaller the African American population the larger the number of voters. Key found this trend to be particularly evident in Alabama, which served as the model for his thesis.

Table 7.8 sets out the county population densities and their relationship to the number of registered African American voters. In the counties where the African American population was 50 percent and higher (there were four such counties in Texas in 1950), the mean number of African Americans registered to vote was 44.9 percent. Conversely, where the African American population comprised less than 10 percent (which was the case in 163 of Texas's 254 counties), the mean number of African Americans registered dropped to 34.7 percent. Overall, at least in Texas, the findings of Key and Bunche are not corroborated, and, in fact, the reverse is true. There is a nearly stable level of voter registration in counties with 20 percent or more Black residents, and the decline that comes when the African American population drops below 20 percent is not as steep as one would imagine. Thus, in Texas, the larger the African American electorate, the larger the number of African Americans registered.

Comparing the Texas data with Alabama—a model southern state, according to Key—we see in figure 7.1 that the African American electorate in Texas does not even remotely come close to what Key predicted would be found in the other 10 southern states of the old Confederacy. Neither Arkansas nor Georgia matched the African American voter registration level found in Texas. A possible explanation for this difference could be the legal activism of African American leaders in Texas, as happened with the pioneering initiative taken against the white primaries, the electoral activism of other African American leaders along with the Black and Tan Republican Party, and the appearance of a New Deal Democratic leader such as LBJ who found ways within the segregated system to reach out in a meaningful way to the African American electorate and increase voter registration and participation.

After the defeat of the white primary in Texas in 1944, "politicians now find time in their crowded schedules to make personal appearances at Negro gatherings. No less personages than Governor Jester and Congressman Lyndon Johnson have put in appearances at the Red Cross Roll Call and Baptist conventions." Even a veteran segregationist such as Congressman Wright Patman "was to be seen putting in an occasional appearance

TABLE 7.8. The Relationship of the African American Population Density to the Mean Number of African Americans Registered to Vote

Percentage of African Americans in the County Population	Number of Counties	Percentage of the Total Number of Counties	Mean Percentage of African Americans Registered to Vote
50+	4	1.6	44.9
40+	3	1.2	47.3
30+	15	5.9	43.7
20+	31	12.2	43.7
10+	32	12.6	38.7
0.1–9.9+	163	64.2	34.7
0	6	2.4	0.0
Total/Mean	254	100.1	42.2

Source: Adapted from the Bureau of the Census, *Census of the Population, 1950,* vol. 2, Characteristics of the Population Part 43 Texas (Washington, DC: Government Printing Office, 1952), Table 12, 43-60–43-62; U.S. Commission on Civil Rights, *Report of the U.S. Commission on Civil Rights, 1959* (Washington, DC: Government Printing Office, 1959), Table 35, 581–86. Calculations prepared by author.

Note: The population data is for 1950 and the voter registration data is for the year 1958.

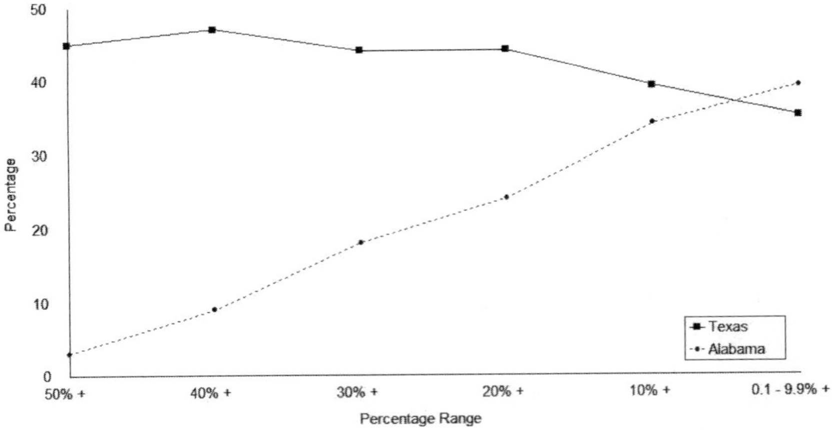

Fig. 7.1. The Percentage of African Americans Registered to Vote in Texas and Alabama by Percentage of County Population: 1958
(*Source:* The Texas and Alabama population percentage for African Americans for 1950 was adapted from the Bureau of the Census, *Census of Population: 1950*, vol. 1, Alabama, and vol. 2, Part 43, Texas [Washington, DC: Government Printing Office, 1952], tables 12 and 42. The registration data for both states were taken from U.S. Commission on Civil Rights, *Report of the United States Commission on Civil Rights, 1959* [Washington, DC: Government Printing Office, 1959], 577–78, 581–86.)

at Negro fish fries and church picnics."[89] Such anecdotes are a powerful testament to the rising power of the African American electorate in the state of Texas.

By 1958, fully 49 of Texas's 254 counties—19.3 percent—had African American voter registration rates exceeding 50 percent. In seven of these counties the rate was 100 percent of the voting age population. The registered voters in these 49 counties represented 16.9 percent of the voters in the entire state of Texas. Four of these counties were in LBJ's Tenth Congressional District (Washington, Lee, Blanco, and Burleson), and two were his home counties (Blanco and Gillespie). It is quite possible that LBJ's "countryside" New Dealism was a source of this electoral motivation.

Texas had nearly twice as many African American registered voters as any other southern state. Only Florida had a higher percentage of registered voters, 39.5 percent, as opposed to Texas's 38.8 percent, but Florida had fewer people.[90] But keep in mind that this is for a single moment in time: 1958.

To develop a time dimension on the African American electorate, we have acquired the best extant data on African American voter registration in Texas from 1867 until 1990. The pattern that emerges is a portrait of an electorate slowly swelling its ranks (see table 7.9). Again, one must keep in mind that the African American electorate in the state was located essentially in the east where the soil had made it possible to grow cotton and nourish slaves. The concentration of this electorate moved between the rural and the urban sectors as the political context went from one of a slave region to a segregated region to a desegregated region, and as the economic context moved from a dying cotton economy to an urbanized environment where newer and better job opportunities existed. Extant electoral data permit us to see not only the sheer size of this electorate but also some of their voting behavior in presidential, congressional, state, and some local elections. As is the case in Georgia's electoral history, a few interested individuals collected such data and preserved it in several manuscript collections and academic publications. And like the Georgia data, this election return data provided insights into the nature of the partisanship of the African American electorate over time.[91]

In the late forties and early fifties, the African American electorate demonstrated both a racial consciousness and to a limited degree an ethnic consciousness in their voting behavior by supporting members of their own race and reaching out to members of other ethnic groups in the state.[92] However, since only a few African American and Latino candidates ran for public office because of the "white only" policy of the Democratic Party in which white candidates were only allowed to run in its primaries, the African American electorate had to vote more often than not for "liberal" Democratic white candidates, even in nonpartisan elections. Moreover, as the Republican Party reached out to the African American electorate, it responded in degree and kind. The old Republican partisanship of the African American electorate did not abruptly fade away; it lingered for a while.

Another clue about the voting behavior of the African American electorate in this era of segregation can be gleaned from the 1958 gubernatorial primary, where they showed a tendency to coalesce behind the Latino candidate. "The vote for Henry Gonzales is one indicator. In all four cities he received 80 to 90 percent of the vote in Negro precincts. In this case Gonzales and earlier Latino candidate support from the African American electorate suggest a voting behavior characteristics of forming elected coalitions with the largest ethnic groups in the state if they are liberal in their appeal."

All of these features of the African American electorate occurred in Texas's large urban centers. Such behavioral features, as Harry Holloway

TABLE 7.9. The Number and Percentage of African American Registered Voters in Texas: 1867–1990

Year	African Americans of Voting Age	African American Registered Voters	Percentage Registered
1867	n/a	49,497	n/a
1900	136,875	n/a	n/a
1910	167,395	n/a	n/a
1920	197,550	27,309[a]	13.8
1930	469,637	3,500[b]	—[b]
1940	540,788	50,000	9.3
1942	549,219	33,000	6.0
1946	566,082	75,000	13.3
1947	570,297	100,000	17.5
1950	582,944	226,495[c]	38.9
1952	595,155	181,916	30.6
1956	619,578	214,000	34.5
1958	631,789	226,495	35.9
1960	644,000	227,000	35.5
1962	662,200	242,000	36.6
1964	680,400	375,000	55.1
1966	698,600	400,000	57.3
1968	716,800	540,000	75.3
1970	735,000	550,000	74.8
1972	879,000	571,000	65.0
1980	1,122,987	620,000	56.0
1990	1,385,784	776,039	56.0

Source: Adapted from U.S. Senate, Executive Document No. 53, "Letter of the General of the Army of The United States: communicating in compliance with a resolution of the Senate of December 5, 1867, a statement of the number of white and colored voters registered in each of the States subject to the reconstruction acts of Congress, with other statistics relative to the same subject," 40th Cong., 2nd sess. (Washington, DC: Government Printing Office, 1868), 11–12; Luther Jackson, "Race and Suffrage in the South Since 1940," *New South* (June/July 1998); U.S. Commission on Civil Rights, *Report of the United States Commission on Civil Rights 1959* (Washington, DC: Government Printing Office, 1959), 512, 581–86. The voting age population data were taken from the *Statistical Abstracts of the United States* for the years 1901, 1913, 1931, 1943, and 1972. For recent years, the data was taken from the Bureau of the Census, *Current Population Report*, Series P-20, 1980, 1990, and 2000.

[a]This is the actual vote for the African American presidential elections in 1920. The election data is taken from the Texas Secretary of State microfilmed data.

[b]This voting data is taken from Paul Levinson, *Race, Class, and Party: A History of Negro Suffrage and White Politics in the South* (New York: Oxford University Press, 1932).

[c]This is poll tax payment and exemption county data taken from U.S. Commission on Civil Rights, *Report of the United States Commission on Civil Rights 1959* (Washington, DC: Government Printing Office, 1959), 581–86, table 35.

indicated, were not the characteristic of the African American electorate in the rural areas of the state.

> The pattern is one in which the East Texas rural Negro is in good part a "controlled" voter who differs much from the city Negro. . . . The Texas rural Negro in this state has legal access to political power which he is unable socially and psychologically to use effectively much of the time. . . . Much of the Negro vote is an adjunct to the white vote, not the independent self willed vote of the city Negro.[93]

Although Holloway acknowledged that in this area of East Texas the African American electorate had some of the highest voter registration rates in the state, when it came time for them to vote, they relied solely on white paternalism.[94] "They are in good part non-voters or voter at the white man's behalf . . . most of them are apathetic and are heavily subject to the white man's influence and to some extent, corruption and the fear of reprisal."[95] For Holloway, the African American electorate might have the courage, fortitude, and self-determination to register to vote by paying their poll taxes, but all of these things fell away when it came time to vote.

Holloway's evidence for this bifurcation of the African American electorate in Texas into urban and rural voters, and then the further bifurcation of the rural African American electorate's political partisan behavior into positive and negative categories, came from Paul Lewinson's 1932 book, *Race, Class and Party*, which suggested that apathy was rampant among the southern African American electorate. Similar comments emerged in sociological and psychological literature that tried to explain the influence of segregation on the personality of the African American. It did not seem to bother Holloway that the work of Ralph Bunche, and to some extent of Key, Robert Martin, and Gosnell, demonstrated from aggregate data that such psychological theories had limited impact. Nor did Holloway look for other evidence from the Texas context. Using his own field observations and participant observations, limited through they were, he drew a negative portrait of the East Texas (rural) African American electorate despite their positive features in regard to registration.

In a later work, Holloway would expand this perspective on the African American electorate in Texas. Writing in a book in 1969 that was based on more field interviews and participant observations, he offered two detailed case studies of this state's electorate. He went to Marion County in East Texas and described the white-led African American voters there as manipulated and their rural context as a traditional culture that was nonparticipatory in nature. Holloway found that white political bosses caused greater turnout for local and county positions held by whites than for state and national positions. Although "[i]n 1964 close to 70 percent of Marion County's Negro adults were registered, a figure well above Austin's 44 percent,"[96] "whites controlled the political and legal system, the economy, and all social and cultural organizations they chose to. Added to this, paternalism in Marion County goes beyond the usual."[97]

Next, Holloway moved to Houston and analyzed African American politics there in great detail. Here he found significant activism among the African American electorate, independence in their voting behavior, and a steady alliance with liberal whites. But in the final analysis, Holloway is very critical of this independence, noting that in Houston, "Negroes affiliated with liberals tied themselves to the losing side and much of what they had achieved was lost when their candidate lost."[98] His point is that liberals rarely won in Texas politics. Therefore, African Americans' independent politics achieved no more than the boss politics of their rural brethren.

In none of his work did Holloway make use of the evidence from the 1920 revolt of the electorate that was indeed centered in rural Texas, nor did he use the work of African American scholars such as Bunche, Robert Martin, and one of his own sources, Henry Allen Bullock. Bullock had supplied voter registration data for the 1957 *Civil Rights Report* that Holloway quoted, but Bullock's work did not inform Holloway's subsequent work or his questionable theorizing about African American voting behavior in the state.

Bullock's 1956 data on the Texas electorate raises serious questions about the usefulness of Holloway's insights. In the rural areas of the state, the African American electorate was not only significantly registered but one-fourth of that electorate was voting. Control of that sizable vote was not quite as complete and systematic as Holloway suggested. Bullock found in East Texas "that the Negro has been most oppressed. . . . And the existence of common enemies has given them a greater sense of identification."[99] Thus, the possibility for independent voting behavior in this rural area had not been fully foreclosed.

Beyond Bullock's data and the 1920 revolt, there is the historical evidence of African American voters for the Populist Party, which was a rural movement. The leading scholar of this period, Roscoe Martin, found that in rural East Texas Populists proactively sought the African American vote: "The People's Party went out to the limit of its means after the colored vote, it recognized the importance of that vote; and it worked long and diligently in its effort to convert it to Populism."[100] He added:

> In the field, organizers went out to effect the organization of [N]egro Populist clubs; [N]egro orators made hundreds of speeches to colored and mixed audiences in the black districts, the colored leader J. B. Rayner, of Calvert, Texas, being especially active in this work; colored picnics and barbecues were arranged, with the dinner preceded and followed by Populist orations; colored days were designated for white Populist camp-meetings; and the [N]egro was given official recognition at the hands of Populist officers which he had not theretofore received."[101]

Martin's findings demonstrate the diverse voting behavior of the African American electorate for the Democratic, Republican, and Populist Parties in the late 1800s. In two counties, the Populist Party received a majority of the African American vote.[102] This diversity suggests independent and sophisticated voting. Additional studies of African American Populism reveal that African American third party voting behavior in rural East Texas was not all controlled, manipulated, or boss-dominated. Some of it arose from sincere African American leadership and community responses.

The African American Populist leader in Texas, John B. Rayner, was able to mobilize African American farmers to be independent in their voting. If Norris Wright Cuney was the preeminent African American leader of the Black and Tan Republicans, "John B. Rayner . . . served as spokesman for Negro Populists from 1894 to 1898 . . . and in 1895 and 1896 he served on the executive committee of the Texas People's party."[103] Throughout the 1894 to 1898 period, Rayner, "a fearless and capable agitator, . . . stumped the countryside for the party."[104] In August 1895, he was one of the featured speakers at a Colored People's Day meeting of Waco Populists and was also at the Milam County meeting of Negro party adherents.[105]

All in all, in 1895 "he addressed meetings in twelve different counties," while "in the 1896 campaign . . . [he] . . . addressed meetings in seventeen counties," and in 1898 he "addressed meetings in nineteen counties."[106] In later years, when the party collapsed in the state, Rayner moved on to other leadership efforts. But his efforts clearly raised the level of Black Populism in the state and with it some degree of independence in the rural vote of the East Texas African American farmer.

The African American electorate in Texas was aggressive, especially so in the rural areas of the state, in becoming registered voters. There are indicators that in both urban and rural areas of the state, they voted in an independent, sophisticated fashion, as well as in a contrite and manipulated manner. In a state where political machines and bosses existed, clearly they had some influence and impact, but the historical and empirical records simply do not support an interpretation of complete and total control.

In San Antonio, African Americans had a long history of voting simply because the white primary law did not apply to nonpartisan municipal elections. Historian Judith Kaaz Doyle wrote, "In the first place, the city's municipal elections were nonpartisan, so white primary directives did not apply to them."[107] Later, she adds, "[d]uring the stormy history of the white primary in Texas the institution sometimes developed loopholes as a result of imperfectly drawn legislation or successful court challenges. . . . Bexar County Democratic officials . . . at times decided that the utility of an organized black vote outweighed the ideological considerations of white supremacy. Thus blacks sometimes voted in nominally white Democratic primaries."[108]

African American leader Charles Bellinger in San Antonio created an African American political machine that used the city's black preachers to organize the black vote. "In the 1930s Bellinger was reputedly able to deliver 5,000 to 8,000 votes," which "made up as much as 25 percent of the total in some city and county elections, despite the fact that blacks made up only about 8 percent of the city's population."[109] This bloc of votes gave African Americans the balance of power in San Antonio.

The 1939 mayoral race in San Antonio attracted national attention because a popular New Deal congressman, Maury Maverick, offered himself as a candidate in the three-way contest.[110] Maverick had a national reputation as a liberal because he was the only southerner to support the 1937 Gavagan Anti-Lynch Bill and FDR's policies. This got him the endorsement of the National Negro Congress, which raised campaign funds for him nationally and locally. Maverick had supported the white primary law and urged local Democratic leaders to enforce it. After his vote for the Anti-Lynch Bill, however, he told local newspapers that he was embarrassed by the support he got from the African American community for doing so.[111]

Opposing Maverick were the incumbent mayor, Charles Kennon "C. K." Quin, one of the three bosses of the citywide machine who had been indicted for corruption but had not been convicted, and Leroy Jeffers, "the assistant district attorney who had [unsuccessfully] prosecuted Quin." Thus, in this municipal election, the African American voters had to make a choice between a "fake and false liberal," a corrupt mayor, and a crusading reformer. They cast 53.4 percent of their vote for the incumbent mayor, 35.4 percent for "Liberal" Maverick, and 11.1 percent for Jeffers.[112] This was sophisticated split-ticket voting for a 1939 African American electorate. They did not follow the dictates of the political machine. Nevertheless, Maverick won; and while in office, with his belief that he did not receive as much of the African American vote as he thought possible, Maverick removed all of the city's Black employees in white collar positions. Next, when complaints came from the National Negro Congress as well as his own "Negro Advisor," he ignored them; and in his 1941 reelection bid he responded to his African American complainers and critics by once again publicizing his liberal credentials—this time by testifying before the congressional hearing on the 1940 antilynching legislation.[113]

African American voters gave him 37.9 percent of their vote, while giving Quin 58.1 percent and 3.9 percent for the four other candidates.[114] Since no one received a majority of the votes, the incumbent mayor, Maverick, found himself in a runoff election with the former incumbent, Quin. Despite the fact that Mayor Maverick had increased his vote among African Americans, he blamed them for splitting their ticket and saw them as "a group of irresponsible blacks stood between him and his cherished goals."[115]

Therefore, in the 1941 mayoral runoff election, Mayor Maverick took a page from Tom Watson of Georgia and turned on the African American electorate. He told white audiences, "We cannot afford to have San Antonio dominated by the colored race." In addition, he said, "he was 'tired of petting Negroes!'"[116]

Quin, who won the runoff, got 64.4 percent of the African American vote, and Maverick got 35.6 percent.[117] Even Maverick's racial tirades had only a modest impact on African American voters. African Americans had in this second mayoral election voted both for a machine candidate and a reform candidate that did not see them as a mature voting bloc.

Collectively, in all three elections African American voters in this city split their votes for both machine and reform politics, even though the reform candidate, Maverick, supported the white primary and ran racist campaigns. Holloway paid this historical example no attention nor did it and the Populist data caution him to qualify his findings and comments. Further, neither of these empirically based cases suggested to him that his two cases needed some reconceptualization.

The culture of white supremacy in San Antonio forced the African American electorate to be sophisticated in voting among a slate of white candidates. Holloway's conceptualization never acknowledged the role that the political context played, and that Black voters had to and did make voting choices inside limited options.

The Partisanship of the African American Electorate

Registration and voting, however, do not encompass the entire story of the African American electorate in Texas. There is also the matter of partisanship. Rural African American voters, in another electoral revolt, had realigned their traditional voting behavior from Democratic to Republican to support Eisenhower. The nature of partisan choice by the African American electorate in both presidential and gubernatorial contests should thus provide us with additional insights into electoral behavior beyond the shadows of manipulation and boss control.

Holloway's data do alert us to two features about one of our two Black Belt counties, Marion County. First, voter turnout was greater at the local level than in the presidential contest. And, second, this county saw an unusual Republican swing to Eisenhower in 1952 and 1956. Given these facts, a statistical and graphical analysis of the partisan vote in the two Black Belt counties was conducted separately on each to determine the appropriate approach. Analysis revealed not only partisan differences in the turnout but a few different breaking points in terms of realignments. Hence, a summary statistic would mask these differences. Therefore, to compensate, we explore the partisanship vote separately. In so doing we can point out both the similarities and differences and the influence of contextual factors on independence in African American voting behavior. Apparently the electorate in the Black Belt county of San Jacinto exemplified greater independence than the electorate in Marion County, but each county did demonstrate some independence. The difference is in degree, not in kind. The partisanship of the Black Belt counties is indeed quite similar.

Figure 7.2 demonstrates that the voting participation of the African American electorate gave Marion County a Republican partisanship characteristic in nine presidential elections from 1872 through 1904. The rise of the poll tax requirement in the state in 1902 caused a decline in voter participation; hence the partisanship of the county shifted to the white-led Democratic Party. However, the diminishing African American Republican electorate maintained a full-scale electoral rebellion in 1920 and significantly reduced the Democratic partisanship of the county. The Democrats recovered by the next election and the few remaining African American Republicans began a new realignment in 1932 that continued through the 1948 election. This dramatic increase in the vote for the New Deal Democrats led to a simultaneous decline in the Republican vote from which it would not recover until the Eisenhower years. In 1956, the shift of some of the African American electorate back to the Republicans gave

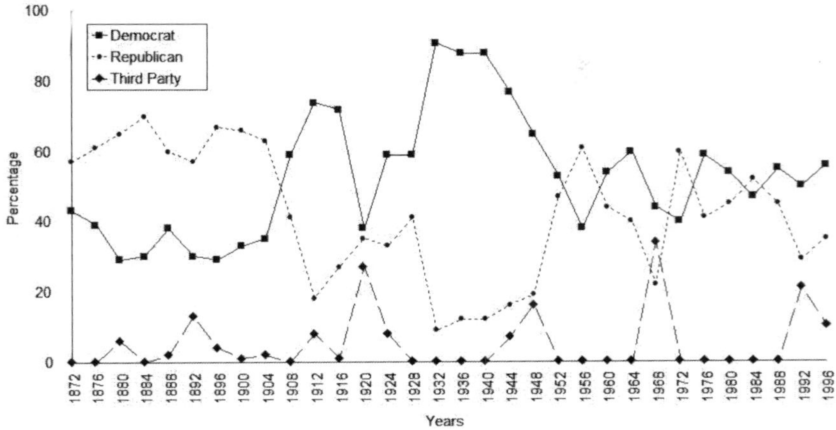

Fig. 7.2. The Vote Percentage by Party in Texas's Black-Belt Marion County in Presidential Elections: 1872–1996
(Adapted from Walter Dean Burnham, *Presidential Ballots: 1826–1892* [Baltimore: Johns Hopkins Press, 1955], 764–813; Edgar Robinson, *The Presidential Votes, 1896–1932* [Stanford: Stanford University Press, 1934], 330–50; Alice McGillivray and Richard Scammon, *America at the Polls* [Washington, DC: Congressional Quarterly, 1998], 730–82, 763–815.)

them the victory in the county. Such a victory would not be seen again until 1972. Native son LBJ brought Marion County and the African American electorate back to the Democratic column in 1960 and 1964.

Third parties historically have been quite active in Marion County. Beside the Black and Tans in 1920, the race-based parties of the Texas Regulars in 1944, the Dixiecrats in 1948, and the American Independent Party in 1968 did well, particularly the Wallace effort, which captured 34 percent of the county vote. But the Democratic partisanship of the African American electorate kept the county in the Democratic column that year. The recent candidacy of native son H. Ross Perot had a good showing, but the Democratic Party still won the county.

In San Jacinto County, the partisanship of the African American electorate parallels that in Marion County, with a few minor exceptions. We see in figure 7.3 that the African American electorate here was Republican from 1872 until 1904 despite very strong third party efforts, particularly in 1892 that captured one-third of the county's vote. In the 1920 electoral revolt, the third party vote was 53 percent of the total votes cast in the county, and the party carried the county. In the subsequent presidential election the white Democrats regained control and held it through 1968.

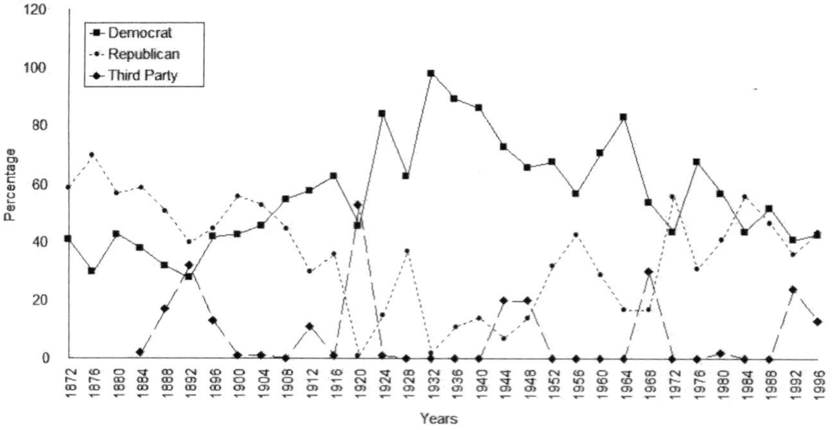

Fig. 7.3. The Vote Percentage by Party in Texas's Black-Belt San Jacinto County in Presidential Elections: 1872–1996
(Adapted from Walter Dean Burnham, *Presidential Ballots: 1826–1892* [Baltimore: Johns Hopkins Press, 1955], 764–813; Edgar Robinson, *The Presidential Votes, 1896–1932* [Stanford: Stanford University Press, 1934], 330–50; Alice McGillivray and Richard Scammon, *America at the Polls* [Washington, DC: Congressional Quarterly, 1998], 730–82, 763–815.)

Although the Eisenhower-led Republicans increased their votes in 1952 and 1956, they never defeated the Democrats, as was the case in Marion County in 1956. Thus, when LBJ ran in 1960, he did not restore Democratic control but merely increased the party's margin by 14 percentage points, followed by another 12 points in 1964. However, without him on the ticket in 1968, the Democratic winning margin dropped a whopping 29 percentage points, significantly more than Marion County's drop in that year. Another native son, George H. W. Bush, helped the Republican Party to win San Jacinto County only in 1984, although he did not carry Marion County.

As for third parties, the race-based Texas Regulars in 1944 and the Dixiecrats in 1948 did significantly better in San Jacinto County than in Marion County, but this pattern did not hold true for George Wallace in 1968. Together, these two counties demonstrate that the African American electorate began as Republicans, rebelled as Black and Tan Republicans, then realigned during the New Deal to emerge during the civil rights era as Democrats. There was a brief moment when they returned to the Republican fold during the Eisenhower years, but subsequent Republican candidates did not maintain this devotion.

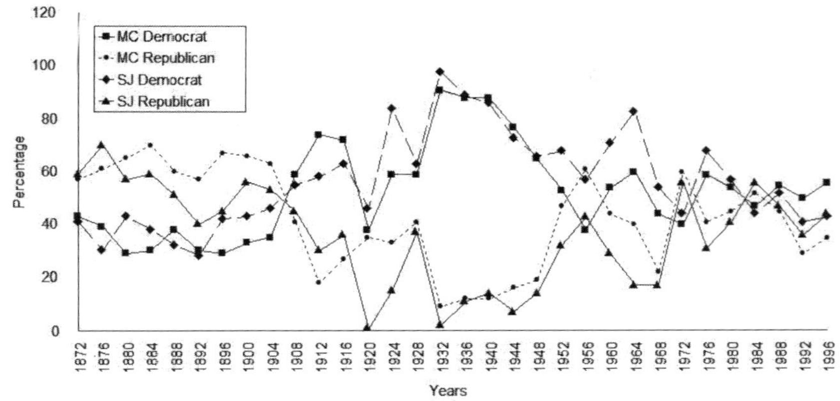

Fig. 7.4. The Vote Percentage by Party in Texas's Black-Belt Counties in Presidential Elections: 1872–1996

(Note: MC = Marion County; SJ = San Jacinto County. Adapted from Walter Dean Burnham, *Presidential Ballots: 1826–1892* [Baltimore: Johns Hopkins Press, 1955], 764–813; Edgar Robinson, *The Presidential Votes, 1896–1932* [Stanford: Stanford University Press, 1934], 330–50; Alice McGillivray and Richard Scammon, *America at the Polls* [Washington, DC: Congressional Quarterly, 1998], 730–82, 763–815.)

In the urban areas where data exist a similar pattern is seen. Further evidence collected from voting data for Fort Worth and Waco reveals a pattern. From 1948 through 1972, urban African American voting behavior in these cities has been significantly Democratic, and during the LBJ years it reached an all-time high, over 90 percent. Only Eisenhower in 1956 was able to capture more than one-third of the African American vote for the Republican Party. Scattered data available for Houston show the same pattern. And in all of these urban areas, none of the third parties, including the race-based ones, received African American votes.

At this point it is useful to examine whether the partisanship patterns of the African American electorate were reproduced at the state level in gubernatorial elections. Did any of the electoral upheavals have their roots in state-level politics? What other partisanship options were left for the African American electorate in a one-party state?

In analyzing the Democratic, Republican, and third party vote in each election from 1873 through 1974, both counties had a Republican Party voting pattern from 1873 through 1890. Then the Democratic Party won almost every election from 1892 through 1974, with only two exceptions in Marion County and four in San Jacinto County.

As we saw at the presidential level, the poll tax along with the Lily-Whitism of the state Republican Party put Republican partisanship into an irrecoverable decline. It would slowly fade at the gubernatorial level even through the Eisenhower years, and it had not recovered by the time the state went to a four-year term for the office of the governor in 1974.

It is notable that in presidential elections, the Republican vote carried these counties until 1908, much longer than in gubernatorial elections. The 1920 revolt gave San Jacinto County to the presidential Republicans in that year, but neither county went Republican in voting for governor. One-partyism at the state level did have an effect.

The coming of the New Deal, aided by individuals such as LBJ, would begin to realign the fading African American Republican electorate into the Democratic Party. This vote would attach itself to liberal and moderate Democratic gubernatorial candidates prior to the passage of the 1965 Voting Rights Act and continue thereafter. Hence, a major alignment of the state's Democratic Party occurred, quietly and slowly, aided by the restoration of the vote after the collapse of the white primaries in 1944.

LBJ and the Collapse of the Poll Tax Barrier in Texas

In Texas's political context, the African American electorate faced and eventually overcame one barrier after another. The Democratic Party, in line with its ideology of white supremacy, had legally constructed each one. Although the African American legal challenge had overturned the white primary law, the state's poll tax barrier remained. This came to an end during LBJ's presidential tenure.

Alwyn Barr wrote, "After the Civil War, Texas Democrats who had fought to protect and perpetuate slavery refused to enfranchise newly freed Negroes in the state constitutional convention of 1866." Then Congress stepped in, requiring "the adoption of a new constitution allowing Negroes to vote and ratify the Fourteenth and Fifteenth Amendments to protect that right." However, "when the Democrats won back control of the state government in the 1873 election,"[118] they called a constitutional convention and authorized a poll tax as part of the 1876 constitution. This tax was then levied by the next state legislature in 1877. By 1902 the legislature had further ruled that the poll tax be paid by January 31 of an election year.

As discussed earlier, this requirement led Donald Strong and others to draw a sharp distinction "between the poll tax as a voting requirement and merely as a revenue measure."[119] They argued that the poll tax in Texas was not designed to disenfranchise African Americans, as it had been in other southern states, and that it was not the main obstacle to African American voting in the state. Instead, the barrier was the white primary. This interpretation concluded with the assertion that "the poll tax has had little or no bearing on Negro disfranchisement, the object for which it was supposedly designed. On the contrary, those kept from voting by the tax have been the whites."[120] Thus, in Texas, unlike the rest of the South, the poll tax has had the reverse effect; it disadvantaged more whites than African Americans.

More recent research conducted since the abolition of the poll tax in 1966 looked at its impact in the Houston metropolitan area. It found that "[t]he most striking feature, however, was the exclusion of the Mexican-Americans by the poll-tax system, for they constituted 5.6 percent of the potential voters but only 1.6 percent of the poll-tax payers." Hence, the end of the poll tax "did increase the number of qualified voters by slightly less than 100,000, and it did improve the proportion of younger persons, those with Spanish surnames, and those in clerical, sales, and skilled occupations."[121] A subsequent study analyzed the effects of the poll tax in the entire state, concluding that "elimination of the poll tax resulted in an immediate increase in the average registration level of about 7.5%."[122] and that the tax had had a negative effect on racial and ethnic groups in the electoral arena.

However, neither the literature on the poll tax written during its use nor the literature written after the collapse of the poll tax paid any attention to the vote to enact the poll tax or to the two failed statewide votes to repeal it in 1949 and 1963. Evidence from these three poll tax referenda offers a different empirical story. Over two-thirds of the Texas electorate voted to enact the law in 1902. Compared to the 1900 presidential and the 1902 gubernatorial elections, the poll tax participants represented 77.5 percent and 91.1 percent of the voters, respectively. This was a substantial turnout.

The initial attempt at a repeal of the poll tax came 47 years after its enactment, in the midst of the growing civil rights movement. The second attempt came 14 years later, when Texans voted on whether the law should be repealed. Each time roughly 56 percent of the voting electorate rejected attempts to repeal the law. On January 23, 1966, with LBJ now president, the 24th Amendment to the U.S. Constitution was ratified, which made poll tax payments for national elections unconstitutional.

This became in effect the first major civil rights law of Johnson's presidency. Throughout his congressional tenure, numerous attempts had been made to pass anti-poll- tax legislation. Each time it failed, and each time, in true fashion of a southern legislator, LBJ had voted against it. Now, he would preside over its acceptance by the nation.

But even with the new constitutional amendment, Texas still did not relent in regards to its own law. It took a U.S. Supreme Court decision (*Harper v. Virginia Board of Elections*) in 1966, which said "that state election codes making payment of a poll tax a prerequisite to voting" were unconstitutional because such codes "contravened the Fifteenth Amendment to the Constitution of the United States."[123] Only then did Texas finally abandon its 1902 poll tax. Even as the political context changed, the state electorate stood firm and continued to embrace their tradition of political inequality.

By disaggregating the total state vote into county-level votes and comparing them across time, additional voting behavior becomes apparent.[124] Five counties—Duval, El Paso, Hidalgo, Starr, and Webb—voted against the enactment of the poll tax in 1902 and then voted each time to repeal the tax. These counties were in opposition to the rest of the state and shared common characteristics: they were Latino and boss-led counties.

Seven other counties—Bexar, Galveston, Harris, Jefferson, Nueces, Orange and Travis—voted to enact the poll tax in 1902 but then voted in 1949 and 1963 to have it repealed. Most are large urban counties where the African American electorates were quite active. Moreover, since these poll tax elections were referenda rather than regular elections, African American voters could vote if they had paid their poll taxes. Of all the Texas counties, only Cameron voted against the enactment of the poll tax, then for the repeal in 1949, and then reversed its tradition and voted to keep it in 1963. In 1902 the Glascock County vote ended in a tie; but in each of the repeal elections, it voted to keep the poll tax. Seen from the county level, 13 counties opposed this voting prerequisite at some point. This is indeed minimal opposition given Texas's huge number of counties. Of these few counties, most were composed of African Americans and Latinos. Thus, the core of opposition to the state's poll tax came from the minority racial and ethnic groups in the state electorate, and even then it was not consistent.

The next step in our empirical analysis is to correlate the percentage of the county vote for and against the poll tax in each of the three referendum years to see if they are connected. The results from this empirical evidence indicate that no relationship is found between the 1902 voting coalition that enacted the poll tax and those in 1949 and 1963 that voted not to repeal it. This should not be a surprise, given that 47 years had elapsed between the 1902 vote and the first repeal attempt.

However, there is a strong relationship between those counties that voted not to repeal in 1949 and those that did so in 1963, as well as among those counties that took the opposite stance. The original coalition of proponents of the tax held together in the 14 years between these votes.

Overall, both sides were strong in their particular positions, but the proponents of the tax carried the day in all three elections. The Texas electorate refused to repeal the tax, even if it did hurt poor whites more than it hurt African Americans. Seemingly, this was unimportant, in consideration of the role that the tax played in suppressing the African American vote. It took the 24th Amendment and the Supreme Court to remove the poll tax in Texas. None of the research conducted to date on Lyndon Johnson has captured this very important linkage and the vital role it played in enhancing the African American and Latino electorate in the president's home state.

The major reason for this omission rests on overemphasizing the legal interpretation in the literature, and the debate that it touched off. This questionable interpretation pushed the three state poll tax votes from view; in fact, none of the literature even touches on them. In the final analysis, attention should have been given to their significance because the poll tax issue changed the electoral context, at least in Texas.

In retrospect, when LBJ arrived as an electoral force in state politics in 1937 and as he evolved to enter the U.S. Senate in 1948, the African American electorate was shedding its initial Republican partisanship and moving toward a Democratic one. It had to overcome the Democratic Party barriers of the poll tax and the white primaries, and the psychologically conflicting ideology of white supremacy. The African American electorate became Democratic in special elections, in selected municipal elections, and in general elections at the presidential level. It would not be until after 1944 that African Americans could vote as Democrats in primary elections. As a result, in 1946 and 1948 they completed their Democratic partisanship journey by voting for LBJ in the congressional and senatorial elections, as we shall see in later chapters. The African American electorate and LBJ entered the Democratic ranks at about the same time in Texas politics and for the same thing—power. As the African American electorate entered the state political arena, it had in the configuration of Texas politics a political ally, the Latino electorate.

The Rise of the Latino Electorate in Texas Politics

Although the state political parties, political candidates, the white electorate, and the U.S. Supreme Court hindered the African American electorate, that is not the case with the Latino electorate. Unlike all other states of the old Confederacy, Texas, with its border with Mexico and its history as a Mexican province, had a large ethnic Latino population. The size of this population made it possible for this group, as voters, to represent a significant segment of the total Texas electorate.

The Latino electorate, much like the African American electorate, gradually evolved to gain power in the Texas political process. The one major difference between the two groups was their geographical location in the state. The African American electorate mostly resided in East Texas, and the Latino electorate was in South Texas; where these areas met is where the two electorates interacted. The African American and Latino electorates also found themselves in close proximity in the urban areas of the state. For the moment, our focus will be on South Texas and its Latino population.

The southern part of Texas was conveyed to the United States in 1848 by the Treaty of Guadalupe Hidalgo, which naturalized all of the Mexican and Spanish people inhabiting the region as U.S. citizens. This area was divided into four counties: Nueces, Cameron, Starr, and Webb. By 1900, due to rapid population growth from natural increases, Anglo-Saxon migration to the area, and Mexican immigration, these four counties were further subdivided into 13 counties.[125] This decentralization of the political units into multiple counties led in part to the decentralization of political power as well. In the early years of the region, there were oligarchies set up by both Anglo and Mexican ranchers and farmers. These individuals centralized power into a few hands that ranged over a large area. These individual oligarchies—through a combination of their political savvy, economic resources, and enlightened social welfare efforts—dominated the area for many years. When these resources proved insufficient or unreliable, they resorted to political corruption in terms of ballot box stuffing, "paying their poll taxes, and voting the alien Mexican," or simply tampering with the election return data. The Latino community benefited little from political participation. To confront this reality, city-based Latinos "organized themselves into a League of United Latin-American Citizens" (hereafter LULAC) founded in 1927 with "twenty local councils, most of which [were] located in town and cities" in South Texas.[126] The electorate was clearly evolving from a dependent to an independent political status. The decentralization of the political units in South Texas thus placed institutional barriers in the way of the concentrated power of the few oligarchies.

The role of the state in the evolution of the Latino electorate did not stop at the politics of decentralization. Texas never devised legal disenfranchisement measures based on ethnicity against the Latino electorate as it did against African Americans. To be sure, "in many counties, unsponsored individual Mexican-Americans meet a barrier to the ballot similar in character if not in degree to that which discourages Negro voting in most of the South."[127] Although "Mexican-Americans suffer unmistakable discrimination and some forms of segregation,"[128] the state of Texas never legally prohibited them from voting. Thus, the problem for them was the independent exercise of their franchise, due to economic dependency. In the absence of state intervention the political machines and bosses filled the political vacuum as they did elsewhere in the region and in the urban centers of the North.

But the Latino leadership fought back. After the organization of LULAC in 1927 came the independent candidacy for governor in 1958 of State Senator Henry Gonzales. Gonzales was able to build group consciousness, political mobilization, and political independence, as African Americans had done in 1920. The establishment of the American GI Forum by Dr. Hector Garcia and the Political Action of Spanish-Speaking Organizations served as a means to challenge and reduce the barriers facing the Latino electorate in the state.[129] These different strategies varied in their impact and influence. One empirical indicator of this growing independence was Gonzales's candidacy.

The Revolt of the Latino Electorate: The 1958 Gubernatorial Election

The revolt of the African American electorate came in 1920, from within the Republican Party; however, the Latino electoral revolt came in 1958 from within the Democratic Party. In the Democratic primaries that year, Henry Gonzales came in second in a four-man race, receiving 18.7 percent of the vote. He outpolled a former governor and U.S. senator who had been a long-time force in Texas state politics. Clearly, this was a major level of voter support for a Latino candidate in the era of segregation.

Table 7.10 offers the empirical data from the 13 Latino counties of South Texas. Gonzales captured eight of them and Price Daniel, a former

U.S. senator, won in the other five, all of which are geographically contiguous from south to north. What one sees here is ethnic consciousness overcoming the tradition and the power of political bosses and machines. When this study broke down the vote for Gonzales in the Latino counties of Duval, Kenedy, Starr, and Zapata, along with Johnson's home counties of Blanco and Gillespie, Gonzales won in both of the boss-controlled counties, Duval and Zapata, but lost in Kenedy County. He lost in both of the presidential home counties, coming in third in each, where he ran against LBJ's friend Price Daniel and the 1941 senatorial candidate, Lee O'Daniel.

Statistically speaking, Gonzales outperformed the leading candidate, Daniel, in South Texas. Gonzales's vote percentages ran from 10.9 percent to 91.6 percent, while Daniel's were 8.0 percent to 79.4 percent. The average vote for Gonzales was 54.6 percent, while Daniel's was 37.9 percent. The overall performance by Gonzales in a historically Latino region of the state was indeed a significant achievement, demonstrating that the Latino electorate could be led away from its past.

Outside of South Texas, Gonzales's candidacy engendered coalition building and alliance formation, in addition to building Latino ethnic consciousness and political mobilization. He won three other counties: two of which, Maverick and Presidio, were on the Mexico border, as well as Kimble County, which is well away from the border and which was a Republican-leaning county. This was not reflective of a major alliance and

TABLE 7.10. The Vote and Percentage in the 13 Latino Counties in the 1958 Texas Gubernatorial Election

	Price Daniel		Henry Gonzales		W. Lee O'Daniel		Joe Irwin	
13 Texas Counties	Vote	(%)	Vote	(%)	Vote	(%)	Vote	(%)
Brooks	569	26.0	1,411	64.6	188	8.6	18	0.8
Cameron	7,665	53.1	5,806	40.2	752	5.2	208	1.5
Duval	776	17.8	3,327	76.5	202	4.6	45	1.0
Hidalgo	8,261	45.5	8,493	46.7	1,174	6.5	244	1.3
Jim Hoggs	285	20.0	1,109	77.8	25	1.8	6	0.6
Jim Wells	2,282	35.0	3,418	52.4	729	11.2	98	1.5
Kennedy	73	79.4	10	10.9	8	8.7	1	1.0
Kleberg	1,555	46.6	1,399	41.9	314	9.4	71	2.1
Nueces	13,058	53.1	8,384	34.1	2,552	10.4	598	2.4
Starr	921	24.5	2,796	74.4	35	0.1	5	0.0
Webb	2,540	24.3	7,670	73.3	224	2.1	34	0.3
Willacy	1,274	59.3	584	27.2	264	12.3	25	1.2
Zapata	72	8.0	826	91.6	4	0.4	0	0.0

Source: Adapted from Mike Kingston, Sam Attlesey, and Mary Crawford, eds., *The Texas Almanac's Political History of Texas* (Austin: Eakin Press, 1992), 252–55.

coalition building, but it was indeed a start, especially given that this was an era of segregation.

Looking at the election return data from the other 241 Texas counties, we see that these counties represent 81.6 percent of Gonzales's total vote. Moreover, we know that more than a few of these votes came from whites since they were cast in counties where Latinos and African Americans were few. This was coalition building, and it would signal to LBJ that this segment of the state electorate was seeking greater independence in voting.

The Partisanship of the Latino Electorate in Presidential Elections

Analyzing the presidential vote for both political parties in two Latino counties, Kenedy and Starr, one finds that there is no clear uniformity; therefore, a summary measurement cannot accurately reflect the true pattern. There is, however, a strong Democratic trend in both counties, with a swing to the Republican Party in different elections. In Starr County, the Republican Party won five of the 32 presidential elections (1872, 1876, 1880, 1892, and 1972), and the Democratic Party won the rest (84 percent). In Kenedy County, which did not exist until 1924, the Republican Party won five of the 19 elections and the Democratic Party the other 14 (74 percent). The Republicans won here in 1940, 1944, 1952, 1956, and 1972.

Using a comparative approach to the Democratic gubernatorial vote in both counties, one finds the levels of support for each party over time. These divergences clearly demonstrate that other contextual factors besides bossism were influencing the partisanship of the Latino electorate in these two counties. Candidate appeal, candidate contributions, and issue concerns clearly could have influenced the outcome in these elections. But no matter what the degree of influence of other factors, in the Latino counties there was a strong Democratic partisanship with only a few deviations.

Shifting to the boss counties, Duval and Zapata, there is a close correlation in the voting trends of the two. In Zapata County, where there were 30 gubernatorial elections, the Republicans won nine and the Democrats won 21 (70 percent). In Duval there were 29 elections; the Republicans won three and the Democrats won 26 (90 percent). In fact, from 1908 through 1996 the Democrats won every election in Duval County. In Zapata County, the Democratic Party won every election from 1924 through the present. The only difference between the two counties is in the level of support for the Democratic Party.

For a further comparative analysis of the Democratic vote in the boss counties, one can consider presidential elections. What one finds are the different levels of support for each party over time, but a thoroughly clear-cut Democratic vote after the first decade of the twentieth century.

Zapata County had a larger Republican vote in presidential elections than Duval and Starr Counties but was quite similar to Kenedy County. Nevertheless, all four counties and both categories reveal a dominant Democratic partisanship in the Latino electorate. Recent Republican efforts have yet to shift them. Moreover, the race-based third parties—1944 Texas Regulars, 1948 Dixiecrats, or the 1968 American Independent Party—received only feeble support. The mean vote in the two counties for Wallace's AIP stood at 3.5 percent. Neither of the other third parties even came close to this. Overall, the Latino electorate tended to stay with the major parties, particularly the Democratic Party, in presidential elections. There is one exception to this pattern in terms of third parties. Native son H. Ross Perot's mean vote stood at 9 percent in 1992 and 4 percent in 1996. He did alter the voting pattern of the Latino electorate in two national elections.

The Partisanship of the Latino Electorate in Gubernatorial Elections

The Latino Democratic partisanship in presidential elections in Latino and boss counties simply reproduced the pattern seen in gubernatorial elections, in a much more heightened manner. There were few Republican gubernatorial candidates in Texas who were attractive to Latinos or who had the possibility of being successful due to the party split between the Lily-Whites and the Black and Tans, and the resultant dominance of the Democratic Party. One-partyism clearly asserted itself here. The above empirical evidence demonstrates that the Democratic tendency was continual in the Latino counties, where it was rarely challenged, except in 1880 when Democrats were defeated in a close race. The Republican victories in national elections failed to influence the Democratic partisanship of these counties. No realignment even took place in the period surrounding LBJ's exit from the political arena in 1968, as happened in many parts of Texas.

Surprisingly, this trend was not found in the boss-led counties. In these counties there was fluctuation up until 1910, when Democratic partisanship settled in and continued until LBJ exited the political arena. Prior to

1910, the Republican Party was able to capture at least one of the boss counties in most state and presidential elections. Early bossism was more flexible and more dynamic than later bossism, which by the turn of the century was a fixture of local politics. Fluctuations occurred in the Republican vote but never to a majority status. When LBJ entered congressional and statewide elections, the boss counties were reliably Democratic. So were the Latino counties.

The African American and Latino Electorates: LBJ as a Merger and Coalition Factor

From the beginning, African Americans and Latinos found common ground and formed, if only transiently, mutual coalitions and unions. Numerous Latinos in South Texas helped African American slaves flee to freedom in Mexico. Noted historian John Hope Franklin writes, "During the 1840s and 1850s, southern Texas became a thoroughfare for slaves crossing the border to freedom in Mexico." Texas law "provided the death penalty for anyone 'enticing a slave from his master,' . . . [but] [t]here was no adequate punishment for those who advised or attempted to induce a slave to run away. Mexicans who assisted slaves had been brought before local authorities but were discharged because they had committed 'no overt act.'"[130]

The 1937 special election and subsequent elections gave African Americans and Latinos common cause to bond together. This is one of the overlooked legacies of LBJ's state politics. Long before the 1937 election, these groups had found other instances of common cause, where they voted or acted in near unison.

In municipal elections, some Latino candidates began to build alliances between the African American and Latino electorates. Because African Americans could not vote in Democratic primaries until 1944, the two had to coalesce around voter revolts and special elections. For example, when the African electorate revolted in 1920, there was only modest support for this Republican effort in the Latino and boss counties. The African American electorate subsequently began a realignment to the Democratic Party; but this process, as we have just seen, had already started in the Latino and boss counties.

The New Deal helped to spur the evolving Latino electorate and the realigning African American electorate on the state level into unified action. LBJ became one of the forces that helped these two electorates to merge, and his candidacy provided the basis for their coalition. Furthermore, LBJ was not passive in this. His candidacies at the congressional, senatorial, and presidential levels were active, if not super active, in molding these two electorates into a force to sustain the New Deal in Texas, to keep his boss, Congressmen Richard Kleberg, in office, and finally to get himself elected to office. It was LBJ who marshaled these electorates into a solid Democratic phalanx, against forces that tried to shift the state in another direction. Today, these two groups maintain the Democrats' partisanship almost alone against a growing Republican Party in the state. Without them, Texas would have shifted to a one-party Republican state. LBJ's pursuit of these two electorates helped to carry his legacy of a compassionate Democratic Party into a new century, as we shall see in the next section.

★ Part III

The Making of a Native-Son Candidate

Lyndon B. Johnson had, as one of his motivations to become a political candidate, his father. Sam Ealy Johnson Jr. had served in the Texas House of Representatives in 1904 and 1905, prior to LBJ's birth. After LBJ's birth, Sam had served in the 35th Called Session (1918), 36th Session (1918), 37th Session (1920), and the 38th Session (1922).

Two occurrences in Sam's state legislative career would be repeated in Lyndon's. First, Sam Johnson participated in a special election on February 15, 1918, to get back into the state House of Representatives after a hiatus of nine years, 1908–17.[1] LBJ was first elected to Congress via a special election in 1937, and he made his first Senate foray in a 1941 special election. Second, the independent Democratic candidate who ran against Sam Ealy Johnson in 1918 declared that he had won and contested the result by asking the state House Committee on Election to investigate Johnson's electoral count. LBJ's victory in the 1948 runoff election led to hearings before the State Party Committee and Supreme Court Justice Hugo Black, and a Senate Election Committee investigation. The parallel between father and son would be quite striking. Most important, Sam Johnson advised his son in his first special election for Congress. Thus, LBJ's personal political ambition was helped in part by his father's own successful political career.

However, LBJ was not the only one of the southern presidents to have a father as a political model and mentor. President Jimmy Carter's father, James Earl Carter Sr., served a term from Sumter County in the Georgia

House of Representatives when Carter was a young man, from 1953 to 1954. Prior to his election to the state House, Carter's father served 10 years on the Sumter County Board of Education.[2]

About his father's influence on his own political ambitions, President Carter wrote, "His accomplishments and the breadth of his interests were astonishing to me. In almost all facets of community life he was a respected leader, including . . . in his newly elected position as member of the state legislature." This helped Carter to think seriously about trying "to follow in his footsteps in this tiny rural community."[3]

There were other political influences from his father. President Carter recalled, "One of the most memorable was in 1934, when [Eugene] Talmadge was running for re-election as governor. Daddy let me go along."[4] Carter recounted that his dad "would put a bed of straw in our two-ton flatbed truck and carry a load of men to Gene's political rallies."[5] And one rally in Albany, Georgia, Carter described Talmadge's speech as follows:

> He recited voluminous criticisms of the New Deal, and how the federal government was trying to control the lives of every free American. Everyone awaited and cheered his declared policy of not campaigning in any county with a town large enough for a streetcar. . . . Like all of his opponents, Talmadge advocated strict racial segregation, but he would always point out a number of black farmers in prominent locations in the crowd who were also his supporters.[6]

Carter concluded by saying, "Our group from Plains was ready to go home after eating, never to forget one of the most memorable events of our lives."[7]

Carter made it clear that his father, like Talmadge, was a rigid segregationist. Although he acknowledged the influence his father had upon his political ambition, Carter recently indicated that some of these memories, while powerful, "are embarrassing."

And Carter's father was not the only family member involved in politics:

> In 1964, when Lyndon Johnson decided not to campaign in the Deep South and received just a handful of white votes in our county, Mama volunteered to manage his campaign office. Almost every day, when she returned to her car she found it covered with graffiti,

the windows soaped over, or the radio antenna tied in a knot. Her only compensation was to be a delegate to the national Democratic convention.[8]

Because LBJ's and Carter's fathers held elected positions, it is possible that there were electoral influences upon the sons as well. Table III.1 provides the election returns where available for Sam Johnson's and Earl Carter Sr.'s general elections. Since the election return data are scattered for all of Sam Johnson's elections, there is no way to conduct a correlational analysis to see if there is a relationship between his elections and those of his son. For the Carters, there is only one election and one county, which is not enough to conduct a correlational analysis at the county level.

Despite these limitations of the empirical data, however, analysis of the incomplete and scattered data permits us to see that one of the counties in Sam Johnson's state House of Representatives district ended up in LBJ's congressional district. It is quite possible that some of the voters for his father might have transferred their electoral support to LBJ in his crucial 1937 special election and in subsequent ones. The same pertains to Carter. In addition, as both of their fathers had died, it is plausible to consider some sympathy votes on their behalves. Thus, there is a possibility of a linkage of influence at the electoral level.

One can see from this overview that the parents' political experiences have been forces in motivating candidates and that those experiences, especially in the cases of Johnson and Carter, might have helped to build an electoral foundation for their sons. The chapters in this section will explore how LBJ fashioned his victorious electoral coalitions in the House and Senate races. Native-son presidential candidates can build on the legacy of their families, particularly those who have been engaged in politics even in the absence of "friends-and-neighbors" voters.

★ 8

The Congressional Vote for Johnson

Lyndon Johnson's victory in the April 10, 1937, special election for the 10th Congressional District seat would be a fateful moment in American history. With this election, American politics, its society, and the political process would change forever. Few saw this at the time, but before LBJ would run his political course from a member of the House of Representatives to United States president, nearly all aspects of the American party system and the political participation process would be transformed. That transformation is still under way today. Surely, President Obama is a beneficiary of the LBJ civil and voting rights legacy.

Fateful moments might not be understood at the time of their occurrence, but they do not go unrecorded. Both the *New York Times* and President Franklin Roosevelt understood the significance of this special election victory in the hill country of Texas. In a front page article, the *Times* called attention to the fact that the youthful new congressman had during his campaign embraced the New Deal and President Roosevelt's plan to enlarge the Supreme Court.[1] President Roosevelt, on a fishing trip in the Galveston area, met with Johnson and Governor James Allred on May 11, congratulated the new congressman, and "invited him to be his guest on the presidential train as far as Fort Worth."[2] At the end of the train ride, President Roosevelt gave the new congressman the name and telephone number of his major political operative in Washington, Tommy "the Cork" Corcoran.

In addition to fateful moments are motive, motivation, and ambition. The fateful moment merely permits these forces to converge. LBJ's father, Sam Ealy Johnson Jr., ended his last term in the state legislature when LBJ was 16 years old. Lyndon was not only proud of his father's public service, he attended several of the sessions in Austin with him. Thus, for LBJ, his fateful moment had a background.

It also had a gestation period. LBJ's family background of public service forged a path in that direction for him. Four years after his father quit the state legislature, the Democrats held their 1928 National Convention in Houston and nominated Senator Joseph Robinson of Arkansas for the vice presidency, in hopes of carrying the South for the party.[3] LBJ was working at his college newspaper, the *College Star*. He got himself accredited as a newspaper correspondent at the convention and saw a southerner nominated to the national ticket at his first national political convention.

Two years later, in 1930, LBJ made a speech on behalf of former governor Pat Neff, who was running for reelection to the state Railroad Commission. According to one observer, LBJ gave the speech because when Neff was governor he had given a job to LBJ's father.[4] Because of this speech, his friend Wally L. Hopkins, who was running for the Texas Senate, asked the new college graduate to help run his campaign. Johnson conducted the campaign operations in "Blanco and Hays Counties, and he did a magnificent job."[5] Like Clinton after him, LBJ got his first campaign management experience by starting at the local level during college.[6] The preparation for his fateful moment continued.

In the fall of 1930, Republican congressman Harry M. Wurzbach—the only Republican in the Texas delegation for more than a decade—died in office and was replaced by a Democrat, Richard Kleberg. Kleberg's father owned the famous King Ranch, the largest in the world. Family, friends, and political acquaintances recommended LBJ to Congressman Kleberg, who took the advice and hired LBJ as his personal secretary for his Washington office. In 1932, Johnson "managed Kleberg's successful reelection campaign. It was a momentous year for elections. . . . [In addition to] Roosevelt's victory, Huey P. Long, already governor of Louisiana, was elected senator as well, and migrated to Washington."[7] This was followed by another successful reelection campaign in 1934 for Congressman Kleberg.

Johnson's payoff from his congressional secretary position was not just learning how to run a successful congressional campaign. He also made numerous high-level congressional contacts, particularly with Congressman Sam Rayburn, who had been in the Texas legislature with his father and whom his father had supported for Speaker of the Texas legislature.[8] LBJ also became acquainted with both Texas senators, Tom Connally and Morris Sheppard, and numerous congressional staff members. By the time he resigned his position in 1935, he had political friends and acquaintances in very high places.

The acquisition of these skills and contacts made it possible for LBJ to be a political player in a much larger political arena than a mere congressional district. He parlayed them into a statewide position, the state director of the National Youth Administration in Texas. President Roosevelt created this agency in 1935 "to get young Americans off the street corners and highways and put them to work, either in school or at jobs."[9] To let them wander and be idle threatened their future and that of the country. "Its annual budget would be $50 million—and it would be administered in each state by a state director."[10] In order to attain the directorship, LBJ enlisted the assistance of Congressman Rayburn, who went to see Senator Connally and asked him to get President Roosevelt to appoint LBJ. Not only was Connally startled at first, for he and Rayburn rarely spoke to each other, but he hesitated to respond to his request. Rayburn persisted and refused to leave Senator Connally's office until he agreed. The White House reacted with amusement to the very thought of entrusting a statewide program to a twenty-six year old utterly without administrative experience. It announced that the Texas NYA director would be DeWitt Kinard. "Kinard was, in fact, formally sworn in to the post."[11] Sam Rayburn then went to the White House, and shortly thereafter the White House announced that a mistake had been made. The NYA director for Texas "was not DeWitt Kinard after all . . . it was Lyndon B. Johnson."[12]

LBJ turned his directorship of the NYA into a bundle of opportunities for the youth of Texas, both white and African American. As one of his biographers noted, his astute management of the NYA post "brought him his first taste of national fame. The organization he built in Texas was used as a model by many other states."[13] Before he completed his stay as state director, "his NYA job allowed Lyndon Johnson to expand not just his organization but his acquaintances. . . . Lyndon Johnson had no trouble meeting the most influential men of Texas."[14] Here was another step to that ever rising fateful moment. Both were now rushing to meet each other.

The NYA post offered LBJ one very unexpected dividend that would provide him with his defining legacy. LBJ captured the support and admiration of the African American community. Most descriptions of LBJ overstate, and even overdramatize, his involvement with his Mexican American students. Many make his teaching career, which he had before joining Congressman Kleberg's staff, the determinant of his later effort to eliminate poverty. Although Mexican American voters were important to Johnson's electoral coalition, African Americans were too, and they ultimately were more important in shaping his legacy. His experiences with African Americans took shape in his NYA years.

For Lyndon Johnson, the fateful moment came "on February 22, 1937, [when] Texas Congressman James P. Buchanan, age seventy, suffered a fatal heart attack in Washington."[15]

The Fateful Moment: The Special Election for the 10th Congressional District

Fateful moments in an electoral democracy are not just the creation of an ambitious individual. They also require changes in the electoral process. The 10th Congressional District was redrawn after the 1934 midterm elections and went from nine counties to 10. This remade district now included Blanco County, the home of the Johnson family. Although LBJ lived in Austin, located in Travis County, the addition of Blanco County to the 10th District gave him his home base where he was better known than in Travis County, where he had a residence that he occasionally visited. However, biographer Robert Caro argued that placing Blanco County in his district worked against LBJ instead of for him: "The candidacy of Lyndon Johnson, 'home man' of the district's smallest county, all but unknown in the others, was not taken seriously."[16] Caro repeated:

> He had been raised in Blanco County, but Blanco, which had not even been part of this huge, sprawling district until the 1935 redistricting, was its most isolated and remote corner, and the smallest of its ten counties; with a population of 3,800, less than 2 percent of the district's 264,000 residents, it was all but ignored in district politics.[17]

In addition to these insights about the poor assistance he would garner from his home county, Caro declared that LBJ's occasional presence in Austin was another significant drawback: "Johnson's limited residence in the district was, moreover, promising to be a major handicap in an area in which the word 'carpetbagger' had a particularly distasteful ring."[18] Therefore, as Caro argued in his biography, the redistricting of the congressional district to include his home county had actually disadvantaged LBJ, and even if it had not, the small "friends-and-neighbors" vote (i.e., the vote from localism) provided by Blanco County would matter little in the final outcome. As we shall see, this is not entirely true.

Data from the Election Register at the Texas Secretary of State's office show the role that Blanco County played in the 1934 and 1936 elections of incumbent Congressman James P. Buchanan. This smallest county in the new district ranks not last but seventh in terms of votes contributed to the congressman's reelection, providing 8.3 percent of the total votes cast. An analysis of the 1934 election reveals that voter turnout was lower in three counties that had much larger populations than Blanco County.

A similar analysis of election data for 1936, a presidential election year and one in which Buchanan had Republican opposition, unlike 1934, creates a new electoral portrait. In a presidential election year, nearly every county increases its voting turnout. In Blanco County, however, the voter turnout remained nearly the same in both elections. Such empirical data suggest that in nonpresidential election years, LBJ's home county could make a significant contribution to an election effort. In presidential elections, the percentage of the vote contributed by Blanco would decrease because of the greater turnout in other counties, particularly the large urban county of Travis. Hence, the empirical data show that the disadvantage that biographer Caro saw was in error, and that, if LBJ ran in a nonpresidential year, he would have an advantage with his home county.

The death of Congressman Buchanan in 1937 came in a nonpresidential election year. Thus an ambitious man and the electoral process converged. Before LBJ could announce his intention to run, however, there was a strong rumor that the congressman's widow would run. On the day of the funeral, February 26, "the district's most prominent politicians returned to the black-draped house in Brenham to pledge the sixty-two-year-old Mrs. Buchanan their unanimous support."[19] LBJ turned to his father for advice, and he urged his son to run because Mrs. Buchanan was too old for a political fight. When LBJ announced, Mrs. Buchanan decided not to run. Buchanan's campaign manager, C. N. Avery, threw his hat into the ring,[20] and the race was on.

Special elections in Texas were a one-shot affair. All parties and candidates entered the same race, and the candidate who received the most votes, a plurality, won. There was no runoff.[21] On March 5, 1937, Governor James Allred set the special election for April 10, allowing forty days for campaigning. LBJ, having announced, hit the ground running without waiting for the governor's announcement. His opponents, accustomed to the leisurely pace usual in Texas elections, had not expected the campaign to start until Allred set a date for the election. But by then, Johnson had already completed a tour of the entire district. "When Avery opened his campaign on March 9, Johnson had already been in the field for a week."[22] Other candidates started even later than Avery.

LBJ's head start paid off. He won in the special election by 3,169 votes, with 27.7 percent of the total vote (see table 8.1). Although the total vote was smaller than that in the 1936 presidential election, it was nevertheless greater than the turnout in the 1934 midterm election. An examination of the county-level results shows that LBJ won six of the district's 10 counties. Most important, he won the large urban county of Travis, despite the strong opposition of Austin's mayor. The wins in Travis and Blanco meant that he won both of his home counties. Although in the final analysis LBJ did not need the 688 votes from his home county, the voting behavior in this county reflected what it had done in 1934. The shift to LBJ simply increased his margin of victory.

In examining the voting age population for each county in the 10th Congressional District, there are new insights. In 1937 there were 164,480 potential voters for the special election. Therefore, LBJ's 8,280 votes amounted to slightly more than 5 percent of the district's potential voters. However, if we use the poll tax receipts as an indicator of eligible voters, the number drops to 64,498 or 44 percent of the voting age population. Of these registered voters, only 48 percent turned out to vote in the 1937 special election. This means that of the registered voters in the district, LBJ received 12.8 percent of the vote. And of the actual votes cast, LBJ's percentage rises to 27.7 percent. In the six counties that LBJ won (Blanco, Burnet, Caldwell, Hays, Travis, and Washington), the mean turnout rate was 47 percent. By any measure the 1937 special election captured the interest of the registered voters. This was more than enough for him to receive a plurality in a nine-man field.

Of LBJ's victorious outcome, Caro reflected, "the deeper in the hills a precinct, the more isolated and remote—and poor—its people, the stronger the showing that Lyndon Johnson made in it. He was the candidate of the Hill Country."[23] He further noted that LBJ's "3000-vote plurality—a

TABLE 8.1. The Results of the 1937 Special Election in the 10th Congressional District

Candidate	Vote	(%)
Johnson	8,280	27.7
Harris	5,111	17.1
Shelton	4,420	14.8
Stone	4,048	13.5
Avery	3,951	13.2
Brownlee	3,019	10.1
Ross	1,088	3.6
Walker	18	0.1
Smith	12	0.0
Total	29,947	100.1

Source: Adapted from the Secretary of State, *Register of Elected and Appointed State and County Officials* (Austin: Election Register Texas State Archives, Microfilmed Copy, 1838–1972).

plurality whose dimensions had been utterly unsuspected—came principally . . . from the people in whom he had invested time no other candidate for Congress had ever given them."[24] Another biographer, Robert Dallek, explains LBJ's 1937 election victory in the following manner:

> Lyndon's aggressive identification with Roosevelt, the stumbling campaign of his opponents, his unrelenting efforts to become known in every corner of the district through personal appearances, newspaper ads, mailings, and radio talks gave him a surprisingly large victory margin on election day. . . . A breakdown of the vote by counties showed that Lyndon finished third in two, second in two, and first in six, including Travis, where he got nearly 3000 of the 10,300 votes. Unlike his opponents, who made strong showings in only one or two counties, Johnson ran well across the whole district.[25]

These electoral explorations, while interesting, did not rely on a systematic or comprehensive review of the election data. Table 8.2, using the demographic categories established for this study, reveals a different type of LBJ victory than that described by his biographers. LBJ ran best in his

TABLE 8.2. The Results of the 1937 Special Election in the 10th Congressional District by Demographic Category

	Urban Counties[b]		Town Counties[c]		Rural Counties[d]		Blanco County	
Candidate	Vote	(%)	Vote	(%)	Vote	(%)	Vote	(%)
Johnson	2,962	28.7	4,399	25.8	231	14.0	688	74.4
Harris	1,483	14.4	2,972	17.4	624	37.9	32	3.5
Shelton	2,167	21.0	1,834	10.8	370	22.5	49	5.3
Stone	297	2.9	3,680	21.6	60	3.6	11	1.2
Avery	1,893	18.4	1,834	10.8	142	8.6	82	8.9
Brownlee	1,023	9.9	1,779	10.4	173	10.5	44	4.8
Ross	479	4.7	546	3.2	45	2.7	18	2.0
Walker	3	—[a]	13	0.1	1	0.1	1	0.1
Smith	4	—[a]	6	—[a]	2	0.1	0	0.0
Total	10,311	100.0	17,063	100.1	1,648	100.1	925	100.1

Source: Adapted from the Secretary of State, *Register of Elected and Appointed State and County Officials* (Austin: Election Register Texas State Archives, microfilmed copy, 1838–1972). The population data for the grouping of the demographic categories were taken from the Bureau of the Census, *Census of Population, Sixteenth Census of the United States—Texas* (Washington, DC: Government Printing Office, 1943), Table 22 "Age, Race, and Sex by Counties: 1940 and 1930," 808–57.

Note: In 1937 there were one urban, seven town, and one rural counties. The home county is Blanco.

[a]Percentage less than .0001.

[b]The urban county in 1937 is Travis County.

[c]The town counties in 1937 are: Bastrop, Burnet, Caldwell, Hays, Lee, Washington, and Williamson.

[d]The rural county in 1937 is Burleson.

home county, getting 74.4 percent of the entire vote cast. He got 28.7 percent of the urban county vote and 25.8 percent of the vote in the town counties in the 10th Congressional District. He performed poorest in the rural county of Burleson, where he got only 14 percent of the vote. LBJ did his best in the most populous county, Travis, where he resided. Hence, our empirical analysis demonstrates that, in his first electoral campaign, LBJ was elected to office by more than rural voters. Voters in the big cities, small cities, and his home folks gave him his winning coalition.

As to the native-son factor in this initial campaign, Key's observation that localism did not hold was quite instructive. The hometown vote helped, but it was not enough on its own to turn the tide. LBJ needed electoral help from large groups of voters outside of his home base, and he got it. On this point, nearly all of his biographers agree that one single factor accounted for his victory. Evans and Novak described it best: "Johnson quickly found that the more he praised Roosevelt, the deeper he buried his opponents."[26]

To empirically test this impression, one can look at the correlations among the Democratic vote for Al Smith (1928 Democratic U.S. presidential candidate), FDR (1932 Democratic U.S. presidential candidate), and LBJ. There is a strong relationship only between those in the 1928–32 Democratic coalition; yet between the 1932 and 1936 voters, there is no relationship at all, meaning that the 1936 FDR vote brought entirely new groups of Texas voters to the Democratic presidential coalition. With such a change in the presidential coalition, there is an effect on the Democratic congressional coalition. In fact, what one finds from the correlation analysis is that there is a negative correlation between the presidential Democratic coalitions, whether led by Smith or FDR, and the congressional Democratic coalition, which LBJ put together in 1937. Part of the reason is that in 1937 the number of registered voters dropped in five counties in the district, and in the 1928 election the Republican Party swept four counties. The Democratic coalition had changed. Hence, it is not entirely accurate to say that Roosevelt's New Deal brought LBJ's voters to the polls; other variables mobilized the voters in this contest. Our findings here are statistically significant.

The African American Electorate and LBJ's 1937 Congressional Election

In fact, one of the groups that LBJ brought to his victorious Democratic electorate was the coalition of African American and Latino voters. Caro declared that African American voters were manipulated into LBJ's coalition:

> The rural "boxes," or precincts, which could be bought by a payment to a local Sheriff or County Commissioner. There were a few of these boxes in the Tenth District, and Johnson had the money to buy them. The district contained a substantial Negro vote—located in several small all-Negro settlements in Blanco County; in Lee County, where there were thousands of black sharecroppers; and in the Austin slums. In Austin and Lee County, at least, the Negro community voted the way its leaders wanted it to vote, and the leaders were for sale—cheap. Johnson had the money to buy them.[27]

African Americans were, in Caro's account, at their best corrupt and manageable voters. But this does not correlate well with the information available at the Johnson Presidential Library. The archival data on the NYA and the unique relationship that Johnson created with the African American community suggest more than managed voting. These documents lend credence to views of the community's supposed appreciation of him when he decided to run for Congress. Caro's failure to acknowledge LBJ's links to the community leaves the African American electorate, who mobilized under severe legal constraints in Texas, as unappreciated victims.

There was more evidence on this point than just the archival data. Contrary to Caro's assertions, the greatest percentages of African American voters were in Washington, Burleson, and Bastrop Counties, and the largest numbers were found in Travis and Washington Counties. The smallest percentages of voters were in Burnet County and in LBJ's home county of Blanco. Overall, African Americans made up 19.8 percent of the *potential* voters in the district; individuals could cast a ballot only if they had paid their poll tax and presented the receipt at the polling place.

If the voting age population is suggestive of potential African American participation, further empirical clues are available from a comparison of the 1920 county vote for presidential electors and gubernatorial candidates with those given to LBJ in his 1937 congressional race. When compared, one sees a significant difference in the voting patterns: few people voted in the gubernatorial contest except in Burleson, Lee, and Travis Counties. And even in these counties the differences are extremely small (see table 8.3). There is another, perhaps more significant, pattern uncovered in this comparison. The counties with the highest African American voting age population gave the highest number of votes to the Black and Tan presidential electors. However, in the gubernatorial election, the large urban counties provided the greatest number of votes. LBJ's second highest number of votes came from Hays County, which is adjacent to Travis County, and his fourth highest vote came from Washington County, the one with the largest number of African Americans of voting age. Although African Americans voted for LBJ in 1937, there were significant restraints on the electorate.[28] But first let us turn to the other ethnic electorate: Latinos.

The Latino Electorate and LBJ's 1937 Congressional Election

Following the Latino electorate in Texas as we did the African American electorate, the next major event is the 1937 special election that sent LBJ to Congress. To explore the Latino electorate's potential participation and relationship to LBJ's initial election, we will begin with an estimation of the size of both the Latino population and the Latino voting age population in the 10 counties that comprised the 10th Congressional District.

Table 8.4 reveals that, based on their 1930 voting age population (VAP)

TABLE 8.3. A Comparison of the Percentage and Votes for African American Republican Presidential Electors and Gubernatorial Candidates in 1920 with the Percentage and Votes for LBJ in His Initial 1937 Congressional Elections

	Presidential Votes		Gubernatorial Votes		The LBJ Votes	
County[a]	(%)	*N*	(%)	*N*	(%)	*N*
Washington	15	471	5	145	31	735
Burleson	23	458	22	439	14	231
Bastrop	7	147	9	180	20	520
Lee	15	331	14	316	19	285
Travis	6	380	6	366	29	2,962
Caldwell	11	218	8	165	38	663
Williamson	2	84	2	77	13	738
Hays	1	16	1	17	50	940
Blanco	1	13	1	12	74	688
Burnet	0	0	.002	2	37	518
Total		2,118		1,719		8,280

Source: Adapted from the Texas Secretary of State, "Register of Elected and Appointed State and County Officials 1920–1922 Election Returns and 1936–1938 Election Returns," in *Election Registers 1838–1972* (Austin: State Archives, 1838–2000, microfilmed copy). Calculations prepared by author.

[a]The counties in the 10th Congressional District have been placed in a rank ordering based on the total number of African Americans in each county in 1920. Hence, the largest number of African Americans lived in Washington County and the smallest number in Blanco County. The names and number of the counties in the Texas 10th Congressional District are taken from the information in the Secretary of State's *Election Registers 1838–1972*.

percentage, Latinos had a double-digit presence in four counties. In 1937 LBJ won six counties; the Latino VAP was in double digits in three (Hays, Caldwell, and Travis) and extremely low in the other three (Burnet, Blanco, and Washington). Thus, the Latino electorate might have been partially mobilized by the LBJ campaign. In LBJ's home county of Blanco, only 50 Latinos were of voting age in 1930. Moreover, in Hays and Caldwell Counties, there was only a small African American VAP, which further suggests a much greater role for the Latino electorate.

Of the relatively small number of Latinos in this congressional district in 1937, many lived in Travis County, in an area known as "Mexican town." Using the contact list for the 1937 campaign found in LBJ's House of Representatives papers, Julie Pycior noted that Johnson visited "the East Austin barrio . . . [and] . . . also recruited Vincent Valdes, an East Austin grocer and officer in the local LULAC Council."[29] In addition, LBJ "paid more attention to the traditional political bosses such as José Salazar, who, according to Johnson aide Sherman Burwell, 'controls 50 qualified Mexican votes' in Kyle."[30] Pycior concluded, "Johnson outspent his seven opponents and sought out voters that the others overlooked, trudging into rural hollows and barrio back alleys. The money and effort paid off. . . . Johnson edged them all out by just a few hundred votes, the smallest margin of any congressman that year."[31] Thus, while statistical data do not exactly pinpoint the role of the Latino electorate in LBJ's initial election, archival, documentary, and interview data suggest that they had an impact, as did the African American electorate.

TABLE 8.4. The Relationship of the Latino Voting Age Population to LBJ's 1937 Special Election Vote: By County

	1930 Latinos Voting Age Population		1937 LBJ Vote	
County	(%)	*N*	(%)	*N*
Hays	31	2,438	50	940
Caldwell	30	4,837	38	633
Bastrop	12	1,479	20	520
Travis	10	4,439	29	2,962
Williamson	9	2,089	13	738
Burleson	8	845	14	231
Burnet	5	309	37	518
Lee	4	238	19	285
Blanco	2	50	74	688
Washington	1	122	31	735

Source: Bureau of the Census, *Census of Population: 1930 Texas* (Washington, DC: Government Printing Office, 1931), Table 13, 975–90, for the Latino voting age population. For LBJ 1937 congressional vote, see table 6.4 in this book.

A degree of credence can be given to the conclusions drawn from the archival data because, long before 1937, LBJ had connected with the Latino community during both his tenure as Congressman Kleberg's secretary and his directorship of the state's National Youth Administration. LBJ had helped the congressman reach out to this voting community[32] and had him use New Deal programs to assist his constituents. "Those in Kleberg's congressional district were particularly fortunate because it boasted more CCC [Civilian Conservation Corps] camps than almost any place in the nation, thanks to Lyndon Johnson."[33] Subsequently, LBJ had used the NYA as a relief agency to help the Latino community throughout the state. Although his administrative efforts had left a lot to be desired, he had reached out in a manner better than most state programs in the South. In Pycior's estimation, "despite its shortcomings, the NYA position gave Johnson an opportunity to translate into action his concern for the plight of Mexican Americans."[34] This engendered a base of electoral support for LBJ in his forthcoming political career.[35] In these close elections, each vote was important.

At the congressional level, the vote of the Latino electorate was helpful in Johnson's initial election in 1937, but it was not critical in his subsequent House elections because he was not threatened by any challenges, as we shall see in the next chapter. But the 1937 special election and the 1958 Latino electoral revolt do not tell the entire story of the Latino electorate; there is the matter of partisanship. It was Democratic.

The African American and Latino Voters in LBJ's 1937 Congressional Election: A Collective Assessment

When we combine what we now know about the African American and Latino voters in LBJ's initial election, a collective portrait can be mapped for the first time. Legal data tell us that both groups could vote in this election. Second, the U.S. Census data tell us that while the population of the counties in the 10th Congressional District varied by race and ethnicity, African Americans had a much greater presence and, therefore, a greater potential electoral impact than Latinos. Nevertheless, Latinos dominate in at least two counties, and each group has a large presence in Travis County. Third, 1920 electoral data reveal that African Americans were mobilized in voting. Although this is essentially reflective of Republican activity, it tells us that there was a potential electorate already waiting to become involved. Both groups could play vital electoral roles.

There is one final part in this composite evaluation. Statistical measures of associations might help to pinpoint this relationship with a greater degree of accuracy. Thus, correlational analyses demonstrate that there was a minor association of the 1930 Latino VAP with the turnout and the LBJ vote in the 1937 election, while there is a completely negative association of the African American VAP with these variables. Hence, one could conclude from the measures of association that there was little, if any, relationship between the electorate and LBJ's victory. But this is the problem with relying on a single source for information. Here the best that can be said is that the measures of association failed to mobilize African American and Latino voters in this special election. It is still very possible that with their help LBJ was elected to Congress and became set for reelection.

The Five Congressional Primaries

When the white, African American, and Latino electorates coalesced in 1937 to send LBJ to Congress, the electoral dimension of his fateful moment in American politics had occurred; and the first step in the remaking of the Democratic Party had commenced. Shortly after the 1937 special election, the process of reelection to Congress was now under way. LBJ would win five primary and general elections for Congress through 1946.

In three of those reelection contests, 1938, 1940, and 1942, LBJ was unopposed in both the primary and general elections, although there were small scattered write-in votes in the 1940 and 1942 general elections. But in 1944 and 1946 there was primary opposition; and in 1944 there also was general election opposition, with an insignificant write-in vote. Therefore, to analyze LBJ's reelection efforts, we will first combine them at the primary and general levels and examine them over time.

Before presenting this analysis, we wish to remind the reader, first, of Key's findings that the native-son variable did not exist in Texas during LBJ's rise to power. Second, remember that LBJ's home county of Blanco had been in his father's state legislative district and that some of its support for his father may have carried over to the son.

Whatever the impact of these factors, however, the newly elected congressman crafted an electoral coalition from his NYA casework and constituent assistance. Clearly he continued that tradition during his first year in office. Here is how one of his biographers described his constituent services:

> Lyndon, when he returned to the Tenth District after his first session, carried some very respectable accomplishments with him. He had

> managed to get a considerable sum in emergency loans for the crop farmers among his constituents. Three PWA (Public Works Administration) grants had been awarded to the Tenth District on his urging—one for a city hall and fire station in Austin, another for a new federal building in the town of Elgin, and a third for a school in, yes, Johnson City. And the town of Lockhart would have postal delivery, which it had never had before. Nothing major, but a not inconsiderable record for a freshman Congressman who had only arrived in May.[36]

But this was not all. As a freshman congressman, after only six weeks in Washington LBJ requested and received an audience with President Roosevelt. At that meeting, Johnson let the president know that he had a

> problem with Milo Perkins, who was then head of the AAA [Agricultural Adjustment Administration] and high among the angels if not the saints of minorities according to then standards. And this was a rather shocking thing, that there would be a complaint against Milo Perkins. Well, it seemed that back in the Tenth Congressional District of Texas, Negroes were not receiving any benefits of the operation of the AAA.

From these reports, we can see that LBJ's efforts encompassed all segments of his electoral coalition. His subsequent reelections, then, demonstrated that he did not rely solely upon the administration of President Roosevelt and the New Deal, nor on the friends-and-neighbors vote. He clearly used casework as a tool to fashion and maintain, if not enlarge, his victorious electoral coalition.

As Johnson's primary election opposition increased, his share of the vote decreased. By the time of his last congressional primary in 1946, LBJ's electoral support moved from 100 percent to two-thirds of the primary vote. In his initial reelection primary in 1938, he increased his total vote from 8,280 in the 1937 special election to 53,248 votes. Every county showed an increase.

In LBJ's second reelection primary in 1940, more ballots were cast in the governor's race than ever before.[37] For the second time LBJ was unopposed and captured 100 percent of the vote. Despite the fact that voter registration (under the poll tax system) declined in two counties (Bastrop and Lee), it increased in the other eight, and more people were eligible to vote in this election than in 1938. LBJ's third reelection primary was a repeat of the second.

Between the 1942 and the 1944 Democratic primaries, the political context in Texas changed, and LBJ's primary electoral coalition underwent a transformation. This was set in motion by a series of national and state forces. Here is how Weeks described it:

> In the presidential election year of 1936 occurred the first of a series of divisions in the [state] Democratic Party that became chronic. In that year the "Jeffersonian Democrats" emerged, but these anti-Roosevelt Democrats were restrained from producing a real split party because of the presence of John N. Garner of Texas on the ticket as vice-presidential candidate. In 1940 with the absence of Garner, with Roosevelt more to the left, and with the presence of "Democrats for [Republican presidential candidate Wendell] Willkie," the opposition to Roosevelt increased—although, it was not as yet sufficiently strong to cause a real break. In 1944, however, the split came with the formation of the Texas Regulars [as a state party].[38]

In addition to the political schism there was an economic factional force. "Oil Texas, Urban Texas, and Cotton Texas" had by 1944 long displaced "hill-country Texas." "The onetime land of the Populists was becoming the land of the oil buccaneers, who were battling government restraints and were wedded to a new laissez-faire. Texas was moving to the right."[39] "Now, in the postwar years, Texas oil was on the march—supplanting cotton as the state's most politically potent industry, an almost unlimited source of campaign dollars to its political friends and a terror to its political enemies." Sam Rayburn, by then Speaker of the U.S. House of Representatives, and "the leading political figures of Cotton Texas were in jeopardy at the hands of the oil buccaneers. . . . Oil Texas launched a serious effort to unseat Rayburn [and LBJ] in the 1944 election."[40]

The final blow to Texas's traditional alignments came when the Supreme Court in *Smith v. Allwright* "struck down the Texas law barring blacks from the Democratic primary."[41] The new Texas Regular Party, which "hoped to siphon off enough Democratic votes to prevent another Roosevelt victory," passed its party's platform, calling for "[r]estoration of the supremacy of the white race, which had been destroyed by the Communist-controlled New Deal."[42] Public sentiment for social injustice and continued segregation once again reared its head. However, the change set into motion by the Supreme Court meant that African American Democrats could now vote for LBJ in the 1944 Democratic primaries.

Collectively, these national, economic, and race-based forces coalesced to change the political context in Texas and brought forth LBJ's first primary opposition. The leadership of the right wing anti–New Deal movement supported "Buck Taylor, the editor of a small Austin paper, the *Middle Buster*." Taylor had been sponsored by the Christian Americans, an antilabor and race-baiting organization, to lobby the state legislatures in Georgia and the Carolinas to pass legislation against labor unions and their African American employees.[43] In his 1944 primary campaign against Johnson, Taylor captured 30 percent of the total vote and carried one county, Washington, with 52.8 percent of its vote. The voters in LBJ's home county of Blanco cast 135 votes for Taylor, for 27.1 percent of the total there.[44]

Looking back at LBJ's first primary opponent, Texas politician and former governor John Connally said, "Buck Taylor, who was a nobody, a ne'er-do-well, kind of a political hanger-on, ran against Lyndon with the support of a great many people. The only reason they ran him was to try to cut Lyndon up. They knew that he wouldn't win, but they wanted to try to destroy Lyndon."[45] Despite Taylor's electoral failure, his presence set into motion future opposition to LBJ's reelection efforts.

LBJ entered his last House of Representatives Democratic primary in 1946 and this time he found himself facing two opponents in the primaries, Handy Hollers and Charles King. Hollers, "a recently discharged army colonel and district judge . . . decided that a great many veterans of the Tenth District were dissatisfied with the way things had been handled while they were away and might, if given a choice, prefer to be represented by someone else in Congress, namely himself."[46] Hollers, who was "said to be an able lawyer, and competent judge, campaigned on two issues only. One, that he was a veteran; two, that Lyndon was a crook." As one observer noticed, Hollers "accused Lyndon of everything under the sun. . . . He accused him of being too close to Roosevelt and then too close to Truman."[47] LBJ, on the other hand, "felt that it was a campaign by some of the major oil companies that didn't like some of his votes, and he in turn attacked the oil companies and campaigned against them far more than he campaigned against Colonel Hollers."[48] It worked well.

Even with two opponents, LBJ captured 68 percent of the vote and won every one of the 10 counties in the district. Neither Hollers nor King was any electoral match for LBJ. In fact, only in Washington County did the two men make it a real contest. In that county Hollers and King got 2,341 votes between them for 47 percent of the total vote, and in Blanco County 29 percent. Clearly LBJ's casework and constituent service helped him

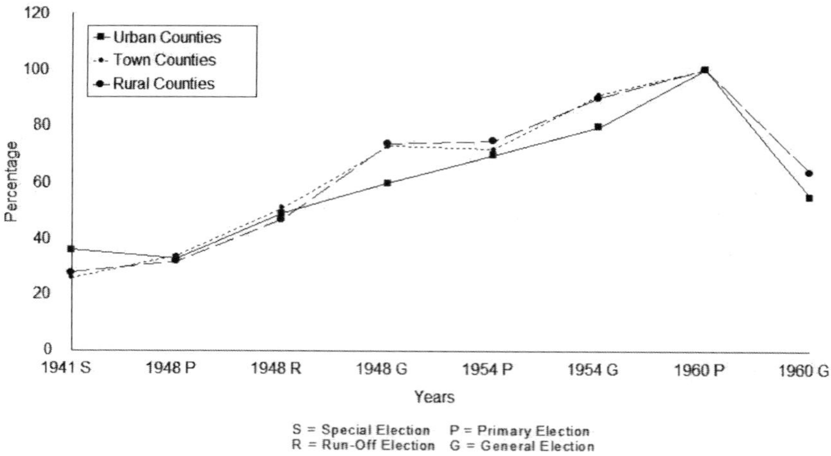

Fig. 8.1. The Percentage of Senatorial Candidate Johnson's Special, Primary, Run-Off, and General Election Vote by Demographic Category: 1941–1960

continue his victorious march toward the presidency. Nevertheless, as opposition began to appear in the primaries, LBJ's voter support started to drop off.

Figure 8.1 permits us to further analyze LBJ's primary votes by demographic categories. In the 1937 special election, he ran best in the rural county, Burleson; but by his initial primary election, LBJ ran equally strongly across the entire demographic spectrum due to a lack of opposition. By the forties, none of LBJ's congressional district was rural, thus the urban and town counties carried the electoral weight.

The Five Congressional General Elections

In a one-party state like Texas, as in much of the South, opposition occurred in the Democratic primary and not in the general election. Hence, what opposition there was came in the primaries. The only opposition LBJ faced in the general elections came from scattered write-in votes in 1940, 1942 and 1944,[49] and a single Republican opponent in 1944, when Arthur Bartelt captured 8.8 percent of the total vote. Bartelt's vote ranged ran from 27.6 percent in LBJ's home county to 3.5 percent in Burleson. This was less opposition than he had faced in the primaries.

Such a token Republican showing was what one would expect in this one-party state.

If we analyze LBJ's general election vote by demographic categories, we see a replication of his primary electoral vote. Beginning with mostly rural support in 1937, a shift to the urban and town counties occurs in 1938. Over time there is a slight tendency for the electoral coalition in the town counties to provide stronger support.

At the county level, LBJ won six of the 10 counties in 1937 and won every one of them in each of the five subsequent primaries except 1944, when he lost one county. In the five general elections, given the one-party nature of the state, LBJ did not lose a single county.

Lastly, in terms of Johnson's congressional elections, his performance in his home county of Blanco is particularly important given the lack of localism in Texas and in terms of the voting behavior of its citizens. In the 1937 special election LBJ got 8.3 percent of his total vote from Blanco County. In the primaries his home county never provided more than 2.1 percent of his total vote. But in the general elections, Blanco County support rose to a high of 9.8 percent in 1938 and dipped to a low of 2.7 percent in 1944, when LBJ faced his first and only Republican opponent. Overall, this sparsely populated county provided only a small percentage of LBJ's overall primary vote. This was not the case in the general election, where the Blanco County vote provided a much higher proportion of the total vote, but the pattern here was erratic. Such was also true of Jimmy Carter's support from Sumter County,[50] although it does not show up in the home counties' support for Clinton, who generally received a consistent level of support in his numerous state races.[51] Home-county support for LBJ was uniform in the primaries but not uniform in the general elections.

Before leaving our discussion of the electoral support that LBJ received from his home county, we move beyond a percentage analysis to examine the actual vote level, to see if the percentage measure masked any patterns in that support. In no uncertain terms, prior to 1937 the district had a tendency to turn out in greater numbers in the primary than in the general election. After LBJ was elected in 1937, this pattern would persist, except in 1944 when he had Republican opposition. The highest voter turnout in this district came in 1938 when LBJ got 53,248 votes in the primary, and the lowest occurred in 1942 when he received 12,799 general election votes.

This pattern of greater turnout in the primaries than in general elections was typical of one-party southern states.[52] A similar situation prevailed for Carter but not for Clinton, where his general election votes tended to be higher than his primary vote turnout.[53] The data on actual votes cast show an erratic pattern that parallels that in the percentage data. Personal factions were ever changing, despite the existence (or nonexistence) of localism. This is the essence of a one-party system.

LBJ's House of Representative Electoral Coalition

LBJ's 11 House elections—one special, five primary, and five general—afforded him an entrance into both Texas state politics and national politics at the same time. Unlike Carter and Clinton, who emerged as native sons from state offices first, LBJ made the strategic choice of going after a congressional seat. However, both Carter and Clinton considered congressional candidacies initially. Carter eventually decided to run for a state senate seat.[54] Clinton actually ran in primary, runoff, and general election campaigns for a congressional seat but lost in the general election.[55] His entrée into politics became a state office, as well. Thus, in many ways LBJ, as the first southern native-son president, crafted a political road map to the presidency.[56]

Given the lack of localism in Texas politics, it is necessary to explore how well LBJ's base electoral coalition held up over time. An answer to this question tells us much about how native-son presidential candidates emerge, even in political climates where the native-son variable is not present. Can casework and constituent service supplant localism? Can personality substitute for the lack of localism?

LBJ's congressional district remained geographically constant over the period in which he served, making it comparable across time with his electoral coalition, which emerged in the 1937 special election and stayed with him to his last election in 1946.

Did the percentage of the LBJ electoral coalition hold together from one election to the next? We begin with the general election data since they offer us empirical insights beginning with the reapportioning of the district in 1934. The electoral coalition of Congressman James Buchanan held at 99 percent between 1934 and 1936. Clearly the Democratic partisans significantly supported the incumbent. But Buchanan's coalition was negatively associated with LBJ's initial coalition in 1937. Congressman Buchanan's long-time campaign manager ran and obviously captured many of his friends and supporters. Thus, LBJ's 1937 coalition had to come from other sources.

LBJ's 1937 coalition did not continue into the 1938 general election, which saw the rise of a different electoral coalition. However, once that coalition took shape, more than 80 percent of it stayed with him across time. That was substantial support. This support dropped only in 1944 when LBJ had his one and only Republican opponent. By the time of his last election, in 1946, nearly 100 percent of his previous electoral supporters showed up to vote for him.

A similar reality prevailed at the primary level. There was a nonlinkage between the 1937 special election coalition and the one that arose in the 1938 congressional primary. But when LBJ ran in his last House primary 99 percent of his previous supporters showed up to vote for him, even though he faced his only primary opposition. Facing these challengers mobilized his factional faithful.

Collectively, LBJ's primary and general election coalitions held together, both in the face of challengers and when there were no challengers. This demonstrates that one can build an electoral coalition, at least in congressional elections, without the variable of localism influencing voting behavior, even in a one-party state like Texas. Candidate personality and casework are effective vote-getters and can replace the friends-and-neighbors vote. Essentially, LBJ's House of Representatives elections not only launched a fateful moment in American politics, they carried that moment forward to a new destiny for American politics. LBJ was well on his way.

★ 9

The Senatorial Vote for Johnson

How is a native-son presidential candidate born? Clinton ran against the only Republican congressional candidate in a one-party Democratic state. Carter ran against a political-boss-sponsored candidate with all the baggage that carries in a small state senate district. LBJ let the death of an incumbent congressman open the door of political opportunity in the district in which he was born. Clearly this was a matter of fate. But it did not happen only in 1937. It happened again in 1941. Less than five years into his House of Representatives career, LBJ had another "sudden death" political opportunity.[1] One of his biographers describes it thusly:

> Senator Morris Sheppard of Texas died on April 4, 1941; he was sixty-five years old. On April 19 Governor O'Daniel announced that a special election would be held on June 28 to choose a successor to Senator Sheppard. Then he appointed an interim senator. . . .
>
> That was Andrew Jackson Houston, the only surviving son of Sam Houston, who had also been a U.S. senator.[2]

Special elections in Texas tended to generate a crowded field of candidates, simply because avenues to political office were few in a one-party state. In addition, in "a special election rather than a party primary, any citizen could get his name on the ballot merely by paying a $100 fee, and twenty-seven candidates besides Johnson had taken advantage of this opportunity."[3] As he had done in his first special election, LBJ quickly distinguished himself from the huge field of contenders by embracing President Roosevelt and the New Deal. FDR also helped LBJ, as he had done in his initial special election: "He arranged for Johnson to see him on April 22, just before his regular Tuesday press conference, so that arriving reporters would see Johnson emerging from the Oval Office."[4] Of this new political opportunity, Mooney wrote, "The Texan emerged with an announcement that he was a candidate for the unexpired term of Senator Morris Sheppard, who had died April 9. He read the announcement from the steps of the White House."[5] A few minutes later, the president at his news conference gave LBJ his endorsement; and in Texas, the *Dallas Morning News* declared in a front-page headline, "F.D.R. Pick Johnson to Defeat Dies."

With this move, LBJ narrowed the political field to himself and three other major contenders. There was Governor W. Lee O'Daniel, nicknamed "Pass the Biscuits Pappy," because he was a flour salesman and "a self-styled . . . politician of extremely conservative views."[6] The other contenders were Martin Dies, a former congressman and onetime head of the House Un-American Activities Committee, and Gerald C. Mann, the popular and able attorney general of Texas. This special election turned into a political circus that provided the rural-born electorate with entertainment mixed with religion in the best southern tradition. LBJ did his absolute best to make the most of his new political opportunity.

Moving the Fateful Moment: The 1941 Special Election for the United States Senate

Fateful moments are always caught up in ever-moving political and social contexts. Political journalist Theodore White described how Texas itself was on the move simultaneously with LBJ's moment, in its effort to expand its wealth and values beyond the southern region and increase the power it had already captured in Washington, DC. He wrote:

> The first sense of the tilt in national leadership from northwest to southwest can probably be dated sometime between 1952 and 1954, when imperial New York sensed a serious . . . trespass on its domain. . . . The trespass came from Texas. There, a handful of uncouth oilmen had begun to invest in congressional candidacies across the nations. . . . Texas was apparently the prime new political challenger to New York . . . Texas, like New York, was an outreach state. . . .
>
> Texas oilmen were beginning to buy their way into national politics everywhere . . . these . . . men had invaded the politics of

> no less than thirty other states, had pumped money into well over a hundred congressional races, and were beginning to act as if they could buy up national politics as they bought horses and oil leases.[7]

However, what White's analysis missed was that while the new rich oilmen were trying to capture national politics as a group, an individual in Texas national politics, LBJ, was himself moving to capture presidential power. He took a step toward this new position in 1941, as he had in 1937 when a legislative death opened up another political opportunity. In the end, LBJ's rise would serve as a check on the rising grab for national power by the new Texas oil barons.

The history of Senator Sheppard's seat goes all the way back to Sam Houston of Texas's independence fame. It was Senator Houston who first held the seat from 1845 to 1861. Six men succeeded him before Morris Sheppard was elected to it in 1913.[8] Senator Sheppard held the seat for 28 years,

> the longest of any Texan . . . [and he] . . . was the first man to gain the Senate office by virtue of an election. Early in the century, the Democratic Party required all candidates for public office to stand for election in the primary. Even senators, who did not normally face voters, had to run. Incumbent Joe Bailey, with scandal nipping at his heels, chose not to run. And in the 1912 primary, Sheppard won a plurality against five opponents.[9]

Upon Senator Sheppard's death, Texas governor Wilbert L. O'Daniel, ever mindful of the historic succession and tradition inherent in the seat, appointed Sam Houston's son Andrew as interim senator to keep this great legacy going. Andrew Jackson "A. J." Houston was in his late eighties. After hearing about his appointment, "he rested for a month, then got on a train and went to Washington where he was sworn in by Vice-President Wallace just ninety-five years after his father had been sworn in."[10] Houston only served 24 days; he "was so ailing and infirm that he could not receive reporters. . . . [His] daughters did not even want him to take the risk of making the long trip to the nation's capital. Six weeks after his appointment, he did journey to Washington, attended one committee meeting, and died."[11]

This choice of appointment by Governor O'Daniel was an attempt to define the "issue" in this special election as one of determining who would carry on this great historic legacy. Others have argued that the appointment of such an old person "would give the governor the minimum amount of trouble should he decide to enter the race himself."[12] The governor was the last of the 29 candidates to enter the race. "He waited until the sixth week of the campaign to do so."[13] Over the 28 years of his tenure, Senator Sheppard had built an electoral following through five Democratic primaries and four general elections. Thus, the question is how much of this coalition did LBJ and the governor draw to themselves in this election.

There were two patterns in the electoral support for Sheppard. The total number of Texans voting for him rose in each primary election. However, this pattern does not hold for the general election, where he received a large vote in presidential years and a small vote in the off years. In each of the presidential years, the general election vote exceeded the primary vote. Such a voting pattern is similar to that found in Georgia, where the primary vote usually exceeds the general election vote.[14]

The second pattern to arise from this analysis of Sheppard's electoral support is the fact that in this one-party Democratic state, the greatest turnout came in the primaries because there were rarely competitors in the general election. The primary vote percentage that Senator Sheppard received depended on the number of candidates running and their popularity. He began with 49 percent of the vote in 1912 but averaged 63 percent across his five primary elections. Capturing the Democratic Party's nomination in the primary was a prerequisite if a candidate wanted to win a Senate seat. The vote percentage in the general election reveals that the Republican Party's senatorial candidate received little electoral support. In fact, Senator Sheppard's average vote was 88 percent, which left only 12 percent for his Republican opponents. Overall, Senator Sheppard had built a much stronger electoral base in the general election than in the primary election; yet his electoral support in the primaries was constantly increasing.

Our analysis of Senator Sheppard's vote is quite revealing. It does not tell us about the nature of its cohesion and stability, nor does it reveal anything about the relationship of one election to another. For that information, it is necessary to turn to a statistical measure of association. Again our correlational analysis indicates the degree of association among Sheppard's various elections in the primaries and the general elections. His primary electoral coalition changed from one election to the next and showed no real cohesion at all. Basically speaking, a different group of individuals voted for him each time.

Probing the general election coalition, there are some minimal relationships visible between the electoral groups in the 1918–24 vote, and between those in the 1924–30 groups. However, between the groups that voted for him in 1930 and 1936, there is a strong relationship; nearly all returned to vote for him in 1936. All of the general election relationships and two of the primary election relationships are statistically significant, meaning that what we found about them is valid and did not occur by chance. Hence, on the surface, Senator Sheppard received rising electoral support, but underneath that support, except in the general elections of 1930 and 1936, there was a lack of cohesion and stability. As Key pointed out, the state electorate was perpetually in flux.[15] Sheppard's electoral coalition was literally up for grabs for another Democrat upon his death, if not before.

Therefore, when the special election for Sheppard's Senate seat took place, on the final official ballot the Democratic Party had 25 candidates, the Republicans two, and the independents and the Communist Party had one each. It should not come as any surprise that the Democratic Party captured nearly 99.9 percent of the total vote in this one-party state. The vote for the two Republican candidates once again reveals the limited influence of the party in the Texas electorate. Additional empirical evidence for this can be observed in table 9.1 where the total vote has been disaggregated to the individual candidate level. Six Democratic candidates received more individual votes than the two Republican candidates combined (344 cumulative votes).

Governor O'Daniel and Congressman Johnson came in first and second, respectively, with only a 1,311-vote difference between them. Nearly all of the biographical studies suggest that on the night of the election, LBJ was ahead by several thousand votes, but his lead evaporated over the next few days as county vote totals changed. Despite his best effort to rally his supporters and the political bosses and machines, he could not regain the lead.

In table 9.2 we examine how LBJ's congressional electorate responded to this 1941 special election. Extant data at both the primary and general election levels show that LBJ did not rally his own congressional base. Counties that had voted for him in the 1940 primary election when he had no opposition did not turn out for him again in the 1941 special election. Barely a third of those who voted for LBJ in 1940 came back to vote for him in 1941 in the three counties for which data exist. Had he rallied just the primary electorate alone in these three counties, he could have won the election.

Moving from the extant primary election data to the 1940 general election data, it becomes quite obvious that had the general election elec-

TABLE 9.1. The Vote and Percentage for Each Candidate of Every Political Party in the 1941 Special Senate Election

Candidate	Votes	(%)
Democrats		
W. Lee O'Daniel	175,590	30.5
L.B. Johnson	174,279	30.3
Gerald Mann	140,807	24.5
Martin Dies	80,551	14.0
Sam Morris	1,654	0.3
Joseph Thompson	431	—[a]
Joseph Bean	242	—[a]
W.W. King	238	—[a]
Cyclone Davis	181	—[a]
Guy B. Fisher	141	—[a]
John C. Williams	128	—[a]
S.G. Newsome Jr.	98	—[a]
W.E. Gilliland	95	—[a]
E.A. Calvin	92	—[a]
Commodore Hatfield	84	—[a]
Bubba Hicks	77	—[a]
W.C. Welch	74	—[a]
Floyd E. Ryan	61	—[a]
Walter Schultz	61	—[a]
A.E. Harding	59	—[a]
Robert Heard	58	—[a]
O.F. Heath	51	—[a]
Dr. John R. Brinkley	36	—[a]
Edwin Waller	23	—[a]
C.L. Sommerville	20	—[a]
Republicans		
Polite Elvins	276	—[a]
Enoch Fletcher	68	—[a]
Independent		
W.R. Jones	258	—[a]
Communist		
Homer Brooks	53	—[a]
Grand Total	575,786	99.6[b]

Source: Adapted from the Texas Secretary of State, "Register of Elected and Appointed State and County Officials 1941–1945," in *Election Registers 1838–1972* (Austin: State Archives, microfilmed copy, 1838–1972). There is also a list of these candidates and their votes in Box 65 of LBJ's Subject File at the Lyndon Baines Johnson Presidential Library in Austin, Texas. Calculations prepared by author.

[a]Indicates less than one hundredth of one percent.

[b]Does not total to 100 percent because the totals for 25 candidates were not summed.

torate responded to his campaign pleas, he also could have won the 1941 special election.[16] Only 39.2 percent of LBJ's 1940 general electorate supporters came back to the polls to support him in 1941. Even a share of the 29,468 missing votes from the 1940 general election surely would have been enough to overcome the 1,311-vote lead with which Governor O'Daniel won.

Although the 1940 vote occurred in a presidential election year, when the voter turnout is supposed to be greater, LBJ's primary vote total for 1942 was 44,656,[17] nearly as high as his 1940 general election vote of 48,442. This suggests that the difference between the presidential year and the congressional year, at least in LBJ's 10th Congressional District, was small. Thus, the turnout or lack thereof that seemingly occurred in the 1937 and 1941 special elections was not totally significant.

TABLE 9.2. A Comparison of LBJ 1940 Primary and General Election Votes with His 1941 Special Election Votes in His 10th Congressional District

County	1940 Primary Election Vote	1940 General Election Vote	1941 Special Election Vote	Difference
Bastrop			1,654	
Blanco			654	
Burleson			950	
Burnet	3,007		1,326	−1,681
Caldwell	4,572		1,203	−3,369
Hays	3,413		1,153	−2,260
Lee			566	
Travis			7,477	
Washington			1,128	
Williamson			2,863	
Total			18,974	
Bastrop		2,976	1,654	−1,322
Blanco		1,574	654	−920
Burleson		2,304	950	−1,354
Burnet		2,495	1,326	−1,169
Caldwell		4,147	1,203	−2,944
Hays		2,800	1,153	−1,647
Lee		1,885	566	−1,319
Travis		20,478	7,477	−13,001
Washington		3,271	1,128	−2,143
Williamson		6,512	2,863	−3,649
Total		48,442	18,974 (39.2)	−29,468 (60.8)

Source: Data adapted from the only three newspapers that reported votes for LBJ: "Official Tabulation of the Primary Election," *The Burnet Bulletin* (August 1, 1940), 2; "The Democratic Primary," *Lockhart Post-Register* (August 1, 1940), 1; "Election Results: Return of Primary Election, July 27—unofficial," *San Marco Record* (August 2, 1940), 5; and Mike Kingston, Sam Attlesey, and Mary Crawford, *The Texas Almanac's Political History of Texas* (Austin: Eakin Press, 1992), 146–49.

Further insights can be had about LBJ's supporters in the 1941 special election if we employ a correlation analysis. Because election data exist for only a few counties in the 1940 primary, it is necessary to correlate the general election vote with the 1941 special election vote. First, however, it must be noted that in the 1941 special election LBJ won only eight of the 10 counties in his district.[18] His mean vote percentage was 51.6 percent, running from a high of 71.6 percent in Burnet County to a low of 32.7 percent in Lee County. His home county of Blanco gave him 61.0 percent, the second highest level of support. There is a poor negative relationship between LBJ's 1940 general election vote and his 1941 special election vote in the 10th Congressional District (= .10). However, a test for statistical significance of this finding reveals that it does not reach a level of reliability. Hence, it is necessary to turn to another analysis for greater insights.

A county-level analysis tells us that LBJ won only 70 of Texas's 254 counties, or 29.6 percent. Of these 70, he won Fisher County by a single vote, and several others with less than 50 percent of the vote, due to the huge number of candidates. Comparatively, Governor O'Daniel captured nearly twice as many counties and won in a majority of them. In fact, the governor won more counties than all of the other candidates combined. Yet even with nearly double the number of counties, he beat LBJ by only 1,311 votes. Thus, it was not so much the number or percentage of counties won as much as it was the number of voters mobilized to turn out that determined the outcome. Seemingly LBJ did as well as the governor but in many fewer counties.

The next question one might ask is "where did LBJ's votes come from in terms of the demographic areas of the state?" Using the types of counties, LBJ won in three of the seven categories: the urban counties, the boss counties, and the Latino counties. Despite the fact that he had become known as a "countryside liberal," providing significant benefits to the poor people in his district, appreciation for these good works had not spread across the state. In fact, he lost one county in his 10th Congressional District, Washington County, to Governor O'Daniel, 1,128 votes to 1,746. He simply did not remobilize his supporters to come back to the polls as they had in the 1940 general election.

In addition to losing the rural vote and one of his 10th District counties, LBJ lost Gillespie County, his home county, where he came in third behind Gerald Mann and O'Daniel. LBJ did beat both men in his resident county, Blanco, but this victory was not enough for him to offset his losses in Gillespie County and be the overall winner in this category. O'Daniel was the overall winner in this home category with Mann coming in a close second. LBJ ran a distant third. Key's analysis about the absence of localism held true in this case.

However, in the boss and Latino county categories, LBJ simply trounced his opponents. In the former category he got nearly 93 percent of the vote and 85 percent in the latter. Prior to the 1941 special election, LBJ sent Judge Manuel Bravo, the political boss of Zapata County, a series of letters requesting his support. A recent biographer of Judge Bravo, Gilberto Quezada, unearthed these letters and noted that "[f]our out of the five border counties voted for Johnson—Zapata and Starr with 91 and 96 percent respectively. Zapata was the only county with a round number of 300 votes, almost as if the number was preplanned."[19] After the election was over, Judge Bravo wrote LBJ about the outcome and indicated that "[w]e have been disheartened with the final count."[20] Shortly thereafter, "[f]rom his office in the House of Representatives, Johnson sent a thank-you note to every member of Zapata's political machine, with a personal message to Judge Bravo: 'For your own fine spirit of loyalty and cooperation, I will ever be grateful. . . . You did your part and we will work together again.'"[21] Quezada further stated that "[t]he 1941 election campaign was the beginning of a lasting friendship between the two politicos."[22]

However, this very strong support from the boss and Latino counties was not enough to overcome O'Daniel's strength in the town counties, especially those located in East Texas where the majority of the African American population resided. Archival documents reveal that LBJ's campaign tried to mobilize this community, and leaders inside the community took it upon themselves to mobilize on his behalf. During the campaign an article appeared in the *Houston Defender* entitled, "Negro Citizens Organize to Push Johnson Cause," which indicated that "Mrs. Lola Ann Cullum was appointed this week by County Judge Roy Hofheinz to serve as South Texas manager for the Lyndon Johnson-for-Senator Campaign Among Negroes."[23] Immediately after she was appointed, Mrs. Cullum formed an executive committee that was composed of some of the most outstanding African American leaders in the state, notably R. R. Grovey, of the Supreme Court case of *Grovey v. Townsend*.[24] The campaign's chairman, Dr. W. M. Drake, announced, "We are urging all Negro voters to vote for Lyndon Johnson because he has a clean record of fair dealings with all races. Therefore, we have decided after studying the records of all the other candidates that Johnson is a safe choice for all the Negroes of Texas to support."

Shortly after this article appeared it brought a letter of inquiry from the Texas representative of the *Pittsburgh Courier*, Mrs. O. J. Cansler, asking if the campaign wanted this African American newspaper with its 12,000 state subscribers to work on behalf of the Johnson campaign. The archival documents simply indicate that the campaign would consider the request.[25]

In addition to Congressman Johnson's campaign efforts to help mobilize the African American electorate on his behalf, there were initiatives from the community's own leadership. Chief among them were the efforts led by J. E. Clayton, principal of Littig High School and first vice president of the National Federation of Colored Farmers. Clayton was also on the staff of the Southern Tenant Farmers Union, as well as on its National Executive Council. Immediately he moved to involve the organization, which had its national office in Memphis, Tennessee. The secretary of the Southern Tenant Farmers Union, H. L. Mitchell, wrote Congressman Johnson saying "that we might give you whatever help we could during your campaign. I expect to be in Texas sometime during the month of June, and will be out among the farm people, and I will do anything that I can for you . . . our mutual friends, Aubrey Williams and Jess Kellam of N.Y.A. both know me well, and I shall look forward to seeing you when I get down to your state."[26] Johnson replied a week later, indicating that he "appreciated your splendid letter telling me of your interest in my campaign for the Senate,"[27] and inviting Mitchell to drop by to see him during his visit to Texas.

Clayton also engaged the editor of the *Houston Informer* newspaper to write an editorial supporting LBJ.[28] A day later, Clayton wrote an "open letter" to the African American electorate urging them to vote for LBJ. He then toured East Texas, campaigning for the Johnson ticket and distributing his open letter to members of his audience and leaders in the area.[29] While in Houston, he got in touch with Freeman Everett, president of the International Longshoremen's Association local, and had him "get the literature in the hands of every colored worker on the waterfront and . . . stickers on the cars."[30]

When Clayton's campaigning efforts attracted the attention of LBJ's own colored committee, its chairman wrote Clayton and requested $100 for him for his own executive committee operation. Clayton refused, saying, "When I volunteered to work for Congressman Johnson, I told him that my services would not cost him a cent. . . . I am operating my office, bearing my own living expenses and giving my time and services and I have not asked anybody for a single cent to help me . . . even though I am a poor man."[31]

Congressman Johnson knew of Clayton's independent efforts in his behalf and wrote, "J. E. Clayton has been working hard among his people all over the state and I am sure that he is producing results."[32] Thus, in LBJ's

1941 senatorial campaign there were both sponsored and unsponsored African Americans working to help him get elected, because both groups saw him as being fair and balanced in his outreach efforts. His constituent service had clearly helped to build Johnson a political base, even among a voting segment that the state of Texas sought to eliminate from the political process, and in a state without friends-and-neighbors voting behavior.

Johnson's "countryside liberalism" did not mobilize only the independent African American leadership; it did the same thing in the Latino community. R. L. de Cordeva, chairman of the Latin American Democrats, which was a confederation of Mexican American Democrats in Texas, wrote an "open letter" to the Latino electorate urging them to vote for Congressman Johnson because he was "convinced that Mr. Johnson is better qualified for this office."[33] He, like Clayton, had driven in the East Texas area and toured South Texas for the Johnson campaign.

Thus, there was some liberalism to be found in both East and South Texas, in areas that also exemplified conservatism. These independent efforts challenged the racial conservatism of the white electorate and those candidates who had voting records that embraced it. Here was a small electoral revolt against the leaders of racial segregation, and they wanted LBJ to carry their torch of racial justice for them.

For all Johnson's efforts, however, the voters were influenced on the day of the election in a negative way by the early returns. When the early returns started to come in, "[t]hey were promising. When Lyndon finally retired for the night, he was ahead by three thousand votes, and when he woke up the next morning, his lead was nearly five thousand. Newspapers all over the state were saying that he had been elected."[34] This news would lead to his defeat. Caro described LBJ as having "violated a fundamental rule of Texas politics: report your key precincts—the ones in which you control the result—only at the last minute so your opponent would not know the total he had to beat; otherwise in a state in which not a few isolated rural precincts were 'for sale,' beating it would be all too easy."[35]

Merle Miller followed up on Caro's insights: "As the days passed, election officials in various counties who had taken the ballot boxes home with them or locked them up or mislaid them, started opening them. . . . Other election officials discovered that they had made errors in giving Lyndon too many votes, and they hurriedly sent in their 'corrected' totals. Most of the 'corrections' were in Pappy's [O'Daniel's] favor."[36] Historian George Norris Green described LBJ's defeat thusly: "[F]or the next several days, a dozen or more east Texas counties kept bringing in 'corrected returns.' A few managed to vote over 100 percent of their potential voting strength. The Johnson forces tried to counter by appealing to George Parr [the Duke of Duval County] for more votes, but Parr . . . refused to do anything more."[37] Now it was all over. Sixteen days after the special election, "[o]n July 14 the state canvassing board came up with its official computations,"[38] announcing that Governor O'Daniel was the winner when the corrected totals were taken into consideration. LBJ had been counted out and as a consequence lost his first and so far only statewide election.

The Next Step to the Fateful Moment: The 1948 Senatorial Primary Election

In 1948 another political opportunity came for LBJ. Former Texas governor and now U.S. Senator O'Daniel decided not to return to the Senate because he was "[o]ut of favor with the national Administration and possessing no independent standing, he could not 'get things done' in Washington for his constituents. . . . He had drawn his chief support from the old folks, the poor, and the farmers. As governor he had been ostensibly concerned with old-age pensions and taxes to finance them. In the Senate, however, his attitude on a wide variety of matters was consistently contrary to the interest of the people whose votes elected him."[39] A Texas newspaper, the *Lubbock Avalanche,* labeled O'Daniel's decision to retire voluntarily as "the one most constructive act in his ten years in politics."

Even before O'Daniel let his political plans be known, LBJ already had decided to run again for the U.S. Senate. Former governor Coke Stevenson announced his intention to run, on January 1, 1948. LBJ formally announced his candidacy five months later, on May 12. [40] By the June 2 filing deadline, 11 candidates had put their hats into the ring. Most observers felt that the race would be between Congressman Johnson and former governor Stevenson, who was known as "Mr. Texas" because of his popularity with the electorate. Among these 11 candidates was a Republican senatorial candidate in the 1922 election, George E. B. Peddy, who had under that party label captured 130,744 votes.[41] He had now switched to the more viable Democratic Party and its primary. His entrance added another heavy hitter to the race.

The primary election was held on July 24, 1948. Former governor Stevenson captured just under 40 percent of the vote. LBJ was second with a third of the vote, and Peddy came in third with nearly 20 percent. This left the other eight candidates with just under 7 percent of the total vote. Under Texas law there had to be a runoff between the two top vote-getters, LBJ and Stevenson. Stevenson had outpolled LBJ by 71,460 votes and 6 percentage points.

In telling this simple fact, writers have employed a wide variety of interpretations around a host of themes, facts, and myths. There was the suggestion that LBJ had to resign his congressional seat to run for the Senate, which was not true and made him seem more desperate. There was the notion that he introduced a wider variety of campaign techniques in the primary by using the radio. Not so. There was an especially popular reference to his use of a helicopter, usually dubbed the "flying windmill." Several writers conclude with the fact that former governor Stevenson drove himself from town to town with no advance planning and no supporting cast of campaign men. Some writers added data about Joe Belden's Texas Poll, which showed LBJ as running behind during the entire primary race, again adding a heightened sense of desperation to the race and again untrue. Next came the discussions about huge expenditures of money, but there is no paper trail to expose the exact amounts.

Once money was introduced into the story, the discussion turned to the buying of votes in the African American and Latino communities. To prove that point, the narratives turn to the number of votes that LBJ received vis-à-vis Stevenson. Little attention was paid to Key's empirical analysis on the point of the manipulated vote. In consideration of boss George Parr's comments and reaction to Stevenson's complaints about questionable voting in "Duval and surrounding counties," Key analyzed "Duval County's performance in a series of state races over a twenty-year period."[42] This analysis revealed that Duval overwhelmingly had supported Stevenson in the 1942 and 1944 gubernatorial races, hence its voting behavior in the 1948 Senate race for Johnson was no different than what it had done in the past for Stevenson.[43] But most of the work on LBJ simply ignored Key's findings.

Lastly, there was the assertion that during the campaign Johnson started to shift to the right. Evans and Novak made the most of LBJ's supposed repositioning: "Now, in his second attempt, he began to do what he would not do in 1941: move rightward with his state, and move fast. . . . In postwar Texas, the mainstream hugged the right-hand bank." Evans and Novak fixed the day of the shift in LBJ's political ideology from countryside liberalism to right-wing conservatism as "April 12, 1945—the day of Roosevelt's death."[44] This makes it appear that LBJ was without any principles, and only single-minded about power.

Alone or in some combination, these factors were used to explain in dramatic fashion LBJ's frenzied campaign and his motivation in the 1948 senatorial primary. Such interpretations craft a one-dimensional portrait because they focus solely upon the candidate and leave out another critical dimension, the Texas electorate, until the end when the reader finds that, despite his strenuous campaign effort, LBJ came in some 71,000 votes behind Stevenson. However, the cause of this second-place finish is to be found not only in the candidate but also in the behavior of the Texas electorate.

In order to get a clear vision of the influential Texas electorate, we turn to their voting behavior in the statewide elections for Coke Stevenson. When LBJ ran against Stevenson in 1948 he had participated in only one statewide election contest, the 1941 special Senate election. Stevenson had participated successfully in nine contests. Hence, an overview of the Texas electorate's behavior in Stevenson's five elections for the lieutenant governor post and four successful elections for governor is needed. They knew this candidate and found him worthy of support. The support that the electorate gave to Stevenson in five of his statewide elections was greater than that given to all 29 candidates in the 1941 election. In addition, in all nine of Stevenson's elections he received nearly double the number of votes that LBJ got in his first and only statewide election.

Therefore, it can simply be said that the Texas electorate responded to Stevenson; it reveals how the electorate turned out in the statewide elections in which Stevenson was a candidate. In four of the nine races, there were more than a million voters. Only twice did his campaigns attract fewer than 500,000 voters, and each time it was in the less important general elections in nonpresidential election years.

The third indicator of electorate involvement was the percentage of the total vote for Stevenson. The mean percentage for Stevenson in the primary elections was 63.3 percent, and 95.8 percent in the general elections. By any yardstick, the Texas electorate had provided Stevenson with a substantial base. If one adds to this the electoral base he had created during his campaigns for county judge and state legislator, it becomes evident that voters in Texas were not only knowledgeable about him but had put him into public office every time he ran.

In all of Stevenson's nine statewide elections, in every region of the state, the Texas electorate responded to him. With the exception of his first primary, which he lost, he won almost every county. The Texas's electorate support for Coke Stevenson was broad-based, covering every demographic region and including liberal, conservative, and moderate counties, and Democratic and Republican counties. In his last statewide primary before the 1948 election, Stevenson won all of the counties. In a primary election this is an exceptional electoral sweep.

Therefore, when one looks at the outcome of the 1948 primary election from the standpoint of the dimension of the Texas electorate, and the fact that LBJ ran only 71,000 votes behind Stevenson, other explanations for the outcome fail to tell the complete story. Using this second dimension, we can revisit the primary outcome and search for additional insight and a more comprehensive perspective that does not focus solely upon LBJ's personal motivation.

Even without this huge electoral base, the Texas electorate significantly responded to LBJ's 1948 campaign. First, in this presidential election year, more than double the number of votes were cast. In this circumstance, LBJ increased his own vote by slightly more than double what he received in 1941. Although this was not enough to win the 1948 senatorial primary, it was a substantial performance given the electorate's past support for Coke Stevenson.

A further look at the response of the Texas electorate to the LBJ primary campaign is displayed in the number of counties won by Stevenson in his previous elections. When compared with earlier data, one finds that 1948 was the first time he had won so few counties since his initial loss in the 1938 primary. Clearly LBJ's campaign seriously reduced Stevenson's support. In fact, in 1948 LBJ increased the number of counties that he won in the 1941 special senate election by six. He won all of his 10th Congressional District counties, capturing 64 percent of the total vote cast. Thus, in total votes and total counties, LBJ managed to capture some of Stevenson's supporters, if not attract new voters into the electorate, and to diminish some of Stevenson's well-established statewide reach.

Key's 1949 finding that localism did not exist in Texas as it did in Arkansas and Georgia finds additional empirical support here, in the decline of the total number of votes and counties for Stevenson, suggesting that some of his supporters dropped away in this election.

By analyzing the 1948 election from the dimension of the Texas electorate, we can now look demographically to see where the strengths and weaknesses of these two candidates lay just before they were to face each other in a runoff election. In table 9.3 we see that LBJ ran behind Stevenson in the urban, town, and rural counties, capturing about one-third of the vote in each and reducing Stevenson's electoral reach below the 50 percent threshold. Only in rural counties did Stevenson even come close to 50 percent. On the other hand, LBJ beat Stevenson in the home, Black Belt, boss, and Latino counties. In the latter two LBJ trounced Stevenson, winning 96.6 percent and 86.4 percent, respectively, although the vote was relatively close in the Black Belt and home counties. However, Stevenson won LBJ's birth county of Gillespie, while LBJ won in his resident county, Blanco. This gave him enough votes to win the entire home counties category, but only by four votes.

At this point a word needs to be said about the political participation of African American voters. As noted earlier, unique contextual circumstances, that is, the 1944 Supreme Court's ruling in *Smith v. Allwright*, permitted African American voters to participate in this election. "The 1948 election was the first Senate primary in generations in which blacks could legally cast ballots. . . . [and in this election] Johnson ran an anti-civil rights campaign yet managed to obtain the majority of black votes in the extremely close 1948 Democratic primary."[45] Cox estimates that 75,000 African Americans voted in the 1946 gubernatorial election. In 1947, on the eve of the 1948 Senate primary, some 100,000 African Americans were registered to vote.

On the date of the primary election, July 24, 1948, "[t]he two largest black newspapers in Houston and Dallas, the cities with the largest black populations," carried "a sample ballot listing all candidates for office. In

TABLE 9.3. The Results of the 1948 Senate Primary Election in Texas by Demographic Category

	Urban Counties		Town Counties		Rural Counties		Home Counties	
Candidate	Votes	%	Votes	%	Votes	%	Votes	%
Johnson	175,315	32.9	186,136	34.1	34,374	31.9	960	44.1
Stevenson	209,053	39.2	212,591	38.9	52,342	48.6	956	43.9
Peddy	109,870	20.6	112,625	20.6	13,261	12.3	255	11.7
Myers	6,334	1.2	6,928	1.3	1,896	1.8	3	0.1
Cortez	8,595	1.6	3,615	0.7	1,034	1.0	0	0.0
Others	24,106	4.5	24,717	4.5	4,796	4.5	3	0.1
Total	533,273	100.0	546,612	100.1	107,703	100.1	2,177	99.9

	Black-Belt Counties		Boss Counties		Latino Counties	
Candidate	Votes	%	Votes	%	Votes	%
Johnson	999	37.3	4,287	96.6	2,578	86.4
Stevenson	858	32.0	94	2.1	139	4.7
Peddy	567	21.2	25	0.6	122	4.1
Myers	90	3.4	1	*	39	1.3
Cortez	13	0.5	9	0.2	65	2.2
Others	151	5.6	24	0.5	42	1.4
Total	2,678	100.0	4,440	100	2,985	100.1

Source: Adapted from Mike Kingston, Sam Attlesey, and Mary Crawford, eds., *The Texas Almanac's Political History of Texas* (Austin: Eakin Press, 1992), 130–33.

the race for U.S. Senate, every candidate was crossed off except the name of Lyndon Johnson."[46] The owner of both papers was Carter Wesley, an African American who had used these papers "in the successful fight against the white primary law and continued the battle for prohibition of the poll tax and enactment of anti-lynching laws."[47] In his editorial Wesley endorsed Johnson with the following comment: "[F]or United States Senator we have chosen Lyndon Johnson, we voted for him rather consistently as Congressman, because though he is no angel, he is about as good as we have seen in the race."[48] Both papers rejected LBJ's opponent, former governor Coke Stevenson, and were highly critical of him. However, ad hoc groups in both Dallas and Houston did form to support Stevenson.

In concert with Wesley's use of his newspapers, Hobart Taylor Sr., owner of the taxicab franchise in Houston, organized get out the vote efforts and provided voters with rides to the polls. Mack Hannah Jr., an active union leader, rallied voters in Port Arthur and Galveston. "In addition to the networks of individuals, other 'political leagues' of black voters were at work. In Dallas, the Progressive Voters League endorsed Lyndon Johnson. . . . In San Antonio Johnson was supported by the Bexar County Colored Voters League,"[49] along with the Bellinger political submachine now run by Valmo Bellinger.

Although neither candidate took any stand on civil rights, Johnson did secure federal funds for the African American Holy Cross Hospital during the campaign, and the word got out. On the Stevenson side, the group who argued in his behalf noted that he did not call a special session of the legislature when the Supreme Court abolished the white primary. A survey of 147 Texas newspapers found that "civil rights was hardly mentioned during the 1948 campaign."[50] But Johnson's constituent service stood him in good stead with the African American electorate, and in the large cities such as Houston and Fort Worth, he won in many of the precincts with a significant number of African American voters.

According to Cox, all of the urban African American precincts save one supported Johnson. When this is contrasted with the rural Black Belt data, we see that the African American electorate truly favored LBJ over Stevenson. Nevertheless, they supported both men. Johnson got the statewide majority of the African American vote, although he lost the election to Stevenson. LBJ's support in the 1948 primary was enough to put a ceiling on Stevenson's long tradition of electoral success. Johnson was able to seriously challenge Stevenson in every demographic group. His competitive showing ultimately forced Stevenson into his first runoff election since his initial statewide race in 1938. LBJ left the 1948 Senate primary as a champion campaigner.[51]

The Capture of the Next Step to the Fateful Moment: The 1948 Senate Runoff Election

The primary election was held on July 24, 1948. The date for the runoff election was set for August 28, 1948, leaving 35 days for Johnson to overtake the lead that Stevenson had built. The other candidates now were gone; it was just Stevenson versus LBJ, a clash between Texas in Washington and a Washington led by Texas. The former was a vision of Texas having a voice in national politics, a voice that would extol conservative aims and aspirations as bred and developed in Texas. It was the voice of Stevenson, "Mr. Texas," as he had shaped it in his effort to achieve and guide his state. It was a state-bred philosophy with little beyond the context of his own strong drive for individual achievement.

The other vision in this electoral struggle was in the throes of becoming. We now know from hindsight that adequate representation for Texas would have required no more than a senator who could articulate a reasoned voice for the state's growing conservatism. But Texas held the kernels of the nation's future. It had African Americans and Latino Americans, both suffering from grinding poverty, racism, and segregation. By all accounts Stevenson was neither able nor willing to expand his vision to extend democracy to these groups, either in Texas or in America. LBJ had read him right. Stevenson was bound by his own narrow and tradition-loaded vision of "Mr. Texas." He could never rise above his own self-definition. Stevenson's Texas-determined conservatism trumped injustice. It was by now a philosophy that could address national problems only from a Texas perspective. LBJ, on the other hand, could adjust and be flexible, and even in the campaign he was, as his numerous biographers have noted, moving from a countryside liberal to a pragmatic moderate. Changing national and state contexts made LBJ aware that inflexibility narrowed his options and his ability to rise in the America political system. Stevenson was intractable; LBJ was in transition. And these visions were about to clash in the 1948 monthlong runoff campaign.

This crucial election was one of the toughest political campaigns in Texas. Mooney wrote, "A week after the [primary] election Johnson was back in full cry. He abandoned his helicopter, announcing that it was too slow for him, and flew from one city to another to go after votes."[52] Stevenson, however, approached the runoff election as he had the primary election and earlier elections. Biographers George Norris Green and Merle Miller described Stevenson's approach to the 1948 primary campaign thusly:

> Stevenson erred by taking to the road in an old Plymouth, not outfitted with a loud speaker, and shaking hands at gas stations and courthouses. After easing into a town, the governor would spend an inordinate amount of time chatting with old friends from legislative or wagon hauling days.[53]

> According to T. Kellis Dibrell, "Coke had an old Ford car, and he'd drive from city to city. There wasn't any advance scheduling; it was a very old-time campaign. He'd come to town, and we'd take him over to the courthouse, he'd shake hands with all the public officials."[54]
>
> Allan Shivers [noted], Stevenson barely campaigned. As I remember, [one individual] was traveling with him, writing his speeches and driving the car and arranging the whole schedule and about the only campaign organization that Governor Stevenson had.[55]

Stevenson's traditional way of campaigning had placed him more than 71,000 votes ahead of LBJ in the primary; therefore, in the crucial runoff campaign he adopted the same tried-and-true style. Caro described Stevenson's strategy for the 1948 runoff as follows:

> During the first two weeks in August, he campaigned as he had always campaigned, driving around the state, shaking hands, talking to handfuls of voters about "principles" and the need for economy and "common sense in government.
>
> Coke Stevenson was not organizing the rural counties. . . . Nothing illustrates the lack of central coordination in Stevenson's campaign more clearly than the situation in two remote counties, Kinney and Hansford.
>
> These two Stevenson strongholds had given the former Governor a combined plurality of four hundred votes in the first primary. Because Stevenson was so far ahead, officials of these two counties felt the ex-Governor would not need their votes in the second

primary—so they weren't holding one. And Stevenson headquarters was unaware of this fact.[56]

In this crucial election, failures such as this helped to ensure the arrival of a fateful moment in American history. LBJ, who was now traveling in airplanes instead of his "Johnson City Windmill," left no political stone unturned.

Election Day fell on a Saturday and the counting, recounting, and correcting continued for six days. The Texas Election Bureau announced the official results on September 3, 1948: 494,191 votes for Johnson and 494,104 votes for Stevenson, giving LBJ a wafer-thin victory of 87 votes. The last corrected votes came in from Precinct 13 in Jim Wells County on Friday, adding 200 more to LBJ's total and pushing him to victory. This sent up charges of fraud and set in motion a series of lawsuits that were filed in county, state, and federal courts simultaneously.

At this point in the discussion of LBJ's runoff victory, most writers shift immediately into an investigation of where the extra 200 votes came from and whether LBJ had a hand in "illegally generating them from the political bosses in South Texas." This approach drops the analysis of the vote and replaces it with a degree of sensationalism. Baum and Hailey wrote: "Robert A. Caro inexplicably refuses to place LBJ's hair-breath margin of victory into the larger context of Texas Democratic Party factionalism. Caro views LBJ's success in 1948 as simply the product of character assassination, novel use of a campaign helicopter, and undisguised theft—not of only some two hundred votes, 'but thousands—many thousands,' in fact."[57]

But political bosses, political machines, and the manipulated Latino vote are not the full story, only part of it. It is now time to move beyond this fixation. In 35 days, LBJ added 88,574 votes to his primary total. Stevenson also increased his vote total over the primary by 17,027 votes, a 3.5 percent increase. For one of the greatest vote-getters in Texas political history, however, Stevenson failed badly, given all of the votes that became available when the other primary candidates were eliminated from the runoff.

LBJ's electoral comeback can be seen in more than the individual votes. It is there in the county votes as well. At the county level we see the remarkable increase in the number of counties won by LBJ. In the primary, he had won 76 counties (see table 9.12), whereas in the runoff he captured 108 counties, close to a 50 percent increase. Stevenson's eroding electoral support is shown in the fact that he had won 169 counties in the primary but only 144 in the runoff. Even with this loss in county strength, Stevenson won 57.1 percent of the counties, but the overall loss in votes cost him the victory. LBJ's victory included the nine counties that George Peddy had won in the primaries. Thus, a total of 34 counties moved out of Stevenson's electoral orbit as LBJ won 32 more, and two more simply withdrew from the voting process altogether.

Two significant players in Texas politics at this time were Jim and Miriam Ferguson, frequently referred to as "Ma" and "Pa" Ferguson. They each held the gubernatorial post in the state in 1914 (him), and in 1924 and 1932 (her). "Jim Ferguson, farmer, lawyer, and banker by trade, directed his campaign appeal (and that of his wife) to the rural voter. The Fergusons were elected by rustics. . . . Jim Ferguson was perhaps the most important leader in the state's politics for two decades."[58] In the Senate runoff election, Ma Ferguson endorsed LBJ. "'Ma had never forgotten that Stevenson had not attended 'Pa' Ferguson's funeral, in stark contrast to Johnson's attentiveness during Ferguson's last illness." Green added that "of the twenty counties that switched from Stevenson to Johnson in the grandest way, half of them were Ferguson's best counties."[59] These counties amounted to one-third of LBJ's voters.[60] This was indeed a tremendous aid in helping LBJ overcome his electoral deficit.

The demographic approach can provide an even more precise analysis of how LBJ put together his electoral comeback. LBJ won in the town, Black Belt, boss, and Latino counties, while Stevenson won in the urban, rural, and LBJ's home counties. In the latter category, as it had been in the primary, there was a split decision. LBJ won in his resident county of Blanco (76.2 percent of the vote), while he lost to Stevenson in his birth county of Gillespie (19.8 percent). Since this had happened in the 1941 Senate special election and in the 1948 Senate primary and runoff elections, it is clear that "friends and neighbors" voting did not occur in the future president's birth county. It should be noted that this county was not in LBJ's 10th Congressional District.

Returning to the county level, it can be seen that, although LBJ again lost the urban county category to Stevenson, he lost by only 1 percentage point, a total of 8,563 votes, but increased his proportion compared to the primary election. According to Cox's precinct analysis, the cause of this increase for LBJ was the support of African American voters. In San Antonio, the African American precincts that had backed Stevenson in the primary switched to LBJ. As they had done in the primary, the African American electorate mobilized to assist a candidate who had readily provided constituent service to them over the years. The limited empirical evidence is clear that in the 1948 runoff election the mobilization of the

African American electorate was part of the cause for the increase in LBJ's urban performance. And in the so-called managed counties—Black Belt, boss, and Latino—LBJ won easily.

In the runoff election Stevenson and LBJ swapped categories. LBJ won in the large town county category, and Stevenson won in the smaller home county category. This is where LBJ overcame his electoral deficit. While the Jim Wells County "vote scandal" tells a very intriguing story, LBJ needed more than those 200 votes to make up for his huge electoral deficit coming out of the primary. In fact, all of the votes that he received from the "managed" counties were not enough to overcome that deficit by themselves; other counties had to help. Those counties that shifted to LBJ, those that in effect remained neutral by not participating, and the managed counties all delivered needed votes.

In his pioneering work on what makes for champion campaigners, Gosnell wrote:

> A plurality is based on four factors: (1) bringing the maximum number of loyal supporters to the polls (activation); (2) winning new or undecided voters (attraction); (3) causing the defection of opposition voters (conversion); and (4) keeping opposition votes at home (reduction).[61]

To this model campaign strategy Gosnell added that an effective alliance had to be made with the political bosses and machines in one's area.[62] Gosnell did not explicitly add the bosses and machines to his campaign model because it revealed an unsavory side to Democratic Party elections in America that smacked of pure corruption, and this was a value that he did not want to embrace. Nevertheless, Gosnell was enough of a careful empirical scholar that he did not overlook the role and function of bosses and machines in shaping the outcome of elections.[63]

LBJ saw and learned about machine politics from the contested election that his father had faced in 1919.[64] He had also learned from being an astute observer of and participant in Texas politics, and he had learned from being a political candidate. He also learned from his first election loss and from his political mentor, FDR, who told him afterwards, "Lyndon, apparently you Texans haven't learned one of the first things we learned up in New York State, and that is that when the election is over, you have to sit on the ballot boxes."[65] LBJ not only fit the characteristics of Gosnell's model campaign, he also played to win over the bosses and machines in his state. It was a fact of political life in Texas.

Caro, who made the most of the corrupt machines and bosses in the Rio Grande Valley and in Jim Wells and Duval Counties in particular, added a value judgment to his story about this feature of Texas politics, by suggesting that it was permitted as long as it stayed within "reasonable" limits. By this he meant that Latino and African American voters should not determine the outcome of the election. In the 1948 runoff, the "wrong people" (i.e., people of color) determined the outcome of the election. This meant that LBJ went beyond the "acceptable" bounds; corruption was acceptable as long as the most "corruptible" element in the state didn't determine the outcome. Such reasoning was a throwback to the Tammany Hall distinction between "honest Graft" and "dishonest Graft."[66] The reality is that LBJ simply outmaneuvered Stevenson in the runoff and won the election across a number of dimensions.

Thus, the stage was set for the general election. Stevenson, whose legal efforts were thwarted at each turn, eventually

> turned desperately to the U.S. Senate Election Committee, whose two investigators started impounding ballots. This action had no effect, since Duval's ballots were accidently burned by the janitor and some of the Jim Wells and Zapata ballots were lost (those entrusted with their safekeeping were baffled as to their whereabouts). The FBI also conducted an investigation, but it was desultory at best, perhaps because FBI director J. Edgar Hoover did not want to offend President Truman.[67]

In the end, LBJ's runoff campaign overcame his electoral deficit, defeated a Texas legend, and sent him into the general election for the Senate. Stevenson's anger and frustration led him to oppose LBJ for the rest of his political life. In the general election, Stevenson endorsed the Republican candidate, Jack Porter, which of course "was a futile gesture in one-party Texas."[68]

The Capture of the Senate on the Move to the Fateful Moment: The 1948 Senate General Election

LBJ did not campaign in the 1948 general election for the Senate. However, he did board President Truman's "whistle-stop" train on September 25, and ride with him from San Antonio to Fort Worth, then join the president in a motorcade to Dallas and Garland. As he had done with

FDR, LBJ made political appearances with Democratic president Truman and associated himself with Truman's reelection bid in Texas, despite the appearance of the Dixiecrat movement there.[69] The presidential campaign apparently took the place of campaigning for the Senate general election. However, Stevenson and the Republicans did not sit idle:

> Texas Republicans came to life and announced that the Democratic nominee would receive more than token opposition this time. Jack Porter, a Houston oilman who had left the Democratic Party in the early forties, carried the Republican banner in the general election. Porter was a vigorous and knowing campaigner. . . . He enlisted the aid of Coke Stevenson, who took to the radio to urge his followers to support Porter.[70]

In addition to Porter, Sam Morris, who had run against LBJ in the 1941 special election for Senate, was running this time as a candidate for the Prohibition Party, a third party that had an electoral history in the state. And in addition, this was a presidential election year.

The result of the 1948 Senate general election surprised no one. LBJ won two-thirds (66.2 percent) of the votes cast. Republican Jack Porter, with the assistance of Coke Stevenson's radio commercials, captured one-third (32.9 percent) of the votes cast. The Prohibition Party candidate, Sam Morris, received less than 1 percent.

Stevenson's endorsement of Porter seemingly helped him significantly. In 1946, the Republican running against incumbent Democratic senator Tom Connally received 43,750 votes, for 11.5 percent. Hence, Jack Porter's 33 percent was indeed a substantial gain, a more than 200,000 vote increase. In the end, however, it did not help because LBJ's increase over his 1948 primary total was 297,368 votes, and 208,794 votes total over his runoff.

The same story can be seen from a county-level analysis. LBJ won in nearly 80 percent of the counties for which data are available, a huge increase from the 43 percent he won in the runoff election against Stevenson. In Erath County, he won all the votes. Johnson won 202 counties to 11 counties for Porter. If we were to include the 41 counties for which the returns were unofficial or incomplete, the story would be the same: 241 counties for LBJ to 13 for Porter. At the county level, LBJ's general election victory was a rout.

LBJ also won five of the seven demographic categories, as reported in table 9.3. Once again African Americans in the big cities rolled out to vote for him, as he won the urban, town, rural, Black Belt, and boss counties.

LBJ lost to Porter in the home and Latino counties—although, of the two counties in each of these categories, only one had complete and official data. But Porter's victory in these two demographic categories was not enough, because there were few votes to be had there, too few to win the statewide election.

However, Porter did win Gillespie Percent, LBJ's birth county, where Porter's vote was so large that he would have earned the entire demographic category in any case, because LBJ could not have gotten enough votes to offset Porter's lead. Coke Stevenson also had won this county and therefore this category from LBJ. Localism was not a staying force for LBJ in his birth county.

On the other hand, the Prohibitionist candidate was not a force in any of the demographic categories. Comparing Morris's 1941 and 1948 votes reveals that he did better in 1948, but it was only a modest improvement. He was, in the end, a nonfactor.

The empirical analysis reveals two major features of the 1948 Senate general election. First, there were a staggering number of counties (16 percent) that failed to report in a proper fashion the correct number of votes. Of these 41 counties, Coke Stevenson had won 27 (66 percent) in the primary election.[71] The general election in 1948 was by far the sloppiest to date in terms of reporting, and there is little information on why. Simply

TABLE 9.4. The Results of the 1948 Senate General Election in Texas by Demographic Category

	Urban Counties		Town Counties		Rural Counties		Home Counties[a]	
Candidate	Vote	%	Vote	%	Vote	%	Vote	%
Johnson	327,532	60.1	309,096	72.8	59,986	74.3	484	14.1
Porter	214,058	39.3	111,719	26.3	19,890	24.6	2,941	85.8
Morris	3,841	0.7	4,084	1.0	919	1.1	3	0.1
Total	545,431	100.1	424,899	100.1	80,795	100.0	3,428	100.0

	Black-Belt Counties		Boss Counties		Latino Counties[b]	
Candidate	Vote	%	Vote	%	Vote	%
Johnson	11,524	75.0	4,174	88.3	14	18.2
Porter	451	22.2	543	11.5	63	81.8
Morris	57	2.8	9	0.2	0	0
Total	2,032	100.0	4,726	100.0	77	100.0

Source: Adapted from Mike Kingston, Sam Attlesey, and Mary Crawford, eds., *The Texas Almanac's Political History of Texas* (Austin: Eakin Press, 1992), 150–53. Calculations prepared by author.

Note: Each demographic category had counties with incomplete and/or unofficial data.

[a]There was only one county in this category, Gillespie, where the election return data was complete.

[b]There was only one county in this category, Kenedy, where the election return data was complete.

put, it appears that there was a major breakdown in the recording and reporting of votes in this race. This gaffe stands alone in Texas electoral history, making the 1948 Senate election a most unusual one in every way.

The second major feature in the 1948 Senate general election is the disappearance of Stevenson's friends-and-neighbors voting. The bitterness and disappointment, and possible dishonesty, that Stevenson and his loyal supporters faced after the runoff election did not transfer, at least in any significant way, to the Republican candidate that Stevenson endorsed. Clearly, Stevenson did not hold together his legendary election coalition, nor could he motivate them enough to initiate a political upset in the general election. The huge following that Coke Stevenson had built in his nine statewide elections had truly faded.

Seen in this election is a clash between personal (candidate) loyalty and party (Democratic) loyalty. Even "Mr. Texas" and his Republican candidate could not move people over the party line despite the perceived morality of his position and the righteousness of his claim. Few of his loyal supporters shifted their party behavior in the 1948 election. Localism in this one-party state was limited to the dominant party.

At this point it is possible to empirically explore the localism factor. Using a measure of statistical association, bivariate regression can tell us how strong Stevenson's electoral coalitions were from one election to the next. Of the six correlated primary/runoff elections and the three general elections, one finds both strengths and weaknesses in Stevenson's voter mobilization efforts and resultant electoral coalitions. At the general election level Stevenson never built or sustained stable electoral coalitions, while at the primary and runoff levels he did so in only three of six attempts. His three successful attempts all came during the initial election to each of his different statewide offices. His stable electoral coalition first appeared between the 1938 primary and runoff election for lieutenant governor. It appeared once again between the 1942 primary and his 1944 election for governor. Last, it appeared between the 1948 primary and runoff election for the U.S. Senate. And in this, his last election, there was only a small increase in the number of voters who voted for him in the primary that returned to vote for him in the runoff. In the 1938 runoff some 53 percent returned to vote for him, while in 1948 some 57 percent returned to vote for him.

However, once Stevenson had captured a statewide office, the weaknesses in his winning electoral coalition began to show. Each time, at the very next election his coalition became unstable. In fact, even when these electoral coalitions showed stability, as in the initial elections, slightly less than half of the original supporters returned to vote for him. Simply put, Stevenson's electoral coalitions fit the patterns found by Key who discovered that personal factions were loose and transient from one election to the other. This was especially true of Stevenson's general election coalitions, and being such they created a major problem when he endorsed the Republican candidate against LBJ in the 1948 senatorial election.

Based on the analysis of the primary/runoff elections to the general election coalitions, there was no relationship between Stevenson's general election voters and the support for the Republican Party. In fact, the relationship is inverse. Thus, if anyone benefited from Stevenson's general election voter coalition it was LBJ, because there is a small relationship between the two. It is possible that 8 percent of Stevenson's voter coalition supported LBJ in the 1948 U.S. Senate general election due primarily to the traditional and enduring Democratic partisanship in the state. Clearly, from the empirical assessment, if Stevenson's electoral coalition existed at all in this election, it was not transferable across partisan lines.

Therefore, despite Stevenson's great popularity and large number of election victories across time and offices in Texas, his electoral coalitions suffered from the same problem that plagued all personal election factions in southern politics: they were not permanent. They had to be refashioned for each election. This made Stevenson electorally vulnerable not only in the different types of elections but also in a political context like Texas where bosses and machines persisted. And the latter had more control over the outcome than did one's personal popularity, whether it arose from charisma or personality, because machines and bosses by their inherent nature would be able to manipulate both a segment of the electorate and some aspect of the counting of the ballots. Governor W. Lee O'Daniel understood this facet of machines and bosses well when he defeated LBJ in the 1941 special election for the Senate, and LBJ and his political operatives understood this better than Stevenson in 1948. Thus, Stevenson's vulnerability and his failure to make the most of the Texas machines and bosses finally caught up with him in the 1948 runoff election for the U.S. Senate.

The Rise to Senate Power on the Move to the Fateful Moment: The 1954 Senate Primary

Although 1954 was a reelection year for LBJ, he entered the Texas political context in only a minor way that year. He basically ignored not only the

1954 general election but the primary election as well. During his first six-year term in the Senate, the bulk of his electoral and political activity came in the 1952 presidential election year and the year following it, rather than in his own election year.

By 1952, several forces in the Texas political context had converged to force LBJ to enter the political arena in a major way. It began even before 1948 when Harry Truman was reelected to the presidency. On December 5, 1946, Truman had signed Executive Order 9808 establishing the President's Committee on Civil Rights.[72] Based on the 1947 report of this committee, President Truman sponsored an equal rights plank at the 1948 Democratic Convention. This simple platform promise caused the Southern delegations to walk out of the Convention. They later reorganized as the States' Rights Democratic Party, which was eventually dubbed the "Dixiecrats" by the newspapers.[73]

In addition to the plank in the Democratic Party platform, however, President Truman had sent to Congress on February 2, 1948, a recommendation for "the enactment of legislation to effectuate some, but not all, of the proposals of his Committee on Civil Rights."[74] It was these organizational and policy actions that set southern political leaders to formulating numerous opposition strategies. As Key noted, the southerners opposed both Truman's nomination and his civil rights program, but they differed among themselves about what they would do if they "lost" at the Democratic National Convention.[75] In Texas in 1948 LBJ had traveled with the president on his train, but he also criticized his civil rights plan. Although LBJ supported Truman's election, 9.3 percent of the Texas electorate voted for the Dixiecrat party.

Once elected, President Truman was "concerned about national security and conservation, [and] wanted direct federal access to the supposedly oil-rich tidelands. . . . [Eventually] federal jurisdiction over the offshore lands was upheld by several Supreme Court decisions" in 1950.[76]

Taken together, these factors served to shape the political response of Texas governor Allan Shivers to the changing national political conditions that had angered his state and his establishment supporters. Therefore, "by the summer of 1951 . . . he signed a bill allowing candidates of one party to cross-file as candidates of other parties."[77] In the following year he joined "with the Dixiecrats to bolt the national Democratic ticket . . . [and] Shivers and his Dixiecrat allies overwhelmingly controlled the state Democratic convention in May."[78] Next, the governor went to the Democratic National Convention and was seated, over the objection of the Loyal Democrats of Texas (LDT) delegation, with the help of LBJ.[79] Governor

Shivers held another state Democratic Convention in the fall just before the presidential election, and endorsed "a Republican for the Presidency." Efforts by Congressman Rayburn, Johnson, and the LDT to the contrary did not help. Governor Shivers and his "Shivercrats," along with the "Texas Democrats for Eisenhower," carried the state in November.

According to some biographers, earlier in 1952 LBJ had entered into a secret agreement with Senator Richard Russell of Georgia, the leader of the Senate Democrats, to support Russell's bid for president. Here is how Evans and Novak described it:

> As early as the 1952 Democratic Convention in the Chicago Stadium, Johnson was eyeing the national ticket. . . . In 1952, . . . Johnson made a secret pact with Russell. He would do all he could to secure Russell's nomination for President. But if Russell failed, Russell then would do all he could to get Johnson on the ticket as Vice-President. Johnson even had a floor lieutenant to help the Russell-Johnson combine.[80]

However, as Evans and Novak explained, "When Adlai Stevenson telephoned Johnson to ask him to introduce the party's presidential candidate at San Antonio during the campaign, Johnson went to Shivers for advice. . . . Johnson's telephone call to Shivers was simply a shrewd political move to deaden the impact of his forthcoming campaign association with Stevenson and to show Shivers that he, Johnson, appreciated the strength of the right wing in the Texas Democratic party."[81] Thus, in this struggle between the liberal and conservative wings of the party, LBJ interacted with both sides and campaigned—not wholeheartedly, argue some—for Democratic candidate Adlai Stevenson in his losing bid both in the state and nationally.

Given this electoral defeat for his party, and despite the assurance from Governor Shivers during that telephone conversation that he would protect Johnson from the state conservative clique in his forthcoming Senate reelection bid, LBJ launched his campaign in 1953. Taking no chances, given his 87-vote victory in 1948 and the defections of the Democratic electorate in 1952, as well as rumors that Governor Shivers might run against him, LBJ arranged "a whirlwind tour of Texas in 1953. He visited every major city. We estimated that he shook about 225,000 hands, made two or three speeches a day; he was hitting big towns, small towns, cities, villages, hamlets. He went through East Texas cafés drinking coffee with people. He hit Amarillo, Lufkin, Tyler; he hit just about everything you could think of."[82] This hectic campaign activity led George Reedy to declare, "Actually Johnson won the 1954 election in 1953."[83]

After Johnson's precampaign massive election tour, only one candidate entered the July 24, 1954, Democratic primary. This candidate, 30-year-old Dudley T. Dougherty, was a "freshman in the [Texas] state legislature."[84] Although he launched his campaign with the first of three telethons and campaigned throughout the state from the back of a red fire truck, LBJ took little notice of his opponent. According to Reedy, "Johnson made only a single speech in Texas during that whole campaign. He never mentioned Dudley Dougherty's name, did not put out any campaign literature, and he only took out one ad."

> Not only did Lyndon not campaign, but his office issued frequent statements saying that he was so concerned with the affairs of the nation and the world that it was simply impossible for him to leave Washington. Indeed, he voted by absentee ballot—to save time.[85]

In fact, when the primary results came in on the night of July 24, LBJ was in a major policy debate on the Senate floor, mired in a filibuster on an atomic energy bill.

Table 9.5 provides the results for this Johnson election without a significant campaign. He captured 71 percent of the vote to the conservative state legislator's 29 percent. This was LBJ's best performance yet in a senatorial campaign; however, in terms of actual votes it was the second best performance of a Democratic primary candidate against him. Only Stevenson had done better. Daugherty's electoral support was an indicator that the rising tide of conservatism was ever so slowly creeping into the voter base in the state's one-party system. It was a harbinger of things to come.

However, if one were to examine this Senate primary only from the perspective of the number of counties won, it would appear that LBJ had

TABLE 9.5. The Vote and Percentage for Each Candidate in the 1954 Democratic Senate Primary Election in Texas

Candidate	Votes	%
L.B. Johnson	883,264	71.4
D.T. Dougherty	354,188	28.6
Total	1,237,452	100.0

Source: Adapted from Mike Kingston, Sam Attlesey, and Mary Crawford, eds., *The Texas Almanac's Political History of Texas* (Austin: Eakin Press, 1992), 134–37.

a huge 98 percent victory and held magical sway over his voters. But the base of the Democratic electorate was sliding toward the hard right in Texas politics. The shift to the Eisenhower-led Republicans in 1952 had cast a spell not only on the elite in state politics but upon the electorate itself. A precise measurement of this shift is not possible given the vagaries of the election data, but the response to a hard-line conservatism suggests some movement inside the Democratic Party's electorate.

The disaggregation of the voters into demographic categories shows more of this shift, as seen in table 9.6. In the seven demographic categories, LBJ's mean stands at 75.1 percent, ranging from low of 67.8 percent in the home counties to 89.6 percent in the Latino counties. He also ran well in the Black Belt counties (81.2 percent), and once again the African Americans in the big cities rallied to his banner.

Overall, both LBJ and his Democratic challenger captured the lion's share of their votes in the town counties, the most populous category of the seven, with the urban counties a close second. Seemingly, the Democratic Party's electoral base in the urban centers of the state was in transition to the Republican Party. The electoral realignment that had started in 1952 was still under way in 1954. This suggests that in another two years, the Democrats' eroding urban base could still be available for the Eisenhower reelection bid. LBJ's primary election result clearly implies this possibility. In fact, two years later, Eisenhower did win the state in the 1956 election. And once again his support came in part from the urban counties. Texas Republicanism in the fifties was emerging in the big urban centers of the state.

TABLE 9.6. The Results of the 1954 Senate Primary Election in Texas by Demographic Category

	Urban Counties		Town Counties		Rural Counties		Home Counties	
Candidate	Vote	%	Vote	%	Vote	%	Vote	%
Johnson	377,813	70.4	401,433	71.5	90,549	74.7	1,190	67.8
Dougherty	158,785	29.6	160,326	28.5	30,715	25.3	620	32.2
Total	536,598	100.0	561,759	100.0	121,264	100.0	1,810	100.0

	Black-Belt Counties		Boss Counties		Latino Counties	
Candidate	Vote	%	Vote	%	Vote	%
Johnson	2,124	81.2	3,485	70.5	3,805	89.6
Dougherty	493	18.8	1,459	29.5	440	10.4
Total	2,617	100.0	4,944	100.0	4,245	100.0

Source: Adapted from Mike Kingston, Sam Attlesey, and Mary Crawford, eds., *The Texas Almanac's Political History of Texas* (Austin: Eakin Press, 1992), 134–37.

Of the shifting Democrats in Texas, Weeks noted, "It is obvious that if the Republican Party is to attain the status of a major party in the South, it must first win permanent rank-and-file recruits who will have to come from the party." Then, regarding those who would be most likely to come and who did come in the fifties, he added:

> Urban and industrial growth and large migrations of outsiders into the developing areas of the South have, however, created a third class, a great new-white-collar, middle-of-the-road middle class, whose political position tends to shift backward and forward between the conservative and liberal poles. In Texas . . . in 1952, they coalesced with the Shivercrats-Republican combination. Among this class are to be found the largest percentage of independent voters and most of the potential Republicans. . . . Many of them are "Presidential Republicans."[86]

LBJ's 1954 U.S. Senate Democratic primary election permits one to see this "third class" of Democrats within the state's electorate and see their continuance from the 1952 election. Clearly, Democratic governor Allan Shivers saw this emerging group in the state's politics as well as in presidential elections. Demographically, this analysis allows us to place this group in its geographical setting in Texas.

The Rise to Senate Power on the Move to the Fateful Moment: The 1954 Senate General Election

Biographers of LBJ barely mention his 1954 Senate reelection campaign. For instance, all that Evans and Novak wrote was a single sentence, which by the way is more than most: "Congress had adjourned to campaign for the November elections, and Johnson, with his own election assured, toured the country to fight for the election of Democratic Senators." Instead, they devoted more attention to this latter, nationwide campaign for other Democrats, which, as they saw it, permitted Johnson to command "headlines as one of his party's chief campaigners, and for the first time he invaded Northern Democratic strongholds that seldom if ever before had heard a southern accent from the political stump."[87] After LBJ "made a whirlwind campaign through the nine states of Colorado, Washington, Montana, Wyoming, Utah, Nevada, Arizona, New Mexico and Minnesota,"[88] he returned to Texas and basically ignored his reelection, as he had done in the 1948 general election, although the Republican and Prohibition Parties had put candidates in the field to oppose him.

The 1954 general election brought more than 600,000 voters to the polls in Texas to choose among the three candidates for the U.S. Senate. In this midterm election, when turnout is always less than in presidential elections, LBJ's opponents together failed to capture one-fifth of the total vote. LBJ received about 85 percent of that vote. The Republican candidate, Carlos Watson, managed nearly 15 percent, which was less than half as many votes as the 1948 Republican candidate had polled with the backing of Coke Stevenson. The Prohibition Party candidate, Fred Sprangler, received just over 3,000 votes, also less than half of what his predecessor had managed in 1948. The best that can be said of these challengers is that they showed up.

More evidence for this ineffective challenge can be found at the percent level, which depicts the percent-level vote: LBJ lost only one county in the entire state. This time LBJ carried both of his home counties. Even more of Johnson's sweeping victory shines through when a demographic analysis is applied to the election return data (see table 9.7). The Texas electorate did not fail to support him in the urban, rural, or town counties, even without his presence on the campaign trail. Seemingly none of the electorate forgot LBJ's thorough political canvass of the state in 1953; he was still connected to his base. LBJ's mean support across the seven demographic categories was 87 percent, although his lowest support

TABLE 9.7. The Results of the 1954 Senate General Election in Texas by Demographic Category

	Urban Counties		Town Counties		Rural Counties		Home Counties	
Candidate	Vote	%	Vote	%	Vote	%	Vote	%
Johnson	272,065	79.9	208,786	90.6	49,227	90.3	2,215	70.2
Watson	65,957	19.4	21,288	9.2	5,218	9.6	932	29.5
Spangler	2,663	0.8	264	0.1	86	0.2	8	0.3
Total	340,685	100.1	230,338	99.9	54,531	100.1	3,155	100.0

	Black-Belt Counties		Boss Counties		Latino Counties	
Candidate	Vote	%	Vote	%	Vote	%
Johnson	1,057	95.0	3,536	84.3	2,433	98.9
Watson	55	4.9	654	15.6	27	1.1
Spangler	1	0.1	7	0.2	0	0
Total	1,113	100.0	4,197	100.1	2,460	100.0

Source: Adapted from Mike Kingston, Sam Attlesey, and Mary Crawford, eds., *The Texas Almanac's Political History of Texas* (Austin: Eakin Press, 1992), 150–53.

came in his home counties (70 percent), and there was no let-up in his solid African American support, which reached 95 percent in the Black Belt counties. His highest support came from the Latino counties with 98.9 percent.

Despite LBJ's strong across-the-board support in this general election, the urban category once again lagged in terms of the level of support, which was down from the primary vote. The town and rural categories still continued to support him at a significantly higher level than the urban areas of the state, by about 90 percent versus 80 percent. As for his Republican opponent, Carlos Watson, his mean level of support across the seven demographic categories was 12.8 percent, ranging from almost no votes in the Latino counties to a high of 29.5 percent in LBJ's home counties. Although Watson did worse than LBJ's Democratic primary challenger, both of them fared well in the urban areas, and Watson was able to draw upon the traditional partisan voting behavior of Gillespie County.

The Dual Election on the Move to the Fateful Moment: 1960 Senate Primary Election

On November 8, 1932, Congressman John Nance Garner, known as "Cactus Jack," ran simultaneously for Congress (from Texas's 15th Congressional District) and the vice presidency, and won both of them.[89] Thus was born the "dual election" in Texas, an election for state office and national office at the same time. In 1956 LBJ had announced for the party nomination at the Democratic Convention, only to lose to Adlai Stevenson and Alben Barkley.

The tradition continued in the 1960 election, with LBJ running for his U.S. Senate seat and the vice presidency simultaneously. In future decades, it happened again in 1988, when Democratic senator Lloyd Bentsen also ran both for reelection to the Senate and as the vice-presidential running mate of Michael Dukakis.[90] The dual election tradition was not only embedded in Texas law, it also was embedded in the presidential ambitions of each man.

No Democratic candidate entered the 1960 Democratic primary against LBJ. Only a few write-in votes were cast, 145, against over 1.4 million votes for Johnson. In this presidential election year, the voter turnout for LBJ was double what it had been in the 1954 primary. Despite some opposition from its liberal wing, the LDT, there was a unified effort by the Democratic Party to return this rising native son to the United States Senate particularly in case the party went down to defeat in the general election. LBJ had reached the apex of his electoral support as a congressman. It was in many ways a good-bye landslide to a career that started in 1937. LBJ had survived Texas politics and its cleavages as well as its ideological struggles. The time for the next step had come.

The Last Senate Election on the Move to the Fateful Moment: The 1960 Senate General Election

Although the Democratic opposition quit in 1960, the Republicans came back for one more chance to defeat him and the Democratic Party in the state. The Republicans fielded John Tower, a member of the Texas Senate, and the Constitutional Party sponsored Bard Logan in the general election. LBJ won 58 percent of the vote and captured nearly as many votes as he had in the primary election. State Senator Tower captured 41.1 percent of the vote, a massive increase over what other Republican challengers had been able to accomplish. Some observers felt that this large Republican vote came because "many Texans expressed their displeasure at Johnson's dual appearance on the ballot."[91]

There was a small increase in support for the third party, as Logan captured nearly 1 percent of the vote. Even the total number of votes for the third party was double what it had been for previous third party candidates. The Texas electorate was now beginning to spill outside of the Democratic Party ranks. The old one-party system in Texas was beginning to slide, and electoral cracks were showing.

Further empirical evidence of this slippage can be seen in the Democrats' loss of county-level support. LBJ had never lost 24 counties to any previous Republican challenger, only to Democratic primary challengers. Even the wavering Gillespie County, LBJ's birth county, went for John Tower in a very big way. The loss in the Democratic base and the gain in the Republican base were now clearly visible.

At the demographic level, the story is even clearer. In this data we can see the areas in which the Republican Party was starting to make inroads. LBJ's mean level of support across these seven demographic categories was down to 69.8 percent, from a low of 43.2 percent in the home category to a high of 94.8 percent in the Latino counties. Here again, the urban electorate was not responding to the native-son candidate in a profound manner, although the African American precincts stayed with Johnson.

Tower proved to be a much more successful challenger than the previous

Republican challengers. His mean level of support was 31.7 percent, with his range going from a low of 5.2 percent in the Latino areas to a high of 56.6 percent in LBJ's home counties. Tower won Gillespie County with so many votes that it overwhelmed LBJ's support from Blanco and won the category. Beyond this continuation of the traditional partisanship pattern, Tower made major inroads into the urban area, coming within 6 percent of winning a majority of the voters there. This is the first time that a Republican had done so well. Even in the Black Belt category, Tower got one vote in every four. Thus, Tower managed to capture the shifting vote in the 1960 campaign, with the greatest inroads coming in the urban areas where transition had been under way since the Eisenhower victories in 1952 and 1956.

In 1960 Tower began to unite urban Republicans with the traditional Republicans and to some degree the conservative Democrats from the Black Belt counties. His strongest support was in the urban areas, where nearly three times as many Republicans voted as in the town counties. Tower's initial candidacy was based upon the rudiments of a newly forming Republican coalition. This was not the end for him. "After he lost the 1960 race and Johnson became vice president-elect, Tower never stopped campaigning for the special election that would be held less than six months later."[92] There he came in first with 32 percent of the vote, while the Democratic candidate, William Blakley, was second with 18 percent of the vote. Tower then won the runoff and became "the first Republican to win a statewide office in Texas since Reconstruction."[93]

The Senatorial Vote for Johnson: The Time Dimension

LBJ's senatorial elections are so unique, or so controversial, that they generally necessitate a singular, case-study-like approach that focuses on each one in detail. Here we will shift the focus, to examine the continuity and connections among these eight elections and search for patterns that may appear when they are viewed over time.

LBJ ran in eight elections the four times that he sought a Senate seat, in 1941, 1948, 1954, and 1960. Analyzing the outcomes of these races offers more insights into LBJ's Senate vote. LBJ captured one-third of the state electorate in the 1941 special election. He showed a slight improvement in the 1948 primary; then he rose to capture one half of electorate in the runoff. In the 1954 primary he won 71 percent of the vote, and topped out with a clear 100 percent in his last senatorial campaign in 1960. Over time, LBJ's performance became stronger with each election.

This data also shows the changes in LBJ's support in the three senatorial general elections. His electoral support increased from 1948 to 1954 but decreased significantly in 1960 when he had a major Republican challenger and also ran simultaneously for vice president. Similarly, because Texas was a traditional one-party state, his general election performance in 1948 and 1954 was higher than in the primary, where numerous challengers cut into the voting power of the state Democratic electorate. Nevertheless, these elections clearly show a rising trend of support for LBJ from the state electorate.

The pattern seen in LBJ's U.S. Senate elections is quite different from the pattern found in his House elections. Especially in the early years, he had few challengers in either primary or general elections, which made his House electoral pattern highly stable. However, that support began to decline as challengers appeared. This trend is almost the reversal of his Senate election performance. One climbs, the other falls off over time.

Moving from the percentage level of support in these eight senatorial elections to the number of counties won by LBJ, we see a continuation of the trends shown. The results reveal that LBJ won more and more of the counties in Texas in each successive U.S. Senate primary election, continuing to expand his electoral base. This was also true in the 1948 and 1954 general elections. Even in 1960 LBJ still captured more than 90 percent of the counties, although this was a decrease from his 1954 performance. Again, LBJ's percentage victories in the general elections were greater than in the primaries because of the large number of Democratic challengers and the lack of strong Republican challengers in this one-party state. Initially, we can see that the Republican Party had a very limited base in the 254 counties of the state.

Disaggregating LBJ's Senate electoral support by three demographic categories—the urban, town, and rural counties—we see that when he started out in 1941, LBJ drew his strongest support from the urban areas of the state. By the 1948 general election, however, the rural and town counties provided greater support, in nearly equal amounts. In all three areas, LBJ's percentage continued to rise through the 1960 primary election. A sharp decline in his support occurred in the 1960 general election, when he did have a serious challenger. The pattern of LBJ's electoral support continued across the three demographic categories; he expanded his base throughout his Senate career and in all of the demographic areas of the state.

Another set of trends is evident in the voting behavior in the racial, ethnic, and boss demographic categories. The dominant support for LBJ initially came in the boss-led category. Beginning with the 1954 primary, the Latino counties led in the level of support for LBJ as the managed counties' support declined. The Black Belt counties displayed a continuous slow rise in support, which peaked in the 1960 primary election, when LBJ received near-unanimous support from all of these groups. Except for the 1948 primary, the Black Belt counties provided more support in every election for LBJ than did his home county category. Similar results occurred in Arkansas for Clinton.[94]

Despite the differences and the shifts in the levels of support, the pattern here is the same as in the other demographic categories and in the primary and general elections. Clearly, LBJ's electoral rise touched all bases—the demographic, racial, ethnic, boss, and hometown folks. However, these rising trend lines peaked in the 1960 primary election and then declined in the 1960 general election.

One of the interesting features here is the fact that friends-and-neighbors voting tended to work only in LBJ's resident county of Blanco and not in his birth county of Gillespie, which had a tradition of voting for Republican candidates. The native-son candidate could not always overcome traditional Republican partisanship, and it was not until the 1954 primary that LBJ could win the majority of votes in this demographic category. This shift lasted only through three elections. Key's observation that localism did not exist in Texas continued, at least in LBJ's senatorial elections, and at least in his birth county, particularly when there was a strong challenger.

Finally, we can see the rise in the number of votes LBJ received as he continued to run for the Senate over these eight elections. Only in the 1954 general election, which was a nonpresidential election year, did the LBJ vote decline. Therefore, it is possible to conclude that not only did LBJ expand his electoral base in the state, but over time the boss county category declined in its importance and was replaced by the Latino and African American vote in the LBJ electoral coalition. Additionally, given the nonexistence of localism, LBJ's senate elections show that a southern native-son presidential candidate can win even without the friends-and-neighbors vote that prevailed in Arkansas and Georgia. The uniqueness of LBJ's elections for the rising native-son theory is indeed insightful, adding much to the case-study findings on Carter and Clinton, who did benefit from localism.

It is notable that both the racial and the ethnic votes strongly supported LBJ's senatorial electoral efforts. Certainly they saw in this native-son candidate something that was promising, even when he backtracked, as he did in his maiden speech on the Senate floor in favor of segregation. They not only joined his electoral coalition but stayed with him as he finally repudiated segregation in 1957 and beyond.

Lyndon Johnson's election and reelections to the Senate placed him in the position to remake and restructure the Democratic Party, in ways unknown since the rise of the party in the nation and the state.[95] Other native sons who came in his wake inherited this legacy of a remade Democratic Party. He would continue this remolding in the vice presidency and then in the presidency. But it was his election to the Senate that put him on the path to those fateful moments.

President Franklin D. Roosevelt and Cong. Lyndon B. Johnson in Galveston, TX, on May 11, 1937. (*L-R:* President Roosevelt, Gov. James Allred, and Lyndon B. Johnson.) *(Photograph courtesy of the LBJ Library.)*

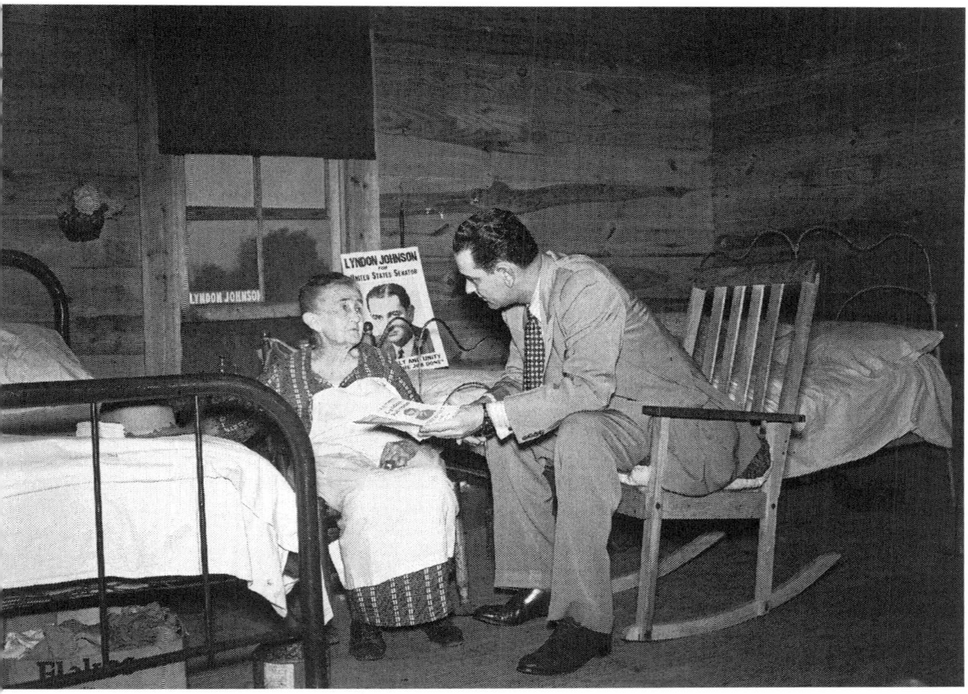

Lyndon B. Johnson's 1941 U.S. Senate campaign stop at the home of 77-year-old Mrs. Mattie Malone in Carthage, TX, in May 1941. *(Photograph by Austin Statesman, courtesy of the LBJ Library.)*

Lady Bird Johnson, Lyndon B. Johnson, and Rebekah Baines Johnson seated at a 1941 campaign event in San Marcos, TX. *(Photograph by Austin Statesman, courtesy of the LBJ Library.)*

Lady Bird Johnson attends LULAC National Convention Picnic in Laredo, TX, during the summer of 1948. She is seated with Dr. Jose Maldonado, LULAC President General (*right*).*(Photograph by Porfirio L. Flores, courtesy of the LBJ Library.)*

Cong. Lyndon Johnson, Ed Cape, and President Harry S. Truman on the 1948 presidential campaign whistle stop tour in San Marcos, TX. *(Photograph courtesy of the LBJ Library.)*

Sen. Lyndon B. Johnson and Sam Houston Johnson look at newspaper headlines proclaiming LBJ's victory in central Texas. *(Photograph by United Press Associates, courtesy of the LBJ Library.)*

Johnson on podium with President Truman, Adlai Stevenson, and Sen. Estes Kefauver at the 1956 Democratic National Convention in Chicago. *(Photograph courtesy of the LBJ Library.)*

Johnson with former President Harry Truman (*center*) and Sam Rayburn (*left*) at the Democratic National Convention in Chicago on August 12, 1956. *(Photograph by United Press Telephoto, used with permission, courtesy of the LBJ Library.)*

Sen. Lyndon B. Johnson campaigning in Brooklyn, NY, with the Hon. Bertram L. Baker (NY State Assembly) and Karen Willis in 1960. *(Photograph by King Photographers and a gift of Bertram Baker, courtesy of the LBJ Library.)*

Sen. Lyndon B. Johnson posing with a group of men, among whom are Dr. Everett Givins (*right*) and some police officers during a Queens campaign stop in 1960. *(Photograph by Frank Muto, courtesy of the LBJ Library.)*

Sen. Lyndon B. Johnson and Lady Bird Johnson campaigning in Beaumont, TX. Cong. Jack Brooks Johnson posing with little boy and girl in traditional Mexican dress and other children. *(Photograph by Frank Muto, courtesy of the LBJ Library.)*

Sen. Lyndon B. Johnson and Lady Bird Johnson visit the Kennedy family residence in Hyannis Port, MA. *(Photograph by Fay Foto Service Inc., courtesy of the LBJ Library.)*

Congressman William L. Dawson posing with Sen. Lyndon B. Johnson at the Capitol. *(Photograph by Frank Muto, courtesy of the LBJ Library.)*

Sen. John F. Kennedy and Sen. Lyndon B. Johnson in 1960 campaigning in Dallas, TX. Piling hands for the camera with the candidates are Sen. Ralph Yarborough (*left*) and Speaker Sam Rayburn (*2nd from right*). *(Photograph by Frank Muto, courtesy of the LBJ Library.)*

President Johnson attends meeting with the National Newspaper Publishers Association in the Cabinet Room of the White House. Attendees included publishers of African American newspapers across the country: John Bogle (*Philadelphia Tribune*), Mildred Brown (*Omaha Star*), C. C. Dejoie (*Louisiana Weekly*), John Sengstacke and Frank Thomas (*The Beacon*). *(Photograph by Cecil Stoughton, courtesy of the LBJ Library.)*

President Johnson meets Civil Rights leaders in the Cabinet Room in April 1968. (*Standing, L-R*: Roy Wilkins, Sec. Robert Weaver, unknown, Vice President Hubert Humphrey, Judge Leon Higginbotham, Sen. Clarence Mitchell III, Dorothy Height, Mayor Walter Washington, Warren Christopher, Whitney Young, unknown, Bayard Rustin, Rev. Leon Sullivan, unknown, unknown, and unknown.) (*Seated, L-R*: Justice Thurgood Marshall, President Johnson, and Clarence Mitchell Jr.) *(Photograph by Yoichi Okamoto, courtesy of the LBJ Library.)*

President Johnson speaking at the 1965 Howard University Commencement in Washington, DC. *(Photograph by Frank Wolfe, courtesy of the LBJ Library.)*

★ Part IV

The Southern Native-Son Presidential Candidate

Of LBJ, journalist Theodore White wrote, "Take Americans like Mr. Speaker Rayburn, like Lyndon Johnson, born on backward farms in a prescientific, pretechnological, preeducational, premedical-care, prepublic-health society."[1] Yet LBJ became a world mover, an American who made a difference: "No President, except Franklin Roosevelt, will have left deeper marks on American history in this century."[2] Both LBJ and FDR used government to attain new levels of individual freedom, but Johnson was unlike Roosevelt. FDR represented what the liberals in the Democratic Party could achieve, such as economic justice and the personal dignity that derived from that justice. But to achieve these social goods, FDR and the liberals bargained away racial justice as a meaningful priority.

LBJ came from the South where political leaders had forced upon the Democratic Party this shifting of political priorities. Southern politicians engineered a Democratic Party of exclusion, and leaders of the Southern Caucus and the liberal wing of the party expected that LBJ would keep the faith. Many anticipated that this would be the flaw in LBJ's presidential character; having grown up in such an underdeveloped society and having risen through the Democratic Party ranks, how could it be otherwise? Novelist Ralph Ellison wrote of a vision "of the flawed white Southerner who while true to his Southern roots has confronted the injustices of the past and been redeemed. . . . So—one hopes, one suspects—is Lyndon Baines Johnson."[3] While LBJ was of the South, he was also quite aware of and sensitive to its problems and the severe disadvantage that they generated for its inhabitants.

Journalists Richard Harwood and Haynes Johnson of the *Washington Post* spoke to the unique dimension that this southerner brought to the Democratic Party: "He did have a feeling for American problems, for poverty, for the disinherited and disadvantaged. . . . He knew what it was to shine shoes and work for a dollar a day. He knew what it was to be hungry."[4] LBJ displaced the liberals and FDR's rhetoric with progressive and populist voices on racial justice and translated them into action.

Historian T. Harry Williams located this feature of LBJ's political leadership not in northern liberalism but in southern radicalism, in its progressive tradition and the homegrown leaders that it generated from time to time. "Occasionally, however, the [southern] system produced leaders who talked about the present, who called for change, who subordinated or spanned race and section—genuine radicals who had to overcome greater obstacles than radicals in other regions."[5] As Williams saw it, a leader in the southern radical and progressive tradition was governor and senator Huey Long of Louisiana.

> The resemblances between Huey and Lyndon are many. They were born into families of similar economic background—average farm families, neither richer nor poorer than others in their immediate area, although, as both came to realize early, poor in comparison with many persons in their states. The Longs and the Johnsons had to work hard to make a living, and although neither family knew real poverty, each had only a secondhand knowledge of real plenty. Huey and Lyndon occasionally exaggerated the hardships of their early lives, but they had experienced some hardship and had seen other persons experience more; both recalled in later years witnessing the tragedy of farms sold under mortgage. Each had fathers and grandfathers who preached Populist philosophies to them, and each grew up in an area that had a tradition of agrarian dissent—Long in Winn Parish in the Louisiana uplands and Johnson in the Texas hill country.[6]

Williams concluded by saying that "[a]lthough Johnson acknowledged a relationship with Long, he placed it in a narrow political context—they were two men who happened to have the same objective in government. The Texan did not seem to realize that the kinship between him and Huey was more than fortuitous or political, that it was a thing of the spirit or self."[7] It was a way of using the political system to help the downtrodden and disadvantaged.

If Williams found LBJ's progressivism embedded in southern radicalism, another historian, Joe B. Frantz, found it in national reform movements and progressive causes.[8] Frantz asserted that Johnson's "support for progressive causes dated back to his days as a National Youth Administration director and New Deal congressman in the 1930s."[9] Even though Johnson supported the Taft-Hartley Act and was against the repeal of the poll tax, Frantz dismissed "this retrogression as pragmatic politics necessary to secure . . . [his] Texas political base." Yet, even before the war, LBJ supported certain segregation measures—even before he became a senator.

Thus, what one finds inside this southern politician are two impulses—one for the cultural values inherent in the South and in Texas, and another for reform and progressive causes. When LBJ became a national political figure, he subordinated the regional impulses to his progressive ones. What sets LBJ apart is not only his ability to rise above his beloved South but that, because of his legislative skills, he was able to put the values and beliefs of his region in reversal.

Biographer Eric Goldman's conclusion that LBJ "was the wrong man from the wrong place at the wrong time under the wrong circumstance"[10] seriously misses the point and is remarkably dubious when one puts LBJ in the company of his southern contemporaries who were also reformers and progressives, such as Senators Estes Kefauver, Albert Gore, Ralph Yarborough,[11] and Claude Pepper, to say nothing of the northern liberals. LBJ succeeded where all of the others failed.

The chapters in this fourth section of the book describe how LBJ worked to obtain the presidential nomination in 1956, 1960, and 1964, and how he put together a 1968 electoral coalition for Hubert Humphrey. This is followed by a discussion of the electoral fortunes of the more recent southern native-son candidates. The section will conclude with analysis of LBJ's legacy 50 years after enactment of his most significant pieces of legislation and the legacy inherited by the Democratic Party and President Barack Obama. Here we see the twofold legacy that this native son left for members of his own party and for the Republicans as well.

★ 10

The Presidential Vote for Johnson

In 1960, "Senate Majority Leader Lyndon Johnson declared his candidacy just five days before the Democratic National Convention, held in Los Angeles."[1] This announcement briefly placed "a stumbling block" in Senator John F. Kennedy's move to the nomination. However, "Kennedy won the nomination on the first ballot. . . . He resented the Johnny-come-lately challenge from Johnson, but the Texan's clout in the Senate and in the Democratic Party . . . and the geographical balance he would add to the ticket led Kennedy to pick Johnson as his running mate."[2] With this choice the die was cast and the fateful moment for the nation, its political parties, the South, and racial and ethnic minorities was now in motion. Soon, this fateful moment would appear.

Before the 1960 announcement, LBJ had declared in 1956 that he was an unannounced candidate in 1952. In at least two of these announcements, LBJ and Kennedy were competitors for the presidency, the 1956 and 1960 years. The origins of Lyndon Johnson's run for the presidency go back at least to 1948, when one of his Senate mentors, Democrat Richard Russell of Georgia, tried to capture the presidential nomination. In the first balloting at the Democratic National Convention he received 266 delegate votes, all from the old Confederacy. However, the Alabama and Mississippi delegations had stormed out of the Convention Hall in protest over President Truman's endorsement of Mayor Hubert Humphrey's proposed civil rights plank, and Russell eventually ended up with 263 votes (21.3 percent) to President Truman's 947.5 votes (76.8 percent).

Russell's grab for the nomination was the first part of the South's strategy to keep the Democratic Party from adopting Humphrey's civil rights plank—the second part was the formation of the States' Rights Democratic Party—and it originated when southern Democratic delegates "persuaded him to allow them to place his name in nomination against Truman's candidacy in a gesture of protest. . . . Russell had hoped to embarrass the president by demonstrating that the push for civil rights would anger white southerners, divide the party, and bring defeat in the fall."[3] However, both this and the Dixiecrat strategy failed. Despite the Truman victory, however, Senator Russell's showing in the National Convention balloting made him a major competitor for the 1952 nomination, and he subsequently turned to LBJ for help.

LBJ, Richard Russell, and the 1952 Presidential Nomination: The Unannounced Candidate

In the fifties, securing the presidential nomination was primarily a national convention affair. It was the politics at the convention, instead of victories in the presidential primaries, that shaped the outcome. But to enhance his chances for a 1952 nomination, Senator Russell ran in two of the 17 Democratic presidential primaries held that year. He captured 1 percent of the vote in the Pennsylvania primary and 54.5 percent in Florida two weeks later. Overall, Senator Russell ended up with 7.5 percent of the total primary vote.[4] The Texas Republican State Executive Council Convention gave him 19 of its votes, and the Georgia Democrats gave him their 28 delegate votes.

In addition to these primary and caucus forays, Senator Russell asked LBJ's help at the 1952 National Convention in securing additional delegate votes. A deal was struck in which LBJ would help Russell win the nomination, and if Russell did not get the nomination, he would help LBJ secure the vice-presidential nomination.[5] Russell lasted through three presidential ballots. On the first ballot, he received 268 delegate votes to Senator Estes Kefauver's 340. On the second balloting, he rose to 294 votes but was again led by Senator Estes Kefauver with 362.5 votes. Then, on the third ballot, Adlai Stevenson surged with 617.5 delegate votes, and Russell faded to 261.[6] Stevenson got the nomination for president, and Alabama senator John Sparkman received the vice-presidential nod.

On all three ballots, LBJ and House Speaker Sam Rayburn held the Texas delegation together to support the Russell candidacy—even when it was clear that it was failing on the third ballot. Only then did Texas switch to Stevenson. The question at this point is whether Russell carried out his part of the bargain for LBJ. Senator Sparkman had been elected as one of the Alabama delegates to the Democratic National Convention and announced his support for Richard Russell.[7]

Then on July 26, five days after the Democratic Convention convened, Senator Sparkman was nominated for the vice presidency "after names of Mrs. India Edwards and Judge Sarah Hughes were withdrawn."[8] Senator Sparkman secured the nomination, but Johnson's name did not seem to appear in the convention's political machinations. This suggested that perhaps Senator Russell, despite getting unified support from LBJ and the Texas delegation—when his own state of Alabama, with only 22 delegate votes, gave him 13 on the first ballot and 14 on the second and third ballots—backed Senator Sparkman despite a split delegation vote. Thus, the extant data hints that Senator Russell did not make much of an effort to push LBJ for the vice presidency. Biographer Robert Dalleck says, "The Georgia senator had no say in the selection of a vice-presidential candidate, and Johnson received no serious consideration."[9] Using an insider's account of no less a personage than Sam Rayburn, who was involved in the backstage selection process, the senator told his own biographer that "Johnson was never even mentioned."[10] Thus, both the extant data and insider information suggest that LBJ's unannounced strategy for getting to the presidential circle was not a promising one. He would not use it again. By 1956, LBJ would be an announced candidate.

Lyndon Johnson, John Kennedy, and the 1956 Presidential Nomination

By the time of the 1956 Democratic National Convention, LBJ was considered to be a likely candidate for both the presidency and the vice presidency. Georgia senators Walter George and Richard Russell had both publicly endorsed LBJ as a possible presidential nominee before the convention. While Russell was unable to get his state delegation to vote for Johnson, he became the Senate majority leader and shielded Johnson from the controversy involving the congressional southerners' attack on the 1954 Supreme Court decision in *Brown vs. Board of Education*.[11] In the Senate, not at the Democratic Convention, is where Russell seemingly helped LBJ's presidential chances. There were other senators who supported LBJ:

> Florida's George Smathers, Louisiana's Russell Long, Arkansas's John McClellan, South Carolina's Strom Thurmond, and other

Southerners endorsed Johnson. From outside the South, only two Senate voices broke the silence: Oklahoma's Robert Kerr and Nevada's Alan Bible.[12]

These endorsements did not translate into delegate votes at the Convention, however. In the first and only balloting, LBJ's convention politics achieved for him only a distant third-place finish, with 5.8 percent of the delegate votes. These votes came from Texas (56), Mississippi (22), Nevada (1), Alabama (1/2), and Massachusetts (1/2). Clearly, the South did not support his bid. Besides Texas, where he controlled the delegation, only Mississippi had given him *all* of its delegate votes. Alabama split its votes among Stevenson (15.5 percent) and a host of other southerners from Kentucky, Georgia, Virginia, and South Carolina. Senator Russell's Georgia cast all of its 32 votes for its native son, Congressman John Davis.

In the end, each of the southern states initially supported their favorite sons. This combined vote total was 125.5 more than LBJ received. But even if he had received all these southern votes, LBJ still would have been left in third place. LBJ's 1956 presidential bid never really got off the ground because Adlai Stevenson was nominated on the first ballot. Even Johnson's home state deserted him. According to Miller, "[t]he Texas delegation wanted to switch over from Lyndon and change its vote, cast its final vote for Stevenson and be on the bandwagon. . . . [but] . . . Texas wouldn't change its vote because it couldn't get a release from Lyndon. It was committed until he released it. So Texas never did cast its vote for Adlai Stevenson."[13]

Initially, Senator Russell had no intention of attending the convention in Chicago. "Disillusioned by his own experience as a presidential candidate in 1952, Dick Russell long since had decided to go fishing during the 1956 convention."[14] It seemed that Russell was abandoning his 1952 supporters and the votes of the Texas delegation that LBJ had held for him. Johnson was convinced that Russell's presence would assist him, but Russell felt otherwise: "Russell, he said, must come out to Chicago with him. He needed his help, his advice, his resourcefulness. Nonsense, said Russell. Even if there was a hopeful prospect for a Johnson nomination, Russell could not help bring it about."[15] As Russell saw it, the governor of Georgia had the state delegation under his tight control, and Russell had no influence with him. Although Russell eventually agreed to go, he was perceptive as he was of little use in LBJ's effort to get the presidential nomination.

Having won the nomination, Stevenson broke with tradition. Instead of selecting his own vice president as a ticket balancer, he "confounded some friends and angered others by throwing the nomination open, and when he confided his plan to the party leaders (including Johnson) there was consternation."[16] Stevenson would let the Convention pick his running mate. "Johnson was under heavy pressure from the South . . . to demand the vice-presidential spot for himself."[17] However, Johnson received only one half of a delegate vote, from Alabama, in the first round of balloting. Texas's delegation cast all of its votes for Senator Al Gore Sr. of Tennessee. Once again the South split its votes among several of its favorite sons. However, Alabama, Florida, Georgia, Louisiana, South Carolina, and Virginia cast at least some of their votes for Senator John Kennedy of Massachusetts. On the first balloting, he received over 300 votes, second to Senator Estes Kefauver. This was indeed a switch for the South, which had traditionally backed southerners.

On the second balloting, the Texas delegation, headed by Johnson and Rayburn, switched from Senator Gore to Senator Kennedy. In the end, Kefauver received 750 delegate votes to 593 for Kennedy. There were no second ballot votes for LBJ. Despite this factual data, however, several biographies, relying upon interviews with LBJ supporters, claimed that LBJ worked the Texas and other southern delegations for Hubert Humphrey. The record does not support this contention. Of all the southern states, only Florida and North Carolina gave Humphrey any votes at all, and that was a one-half vote each. Whatever backroom politics LBJ conducted on Humphrey's behalf, it did not show up in the final voting.[18]

In the presidential sweepstakes, LBJ's support was essentially limited to two states, Texas and Mississippi. Despite his major leadership position in the Senate, Johnson's 1956 effort and his numerous endorsements did not translate into unified southern support for him. Of this limited effort, one of his biographers asked, "Why, instead, did he wage an ill-planned, ill-conceived, ill-executed campaign as part favorite son, part dark horse under the ludicrous slogan of 'Love That Lyndon'?"[19] The answer given, regarding the nature of factionalism in Texas's Democratic Party, is too pat. Despite the fact that Governor Shiver had switched to Eisenhower in 1952 and 1956 and that the liberal wing of the party did not want LBJ, there were other causes.

There was the "favorite son" strategy of other southern states. There was the inability of his Senate admirers, such as Russell, George, and Bible of Nevada, to sway their state delegations into LBJ's corner. There was the inability of his House mentor, Sam Rayburn, as well as former colleagues in that body, to sway members of the House of Representatives to back LBJ. There was no strong regional support for LBJ despite the fact that he was from the largest state in the region. The best that can be said is that LBJ was now at last visible in national politics and that he had a major institutional power base in the Senate. Caro claimed that Johnson wanted to avoid the southern label and refused to commit to numerous southern leaders early, so they shifted to Stevenson before the North did.

In the end, LBJ's second strategy to enter the presidential circle, one with a Senate-based leadership focus and a unique legislative record with a national orientation, coupled with astute national convention maneuvering, ended in a failure. However, LBJ made the very best of his unsuccessful efforts. "Lyndon had shrewdly satisfied southerners by opposing Estes [Kefauver] and northerners by backing Gore, Humphrey and Kennedy in succession"[20] and by trying to trade the Texas delegate "votes for 'something on civil rights that will not hurt my people too much.'"[21] However, there is no record to show how delegates felt about LBJ after the Convention. This conclusion also contradicts the Convention voting record, where Kennedy got many of the southern delegate votes long before the Texas delegation switched. Clearly LBJ was not leading the other southern delegations.

Moreover, this conclusion does not address the rising competition as well as cooperation between Kennedy and Johnson for entrance into the presidential circle. Much has been made of their rivalry for the presidency, and some have even said that it was the root of Johnson's later feud with Robert Kennedy.[22] But the evidence for this rivalry has been based on the memories of political operatives from both camps. The 1956 Democratic National Convention delegate voting gives us the first public evidence of its magnitude, and its two dimensions of competition and cooperation.

Lyndon Johnson, John Kennedy, and the 1960 Presidential Nomination

To improve his chances for the presidential nomination, Kennedy ran in the May 10 West Virginia primary in the hope that this would so impress the party elites that they would be able to secure the nomination for him.[23] Kennedy not only defeated Humphrey in West Virginia, he won all seven of the Democratic presidential primaries. "Over a period of four years Kennedy built up an organization of determined young men, aided by some older professionals of the party, in a determined drive toward the nomination."[24]

Although LBJ did not formally announce his candidacy for the Democratic Party nomination until July 5, 1960, just prior to the opening of the Democratic National Convention on July 11, he had participated in the Oregon presidential primary on May 20. The results of LBJ's first and only presidential primary that year was anything but promising. He received less than 4 percent of the vote, coming in fifth to Kennedy's overwhelming 51 percent, although he did outperform Adlai Stevenson. "Johnson's problem was to establish a major beachhead of delegate support outside the South, which he was never able to do."[25]

Overall, LBJ captured a few primary votes from other states as a write-in candidate. Combined with those he received in Oregon, his total was only 15,593, 0.3 percent of the votes cast in all the primaries. Kennedy ended with 1,897,253 votes, for 32.5 percent, and won easily. Having lost in the presidential primaries, LBJ turned to his friends in the Senate and House to turn their state delegations toward him at the Democratic National Convention. Not only did many of these individuals owe him political favors, many had received campaign funds from the Senate Democratic Campaign Committee that Johnson controlled through his aide Bobby Baker. LBJ's fallback position rested on the delegates that could be shifted to him during the Convention's presidential voting.

On the first balloting, LBJ received 26.9 percent of the votes, a respectable showing but barely half as many as Kennedy. This was not enough to stop a first ballot nomination for Kennedy, who received 53 percent of the votes. Even the addition of the 53 delegate votes that went to favorite sons from Florida and Mississippi could not have stopped Kennedy's sweep of the Convention if they had shifted to LBJ.

Disaggregating the votes by region provides additional information regarding the candidates' bases of support. Looking at the 409 delegate votes that LBJ received, one finds that of the South's total delegate votes, he received 80 percent (281.5) while Kennedy received only nine votes for 2.6 percent of the total. Not only did Kennedy not do well in the region, he did not do as well as he had in the 1956 balloting for the vice presidency. Even the southern favorite sons did better than Kennedy. Such a dismal showing the second time raises the question of why he received such strong support from the region in 1956. Outside of the South, however, LBJ took 10.9 percent of the delegate votes, while Kennedy captured 797 votes for 68.1 percent, nearly double the number LBJ received in the entire country. Clearly Kennedy's strength was outside the states of the old Confederacy, whereas Johnson was still a southern candidate.

While LBJ's fallback position of relying on deal-making at the National Convention never really materialized, it was clear that he had nearly unified the regional vote in support of his effort and expanded his presence into areas outside the South. In fact, he had more support outside of the South than Kennedy had been able to amass inside of the South. LBJ's political base had significantly advanced in 1960 but not enough to capture the nomination. However, there was no arguing that LBJ could both balance the ticket geographically and bring some degree of strength to it. Therefore, when Kennedy made the decision to give LBJ the vice-presidential position, it was seen as a wise political calculation, personal likes and dislikes notwithstanding. Although this action caused "major dissatisfaction among Northern liberal groups . . . Johnson's nomination was seconded by Rep. William L. Dawson (Ill.), a prominent Negro leader."[26] Prior to Johnson's nomination, Kennedy's nomination had been seconded by another African American, D.C. national committeeman-elect Frank Reeves.[27] LBJ was nominated by acclamation on a voice vote. The addition of LBJ enabled the Kennedy-Johnson presidential ticket to become a winner. LBJ's 1960 strategy proved better than his 1952 and 1956 strategies.

Lyndon Johnson, John Kennedy, and the 1960 Presidential Election: The Vice Presidential Victory

Prior to the 1960 presidential election, Texas Democrats had refused to support the party's 1952 nominees despite the fact that the party had a southern native-son vice presidential candidate on the ticket, Senator John J. Sparkman of Alabama.[28] Nor did they support the 1956 presidential nominee, although he too was a southern vice presidential candidate, Tennessee senator Estes Kefauver.[29] In two successive elections, the popular Democratic governor, Alan Shivers, had led party members to cross over and vote for the Republican candidate, Dwight Eisenhower. It certainly did not hurt that Eisenhower was born in Denison, Texas. This Republican native son, running in a one-party Democratic state, won the state with the help of splits in Democratic Party ranks. In 1960 Shivers "came back into the picture during the campaign in behalf of the Texans-for-Nixon" even as "the nomination of Johnson for the vice presidency was a gamble [because of] . . . his seeming surrender of Southern principles by teaming up with Kennedy."[30]

The other matter that confronted Johnson in 1960 was Kennedy's Catholicism. Shortly after the Democratic Convention, the Baptists in Texas launched an attack: "A sermon by Rev. W. A. Criswell, of the First Baptist

Church of Dallas, critical of Kennedy and his Catholicism was circulated in the thousands during August."[31] Nationally known journalist Samuel Lubell found in face-to-face interviews conducted throughout the state in September "that the Protestant ministers were the chief agents in keeping alive the religious issue. . . . [and that] . . . Lyndon Johnson's influence on Texas voters . . . was only marginal."[32] Like other party-bolting incidences, the religious issue was not new in Texas. In 1928 New York governor Al Smith's Catholicism cost him "many votes in Texas and the South."[33]

Finally, there was the politics of resentment in the Texas electoral context in 1960. Every observer of the state electorate mentioned the fact that LBJ's "law," which permitted him to run for two offices simultaneously, engendered a great deal of resentment among the populace. This resentment was played upon not only by Republican critics but by his Democratic enemies as well. Numerous analysts have alleged that it hurt him in the Senate race, given the huge vote for his Republican opponent, John Tower, or that it reduced his presidential vote. Hence, beside the party-bolting and religious issues, there was electoral resentment to hamper the presidential election outcome in Texas, the native-son vice presidential candidate's credentials notwithstanding.

The results of the campaigning undertaken by Lyndon Johnson, Sam Rayburn, John Kennedy, and their families served as a good mobilizer. Even former president Truman entered the state "on October 9th . . . [and] . . . started his short but scorching campaign . . . telling his Baptist brethren as well as others that 'if you vote for Nixon you ought to go to hell.'"[34] In addition, the Democratic Party sent "nineteen United States Senators campaigning in the state during the final two weeks before the election."[35] The Kennedy-Johnson ticket won by 2 percent of the vote. They got 46,233 more votes than the Nixon-Lodge ticket. Despite "a record turn-out of voters" in Texas, the presidential vote was very close. The Republican Party made its best showing in the state to date, winning 48.5 percent of the total votes.[36]

At the county level, the Republican Party lost ground over what it had accomplished in 1956. In this election the Republicans captured less than one-third of Texas's counties. "Of the 254 counties of Texas, 166 voted as they did in 1956, Kennedy holding 105 of Stevenson counties and Nixon 61 Eisenhower counties. . . . The remaining 88 of the 254 counties of the state . . . shifted their 1956 party support in 1960. Kennedy and the Democrats made the greatest gains, winning 69 counties which voted for Eisenhower in 1956. Nixon's gain . . . [occurred] in only 19 of the 1956 Stevenson counties."[37] Under the campaign of a native-son candidate, the county-level base of the Republican Party shrank considerably with its remaining votes based in the suburban areas of the major metropolitan counties.

Next we turn to a demographic analysis of the 1960 presidential election returns, shown in table 10.1. The penetration of the South by the Eisenhower ticket occurred primarily in the urban and suburban counties.[38] Clearly this was the case in Texas as well. It was helped along by the active endorsement and campaigning for the Republican Party by former governor Allan Shivers. "In the opinion of one experienced news commentator, the Shivers' threat ranked second only to the explosive potential of the religious issue."[39] Given the activism of several Protestant ministers in the larger cities against Kennedy's Catholicism, these variables coupled to give the Republicans the dominant vote share in the urban demographic category.[40] In the town and rural demographic categories, however, the influence of the Rayburn-Johnson forces held sway, and Kennedy won by almost 10 percentage points.

In the special demographic categories, the Kennedy-Johnson ticket won the Latino counties with 92.1 percent, the boss counties with 80.7 percent, and the Black Belt counties with 61.9 percent. They lost one home county, Gillespie, and won the other, resulting in a significant loss for the entire category. Gillespie County had had a partisan history of voting Republican since the Civil War; and despite the fact that LBJ had been born there, it did not support him in his vice-presidential bid. With a large vot-

TABLE 10.1. The Results of the 1960 Presidential Election by Demographic Category

	Urban Counties		Town Counties		Rural Counties		Home Counties	
Candidate	Vote	%	Vote	%	Vote	%	Vote	%
Kennedy/Johnson	715,775	48.3	359,569	54.5	80,347	53.2	1,646	33.7
Nixon/Lodge	749,870	50.6	296,295	44.7	69,667	46.2	3,224	66.1
Others[a]	16,697	1.1	4,562	0.7	892	0.6	11	0.2
Total[b]	1,482,342	100	660,426	99.9	150,905	100	4,881	100

	Black-Belt Counties		Boss Counties		Latino Counties	
Candidate	Vote	%	Vote	%	Vote	%
Kennedy/Johnson	2,019	61.9	4,478	80.7	4,129	92.1
Nixon/Lodge	1,190	36.5	1,069	19.3	354	7.9
Others[a]	52	1.6	2	0.0	2	0.0
Total[b]	3,261	100	5,549	100	4,485	100

Source: Richard Scammon, ed., *America Votes 4* (Washington, DC: Congressional Quarterly, 1962), 391–95.
[a]Others = Constitution and Prohibition Parties.
[b]The total vote excludes the write-in votes (175) from the analysis.

ing age population, Gillespie County's partisan voting history took priority over the influence of the friends-and-neighbors voting factor.

The native-son-led Democrats were able to reverse the Republican voting trend of 1952 and 1956 in Texas and restored the party to the victory column in 1960. The Democratic Party had not carried the state in a presidential election since 1948. But with LBJ, the party changed its electoral fortunes and gave him its 24 electoral votes and the victory. With Johnson on the presidential ticket, the Democratic Party made a comeback. Outside of Texas there was a similar result: the Democrats won Alabama, Arkansas, Georgia, Louisiana, North Carolina, and South Carolina. The native son influenced his state and the South from the second spot on the ticket.

LBJ's Dual 1960 Elections: A Comparison of the Senate and Presidential Votes

To establish a comprehensive empirical portrait of LBJ's influence on Texans' voting behavior, given his second spot on the ticket, we turn to the uniqueness of his dual elections in 1960. To date, no other writers have made use of these two simultaneous elections. A few have merely mentioned it, while others have focused on the large number of votes that Republican state senator John Tower received in the Senate race.[41] No one has made a statistical analysis of the data from these elections to examine LBJ's role in the number-two position on the ticket.

In 1959 the Texas legislature passed a law that allowed LBJ to run for two offices at once. It also changed the dates on which the first and second Democratic primaries would be held, moving them from late July and late August to early May and early June, respectively. This change kept the second or runoff primary from falling too close to the date of the Democratic National Convention, which opened on July 11 in 1960. Therefore, when LBJ won the first Democratic primary on May 7, where he was unopposed, with more than 1.4 million votes, he was "certain of his Senate seat in the event of his failure to win the Democratic presidential nomination."[42] No Republican opponent had ever come close to defeating him in any of his contested House or Senate elections. In fact, Johnson did not even announce his bid for the presidency until July 5.

Thus, analyzing the votes received by Johnson in his 1954, 1956, and 1960 contests offered a comprehensive portrait of his Senate elections. He increased his Senate primary vote by more than one-third between the 1954 and 1960 primary elections. This was followed by a staggering 59 percent increase in his general election vote from 1954 to 1960. In the 1954 primary he had only a write-in opposition of 145 votes, but in the general election, with strong opposition from Senator Tower, he still increased his vote significantly. Thus, despite the writers who claim that the dual election law angered Texans, it surely did not halt more individuals from voting for Johnson.

The primary vote for LBJ was higher than the general election vote, a pattern that is common in Texas and most one-party states. Usually more individuals turn out in primaries rather than general elections because it is in the primaries where the choices are actually made. But in this primary, a staggering number of individuals turned out to vote despite the fact that LBJ had no primary opposition.

Shifting to the presidential level, there was a 26.4 percent increase in the vote for the Democratic Party's presidential candidates between the 1956 and 1960 elections. This increase is far less than that for LBJ in both the Senate primary and general elections, as is the raw vote increase. Clearly, *LBJ outran the Democratic presidential ticket in his Senate election.*

In comparing LBJ's performance in his 1960 senate election race with that of the Democratic presidential ticket, Johnson's Senate primary vote was more than 230,000 votes greater than Kennedy's presidential vote; and even his general election vote was more than 140,000 votes ahead of the Democratic Party presidential ticket. His performance against the Republican presidential ticket was even greater. Hence, the theory that resentment assisted Tower's candidacy does not find support in this analysis. Instead, what we see here is that the local native son outperformed, with the state electorate, the nonnative son who was heading the ticket. This suggests that the additional votes that LBJ brought to the contest were more than enough to provide the thin margin of victory with which the Democratic Party won the state in the presidential election.

To gain further insights into the relationship between the LBJ Senate vote and the Kennedy-Johnson presidential ticket, we turn to a correlation analysis. The empirical findings reveal there is a moderate but highly significant relationship between the Senate and presidential general elections of 1954 and 1960. Because of this high level of significance, one can predict from LBJ's 1954 general election vote that one-third (36 percent) of his electoral coalition would follow him into the 1960 elections.

There is an almost perfect relationship between LBJ's 1960 Senate general election and the 1960 presidential election. Again, this is a highly significant finding with little probability of the relationship occurring by chance. Seemingly 9 out of every 10 LBJ Senate voters also cast a ballot for him on the Democratic presidential ticket. LBJ's electoral coalition not only supported him across time but across elections. *Localism might not be influential in shaping presidential voting behavior, but the native-son variable is indeed important, and it can operate in an electoral context that is devoid of localism.* This is why it is so important to separate Gosnell's identification of the variable from the manner in which Key reidentified it. LBJ's elections are the very first that enable scholars to see, at least in the South, the native-son variable operating outside of this context. Such a finding places in question the combining of these two contextual forces by Lewis-Beck and Rice.[43] *Localism does not have to be present for the native-son candidate to have a home-state advantage.*

In the final analysis, LBJ brought strength not only to the Texas presidential ticket but also to other states in the region—Alabama, Arkansas, Georgia, Louisiana, North Carolina, and South Carolina—as Steven Rosenstone found in his work.[44] The theory that southern regional leaders can shape party politics finds additional empirical support in LBJ's presidential electoral coalitions.

LBJ and the Fateful Moment: November 22, 1963

If the 1960 presidential election put LBJ in reach of the fateful moment, which occurred at 1:30 p.m. Eastern Standard Time (12:30 p.m. in Dallas, Texas) on November 22, 1963, that moment came when he took the formal oath of office on Air Force One at 2:30 p.m., framed by his wife on one side and the president's widow on the other. "The Oath of Office was administered by Federal Judge Sarah T. Hughes of the Northern District of Texas."[45] President John Kennedy's assassination that afternoon elevated Vice President Johnson to the Oval Office. This moment would forever change American history and its party politics. In the words of journalist Theodore White, "Only once before, with the killing of Abraham Lincoln, had a President of the United States been cut down so swiftly in so turbulent a passage of rushing history."[46] One of the main features of this "passage of rushing history" was "the civil-rights problem—the nation's most vivid concern, the most important unfinished business of Kennedy before Congress."[47] In the confusion of this fateful moment, LBJ had to step into this vast vacuum and tell Americans, governmental officials, southerners, Texans, and politicians alike, "which direction he meant, now and in the next year, to take the American people."[48] He had to define the new America.

On November 27, 1963, President Johnson addressed a joint session of

Congress: "'Our most immediate tasks,' he said, 'are here on this Hill.'"[49] As he saw it, the future lay in the hands of Congress. He told both Congress and the nation that the future required the nation and its institutions to move past the moment of hesitancy.

> This nation has experienced a profound shock, and in this critical moment, it is our duty, yours and mine, as the Government of the United States, to do away with uncertainty and doubt and delay, and to show that we are capable of decisive action; that from the brutal loss of our leader we will derive not weakness, but strength; that we can and will act now.
>
> Today, in this moment of new resolve, I would say to all my fellow Americans, let us continue.
>
> This is our challenge—not to hesitate, not to pause, not to turn about and linger over this evil moment, but to continue on our course so that we may fulfill the destiny that history has set for us.[50]

Johnson went on to tell Congress of its key priorities:

> First, no memorial oration or eulogy could more eloquently honor President Kennedy's memory than the earliest possible passage of the civil rights bill for which he fought so long. We have talked long enough in this country about equal rights. We have talked for one hundred years or more. It is time now to write the next chapter, and to write it in the books of law.
>
> I urge you again, as I did in 1957 and again in 1960, to enact a civil rights law so that we can move forward to eliminate from this nation every trace of discrimination and oppression that is based upon race or color. There could be no greater source of strength to this nation both at home and aboard.[51]

With these words, President Johnson had fashioned, at least at the rhetorical level, a new America, one that would integrate all of its citizens into the democratic experiment on an equal basis. On the next day, which was Thanksgiving, Johnson made another effort to shape the future as he saw it by telling the nation what its chief priorities were in the aftermath of that fateful moment in Dallas. He asked the nation "to hasten the day when bias of race, religion, and region is no more, and to bring the day when our great energies and decencies and spirit will be free of the burdens that we have borne too long."[52]

Thus, within the span of two days, President Johnson had given both Congress and the American people their priorities. At the conclusion of his Thanksgiving Day message, he told the nation of his own role in this new venture for the future: "I pledge to you the best within me to work for a new American greatness, a new day when peace is more secure, when justice is more universal, when freedom is more strong in every home of all mankind."[53]

With these words, President Johnson created a rhetorical portrait for the future, one that all Americans could now proceed toward. Almost immediately after laying out his vision, the president moved judiciously to make it a reality. "In a seven-day period from November 29th to December 5th, one by one, he called to the White House every major Negro leader of the country: first, Roy Wilkins of the NAACP on the Friday following the assassination; Whitney Young of the Urban League the following Monday; Martin Luther King, Jr., on Tuesday; James Farmer of CORE on Wednesday."[54] At the same time, "Johnson called in businessmen, he called in labor people, he called in church people, and he called in ethnic groups . . . and told them, 'I need you.'"[55] In so doing, he drew upon his political power base in every sector of society to make his top priority a reality.

All of this groundwork came to fruition on July 2, 1964, when the President signed the comprehensive 1964 Civil Rights Act, which was followed by the 1965 Voting Rights Act and the 1968 Fair Housing Act.[56] With these pathbreaking pieces of civil rights legislation, the new America had arrived. And with the 1964 Civil Rights Act, the context for the 1964 presidential election had been set. President Johnson had set into motion the changes not only for the Democratic and Republican Parties but for the very essence of America's democracy.

Lyndon Johnson's Presidential Election: The 1964 Democratic Landslide

Jake Pickle, LBJ's longtime political assistant and congressional staff member, won the 10th District Congressional seat in November 1963 and arrived in Washington the following January, on the eve of the passage of the landmark 1964 Civil Rights Act. During his congressional campaign, Pickle met "with a group of black ministers and community leaders to discuss the bill."[57] Although the meeting had been set up by his longtime friend, Frank Erwin, chairman of the University of Texas Board of Regents, who favored the bill, Pickle remained noncommittal. All that he would say was, "I'll read the bill and be open-minded."[58]

In his memoirs, Congressman Pickle revealed:

> Finally the vote was taken. As the roll call began, I still wasn't sure how I would vote. But I knew the bill wasn't the terrible miscarriage of justice that many Southerners claimed. So I voted for it. I was one of only six Southerners to do so. The others were Claude Pepper of Florida, Charles Weltner of Georgia, and fellow Texans Albert Thomas, Henry B. Gonzalez, and Jack Brooks.[59]

What had made up the new congressman's mind? He wrote, "[E]ach night I pored over the bill. I began to realize it wasn't anticonstitutional or punitive to states at all. It simply said that we shouldn't discriminate among races. I couldn't argue with that." Nevertheless, after this positive vote, "Most members—and I was one—wanted nothing more than to get out of there." He and several of his Texas colleagues went out to drink and talk about their congressional action. "The consequences of the vote I had just cast weighed heavily on my mind. Had I sabotaged my Congressional career just as it was beginning?"[60]

Of the 23 members in the Texas House of Representatives delegation, only four voted for the 1964 Civil Rights Bill and with the president. Congressman Pickle's experience was simply a microcosm of the larger misgivings about the new Democratic Party that were taking shape just as the 1964 presidential election season was getting under way. Candidates such as Alabama governor George Wallace, a Democrat, and Republican nominee Barry Goldwater tried to mobilize those fears and instill dread in the electorate.[61]

First came the Democratic primaries, held in 16 states and the District of Columbia. Table 10.2 displays the outcome of these primaries. President Johnson did not personally enter any of these campaigns; instead, he used favorite sons, stand-ins, and surrogates, capturing 17.7 percent of the total pledged vote. His closest opponent was George Wallace, who received 10.8 percent of the vote. Robert Kennedy received 0.5 percent, which is quite low in light of the huge demand from Democratic Party members for Johnson to select him as his running mate. This support did not show up in the primary vote, however. White stated that "Lyndon Johnson learned from the polls . . . that he was completely free to choose as Vice-President any running mate he fancied."[62] In fact, neither Kennedy nor Wallace received any formal notice from President Johnson. "From his November [1963] accession to the Presidency until late May, Johnson made only two 'political' speeches—both at fund-raising dinners to which John F. Kennedy had previously committed the President."[63] Wallace's showing in the midwestern primaries was seen as a backlash to Johnson's policies, but it was to be expected and was more of "a *potential* threat, not yet a *real* threat."[64] Thus, the Wallace foray could be relegated to a low priority.

At the 1964 Democratic National Convention there arose a moment when the rising opposition could have coalesced. It was the moment of the Mississippi Freedom Democratic Party's challenge, with a dynamic presentation made by spokeswoman Fannie Lou Hamer about the nature, scope, significance, and brutality of political discrimination in the state of Mississippi.[65] Two delegations had come from Mississippi claiming to represent the true Democratic Party there. The all-white delegation claimed to have official sanction under the state's rules. The racially mixed delegation of the MFDP offered the Credentials Committee the results of their "freedom elections" and "freedom conventions," arguing that they were the "right" party and had morality and conscience on their side (as well as their adherence to the rules and regulations of the state, although they were not state-sanctioned).[66] If the Democratic National Convention had

TABLE 10.2. The Number and Percentage of Votes for President Lyndon Johnson in the 1964 Democratic Primaries

Candidate	Vote	Percentage
Unpledged delegates	2,705,290	43.3
Johnson	1,106,999	17.7
Wallace	672,984	10.8
Reynolds	522,405	8.4
Porter	493,619	7.9
Welsh	376,023	6.0
Brewster	267,106	4.3
Robert F. Kennedy	33,810	.5
Henry Cabot Lodge	8,495	.1
Scranton	8,156	.1
Edward M. Kennedy	1,259	—
Nixon	1,065	—
Goldwater	796	—
Stevenson	452	—
Humphrey	323	—
Rockefeller	109	—
Others	48,544	.8
	6,247,435	99.9

Source: Congressional Quarterly, *Guide to U.S. Elections*, 3rd ed. (Washington, DC: Congressional Quarterly, 1994), 516–18.

responded to the South Carolina Progressive Democratic Party's similar challenge in 1944 and 1948 with more than "political promises," a major precedent would have been in place.[67] Such was not the case in 1964.

When the Credentials Committee took more than three days to decide, pressure from the White House and prospective vice-presidential candidate Hubert Humphrey caused it to seat the white delegation and offer the MFDP a compromise: two delegate votes, honored status for its delegates, and a promise that racial discrimination would not be permitted to prevail at subsequent Democratic National Conventions. The MFDP refused to compromise their consciences and devalue the sacrifices they had made to get to the Convention, and they returned to Mississippi. The MFDP and its supporters provided the state's only votes for President Johnson in the 1964 election.[68] The state itself cast its popular and electoral votes for Barry Goldwater and the Republican Party.

Some of the vast literature on this issue has considered that President Johnson might have felt the need to apply pressure on the Credentials Committee's leadership, key civil rights leaders such as Martin Luther King Jr. (whose efforts to persuade the MFDP leadership failed because the MFDP were suspicious of his motives), and the MFDP delegates because he was concerned that Robert Kennedy and some of his allies would try to use the MFDP controversy to vault him into the vice-presidential position.[69] The president's pressure tactics at the 1964 Convention eliminated this potential route to the presidential circle. A recent work has revealed that the White House even used the FBI to wiretap Convention participants who might have supported the morality-based MFDP challenge.[70] With the MFDP issue resolved, Johnson was unanimously nominated for the presidency. He selected Senator Hubert Humphrey of Minnesota as his vice-presidential running mate. In November 1964, Johnson and Humphrey swept the country.

> Goldwater never had a chance. Johnson won the greatest popular majority in American history. He won 44 states and an even higher share of the popular vote, 61.0 percent, than Roosevelt's 60.8 percent in 1936. Goldwater, with just 38.4 percent, was buried.
>
> While Goldwater won only six states, . . . he won . . . his home state, Arizona [and the five Deep South states]: Alabama, Georgia, Louisiana, Mississippi, and South Carolina.[71]

The results of the election in LBJ's home state were quite informative. This time, as head of the ticket, he received 12.8 percent more of the state's vote than he had in the number-two spot on the ticket in 1960. More of the electorate turned out in 1964 than in 1960, and the vote for the Democratic Party increased by 495,253 votes (29.8 percent). The Republican vote decreased, by 163,133 votes (14.5 percent). In a state where friends-and-neighbors voting did not exist, LBJ's home-state advantage showed.

At the county level, this native-son candidate had an even greater impact on the electorate, capturing 93.7 percent of the counties, leaving 16 counties for Goldwater. The Democratic ticket, which won 174 counties in 1960, had increased that to 238 by winning 64 (26.9 percent) more in 1964. Simultaneously, the Republican Party total dropped from 80 to 16 counties. The rising Texas Republican Party could not effectively compete with this native-son presidential candidate. The impact of the Johnson-Humphrey ticket said much about how the state's electorate embraced the new democratic America. None of the four congressional candidates who had voted for the Civil Rights Act lost.

At the demographic level, LBJ's victory was broad-based across the entire state. He swept every one of the seven demographic categories, ranging from 91.7 percent of the vote in the boss counties to 61.3 percent in the urban counties (see table 10.3). He defeated both urban and traditional Republicanism, changing, if only temporarily, the Republican partisanship of his birth county's voters. The Republican Party here received only one-third of the votes cast compared to two-thirds in the 1960 election. The 1964 election shows that the native-son variable can activate inopera-

TABLE 10.3. The Results of the 1964 Presidential Election by Demographic Category

	Urban Counties		Town Counties		Rural Counties		Home Counties	
Candidate	Vote	%	Vote	%	Vote	%	Vote	%
Johnson/Humphrey	1,053,796	61.3	438,875	64.5	109,389	68.1	3,461	63.5
Goldwater/Miller	661,936	38.5	241,082	35.4	51,097	31.8	1,985	36.4
Others[a]	3,756	0.2	1,040	0.2	244	0.2	2	0.0
Total[b]	1,719,488	100	680,997	100.1	160,730	100.1	5,448	99.9

	Black-Belt Counties		Boss Counties		Latino Counties	
Candidate	Vote	%	Vote	%	Vote	%
Johnson/Humphrey	3,052	70.5	5,441	91.7	4,171	85.3
Goldwater/Miller	1,270	29.3	488	8.2	708	14.5
Others[a]	7	0.2	7	0.1	9	0.2
Total[b]	4,329	100	5,936	100	4,888	100

Source: Adapted from Richard Scammon, ed., *America Votes 6* (Washington, DC: Congressional Quarterly, 1966), 399–403.

[a]Others = Constitution Party.

[b]This analysis excludes the write-in vote.

tive friends-and-neighbors voting behavior. Pride in the native son does have influence.

Another unique feature seen in the 1964 vote is that the boss counties led the way, whereas in 1960 the Latino counties had done so. In both the 1960 and 1964 elections, however, the Latino counties gave a higher percentage of their votes to LBJ than did the Black Belt counties, although both gave their greatest support in 1964. Put differently, the influence and impact on the state electorate of the native-son candidate are weaker when he is in the second position on the ballot. This is as true of the racial and ethnic group categories as it is of the demographic categories—urban, town, and rural. Because of the uniqueness of Texas politics, the composition of the LBJ vote permits us to see the influence of the native son in ethnic political districts, as well as in the political-machine-run counties, a perspective that the voting statistics on Carter and Clinton are unable to provide.

Gosnell's original observation that a native-son candidate shapes his state's voting behavior receives empirical support here because these case studies permit us to see this variable in greater detail. Drawing from the Carter, Clinton, and now Johnson case studies, we know that in the top spot, and to a lesser degree in the second spot, southern native-son candidates impact all the demographic categories: the home county category, and the racial, ethnic, boss, and machine categories. He can also reverse the Republican Party fortunes in the state under certain conditions.

Johnson's Withdrawal from the 1968 Election

By 1968, the new public policy initiatives that Johnson had passed, and the bold steps that he had taken to make this nation an integrated democracy, fully involved the mission of social justice. The deteriorating war in Vietnam had generated vast amounts of negative public opinion against his administration and the Democratic Party. Taking advantage of his declining popularity, several members of his own party announced that they would challenge him for the nomination. This group included Minnesota senator Eugene McCarthy, Senator Robert Kennedy of New York, and a host of favorite son candidates.

The first presidential primary of 1968 was held on March 12 in New Hampshire. President Johnson received 49.6 percent of the vote, with antiwar candidate Eugene McCarthy close on his heels with 41.9 percent of the vote. Nineteen days later, Johnson withdrew from the race. Even then, his name appeared on the ballot or as a write-in candidate in seven of the 15 primary elections, where he captured 383,048 votes and 5.1 percent of the total votes, finishing in fifth place.

In withdrawing from the race, President Johnson handed the civil rights torch to his vice president, Hubert Humphrey of Minnesota. Because of Humphrey's late entry in the primaries, however, McCarthy and Kennedy beat him in every contest he entered. Even President Johnson, who had already withdrawn from the race, beat the vice president in the May 28 Oregon primary. In the overall primary vote, Humphrey received only 166,463 votes for 2.2 percent of the total.

The presumptive favorite, Senator Robert Kennedy, was assassinated on the night of June 4, after winning the California primary. As a result, when the Democratic National Convention convened on August 26, Vice President Humphrey received the nomination on the first ballot, without ever having won a single primary. The LBJ era was at an end.

Many writers have attributed LBJ's decision not to run for reelection to McCarthy's strong showing in the New Hampshire primary. However, this overly simplistic explanation fails to take into account a host of other possibilities, including an attempt by LBJ to save his party's presidential future, given the Republican Party's gains in the South in response to Johnson's support for civil rights. Such an explanation cannot be dismissed, given LBJ's long commitment to his party at both the state and national levels.

On March 31, 1968, at 9:00 p.m., President Lyndon Johnson addressed the nation from the White House. He said, "In these times as in times before, it is true that a house divided against itself by the spirit of faction, of party, of region, of religion, or race, is a house that cannot stand. . . . There is division in the American house now. There is divisiveness among us all tonight. And holding the trust that is mine, as President of all the people, I cannot disregard the peril to progress of the American people and the hope and the prospect for peace for all people." Therefore, "I have put the unity of the people first, *I have put it ahead of any divisive partisanship*" (emphasis added). Having made these points about the role and duty of the president during a war, and during a crisis precipitated by that war, President Johnson told the American people, "Accordingly, I shall not seek, and I will not accept, the nomination of my party for another term as your President."[72]

At the news conference that followed his address, President Johnson let it be known that there was a historical precedent for his action. It was "16 years ago this week—that President Truman made a similar announcement, March 29, 1952."[73] President Truman's withdrawal also had been an effort to save his party's presidential future. In his address at the Jefferson-Jackson Day Dinner, President Truman said to his fellow Democrats, "I shall not be a candidate for reelection. I have served my country long, and I think efficiently and honestly. I shall not accept a re-nomination. I do not feel that it is my duty to spend another 4 years in the White House."[74] He then closed this nationally televised address with a discussion of his own partisan hopes:

> We must always remember the things the Democratic party has done, and the high ideals that have made it great. We must be true to its principles and keep it foremost in service of the people.
>
> If we do that, we can be sure that there will be a Democratic President in the White House for the next 4 years.[75]

Although the record shows that Texas congressman Sam Rayburn, Speaker of the House of Representatives, was at this dinner, it is not clear whether Senator Johnson was there. But surely he learned of the partisan context in which President Truman's withdrawal occurred and realized the opportunity that it opened up for his mentor and colleague, Senator Richard Russell of Georgia, for his own vice-presidential ambitions.

Speaking the next night at a DNC reception, President Truman told his audience:

> There is one thing I overlooked late night. I failed to say, after I had made the announcement that I did not intend to run for reelection, that I will be just as enthusiastically working for the Democratic ticket as if I were on it.
>
> I am just as sure as I stand here that the Democratic Convention in July will nominate a winner.
>
> I will be in there, just the same as if I were the nominee—because I am that kind of Democrat. . . .
>
> Now the Democratic Party is, as I said last night, the salvation of the world and of this great country of ours. And we must not, under any circumstances, let down on that theory.[76]

No one could escape the partisan nature of President Truman's withdrawal. He spoke to a Democratic audience, even though it was broadcast nationally. President Johnson spoke to a national audience. President Truman committed himself to a Democratic victory in November. President Johnson committed himself to unity, consensus, and a later announcement of who he supported for president. President Truman not only sharply criticized the Republican Party and its "white is black" campaign slogan but spoke glowingly of the Democratic Party's past accomplishments and of its forthcoming victory.[77] President Johnson declared his nonpartisanship but cast his speech in such heroic terms that it seemed nonpartisan in putting country above politics. It said that the Democratic Party could rise above mere politics. And before he ended his news conference, President Johnson told his audience that the Democratic Party had done this before.

Both Democratic presidents had taken the high road. Both had seen that their party could not win with them as the nominee because of the political baggage they carried. Both knew that they would be lightning rods, attracting all sorts of political criticism, not only from within their parties but from outside as well. Both men had to withdraw, yet they did it differently. President Truman was quite explicit in his withdrawal announcement that, while he could not win for the party, the party itself deserved to win nevertheless. President Johnson used an indirect tactic. He made the Democratic Party leadership look heroic—and through its leader, a party that would do the right thing in a crisis situation. Here was a party with the American people and their political system as its central concern. Such a political party was not merely greedy for political power, it was a party of justice, of commitment, and of concern for the American people. Its goal was not simply advancing its leaders to political power, but advancing the needs of the American people.

Johnson's indirect strategy said to the American people, "you can under any circumstances trust and depend on the Democratic Party." It is a party working for the American people and should be given another opportunity with another presidential leader to serve the American people. Seen in this light, Johnson's withdrawal was like Truman's, despite the fact that they used different political tactics. While Hubert Humphrey came closer than Adlai Stevenson to winning the election, both efforts failed. Each time the Republicans captured the White House.

The Presidential Vote for Johnson: A Composite Portrait

Looking at this native-son presidential career, we can see that he (1) used convention politics to capture the presidency, (2) made limited use of presidential primaries to capture the presidency, and (3) used the electoral route to win once he had the vice presidential and presidential nominations.

In examining the delegate votes for LBJ at the national party conventions in which he was either a presidential or vice-presidential candidate, one sees another empirical portrait of a southern native son. He got nowhere in 1952 using national convention politics to secure the nomination for the second spot. In 1956 these same tactics barely registered his presence at the convention. All that can be said is that he became visible among the numerous contenders. Then in 1960, his convention tactics got him a little more than a quarter of the delegate votes, which put him in second place. The need to have the ticket balanced in that year ended up with his key supporters securing for him the vice-presidential position. He finally was in the presidential circle upon his third convention effort. At last, in 1964, LBJ "became the second Presidential candidate in the history of the Democratic Party to be nominated by acclamation," following the precedent set by Franklin Roosevelt in 1936.[78] Overall, it was national convention politics that enabled Lyndon Johnson to capture the vice-presidential spot and with it the presidential post. As a native-son presidential candidate, he did not fail to make use of the presidential primaries to reach the White House. However, as the record shows, LBJ did not get involved in presidential primaries until 1960, and even then he entered only one, although he did receive write-in votes in four other states. By 1964, when he was already president, he was on the ballot in only two states, and in six he appeared as a write-in candidate. Finally, in 1968, although he was no longer a candidate, he still appeared on the primary ballot in four states, and received write-in votes in three more. Clearly, LBJ's sporadic use of the presidential primaries had little impact on his presidential career. National convention politics were more successful for him.

LBJ's support in Texas as vice president and then as president increased significantly from 1960 to 1964. The pride of the Texas electorate for its native son clearly showed. In 1964 LBJ carried nearly every one of the counties in the state.

Analyzing this huge victory in terms of demographic categories provides a comprehensive look at both elections. In the urban, town, and rural counties, the huge support for LBJ is apparent—each gave him a major increase in votes, with the greatest support coming from the urban areas. Here not only did LBJ stifle the rising urban Republicanism in the state, but he got urban Republicans to vote for him. Although Goldwater had concentrated on Texas almost more than any other state, visiting it six times during the campaign and increasing his sojourns as Election Day approached, his strategy rested upon a "'backlash' of whites voters" coupled with urban Republicans to win the state.[79] But in 1964 neither the expected backlash nor the surge in urban Republicans developed, and the Goldwater-Miller ticket lost *all* of the ground captured by the Eisenhower-Nixon ticket in 1952 and 1956. Weeks concluded, "In general, the twelve-year dream of a two-party system in Texas had been rudely dissipated."[80]

Additional evidence of the Republican setback in the 1964 election can be seen in all four demographic categories—home, Black Belt, boss, and Latino—where the Goldwater-led ticket floundered. Even traditionally Republican Gillespie County, where the president was born, bounced back into the Democratic column. If urban Republicans gave way to the native-son factor, so did traditional Republicanism in this particular county.

Despite the fact that the Republican Party in 1964 had "a smooth-working, efficient, [and] energetic" statewide organization that was significantly more advanced than the Democrats, a Democratic landslide occurred in the state in every demographic category.[81] "More votes were cast than were expected, and a bumper crop of Democrats turned up. According to one report, about 400,000 Texans who had never voted before in a presidential race showed up at the polls. The totals indicate that most of them were Democrats."[82] In addition, "even ultra-conservative Republicans . . . in the higher-income brackets tended as the campaign progressed to shift their support to Johnson."[83]

Why did this landslide appear? According to Weeks, Goldwater's defeat in Texas rested in part on "the fact that Johnson was a native son of Texas who had lived his entire life in the state."[84] Rising therefore from this composite portrait is the fact that a native-son presidential candidate can influence the state electorate from both the first and the second spot on the ticket. His greatest influence seems to come from the first spot, from which the native-son candidate can engender an electoral landslide and voter realignment in the state, at least at the presidential level. Thus, our question at this point is a simple one: Can such a voter realignment outlast the president's term in office?

★ 11

Johnson's Postpresidential Influence

The 1968 Presidential Election in Texas for Vice President Humphrey

In my initial case study of another southern native-son presidential candidate, Jimmy Carter, Vice President Walter Mondale's 1984 presidential run offered a wonderful opportunity to enrich the theory of a native-son presidential candidate. Our extensive statistical exploration revealed that the former president was able to generate enough support for Mondale that this nonsoutherner was able to regain his political momentum in Georgia's presidential primary. There, Mondale was able to pull away from the crowded field of Democratic contenders and become the leading contender for the party's nomination.[1]

Although Mondale captured the nomination at the Democratic National Convention on the first ballot, he lost in the general election to Republican president Ronald Reagan. Here, Mondale did worse than he had done in the primary elections, and Carter's postpresidential influence faded at the presidential level. Mondale even lost in Carter's home county of Sumter, where he received only 45 percent of the vote to Reagan's 55 percent. Carter, in the final analysis, could not sway voters even in his own home county to vote for his former vice president.

This initial finding about the native-son president having influence for his former vice president in the primary but not in the presidential election stood alone at first. Then, Walton's second case study on President Clinton, which came out prior to Vice President Al Gore's 2000 election effort,[2] revealed that although Clinton endorsed and supported his vice president, the Gore campaign made only limited use of him. The end result was that neither Arkansas, nor Tennessee, nor any southern state supported Gore. The implication from the Clinton study was that a scandal-laden native-son president could not help his vice president in either the primary or the general election. Therefore, the results from the two case studies showed that it is possible for presidential influence to be found in the primary under certain conditions but not in the general election.

President Johnson's 1968 endorsement of his vice president, Hubert Humphrey, offers new empirical evidence with which to once again probe this dimension of southern native-son presidents. And since Johnson's postpresidential strategy is the initial one, predating both the Carter and the Clinton efforts, it sets the foundational base for the model.

Prelude: Johnson's Selection of Senator Hubert Humphrey for Vice President

Prior to our analysis of LBJ's endorsement of Vice President Humphrey in 1968, it is crucial to analyze Johnson's initial decision to select Senator Humphrey as his running mate in 1964. These decisions are interconnected, and one provides a political context for the other. Political scientist Gerald Pomper wrote, "The nomination of Hubert Humphrey as the 1964 Democratic candidate for Vice-President constituted one of the most unusual incidents in recent political history."[3] What had made this so was the assassination of President John F. Kennedy. "After the assassination, Robert Kennedy [the attorney general] became the object of deep emotional support . . . early in 1964. In the New Hampshire primary, through write-in votes, 25,000 Democrats indicated their preference for him as the Vice-Presidential candidate."[4] This shift of sympathy to the martyred president's brother and the rising political support for him jeopardized a long and established tradition in American politics, the relative freedom of the presidential candidate to select his own running mate.[5]

In addition, "[f]or Lyndon Johnson, . . . it was essential to prove that he could draw from the American people their own voluntary approval of his national leadership."[6] To select Robert Kennedy would be to trade on the Kennedy name and on the rising emotional support growing out of the tragedy. In such a political context, it would never be clear that Johnson had acted on his own. There would have been the argument, as journalist Robert Sherrill declared, that he was an "accidental" president, and one that was reelected by an accident as well.[7] For a man who had sought high office for most of his political career, such an assessment overlooked his qualifications and, more important, his achievements in office. The emphasis would have been on *how* he got the office, not on his experiences and his ability to attain it. This was not a question of the loss of presidential prerogative, but of the loss of LBJ's ability to define his own presidential legacy.

Coupled to this second problem is the story of the "enmity" or "indifference" that existed between the two men. At the 1960 Democratic National Convention Robert Kennedy told LBJ that he could not have the vice president position.[8] Some journalists offer the interpretation that personal jealousies and rivalry made the entire matter a question of the president's giant ego and revenge.[9] This group argues that Johnson's public announcement on June 30 that he had removed from consideration all "members of the cabinet or those who meet regularly with the cabinet"[10] referred specifically to Kennedy.

A third potential problem for LBJ was the seating challenge brought by the Mississippi Freedom Democratic Party at the 1964 Democratic National Convention because it threatened to disrupt the convention before a nationally televised audience. Some saw the challenge as causing a Convention floor fight, particularly if it was engineered by the disgruntled Kennedy forces. Taking this possibility as a point of departure, several analysts argued that the president gave the task of solving this problem to Senator Humphrey as an "acid test" as to whether he would be selected for the job. Pomper explained, "The Senator was in a delicate position. Since he was relatively weak in the South, he had to conciliate that section. A walkout by Southern delegates, moreover, might convince the President and the party that the ticket required a more moderate candidate for Vice-President."[11]

These three problems—the loss of informal presidential power, the loss of a presidential legacy, and the loss of a harmonious Convention and the southern electoral vote—dominate in different degrees the vast literature on President Johnson and the 1964 National Convention. Overall, the personal enmity between Johnson and Kennedy overshadows the explanation. But the problem with this single explanation is that it is event and time bound and does not permit one to connect the 1964 selection of the vice president with his 1968 endorsement. It makes American politics a politics of personalities and not the politics of continuity and relationship that it is. American politics has always been more than a mere struggle between candidates. It clearly has been both men and ideas. And in 1964 it was both.

Finally, President Johnson's selection of Senator Humphrey presents a case study in decision making and problem solving. Nearly every presidential scholar makes the case that crisis management is at the center of presidential leadership.[12] They see this one factor as defining and separating great presidents from average ones. If this is so, then in this instance the question is how did President Johnson, faced with this crisis in selecting his vice-presidential running mate, choose Humphrey?

As for the problem of the loss of informal presidential power, this crisis reveals that the president used a number of political techniques to maintain that power. First, "he began to create an extensive public list of possible running-mates. Inclusion of Sargent Shriver [brother-in-law of Robert Kennedy and director of the Peace Corps] served to decrease the concentration on Robert Kennedy as the political heir of the late President. The addition of other names served to prevent a concentration of support or opposition on any other single possibility."[13] In addition to a public list, the White House took a poll of the American public. "[M]ost of all Lyndon Johnson learned from the polls . . . that he was completely free to choose as Vice-President any running mate he fancied. No name suggested in any Quayle poll as Johnson's partner added to or diminished the President's winning margin more than 2 percent."[14]

Next, President Johnson discussed names with Richard Daley, mayor of Chicago, African American civil rights leaders, business and labor leaders, southerners, big-state governors, and a host of advisees and advisers. He even raised the question to Senator Humphrey at a White House meeting. Contact was made with all fifty state Democratic Party chairs to get their insight. Even delegates were contacted. All elements of the Democratic Party had input.

Before all of the advising was over, President Johnson let Senator Humphrey make his own personal case as to why he should be the choice. Humphrey and his staff developed a strategy for selecting "the next best man." "All efforts were directed toward convincing significant persons and groups that the running-mate should be selected strictly on grounds of ability, rather than narrow electoral appeal."[15] Senator Humphrey had the experience, the appeal, and the entrée to most of the groups inside the Democratic Party. He even used some of his Senate colleagues to make his case to the president. Humphrey did have opposition, but it was limited to specific Democratic constituencies. Only with southerners did he have a serious weakness due to his long record of support for civil rights. But even here he was more preferred than Robert Kennedy and was endorsed by some of his southern colleagues. He also lacked support from machine politicians from cities such as Chicago and New York, due to their loyalty to Robert Kennedy and the idea of another Catholic president. But the city politicians were not powerful enough or unified enough to prevent Humphrey from becoming vice president.

In making his decision, the president made use of time itself. "Johnson played a waiting game, expecting the emotional reaction to the assassination to subside, while he preserved his freedom of choice. By delaying his elimination of Attorney General Kennedy to the last possible moment, the hot passion of the moment of the assassination permitted perspective to enter into the mind of the 'attentive public.'"[16] The media opinion leaders even supported the president's freedom of choice in this matter. In addition, by delaying his decision, Johnson let the nomination of Goldwater be "turned to Humphrey's advantage. Geographically, the nomination made the Mid-West, where the Minnesotan was strongest, the crucial area for November. . . . The Democrats could now regard the East as relatively safe, making it unnecessary to nominate a candidate from that area, such as Robert Kennedy."[17]

The selection of Humphrey revealed several aspects of the office of president as well as the diverse coalition of the Democratic Party over which LBJ presided. LBJ solidified the right of the president to select his choice for vice president, as well as allowed Humphrey to seek consensus from the diverse party that now existed. The various Democratic constituencies were emotionally and politically affected by Kennedy's death. LBJ's process of allowing Humphrey to build his case for the vice presidency continued the redefining of the Democratic Party. This new party at times allowed for consensus to develop among diverse interests, but it would be difficult for this rebranded party to continue to coalesce in the future.

However, this case revealed that the president would have a series of problems facing him with his endorsement of Vice President Humphrey in 1968. As we shall see, Johnson went about making his endorsement in a simpler, step-by-step problem-solving manner that would in the end optimize his party's chances.

President Johnson's 1968 Endorsement of Vice President Humphrey

In 1968 LBJ was plagued by not only Vietnam but the possibility of a race war at home. LBJ began to consider not seeking reelection and announcing this at the State of the Union address. Johnson had several conversations with Health, Education and Welfare Secretary John Gardner, who later stated:

> "I had become increasingly concerned about the state of the country, about the war, about the riots, about the course of events as I saw them . . . We were discussing what could be done to insure the reelection of President Johnson. . . . And I found to my consternation some time in early January that I did not think that the president should run for reelection. . . . I wrote a letter of resignation [for Johnson], took it in and handed it to him, and he read it and laid it on the table and asked me why I did it. . . . And I said, "Well, I just don't believe that you can unite the country. I just think that we're in a terrible passage in our history and that you cannot do what needs to be done, with the best will in the world. I just think that is not in the cards for you. . . ." And he said, "Well, I've had the same thoughts myself many times."[18]

LBJ decided to delay the announcement because he did not want to appear as a lame duck too early, but the longer he waited could possibly advantage Robert Kennedy.

Once March arrived it showed itself to be "one of the most tumultuous months in American political history."[19] By the time of the spring primaries, the Democrats were clearly divided into two camps, one prowar and the other antiwar. Antiwar liberals were "willing to go to any lengths to stop the war and get rid of LBJ," even if it meant losing the election.[20] Southern Democrats were joining the GOP to block further programs to advance the Great Society initiative, while white urban ethnics were attracted to George Wallace as a response to the increasing racial tensions in their communities. The diverse coalition and emphasis on government activism to advance social and economic equality that began under Roosevelt was now in jeopardy of completely falling apart under Johnson. LBJ decided promoting himself was not worth sacrificing his party or his nation. Johnson delivered his announcement to withdraw from the presidential campaign on March 31.

At the news conference following Johnson's announcement of his withdrawal from the 1968 presidential race, a reporter asked, "Do you have a candidate for the Democratic nomination?" The president answered by saying, "No. I made that clear, how I felt about that." In his withdrawal speech, he had stated, "With America's sons in the fields far away, with America's future under challenge right here at home . . . I do not believe that I should devote an hour or a day of my time to any personal partisan causes."[21]

Despite any private commitments that LBJ might have made to friends, supporters, or individual candidates such as his vice president, he did not make a public endorsement. On August 28, he sent a message to the Democratic National Committee, which

> was read to delegates by Convention Chairman, Representative Carl Albert of Oklahoma. . . . The next day, following the nomination of Vice President Hubert H. Humphrey, White House Press Secretary George E. Christian issued the following statement: The President called the Vice President in Chicago to congratulate him on the nomination. As the President said yesterday, all viewpoints have been expressed in the Convention. Now that the party has nominated an excellent and an especially well-qualified candidate for President, President Johnson hopes that all Democrats will unite behind him and move forward to victory in the election.[22]

LBJ's public endorsement of his vice president seemingly followed the model created by Harry Truman in his withdrawal from reelection in 1952. Although President Truman worked at the 1952 Democratic Convention for Averell Harriman of New York, he finally endorsed the Convention nominee, Adlai Stevenson.

President Johnson began to deviate from the Truman model when he sent a telegram to the Texas Democratic Party Convention on September 17, 1968. In it, he asked the Convention delegates "to give the same loyalty to Hubert Humphrey that he has given to the Democratic party all his life. I ask you to work as hard for him as he has worked for America." He continued:

> Texas is a critical state in a critical election. This year, again, our party and our people look to your unity and your leadership for strength. I know you will not fail them. I know that Hubert Humphrey and Ed Muskie can count on you to carry the banner of victory into every precinct, every town and every county of our great state.[23]

With this telegram, Johnson was formally asking the delegates and leaders of the state party to transfer their support to this nonsouthern Democratic presidential candidate. In this instance, the Democratic ticket had two liberals and no southerners. The president asked his now conservative state party not to switch its allegiance.

A week later, September 26, 1968, the president sent another telegram to Texas Democrats, to the "Co-chairman of the campaign organizing Workshop of the Texas Democratic Party." Meeting in the Hotel Texas, in Fort Worth, the workshop was headed by Congressman Jim Wright and party leader Will Davis. In this second telegram, this native-son Texas president said, "America needs Hubert Humphrey and Ed Muskie. And I am proud that Texas is leading the way to assure their victory in November."[24] And before this assertion, President Johnson gave the members the famous Johnson treatment: "I salute you, my dear friends, and the fine men and women who were working with you to make Texas a Hubert Humphrey state. No responsible Democrat can sit out this crucial election."[25]

Beyond these two telegrams to rally the Texas Democratic Party behind his vice president, Johnson spoke at a Democratic Party rally in the Houston Astrodome on November 3, 1968, with Mrs. Muriel Humphrey and other political leaders and dignitaries in attendance. At this rally, President Johnson declared, "My dear, beloved friends, I pray that Texas will lead the way" in this election. Resolve "that union is good for Texas, for this region, and for our entire nation."[26] Then the president closed his address to the party faithful by once again asking the state's electorate to give the Democratic Party a victory by electing the party's nominee, Hubert Humphrey, as president.

Although the president endorsed Humphrey to the entire nation at his White House news conference of September 6, it was clear that he was taking every opportunity to work the Texas Democratic Party on behalf of his vice president. Like Truman, Johnson had now become fully partisan. Unlike Truman, however, who made his withdrawal at a partisan affair, remained partisan in his speeches, and continued to be partisan thereafter, Johnson started out as nonpartisan during his announcement and continued to be nonpartisan up until the Convention, but became fully partisan, at least at the public level, after the Democratic Convention made its nomination. And once becoming fully partisan, he made every effort to swing his southern state behind not only his vice president but behind a fully liberal ticket at that. Here was a Democratic presidential ticket that was not balanced, at least ideologically, and not focused on appeasing the South.

The 1968 General Election: LBJ and Humphrey

Throughout the campaign season, President Johnson made stops for the Humphrey-Muskie ticket in Kentucky, West Virginia, and Texas and gave several national speeches from the White House and before the Democratic National Committee meeting in New York City.[27] But it was quite clear that the president did not let up on his own home state. His efforts at home were significant.

The Republican Party, in an effort to capture the South, adopted a new "southern strategy" based on an approach proposed by Richard Nixon's political adviser, Kevin Phillips.[28] Their law and order theme carried numerous code words to attract the white southern backlash vote against the African American social revolution. The Republican Party thus hoped to make further inroads into the region beyond those made by Goldwater when he cracked the solid Democratic South with five states in 1964 due to his opposition to the 1964 Civil Rights Act.

In addition to the Republican Party's new southern strategy, there was the homegrown rebellion led by Alabama's defiant governor, George Wallace. He had tested the political waters in 1964 when he entered several midwestern state primaries in an effort to give the South new political allies outside of the region.[29] These forays convinced him of the possibility of a mass national base. When he was rejected for the vice presidential spot on the Republican Party ticket by Barry Goldwater in 1964, he launched the American Independent Party and ran on a race-based, conservative states' rights ticket that declared itself against civil rights for African Americans.[30]

On November 5, voters went to the polls to decide among the three political parties. Humphrey carried Texas and captured all of its electoral votes. The Democratic victory was a slim one, not quite as large as it had been in 1960. The white supremacist backlash was now in full view. Support for Wallace "came largely from the extreme right wing, which in itself includes many cross-currents of racial and economic interest."[31] According to Weeks's analysis of Texas presidential politics, "a great deal of Wallace's support came from the southern-oriented section of East Texas, but he also made inroads into other normally Democratic areas, such as the industrial suburbs of Houston, Beaumont, and Port Arthur."[32] The Wallace electoral inroads coupled with Nixon's "southern strategy," which employed code words to attract the "white backlash" vote, reduced the Democratic vote percentage to less than 50 percent. In fact, it was only 41.1 percent.

Weeks described how this very narrow victory occurred in 1968:

> The outgoing chairman of the State Democratic Executive Committee, Will Davis, was primarily responsible for managing the effort of the moderate and conservative Democrats. This uneasy coalition between the two factions, and Humphrey's second swing through Texas late in October, gave the impetus necessary to lift the morale of Democratic supporters in the state to the point of producing the slim plurality which was eventually delivered for the party.[33]

Although the account fails to note President Johnson's effort in the state in behalf of his vice president, the candidate's plurality instead of a major victory attests to Johnson's influence, even at a diminished level. Additional evidence of the president's leadership is evident in the election results: the Democratic Party won more than twice as many counties as did the Nixon-led Republicans. The county-level data also show that the Democrats swamped Wallace's third party, which won only 6 percent of the counties in the state. The Democratic victory at the county level nearly matches its 1960 performance, when it won 174 counties, but it falls far short of the party's county-level victory in 1964, when it won 238 counties.

Even the Republican's 1968 performance fell short of their 1960 victory in 80 counties, but it was far more than the 16 they captured in 1964. The Democratic Party in 1968 maintained a substantial dominance of the state's voting electoral base at the county level.

Disaggregating the Democratic Party's slim victory in the 1968 election by demographic categories, it is possible to see where the Republican Party and the American Independent Party made inroads into the Democrats' 1964 voter realignment and landslide support. Clearly, as shown in table 11.1, this 1968 vote for Humphrey reveals a resurgence of urban Republicanism in Texas in 1968. The Nixon-Agnew victory in the urban counties is reminiscent of the Eisenhower-Nixon victories in 1952 and 1956.[34] LBJ's 1964 victory in these counties declines under the inroads the Wallace ticket makes. No other third party had garnered so much support in the urban sector before, nearly 18 percent of the vote.

Elsewhere, traditional Republicanism, like urban Republicanism, reemerged and surged forward. The vote for the Republican Party in LBJ's home county of Gillespie was nearly 72 percent. The vote in Blanco County, which gave the Democrats a plurality of 43 percent, was not enough to offset the huge Republican gains in Gillespie County. Hence, the Republicans received 64 percent of the vote in the home county category. In the absence of a native son on the Democratic ticket, urban and traditional Republicanism made a comeback, and Republicans won two of the seven demographic categories.

Wallace, on the other hand, did not win a single one of the demographic categories, but he performed strongest in the Black Belt counties, capturing 32 percent of the total vote. This was followed by the town counties, where he got one-fourth of the vote, and the rural counties, where he got over one-fifth of the vote. His poorest performance was in the Latino and boss counties.

The Democrats, with vigorous support from LBJ, captured five of the seven demographic categories. Their highest level of support came in the boss counties, with 85.8 percent, followed by the Latino counties, with 72.5 percent. The Black Belt, rural, and town counties came in with under 50 percent each. Thus, the machine, ethnic, and racial counties gave the Democratic ticket its best support in the 1968 campaign, followed by rural and midsize areas of the state.

Overall, Texas was "the only former Confederate state to remain in the Democratic Party column in the 1968 presidential election."[35] Weeks remarked that "the state seemed to come out in the campaign year of 1968 remarkably unchanged. . . . [and] went largely back to normal—a one-party state with its politics mainly confined to the factionalism of the Democratic Party."[36]

The question, however, is what degree of support did President John-

TABLE 11.1. The Results of the 1968 Presidential Election by Demographic Category

	Urban Counties		Town Counties		Rural Counties		Home Counties	
Candidate	Vote	%	Vote	%	Vote	%	Vote	%
Humphrey/Muskie	842,726	40.5	342,870	40.3	68,765	41.9	1,345	24.2
Nixon/Agnew	867,202	41.7	303,639	35.7	60,143	36.7	3,559	64.0
Wallace/LeMay	371,339	17.8	204,981	24.1	35,039	21.4	655	11.8
Total	2,081,267	100.0	851,490	100.1	163,947	100.0	5,559	100.0

	Black-Belt Counties		Boss Counties		Latino Counties	
Candidate	Vote	%	Vote	%	Vote	%
Humphrey/Muskie	2,495	48.3	4,887	85.8	4,022	72.5
Nixon/Agnew	1,018	19.7	635	11.2	1,450	26.1
Wallace/LeMay	1,650	32.0	173	3.0	78	1.4
Total	5,163	100.0	5,695	100.0	5,550	100.0

Source: Richard Scammon, ed., *America Votes 8* (Washington, DC: Congressional Quarterly, 1970), 366–70.
Note: The total vote excludes the write-in votes (489) from the analysis.

son garner for his vice president? How much of his electoral coalition did he transfer beyond rhetoric? The raw voting data tell us that he transferred some of his support, but at a diminished level.

Using bivariate regression (see table 11.2) one can see the level of association between Johnson's and Humphrey's votes, as well as that for Carter and Mondale and for Clinton and Gore. Insights from these three case studies provide significant empirical data on the postpresidential influence of southern native-son candidates. First, in table 11.1 we see that Johnson's 1960 and 1964 vote is strongly correlated with the 1968 vote for Humphrey, the 1964 vote more so than the 1960 vote, when LBJ was second on the ticket. If this strong correlation were projected into the 1968 election, 58 percent of LBJ's voters could have been expected to vote for Humphrey. Using the 1964 vote in the same manner, 76 percent of LBJ's voters could be expected to support Humphrey. Our findings in both of these correlations are significant at the .01 level, meaning that they have little relationship to chance. President Johnson's influence was quite helpful to Humphrey.

The Coattails of Other Native-Son Presidents

As for Carter's influence for Mondale in the general election, there is a minimal, poor relationship between President Carter's 1976 vote and Mondale 1984 vote. But President Carter's 1980 vote shows a strong relationship to Mondale's 1984 vote. We can predict that 56 percent of Carter's 1980 voters joined Mondale's 1984 electoral coalition in the state. This finding also is highly significant. Thus, with so little of the Carter voter transferring to Mondale, there was little chance of Mondale winning the state over President Reagan.

But at the primary election level, the story is quite different. Carter's 1976 and 1980 primary vote percentages do not correlate even minimally with Mondale's 1984 percentage. From this statistically significant finding, it seems that Carter's electoral coalition did not really shift in any serious way to Mondale's winning primary electoral coalition.

In terms of President Clinton's influence in Arkansas for his vice president, Al Gore, in the 2000 presidential election, one finds a very strong relationship between Clinton's 1992 and 1996 elections and the Democratic presidential nominee's vote in 2000. In fact, the relationship is the same for both elections: the same large percentage of Clinton voters gave their support to Gore. Democratic Party loyalty was not only very high in

Arkansas, but higher than in the other two states. The Clinton voters transferred to Gore in huge numbers. Nevertheless, Gore lost the state to the Republican Party in the general election.

Similarly, in the primary election, there was a very strong relationship between President Clinton's voters and those for his vice president, particularly the 1992 voters. More of the voters in Clinton's 1992 electoral coalition transferred to Gore's 2000 electoral coalition than did the 1996 voters. This latter group simply did not take to the Gore campaign. Part of the reason for this might be due to the fact that the Republican Party had surfaced in the state to capture the gubernatorial post in the aftermath of the Clinton scandals. Hence, members of the original Clinton coalition appeared to have been more loyal than the more recent ones. Finally, there was little opposition in the 2000 presidential primaries, certainly not as much as in 1992 and 1996.

Collectively, these three results give us an interesting theoretical perspective on the postpresidential influence of southern native-son presidents on behalf of their vice presidents and former vice presidents in presidential elections in their respective home states.

The Postpresidential Influence of Three Southern Native-Son Presidents: A Comparative Perspective

We have empirical evidence from two state presidential primaries—Georgia and Arkansas—that when localism is present in a crowded candidate field, the native-son's postpresidential influence can be significant enough to give his vice president or former vice president the ability to build an electoral coalition strong enough to win the state. Regardless of the nature of the challengers in presidential primaries, strong or weak, this influence can be quite helpful in overcoming them, even in a crowded field.

At the general election level, the nature of the Republican challenger becomes a central factor in determining the scope and significance of the former president's influence. Here, three states provide the evidence. LBJ's experience reveals that the native-son postpresidential influence can be so powerful as to contribute to winning the state for his vice president. On the other hand, the experiences of Carter and Clinton say that the presidential influence can be so small that the former vice president or vice president, respectively, will lose the state.

A moderating factor for LBJ's postpresidential influence was the strength or weakness of the Republican Party nominee. LBJ's opponent in

1964, Barry Goldwater, alarmed the voters in Texas to such an extent that he mobilized more Democrats to come to the polls, and he motivated Republican voters to switch their votes to the Democrats. Nixon's policies were not as controversial, so his "southern strategy" on race found serious competition from another native son, Wallace of Alabama. This reduced the success of the Republicans, enough to give LBJ's influence strength to carry the state. Hence, it was not so much Nixon the candidate as it was the limited appeal of his strategy in the Texas context against an outspoken segregationist such as Wallace. It is quite possible that without the presence of Wallace, the Republicans would have prevailed as they did after 1968.

These case studies demonstrate that southern native-son presidents can not only influence the voter turnout and party fortunes in their respective states in general elections, they can, in some instances and under certain circumstances, influence the electorate in favor of their vice presidents or former vice presidents and help them win in both primary and the general elections, provided that their Republican opponents meet certain criteria. Each of these case studies adds further richness to the theory of the native-son presidential candidate.

Table 11.2 offers empirical evidence for such a theory. LBJ's electoral support in both 1960 and 1964 shows a high association with the 1968 state vote for Democrat Hubert Humphrey. The r^2 tells us that one could predict that 58 percent of LBJ's 1960 support and 76 percent of his 1964 support would stay loyal and vote for his vice president, Hubert Humphrey.

For Carter, only his 1980 voter support has a high correlation with the Walter Mondale vote. Here 56 percent of Carter's 1980 vote could have been predicted to vote for his former vice president, Walter Mondale, in 1984. This is half of his electoral support.

Clinton's 1992 and 1996 general election support correlates almost perfectly with the vote for his vice president, Al Gore. This permits one to predict that in Arkansas 86 percent and 87 percent of Clinton's 1992 and 1996 voters would support his Gore. Although Clinton's support for his vice president is higher than that for both Johnson and Carter, it is only Johnson who was able to carry his home state for his vice president. Neither Carter nor Clinton were able to achieve that. Yet they did have some influence.

Collectively, these findings conflict with the scholarly literature on postpresidential influence. There is limited research on the subject and the qualitative models that have been created to detect the influence of expresidents do not even consider helping their vice presidents or former vice presidents become presidents. In the pioneering article, Irina Belenky creates six categorical models and places LBJ in one entitled "Exhausted Volcanoes." Of this categorical model, Belenky says that it is a "metaphor" for "the six ex-presidents who did little or nothing of consequence in their retirement years. Ill health, personal temperament, and individual circumstances are among the causative factors that explain their torpor after so many years of high excitement and ceaseless activity."[37] Then Belenky describes Johnson as an ex-president who simply gave up: "The realization that the controversy over the war in Vietnam had all but destroyed his presidency left Johnson, at 60 years of age, anguished, and exhausted. He would spend his remaining four years in lonely, bitter semi-exile at his Texas ranch."[38]

Accepting this initial categorization, the second article on this topic says, "Like [Woodrow] Wilson, Lyndon Johnson (four years) was too ill throughout much of his postpresidency to accomplish little more than pen his memoirs."[39] However, this article does look at the area of electioneering as a possible source of influence, and the authors declare, "Typically, however, former presidents influence electoral politics indirectly

TABLE 11.2. The Post-Presidential Influence of Presidents Johnson, Carter, and Clinton in Their Vice President's Presidential Elections: A Correlational Analysis

Years	Election	dF	r	p	r^2
A. **LBJ**					
1960–1968	General	252	.76	.01	58%
1964–1968	General	252	.87	.01	76%
B. **Carter**					
1976–1984	Primary	157	.06	.01	0%
1980–1984	Primary	157	.45	.01	20%
1976–1984	General	157	.40	.01	16%
1980–1984	General	157	.75	.01	56%
C. **Clinton**					
1992–2000	Primary	72	.69	.01	47%
1996–2000	Primary	72	.50	.01	25%
1992–2000[a]	General	73	.93	.01	86%
1996–2000	General	73	.93	.01	87%

Source: The general election data was taken from Alice McGillivray and Richard Scammon, eds., *America At the Polls, 1960–1992*, vol. 2 (Washington, DC: Congressional Quarterly, 1994), and Richard Scammon, Alice McGillivray and Rhodes Cook, eds., *America Votes 24* (Washington, DC: Congressional Quarterly, 2001). The primary election data for Carter was taken from the *Georgia Official and Statistical Register*, while the election data for Clinton was taken from several Secretary of State Reports.

[a]The Arkansas Secretary of State Report for 2000 does not record any votes for Arkansas County. Hence, it was dropped from all three calculations: 1992, 1996, and 2000.

dF = degree of freedom; p = level of significance.

and from the sidelines."[40] Then, they offer the example of Clinton raising "millions for both Vice President Al Gore's 2000 presidential campaign and his wife Hillary's successful U.S. Senate campaign."[41] And this is where they leave the matter. But this chapter's analysis reveals far more than the current literature on the subject.

Lastly, the president's influence is in the general election rather than in the primaries for all three southern native sons. Here is where their post-presidential influence is the greatest.

★ 12

The Regional Vote

Johnson, Garner, Carter, Bentsen, Clinton, and Gore

In 1928, "[t]he Democrats held their convention in Houston, the first party convention in the Deep South. The urban element of the party wanted to nominate Al Smith, the four-time governor of New York State. . . . They nominated Smith and selected as his running mate Senate Minority Leader Joseph Robinson of Arkansas."[1] Selecting Houston as their convention site and a southerner as their vice-presidential candidate was the Democrats' "southern strategy."[2] They had hoped that this strategy would prevent the Republicans, led by President Hoover, from making inroads into the region using Smith's Catholicism as a cleavage issue. This strategy was not effective. Hoover won 40 states and became the first Republican since Reconstruction to make appreciable inroads in the formerly Solid South, winning Florida, North Carolina, Tennessee, Texas, and Virginia. Smith won only seven states, six in the South plus Massachusetts.[3]

However, present at the historic 1928 Convention was none other than Lyndon Baines Johnson, who "had wangled tickets as a representative of [his] college newspaper."[4] "Johnson used his association with the *College Star* to gain credentials as a correspondent. There Johnson saw the first native-son southerner nominated for the second spot on the Democratic presidential ticket. "Senator Joseph T. Robinson . . . was nominated on the first ballot with 914 votes. Senator Alben W. Barkley of Kentucky finished a distant second with 77 votes."[5] The logic of the situation was quite clear to LBJ: southerners were a force in national party politics.

John Nance Garner: The Pioneer Southern Native-Son Presidential Candidate

Four years later, the Democratic National Convention moved to Chicago, where Texas's long-time congressman John Nance Garner became a candidate and ended up as Franklin Delano Roosevelt's vice-presidential choice. Garner was first elected to Congress to represent the 15th District in 1902.[6] By the time of the 1932 Democratic National Convention, Garner had been in Congress for three decades and had served for nearly 16 terms. Moreover, in 1932, Texas would permit him to run for both his congressional seat and the vice presidency, as would LBJ in 1960 and Lloyd Bentsen in 1988. Hence, in many ways Garner was the pioneer Texan and southern presidential candidate.

The 1932 race gave LBJ a view of "Cactus Jack" Garner's preconvention politics, which involved the selected use of the rising presidential primaries. Garner's name was entered on the ballot of two of the 16 states and appeared as a write-in candidate on a third one.[7] In table 12.1 one can see

TABLE 12.1. The Votes and Percentages for Congressman John Nance Garner in the Presidential Primaries: 1932–1940

Date of Primary	States	Votes	Percentages	Positions
1932 Primaries				
April 12	Nebraska	27,359	19.0	2nd
May 3	California	222,385	41.0	1st
May 10	Ohio	72	write-in	6th
Total[a]		249,816	8.5	4th
1936 Primaries				
April 7	Wisconsin	108	0.0	2nd
Total		108	0.0	8th
1940 Primaries				
April 2	Wisconsin	105,662	24.6	2nd
April 9	Illinois	190,801	14.0	2nd
May 7	California	114,594	11.7	2nd
May 17	Oregon	15,584	12.4	2nd
Total		426,641	9.5	3rd

Source: Adapted from Congressional Quarterly, *Guide to U.S. Elections*, 3rd ed. (Washington, DC: Congressional Quarterly, 1994), 500–505.

[a]The total votes and percentages were taken from all of the primary candidates in each election.

the results of this preconvention strategy. In Nebraska Garner came in second in a three-way contest and captured 19 percent of the total vote. FDR won the primary with 64 percent of the vote. Garner, however, had established a political presence in the Midwest, outside of his region. He then won California over both FDR and Al Smith with 41 percent of the total vote, establishing his support in the largest state in the West as well.[8]

Then, on May 10, in the Ohio primary, Garner appeared not on the ballot but as a write-in candidate. Of the six candidates on the ticket, he came in dead last.[9] Garner did not enter any of the other primaries. However, his strategy of the selected use of presidential primaries to reveal to the party leadership that he was more than just a southern candidate enhanced his political prospects at the 1932 Convention.

Garner selected another Texas House member, Sam Rayburn, as his convention manager and spokesperson. This proved to be quite significant because FDR had won only nine of the 16 primaries and arrived at the Convention with only 45 percent of the total vote and not enough delegates to win on the first ballot. Garner had won 9 percent of the primary vote. Therefore, FDR's campaign manager James Farley had to conduct the "negotiations with Sam Rayburn . . . and through him was able to persuade Garner to agree to withdraw his candidacy after the third or fourth ballot in favor of Roosevelt's nomination."[10]

When the presidential balloting began, "out of 1,154 votes cast in the first ballot, Roosevelt received 666, Smith 201, Garner 90, and the remainder were scattered for the most part among favorite sons."[11] Finally, "[i]t was William G. McAdoo who was given the task of announcing on the fourth ballot the switch of the California delegates from Garner to Roosevelt."[12]

In fact, before the switch was made, Garner got 90 ¼ delegates' votes on the first and second ballots, and then rose to 101 ¼ delegate votes in the third balloting.[13] Garner's convention strategy not only increased his total delegate votes but ended up with him getting the vice-presidential spot despite the fact that in all four convention ballots, the second highest delegate vote-getter was former party nominee Al Smith. Smith's total ran from a high of 201 ¾ delegate votes on the first ballot to a low of 190 ½ delegate votes on the fourth and final ballot. Yet, despite Smith's strong support at the Convention, FDR selected a Texan, John Nance Garner. Here was another lesson for LBJ about southern power in the national party: southern delegates defeated the party's attempt to do away with the two-thirds rule that gave the region veto power over candidates inimical to its interest of segregation.[14]

Therefore, after the fourth ballot and FDR's capture of the party nomination, "[t]he convention then proceeded without a hitch to nominate Garner for Vice President. The deal was clear to all. Garner had been persuaded to give up the [House] speakership for the Vice Presidency. The arrangement was agreeable to Roosevelt, [William Randolph] Hearst, and the delegates from Texas and California."[15] Therefore, a major lesson from the 1932 Democratic National Convention for LBJ was not only the selected use of presidential primaries but the shrewd politicking at the Convention that offset the power of other and better primary performers. There was not only the need for ticket balancing but also a successful presidential candidate might want his own people in powerful positions in Congress as well.

In 1936, as shown in table 12.1, Garner's name appeared on the presidential primary ballot only in Wisconsin. FDR won the primary with more than 1.4 million votes, nearly 100 percent of the turnout. Vice President Garner came in second with 108 votes and Al Smith received 46 votes.[16] "President Roosevelt was renominated by acclamation. . . . [and] the renomination of John Nance Garner for Vice President was also by acclamation."[17]

When it became clear that FDR would seek a third term in 1940, several of his cabinet secretaries broke with him and announced their own presidential candidacies as contenders for the mantle that they had thought he would lay down. Once again, "Cactus Jack" went all out to capture the nomination. He entered four state presidential primaries in the Midwest and West. Although he won none of them, he came in second in all four.

He then moved to the National Convention to defeat the President's renomination efforts. This failed, however, because FDR got a first-ballot victory. Nevertheless, Garner did receive 61 delegate votes, extending his reach a bit beyond the 46 brought by Texas.

LBJ thus saw a member of the president's own party challenge him for the nomination. President Johnson would experience this himself in 1968. Overall, the presidential candidacies of southerners Robinson and Garner were instructive for this rising native son who was now in Congress and starting his own climb up the political ladder. The efforts of congressional powerhouse "Cactus Jack" Garner showed how political power could be converted into presidential candidate success.

But the story of "Cactus Jack" is not all positive. In his political rebellion against the president, he lost not only his vice-presidential power but his presidential potential as well. And with his personal defeat came the defeat of southern power, at least for a time. In 1940, FDR nominated Henry Wallace for the vice presidency, and in 1944 he nominated Harry Truman. Neither man came from the South. No other southerner would get into the vice-presidential office until President Truman chose Alben Barkley of Kentucky; and Kentucky was not necessarily regarded as a "southern" state by the old Confederacy. In the end, Garner's pioneering efforts provided both strengths and weaknesses from which LBJ could learn.

Breaking the Glass Ceiling: LBJ as the Innovative Southern Native-Son Presidential Candidate

Prior to the rise of LBJ, southern candidates such as Senator Robinson (Arkansas), Senator Sparkman (Alabama), and Senator Kefauver (Tennessee) had advanced as far as the vice-presidential nomination. LBJ's mentor, Senator Russell of Georgia, did not even make it that far. But his own Texas colleague, Congressman Garner, and Senator Barkley of Kentucky did eventually become vice presidents. However, the highest achievement of southern native-son presidential hopefuls outside of their region was limited to the vice presidency.[18] LBJ became the first southern politician to break the glass ceiling and rise from the vice-presidential spot to the presidency. In this way he became a model and political symbol for subsequent candidates, such as Governor Carter, his own friend Texas senator Lloyd Bentsen, Governor Clinton, and Senator Al Gore. Indirectly, LBJ was a symbol of political possibility for Congressman George H. W. Bush and Governor George W. Bush on the Republican side, as well as for African American senator Barack Obama. While one might mention Dwight Eisenhower, who happened to be born in Texas but resided in Kansas, as a direct influence, it goes without saying that LBJ showed numerous ambitious southern politicians and an African American one that it was possible to see and achieve beyond the vice-presidential position.

In fact, his indirect influence went beyond the Democratic and Republican Parties in influencing southern native-son presidential candidates from the region to toss their hats into the presidential ring and expect victory. To date, H. Ross Perot, another Texan, ran for the presidency on a third party ticket in both 1992 and 1996. Perot's surprise showing in 1992, when he captured some 19 percent of the vote, made him a serious challenger not only in the state but in the entire country.[19]

George C. Wallace ran in 1968 on the American Independent Party ticket not so much in terms of using LBJ as a political model but more as someone to oppose for changing the system of segregation and racial discrimination upon which the region had grounded its politics, policies, and culture. Wallace was, in a word, a "protest" candidate because of his hope was to return the Democratic Party from LBJ's innovative public policies in race relations back to being a party that embraced and permitted racial segregation to exist despite the existence of the 13th, 14th, and 15th Amendments in the Constitution.[20] Wallace's efforts were designed to recommit the Democratic Party to the southern way of life and its racial hierarchy. Thus, unlike other regional candidates, who hoped to win, Wallace sought to protest and punish.

LBJ's innovations affected both of the major political parties as well as third parties, and led to the rise of future presidents: two southern Democrats, two southern Republicans, and one African American. This in retrospect has given LBJ a leadership role in national politics, via his own Democratic Party, and simultaneously in providing the Republican Party with its new base of rebirth in the South and the nation.[21] In fact, LBJ's legacy to American politics is that he remade the Democratic Party, and then, through influencing other southerners, kept the Democrats victorious on the local and national level with Presidents Carter and Clinton and broke up the solid Republican South, at least temporarily.

The rise of a two-party system in the South and in LBJ's own state of Texas is due in part to southern Republican leadership that emerged in the nineties with Newt Gingrich, Trent Lott, Dick Armey, and Tom DeLay, who based part of their political philosophies and campaign appeals on an enduring cultural history that is opposed to racial equality and inclusive democracy. This leadership and political model exists in the power currently held by southerners Mitch McConnell, Ted Cruz, and Pete Sessions in the U.S. Congress. The transference of Wallace's protest and punishment to the Republican Party in the South has revitalized and renourished it. Thus, LBJ's political innovation improved the political opportunity for politicians both inside and outside of his native South and his native state of Texas.

Transforming the party, the political process, and the party system, and setting into motion the realignment of the southern electorate—to say nothing of bringing new entrants into the electorate with the 1965 Voting Rights Act and forcing a mobilization of the white electorate—are all a result of LBJ's innovations. He impacted and reshaped all four of Key's original functional typologies: (1) party-in-conflict, (2) party-in-the-electorate, (3) party-in-the-organization, and (4) party-in-the-government. This then was a clear breakthrough for the region in national and state politics. A regional leader had reshaped national party politicians and left a political legacy and a new political dialogue for major and minor parties.

Regionalism: The State Portrait

Texas is by far unique among the southern states when it comes to native-son presidential candidates. Unlike Arkansas and Georgia, which only recently produced winning native-son presidents, and Tennessee, which only recently produced two native-son vice-presidential candidates—Estes Kefauver in 1956, who lost, and Senator Al Gore Jr., who won in 1992 and 1996—Texas has produced winning native-son presidents of both major parties, native-son vice presidents, and a controversial third party presidential candidate, H. Ross Perot. In the twentieth century, the Texas electorate has seen a wide variety of native-son candidates, although it has given them different levels of support over time.

In 1932 and 1936, Garner won two terms as vice president, and ran his own presidential campaign in 1940. In 1944, Texas launched its own state-based third party, the Texas Regular Party, supported and aided by Garner.[22] This short-lived party melted into the States' Rights Democratic Party in 1948, headed up by another native-son southerner. Senator John Sparkman of Alabama appeared on the 1952 ticket, followed by Estes Kefauver in 1956. LBJ began his presidential quest in 1956 as well. Texas senator Lloyd Bentsen tried for the presidency in 1976 and received the vice-presidential nomination in 1988. Another Texan, millionaire H. Ross Perot, got on the ballot in all 50 states in 1992, and he ran again in 1996.[23]

Two native Texans appeared in the 1980 Republican primaries, congressman George H. W. Bush and former governor John Connally. Bush wanted the top job but won the vice-presidential spot in both 1980 and 1984. Seeking to rise to the presidency, Bush ran in 1988 and found himself facing another Texan, Senator Lloyd Bentsen, in the vice-presidential spot on the Democratic ticket. Bush's victory in a sense replicated what LBJ had accomplished on the Democratic ticket by moving from the vice presidency to the presidency.

In 1992, Texas again found itself with two presidential candidates, Bush and Perot, although this time both lost. Nevertheless, another southern native son, Governor William Jefferson Clinton of Arkansas, won in 1992 and repeated the feat in 1996. Texas was once again back in play in the 2000 election when the Democrats nominated Senator Al Gore of Tennessee, and the Republicans nominated the Texas governor, George W.

Bush, who won. Thus, within a span of 68 years, the state had represented both parties in the White House.

However, it must be noted here that the senior President Bush moved to Texas, whereas the son was born in Texas. Therefore, Bush senior is technically a resident Texan, not a native son, according to the definition of the concept. Republican Dwight D. Eisenhower was born in Denison, Texas, but resided in Kansas at the time of his 1952 and 1956 presidential elections. If a person merely resides in the state, he or she is an "adopted son."[24] Usually, adopted sons are running in states "not . . . of their birth" and "can expect to receive lower levels of support" than if they were born in these states.[25] The adopted son does not get the same friends-and-neighbors effect, win as many votes, or affect the turnout of the state electorate as much as a native-born candidate. It is this differentiation that mediates the impact of this variable on the state's electoral behavior.[26] It is important that this distinction be made if a properly nuanced theory is to be developed.

Overall, Texas has produced two native-son presidents and one adopted native-son president. Similarly, the state has had five vice presidents: Garner twice, LBJ once, and Bush senior twice. Plus, there have been several native sons seeking the party presidential nomination: Bentsen, John Connally, Perot, and most recently Rick Perry. Hence, none of the southern states have approached Texas's number of candidates or number of victories. Texas indeed has been unusual in the South's effort to play and win in the presidential sweepstakes.

Having now shown that there were numerous native-son presidential candidates and contenders who sought the nomination for both major parties and for a third party in the state's political context from 1932 through 2000 (as well as the other southern regional candidates like Robinson, Carter, Clinton, and Gore), it is now possible to see in clear-cut empirical terms how the Texas electorate responded to both local native sons and the regional ones.

Before developing a collective portrait of the support offered by the Texas electorate to these native-son candidates, it is necessary first to more thoroughly examine the performance of congressman and vice presidential candidate John Nance Garner in the presidential primaries of 1932, 1936, and 1940. Garner's success in three presidential primaries helped to set the stage for LBJ's later efforts.

By 1932 this Texas native son felt that his time had come to move out of Congress and into 1600 Pennsylvania Avenue. Hence, in order to convince the party leadership of his power to attract votes outside of the

South, Garner entered two western state presidential primaries. In head-to-head competition with Al Smith, Franklin Delano Roosevelt, and other presidential hopefuls, Garner, as table 12.2 reveals, won the California presidential primary, came in second in Nebraska, and received a few write-in votes in Ohio. Of all of the candidates entering the primaries, Garner came in fourth with less than 9 percent of the vote.

Entering the Democratic National Convention that year with congressional experience, the support of western states and the Texas delegation, and possibly the South's support, Garner won the vice-presidential spot. Clearly, here was a major lesson for the ambitious LBJ. A Texan had moved into the White House without the support of the eastern and midwestern wings of the Democratic Party. Liberals within the party and the primaries had been deliberately sidestepped.

Three years after LBJ had himself entered Congress in 1937, Garner broke with FDR over his running for a third term, his own distaste for New Deal policies, the Court packing plan, the party purges in the South, and his own driving presidential ambition, and offered himself for the Democratic Party nomination in 1940. FDR's own leading political pollster and forecaster, Emil Hurja, supported Garner in his nomination drive. "[In] March 1939, Vice-President J. Nance 'Cactus Jack' Garner was leading in the public-opinion polls as a favorite for Democratic nomination."[27] Hence, "Hurja had become a 'Cactus Jack' supporter and predicted that he would win the Democratic nomination for the presidency in 1940."[28] In addition, *Time* magazine reported in this time frame that "54 percent of all Democrats are now opposed against a Third Term."[29]

TABLE 12.2. The Differences in the Votes for the Democratic Party's Presidential and Senatorial Votes in the Primary and General Elections for Native Sons Johnson and Bentsen

Year	Democratic Party Primary Senate and Presidential Vote		Democratic Party General Election Senate and Presidential Vote	
1960	LBJ Senate Primary Vote:	1,407,109	LBJ Senate General Vote:	1,306,625
	Democratic Party Presidential Vote:	1,167,932	Democratic Party Presidential Vote:	1,167,932
	Difference:	+239,177	Difference:	+138,963
1988	L. Bentsen Primary Vote:	1,365,736	L. Bentsen Senate General Vote:	3,149,806
	Democratic Party Presidential Vote:	2,352,748	Democratic Party Presidential Vote:	2,352,748
	Difference:	−987,012	Difference:	+797,058

Source: Adapted from table 8.10 for the LBJ data and from Richard Scammon and Alice McGillivray, eds., *America Votes 18* (Washington, DC: 1989), 431, 436, and 442 for the data for Senator Lloyd Bentsen.

Encouraged by such experts and public opinion insights, Garner made an effort to capture the party's nomination by once again running in the presidential primaries of four western states during April and May. But Garner this time failed to beat the incumbent president in any of the primaries. He came in second in all of them; FDR beat him in all of them. Garner's best showing came in Wisconsin where he captured one-fourth of the total votes cast. And this time he came in with less than 10 percent of the vote for a third-place finish, only a slight improvement over his 1932 attempt, and was replaced by Alben Barkley of Kentucky. Garner had let his presidential ambition move him out of the White House and the House of Representatives and back to Texas. Nevertheless, this Texan's use of the western and midwestern states to support his presidential ambition would be repeated by Senator Russell of Georgia in his 1952 drive, and again by LBJ in 1956 and 1960. Southerners, in order to protect segregation from federal intervention, tried using midwestern and western presidential primaries as a tactic, although it did not always prove successful.

Beyond Garner's use of presidential primaries, his role in a political context is worth examining as he gained support for the Democratic Party in Texas and influenced the Texas electorate's voting behavior. In 1928, with Senator Joseph Robinson of Arkansas on the ticket, the Democratic Party failed to carry the state of Texas,[30] losing to the Republican Party by more than 30,000 votes. But in 1932 and 1936, with Garner on the Democratic ticket, the state electorate responded significantly by nearly doubling the vote for the Democrats over the 1928 total. The Democrats would go on to win all of the state's presidential votes until Eisenhower's victory in 1952. With LBJ on the ticket in 1960 and 1964, and with Vice President Humphrey on the ballot in 1968, the Democrats recaptured the state. Since then, Texas has seesawed back and forth between the two parties, favoring Nixon in 1972, Carter in 1976, Bush senior in 1980, 1984, and 1988, and Bush junior in 2000 and 2004, renewing the Republican tradition of victories in the state. Democratic native-son Lloyd Bentsen failed to win Texas as the Democratic vice-presidential candidate in 1988, while Clinton did in 1992 and 1996, but Gore lost in 2000, as did Kerry in 2004 and Obama in 2008 and 2012.

Thus, the state has shifted from supporting native-son Democratic presidential candidates to supporting Republican native sons who might be able to sustain their current ascendancy despite the presence of racial and ethnic minority voters in the electorate. A visual picture of this realignment is presented in figure 12.1. Here we see several temporary third party realignments. The Garner-aided Texas Regulars got 12 percent of the vote

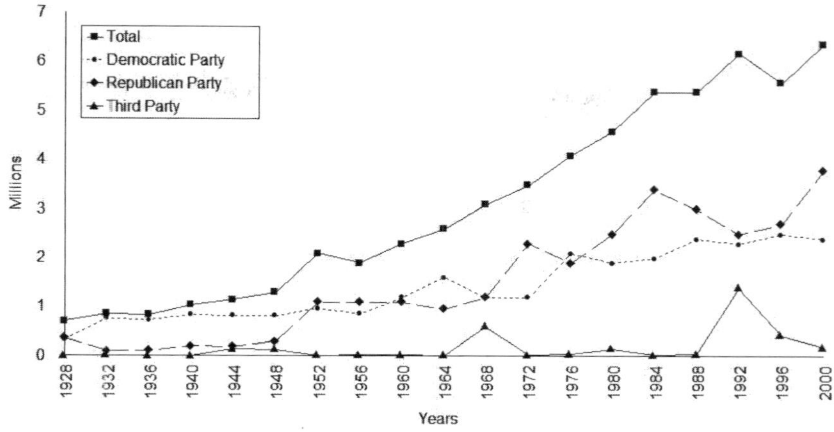

Fig. 12.1. The Number of Total, Democratic, Republican and Third Party Votes Cast in Texas Presidential Elections: 1928–2000

in 1944, the Strom Thurmond-led Dixiecrats got 10 percent in 1948, Wallace's revolt got 19 percent of the vote in 1968, and Perot got 22 percent of the vote in 1992 and 7 percent in 1996. Such third-party activity, led by intrastate and regional hopefuls, did not affect the Democratic Party until 1992. The party's strength was such that it could withstand strong third-party realignment efforts and still win the state. However, as the Republican Party has grown and matured, Perot's significant challenge has seriously weakened the Democrats' support among the state's electorate.

A third empirical marker of the rising Republican success in Texas can be seen in figure 12.2, which delineates the percentage of counties won by each party in presidential elections. The Democrats won the lion's share of the counties up through the sixties, with the exception of the Eisenhower years. In 1932, Garner won every county in the state, a feat that is still unequaled. Since the sixties, the Republicans have won the majority of counties, with the exception of Carter in 1976.

Finally, there is the matter of the demographic responses to Texas and southern presidential candidates. Figure 12.3 offers a longitudinal perspective on the electoral behavior in the state for these candidates. Of the 13 elections involving local or regional candidates, the Democratic victory in the urban counties was lowest among the three types of counties (urban, town, and rural). After Carter won the state in 1976, the Democratic decline continued across all categories, the presence of Bentsen on the

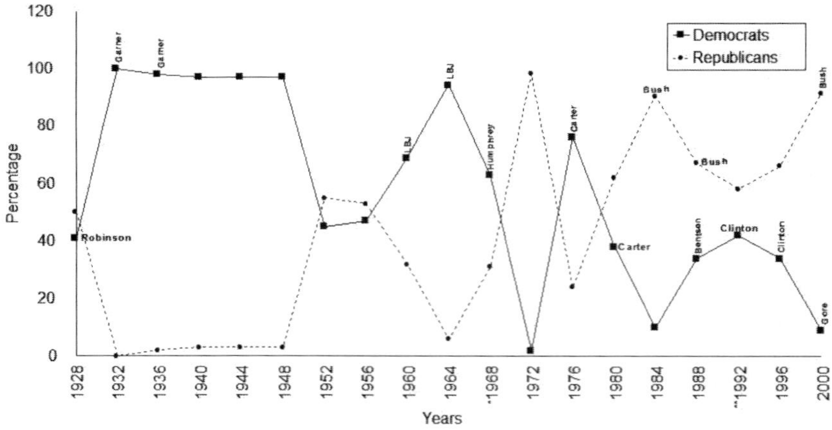

Fig. 12.2. The Percentage of Counties Won by the Democratic and Republican Parties in Texas Presidential Elections: 1928–2000
([*] In 1968, a third party, George Wallace's American Independent Party, won 16 counties with 6.3%. [**] In 1992, a third party, Texan H. ross Perot's United We Stand American–Independent Party, won 4 counties for 1.6%.)

ticket in 1988 notwithstanding. And with no native son candidate running in 2000, the Democratic Party was reduced to only one-third of the vote in the urban areas.

The Democrats' hold on the electorate in the town counties has not been as erratic as in the urban areas. Here they won eight times to the Republicans' five, although again Perot diminished the Democratic vote in 1992. Greater inroads were made by Bush in 2000 in these Democratic town areas than in the large cities. Possibly, the urban centers' large African American and Latino populations dampened the Republican incursions. In the rural county category, the turnout is similar to the urban counties, with one exception. In the 2000 election, native son George W. Bush made the largest incursions as this Democratic stronghold faded significantly. In short, Bush combined urban and rural Republicanism in the state more than either his father or Reagan had done. Although the Republicans would sweep the Democrats in all of the major demographic categories in 1980 and maintain that hold throughout the eighties and nineties, the younger Bush would penetrate the Democratic electorate more deeply across the board than previous Republicans.

Switching from the major demographic categories to the home, racial, ethnic, and boss counties, as shown in figure 12.4, the pattern seen in the

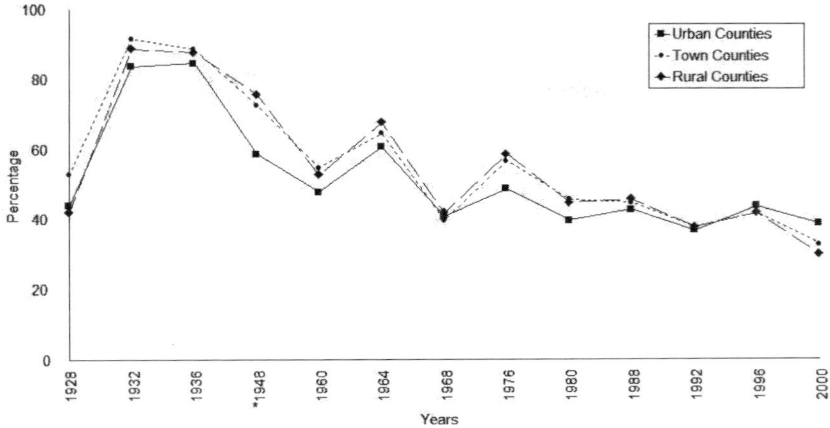

Fig. 12.3. The Percentage of the Democratic Vote for Texas and Southern Native-Son Presidential Candidates by Three Demographic Categories
([*] In 1948, not all of the Texas counties reported their official results in time to be put in the official Secretary of State Report. In fact, the book by Alexander Heard and Donald Strong indicates that for 37 counties in the state, the election data had to be gathered from an unofficial source, a "mimeographical for" using the "Texas Election Bureau" data issued by the Secretary of State. These 37 county results are listed as "unofficial complete" or "unofficial and incomplete." The other book that reports this data is Alice McGillivray and Richard Scammon, eds., *America at the Polls, 1920–1956*, vol. 1. They do not note this data problem. Yet they say in a note that "data from the first of the American Institute of Public Opinion have been used to supplement the incomplete state canvassed returns" (782). How the AIPO got this missing election data, they do not say. These two data sources are significantly dissimilar for Hidalgo County vote for the 1948 Dixicrats. I used the Heard and Strong data for this county and their entire data for the Dixicrat vote.)

major demographic categories is nearly repeated with several key exceptions. In LBJ's home counties, the Republican tradition of Gillespie seriously eroded and diminished the share of the Democratic vote given by Blanco. Thus, the Democratic Party's victories in LBJ counties have been fewer and much smaller since LBJ's time in office. By the 2000 election, the Democrats were getting less than 20 percent of the vote in these counties. Again, Key's observation that there was no friends-and-neighbors voting in Texas continues to hold for Johnson's counties. In recent years, even Blanco County has switched to the Republican Party. It has not supported a Democratic candidate since 1968.

The Republican realignment of LBJ's home counties has not occurred in the other demographic categories. In the Black Belt counties, the Dem-

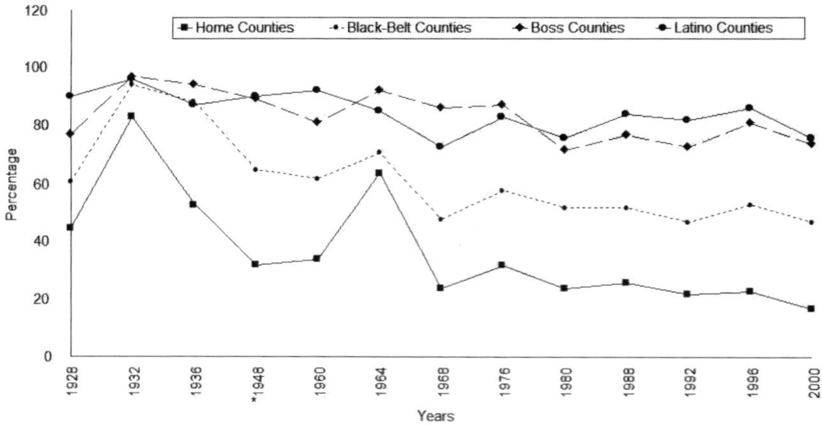

Fig. 12.4. The Percentage of the Democratic Vote for Texas and Southern Native-Son Presidential Candidates by Four Demographic Categories (** see note at figure 12.3.*)

ocratic Party has won 12 of the 13 elections. This may be due in part to the fact that in 1970 there were no more African American majority town counties. For our analysis, we switched to Waller County as representative of the Black Belt, even though then it was only 40 percent African American in population. The Republican Party did not carry it until 2000.

In the boss counties, as well as in the Latino counties, the Democratic Party was able to win all 13 elections. The Republican Party was unable to shift in any significant manner the voting patterns in these counties under any leadership. For almost three-quarters of a century, these counties have remained a bedrock for the Democratic Party, and at very high levels. Third parties, even in combination with the Republican incursions, have not been able to diminish the traditional voting patterns since the days of Garner and LBJ. The linear decline seen in the urban, town, rural, and home county categories is not reproduced in the Black Belt, boss, and Latino counties.

LBJ and Garner clearly dominated their eras in terms of state electoral support for the Democratic Party. And part of this legacy continues in several of the county categories in the state. But beginning with Hoover, and with Eisenhower and Nixon in between Democratic victories, and continuously since Reagan, the Republican Party has captured the state in presidential elections. But this capture has not come at the expense of racial and ethnic voting, as the data show. Essentially, this Republican support has gone from an urban base, as Weeks showed, to slowly capturing the town and rural categories. LBJ could win big in the urban counties of the state, but the Democratic Party was never strong in the large cities, except during the "Cactus Jack" era. Here the big oilmen had wealth and continued to keep the Republican Party in power. Later, the shift of the white electorate to the Republican Party in the town and rural counties pushed the Democratic Party into a decline in the state, and by 2000 the Republicans were stronger in these areas of the state than in the urban areas. This is a new and different Republicanism because it carries with it some of the rural-based ideas of race.

George W. Bush's performance outpaced that of both his father and Reagan in the state. Native sons Garner and Johnson outperformed them all. However, all of the other southern candidates have performed less well in Texas than the home-grown native sons. Only Carter won the state, while Clinton, Gore, and Bentsen lost. The only other Democratic victor in the state was LBJ's endorsed vice president, Hubert Humphrey.

Regionalism: The Vice-Presidential Dimension

Hubert Humphrey and Lyndon Johnson had entered the Senate together in 1948, and over time they became working colleagues and friends. The South-Midwest connection that had started with Garner and was continued by Russell also was employed by LBJ in his 1956 campaign. Southern Democratic leaders felt that they fit better with the Midwest than the East and New England where the liberal candidates emerged. Their idea was that segregation as a regional public policy would get more support from the Midwest than from the eastern party leaders.

In 1948 Humphrey, then the mayor of Minneapolis, was an outspoken critic of segregation. In fact, it was his leadership at the 1948 Democratic convention that forced the walkout of delegates from Alabama and Mississippi.[31] Humphrey's stance and his presidential ambition during the fifties and in the 1960 presidential primaries left him vulnerable to southern politicians such as LBJ who sought to use him to derail the political efforts of the Kennedys, and others such as W. Averell Harriman of New York, who had been stereotyped as political liberals. In order to win the presidency, Humphrey would have to be persuaded to "see" and "understand" the southern way of life—meaning segregation. Humphrey had a friend in the South, if he could be a friend to the region.

Thus, in 1964, LBJ chose Humphrey not only as a ticket-balancer, like

FDR had chosen Garner, but also because Humphrey spoke the language of the liberal wing of the Democratic Party that was embedded in the East and the New England states. Humphrey had proven that he could modify his "flaming liberalism" in his negotiation of a political compromise to the Mississippi Freedom Democratic Party challenge. This permitted Humphrey to talk with the southern delegations, particularly the Mississippi delegation, and show them that he was a man with whom they could reason. Humphrey became a political symbol at the 1964 Democratic National Convention to the southern delegations that they had less to fear from him than they had thought. Here was a midwesterner, from an area to which the South had traditionally reached out in its presidential ambitions, now reaching out to them on their own turf and over an issue that they understood—party discrimination against Black voters—and resolving it in such a manner that segregation would not completely die.[32] Humphrey did not distrust the white racist Mississippi Democratic Party; he merely asked it to make some reforms, in effect telling the party leaders that they would still be in control of their party, they would just have two "honorary" members.[33] This liberal was willing to work with political segregationists to attain his vice-presidential ambition. But even this minor concession was too much for the white Mississippi Democrats who walked out of the Convention.

So did the MFDP. They let it be known that this political compromise made by Humphrey was not responsive enough to the suffering that they had endured to make the party inclusive. The failure of the Humphrey compromise was blamed on the MFDP's militancy and their being unsophisticated in political matters. Some writers argued that theirs was a moral challenge rather than a legal one, and therefore it got a better response than it deserved. Still others argued that LBJ wanted a unified Convention, and this compromise was an attempt to attain that goal. And some observers pointed to the nonviolent tactics of the MFDP delegates and implied that, while the white Democrats at the convention might have been racists, they were at least well behaved.[34] However, the legacy of political violence in Mississippi alone would have weighed against the acceptance of this symbolic compromise. Common decency, if not their own consciences, required their refusal.

Regionalism: Texas in Comparison

Following in the ticket-balancing tradition, in 1988 Michael Dukakis selected Lloyd Bentsen as his vice-presidential nominee. His selection counterbalanced the Republican selection of George H. W. Bush as their presidential nominee. Thus, in 1988 Texas had the unusual situation of candidates from the state representing each of the major parties. Even more unusual was the fact that Bentsen was permitted to run for the Senate and the vice presidency simultaneously, as had LBJ before him.

But the comparison does not stop there. In 1960 and 1988 LBJ and Bentsen received more votes as senatorial candidates than they did as vice-presidential candidates. Table 12.2 displays the differences in the votes LBJ received for the presidential ticket as opposed to those Bentsen received. The vote difference is indeed significant, and if Bentsen had gotten these additional votes for the vice presidency, the Democratic Party could have carried the state. Although it did not happen, it is an indication that more Texas voters wanted Senator Bentsen in the Senate than in the vice presidency.

Therefore, in a head-to-head ticket-balancing match in 1988, the Republican Party adopted son beat the Democratic Party native son. In addition, the Democrats lost the South as well as Texas. The Texas electorate preferred a local president to a local vice president. Bentsen went back to the Senate and went on to become secretary of the treasury during the Clinton presidency.

The 1988 response of the Texas electorate suggests a wider probe of Texas in regard to other states in the South. First of all, in analyzing the regionalism variable in the native-son perspective, one can look at the percentage of the electoral vote provided by the South and that provided by Texas itself. Over time, the 11 states of the Old Confederacy provided from one-fifth of the total electoral vote to just one-third, while Texas provided from 4 percent to 6 percent. Winning the region or the state, or both, would give candidates a sizeable amount of electoral support in the presidential contest. As the 2000 election revealed, had George W. Bush lost one southern state he would have lost the presidential election; and had Al Gore won even one southern state, he would have won the election.

Texas's share of the total number of electoral votes in the South over time remained relatively stable. When LBJ, Humphrey, and Carter ran, Texas had about one-fifth of the electoral votes in the region. Given that Texas currently has the second-largest number of electoral votes of all fifty states, it will continue to be a major force in regional and in national politics. The future portends a significant role for this state as a producer of presidential candidates and as a ticket balancer in national politics.

★ Part V

The Native Son and the Democratic Party

In 1964, Lyndon Johnson won the presidency with the largest majority in American history: 44 states and 61 percent of the vote.[1] Yet in the loss, Goldwater's campaign transferred the Deep South from the Democratic Party to the Republicans. In addition to his home state, Arizona, Goldwater won five southern states—Alabama, Georgia, Louisiana, Mississippi, and South Carolina. These states deserted LBJ because he had moved toward reform and progressive legislation on civil rights. Goldwater "accepted the support of southern racists, thereby capitalizing on a white backlash in the South against the civil rights movement and the Democratic Party for introducing the Civil Rights Act of 1964, even if Republicans helped to pass it. . . . The shift was monumental: after 1964, Republicans controlled the southern white vote."[2]

Courtney Brown's research revealed that a dual realignment had occurred in the 1964 election.[3] The Republican response to LBJ's public policies and his presidential campaign reimaged the Republican Party, transformed its electoral base, gave the South an invitation to join, and offered it a potential new leadership role in party affairs. It also gave the South a chance to shape the Republican Party's philosophy and public policy agenda.[4] Eventually the Republican Party added racial conservatism to its traditional philosophy of economic and governmental conservatism.[5]

Simultaneously, LBJ's reimaged the Democratic Party, permitting it to solve a major contradiction that had existed since the Civil War and to realign around another issue: racial equality. Those who could embrace this issue and governmental intervention to resolve it remained within the

Democratic electorate. Those who could not make the adjustment re-aligned to the Goldwater-led Republicans.[6]

The leadership of FDR, a New Yorker, had reimaged the Democratic Party in the thirties and forties around the issues of economic equality and government intervention to resolve the crisis of the Depression.[7] LBJ had seen the role that FDR had played in Democratic Party politics, and he had seen it succeed. The transformation that FDR had set in motion caused a dual realignment within both parties.[8] The greatest difference here was that FDR had nearly four terms in which to remake the Democratic Party, the Republican Party, and the American party process; LBJ had less than two terms. Yet both men had transformed their party. They had set the public policy agenda, and each time the Republican Party had merely responded. And each time the remade Democratic Party lost some governing power, in Congress or in the White House, or both.

Republican Abraham Lincoln had also reimagined and remade his party in the 1860 and 1864 elections with his war policies and the Emancipation Proclamation, "to correct things felt to be imperfect in the founders' own achievement."[9] Garry Wills adds, "Lincoln had revolutionized the Revolution, giving people a new past to live with that would change their future indefinitely."[10] In so doing, he had altered the very face of the Republican Party, helping to make it a major political party in only two elections.[11]

Finally, there is Brown's keen observation about the native-son candidate and the Democratic Party: "The region [South] was in the midst of a major electoral reorientation [in 1964], only part of which was completed by the time the election took place. Both Democratic and Republican voting in the Deep South was just beginning to put on entirely new electoral faces. . . . [T]he 1964 election was merely one stop, however important, on a longer path of electoral evolution."[12] LBJ, as a native son in the Democratic Party, left an electoral legacy that still challenged the party in the election of 2000. This legacy encompassed both the Democratic Party and the Republican Party, as well as the American political process. Carter, Gore, Clinton, and Obama followed LBJ and found this legacy challenging.

Although party scholarship in the past has paid only minor attention to the native-son variable, this LBJ case study should remind future researchers that it is a powerful and valuable variable that must be considered if we are to understand presidential party leadership in general and in the Democratic Party in particular. In the end, "the flexible, inventive, more volatile characteristics of Johnson were in a sense really the human characteristics of his party."[13] And once he left politics, he left the party to the politics he had created.[14]

★ 13

The LBJ-Remade Democratic Party in Presidential Elections

From Remaking to Reimaging

Lyndon Johnson's former political adviser, Harry McPherson, discussing the role that President Johnson had played in remaking the Democratic Party, observed in 1988 that the party was "indeed successful in the off years. But in the race for the White House, their nominee has been rejected in four of the five contests since 1968." The key reason for this failure "lay in the white man's view that the Democrats had cast their lot with black Americans, to the ultimate disadvantage of whites. Thus, the party of 'inclusion,' having extended the suffrage to women and blacks, has lost the original voters, the white males, and with them . . . the Presidency."[1]

McPherson continues, "A Southern President, Lyndon Johnson [was] part of that combination of forces . . . insuring full participation by blacks in the country's . . . life . . . [B]lack inclusion was the stated goal; . . . the Democratic Party was the means."[2] However, the electoral consequences of this social justice have been the exodus of white males from the Democratic Party and the concomitant loss of the presidency. Thus, LBJ's groundbreaking public policies for racial justice realigned the Democratic Party, and with it the Republican Party as well.

McPherson's observation was merely a harbinger of things to come. Between 1988 and 1992 a flood of books and articles began to promote this theme.[3] Another author, William Mayer, promoted a thesis of Democratic disunity: "Republican presidential victories are built on a foundation of Democratic disunity. The Democrats would win most presidential elections if only they could maintain some minimal level of harmony within their own ranks. More often than not over the last twenty-five years, this has proven beyond their capacity"[4] Race was simply one of many divisive issues inside the party and therefore not the only factor that had crippled its chances for victory. Despite its empirical evidence, however, Mayer's point was lost in the flood of works to the contrary.

Another argument put forth during this period viewed the Democrats as the "party-of-nonvoters": "The policies adapted by Democrats in the sixties weakened their ties to their historic constituencies and this depressed turnout of their potential base. . . . That turnout has fallen, particularly among lower-class voters, because the Democrats have moved to the right, abandoning their working class and poor constituencies as they have become more like Republicans . . . the Democrat Party did not turn less liberal; it embraced a different version of liberalism that has demobilized its potential electorate."[5]

The question of race and African Americans, while not prominent, entered the argument nevertheless. The theorists of the "party-of-nonvoters" took great pains to point out "that even extraordinarily high turnout rates among poor, Hispanic, and black adults eligible to vote would not have won the 1988 election for Dukakis and Bentsen."[6] The inclusion of these new voters as a consequence of the 1964 Voting Rights Act was not enough to offset the white defectors from the party. Thus, while rarely out front as a reason, race became the centerpiece of the theme of the "party-of-nonvoters." LBJ was always present as an undercurrent in these arguments as the original cause of the party's decline; he had set the matter into motion.

But this thematic framework faded, as did the "disharmony" theme. Both gave way to the constantly repeated idea that McPherson had noticed: "Giving African Americans their constitutional rights and accompanying civil rights had led to the destruction of the Democrats' New Deal Coalition." LBJ, these theorists argued, had brought about this situation.

Before the 1992 presidential election, the solution was put forth that the party should distance itself from African Americans. African American sociologist Wilson Julius Wilson wrote:

> An emphasis on coalition politics that features progressive, race-neutral policies could have two positive effects. It could help the Democratic Party regain lost political support, and it could lead to programs that would especially benefit the more disadvantaged members of minority groups—without being minority policies.[7]

Pollster Stanley Greenberg argued:

> Great Society Liberalism was forged in a decade of historic upheavals. Innovative and optimistic, it advanced new concepts of justice and altruism that associated the Democrats with advancing civil rights and fighting poverty. . . . Liberalism emerged from this period with a narrowed image of its constituencies. . . . And, for many, that meant blacks.[8]

Greenberg urged the Democratic Party to reconstruct its political vision so that it "could serve simultaneously as a party of the people and a party of the nation."[9] Race had to become a nonconcern for the party. Race had to be dropped; LBJ's policies had led to "the defeat of national Democratic candidates and the decomposition of Democratic models."[10]

Conservative Democratic politicians formed the Democratic Leadership Council (DLC) to move the party beyond its identification with African Americans.[11] Governor William J. Clinton, one of the founders of the DLC, became a candidate for the Democratic nomination in 1992, calling himself a "New Democrat." In the 1992 campaign race was never raised as an issue. This was an unstated attack on LBJ's remaking of the Democratic Party. The DLC approach, with its emphasis on race-neutrality, was one-dimensional and absolutely inadequate. Clinton was not, as he thought, a remade Democrat, but rather a follower in a process made possible by Johnson's pioneering native-son presidential candidacy.

The Party Literature: Missing the Native-Son Presidential Variable

From Harry McPherson's perspective, LBJ's role in remaking the Democratic Party was costly to the party, leading to the loss of the South and the party's lack of success in subsequent presidential elections. For McPherson, victory should have taken priority over political equality, Democratic inclusion, and simple justice, even if it meant that segregation, white supremacy, and the southern way of life remained intact. This at least would have kept the Democratic Party winning in presidential elections. However, the party's losses could just as easily have happened because of other variables in the electoral and political process. The Democrats could have nominated a weak candidate or the Republicans a strong one.

Both before and after McPherson's observation, the academic literature had declared that LBJ's actions were not possible or even conceivable. Presidents were titular heads of their party organizations and therefore did not have the power to reshape their political parties. Only the party-in-the-electorate through an electoral mandate could provide such direction for party changes in direction and public policy. However, finding a clear-cut mandate and grasping its "electoral meaning from . . . a single election is not possible."[12]

Democratic theorist Robert Dahl wrote that it is impossible to determine presidential mandates from elections; only opinion surveys of the electorate can offer support for such a mandate. In addition, he posited "for most presidential elections before 1940 a valid reconstruction of the policy views of the electorate is impossible or enormously difficult, even with the aid of aggregate data and other indirect indicators of voters' views." Even after 1940, "the existence of surveys since then would not necessarily have supported such claims."[13]

> 1964 was a landslide election, as was 1972. . . . "Johnson's and Nixon's specific claims of meaningful mandates do not stand up well when confronted by evidence." To be sure, in both elections some of the major policies of the winners were supported by large majorities among those to whom these issues were salient. Yet "none of these policies was cited by more than 21% of respondents as a reason to like Johnson, Nixon, or their parties."[14]

In the end, Dahl concludes that the presidential mandate "is not only morally wrong but politically and historically illusory."[15]

Thus, in Dahl's analysis, the chance of an election mandate telling the Democratic Party how to deal with segregation and its southern problem is both nil and nonsensical. Such a mandate has not spoken to Democratic leaders since the unified southern bloc first appeared in national presidential elections in 1880 and fastened segregation up on the Democratic Party. What one finds in every subsequent election through 1964 is, at best, an array of new strategies by which the southern Democrats might maintain their hold over the party. And this southern influence is what kept the Democrats from using their national power to intervene in the illegal, immoral, and antidemocratic practice of segregation.

Thus, remaking the Democratic Party was either *undesirable* or *impossible*. Yet LBJ did both when he used the 1964 Civil Rights Act, the 1965 Voting Rights Act, and the 1968 Fair Housing Act, as well as other public policy enactments, to redesign and reshape the political image of the

Democratic Party. It became the party of inclusion and the party that provided African Americans with their constitutional rights. It was indeed a political breakthrough, on two levels.

First, the tradition of the Democratic Party and its antecedent organizations—the Jeffersonian Democrats and the Jacksonian Democrats—had been to oppose the voting rights of free men of color.[16] In all of Texas's statewide referenda on whether to give African American freedmen the right to vote, the vast majority of Democratic Party supporters opposed the extension of suffrage rights. Moreover, the majority held that African Americans were biologically inferior to whites and therefore not fit for citizenship, that they had no claim to the constitutional rights created in 1787 and no rights that any whites needed to respect.[17] From 1840 through 1880, as the Democratic Party transformed itself from an elite political party to a mass-based party, the key party leaders pushed these ideas. The resultant image was of a white Democratic Party and government led by whites from a two-party system. Only in a few locales did an exception to this image emerge.

After the Civil War and the adoption of the 13th, 14th, and 15th Amendments, which made African Americans citizens and gave them the right to vote, northern Democratic leaders accepted the law but refused to use the power of the federal government to protect the rights of these newly minted citizens. Southern Democratic leaders were even more reactionary and slowly put into place a series of political strategies to block the national Democratic Party from using the federal government to interfere with their segregated way of life, which was based on the unscientific notion of inferiority.

The southern Democratic strategy was in place by 1880, and the reversal of civil rights policies came during the two administrations of Democratic president Grover Cleveland. The white control of the federal bureaucracy started during the presidency of Democrat Woodrow Wilson. Soon, this power led to the rise of the legislative organization known as the Southern Caucus or the Constitutional Democrats, headed by Senator Richard Russell of Georgia. Piece by piece, southern Democratic leaders reshaped the national party to conform to the southern mentality.

This southern dominance was in place when LBJ arrived in the House of Representatives in 1937. In fact, he paid homage to it and to Senator Russell's power and leadership when he made his first speech as senator in 1948, attacking President Truman's civil rights program, defending segregation, and declaring that the white South should be left alone. But LBJ attacked Truman's civil rights proposal as an invasion of the procedural rights of senators, not as a matter of Negro inequality as other Southerners did. He declared:

> What have these filibusters accomplished? . . . I want to list the bills which, so far, have failed to become law because of filibusters:
>
> First. The Force Bill of 1890.
>
> Second. The Armed ship bill of 1917, which was actually not necessary since our merchant ships were armed under another existing statute.
>
> Third. The Antilynching bills.
>
> Fourth. The Anti-poll-tax bills.
>
> Fifth. The FEPC [Fair Employment Practices Committee] bill.
>
> That, Mr. President is the list, the casualty list of filibusters. . . . Only five bills can truthfully be listed as victims of the filibuster.[18]

Therefore, according to Senator Johnson, who had been "a member of the Senate only 2 months,"[19] to vote on a resolution of cloture to limit each senator to one hour of debate on President Truman's new civil rights bill would harm freedom. Senator Johnson argued, "I believe the freedom to speak—the freedom of unlimited debate somewhere in our law-making process—is the keystone of all our other freedoms."[20] Thus, the argument here was not against giving African Americans their civil rights but the right of each senator to have unlimited debate. The Civil Rights Bill was defeated. Other southern Senators usually denied African American equality with a mixture of claims to white supremacy, cries of Negro inferiority, and worry over the need to protect white womanhood.[21] LBJ's rhetoric was devoid of the racial diatribes that flowed from his fellow southern congressmen.

Even before he moved to the Senate, LBJ had supported the South's position on poll taxes, on antilynching legislation, on white primaries, on limited African American voting, and on segregation as a way of life. But here and there he made small changes. First, he accepted African American voters into his electoral coalition, particularly in the special elections for the House and Senate in 1937, 1941, and 1948. When the Supreme Court made the white primaries unconstitutional in 1944, LBJ sought out

African American voters. His initial Senate speech saddened them, but their protest did not get a retraction from him. Even so, he sought out midwestern African American leaders in the 1956 presidential primaries.

Second, LBJ refrained from signing the Southern Manifesto that denounced the 1954 Supreme Court decision in *Brown vs. Board of Education of Topeka, Kansas.* Along with Senator Gore of Tennessee and Senator Kefauver of Tennessee, LBJ declined to go along with his fellow southerners. Senator Russell, who hoped for an LBJ presidential bid, permitted him to opt out. LBJ then helped Congress to pass the 1957 Civil Rights Act and added to this the 1960 Civil Rights Act, working to form both laws so that they would not "hurt the South" too much.

Third, LBJ accepted the vice presidency from liberal easterner John Kennedy in 1960. Here was another break with the southern political strategy. Johnson refused all attempts by his southern colleagues to get him to bypass the vice presidency and wait for a better time to get the top spot. These initial shifts, distancing him from the standard southern position, became major when he confronted the southern way of life from the presidency. It came with his speech to the nation after Kennedy's death in 1963. Yet most of his fellow southerners felt that this was simply a political tactic.

The fourth and most profound shift came when LBJ confronted Russell with the passage of the 1964 Civil Rights Act, the 1965 Voting Rights Act, and the 1968 Fair Housing Act. With these Acts, LBJ opposed the long tradition of the Democratic Party and its long-standing commitment to segregation, biological inferiority, and white supremacy that had begun with the Jeffersonian Democrats.

To make the point even more poignantly, Johnson not only confronted southern power in the Congress, he invited George Wallace to the White House and tried to influence him to permit African Americans to vote in Alabama. Wallace was the most outspoken of the southern Democratic leaders and had by 1964 started a grassroots movement inside the Democratic Party in the Midwest to cultivate opposition to the party's use of federal intervention to eliminate segregation.[22] Blue-collar workers in these states responded in large numbers to Wallace.

LBJ not only rebuked Wallace, Russell, and other weary supporters of this Democratic Party burden, he undercut that tradition with major African American cabinet, subcabinet, and Supreme Court appointments. He used an executive order to select an African American mayor for the District of Columbia. Johnson even transformed a long-standing party tradition by appointing African Americans to national party positions.

Could LBJ have waited for a bipartisan approach to the problem of exclusion and inequality? The truth of the matter is that it was Republicans Everett Dirksen in the Senate and William McCulloch in the House,[23] working with northern House Democrats, who passed the defining civil rights legislation of the sixties. Table 13.1 shows that most southern Democrats were opponents of this legislation. Had the Republicans not joined the enacting legislative coalition, it never would have passed. The Republican Party, which had few seats in the South at time, had little to fear from the southern electorate. Southern Democratic strategists had not counted on being abandoned by the Republicans at this crucial moment. In the past, simple arguments about states' rights and federal intervention had been enough to get Republican support. LBJ changed all of that with his

TABLE 13.1. Party Support Ratios for the 1957, 1960, 1964, and 1965 Civil Rights Acts

Total Party Categories	Proportion of Yes Votes	Proportion of No Votes	Total Number of Votes	Proportion of Yes Votes	Proportion of No Votes	Total Number of Votes
	House 1957 Act			Senate 1957 Act		
Total Vote	78	22	358	80	20	75
Republican Vote	91	9	166	100	0	37
Democratic Vote	61	39	210	61	39	38
Northern Democrats	99	1	107	100	0	19
Southern Democrats	21	79	103	21	79	19
	House 1960 Act			Senate 1960 Act		
Total Vote	75	25	383	79	21	90
Republican Vote	91	9	135	100	0	29
Democratic Vote	67	33	248	68	32	60
Northern Democrats	99	1	149	97	3	37
Southern Democrats	18	82	99	22	78	23
	House 1964 Act			Senate 1964 Act		
Total Vote	69	31	420	81	19	94
Republican Vote	80	20	172	100	0	0
Democratic Vote	61	39	248	72	28	64
Northern Democrats	97	3	145	100	0	42
Southern Democrats	11	89	103	18	82	22
	House 1965 Act			Senate 1965 Act		
Total Vote	82	18	402	80	20	96
Republican Vote	85	15	131	94	6	32
Democratic Vote	80	20	271	73	27	64
Northern Democrats	100	0	180	100	0	42
Southern Democrats	41	59	91	23	77	22

Source: Cheryl M. Miller and Hanes Walton Jr., "Congressional Support of Civil Rights Public Policy: From Bipartisan to Partisan Convergence," *Congress and The Presidency* 21 (Spring 1994): 16.

great legislative skill. Abandoned by their former allies, the infamous Southern Caucus collapsed, as did Wallace's forays into the Midwest Democratic primaries. LBJ prevailed and the southern tradition of tyranny and inhumanity deteriorated.

However, the presidential Republicans did not follow the lead of the congressional Republicans. Barry Goldwater's opposition to the 1964 Civil Rights Act became the new position of the Republican Party. He transformed the economic and politically conservative Republican Party into a racially conservative party. The party fought out this new ideology in the 1964 election and won five of the Deep South states. A new Republican Party had been formed.

According to Courtney Brown, two landslides occurred in the South in the 1964 presidential election. Many southern white Democrats realigned to the Republicans, while many others realigned with the rest of the Democratic Party in the nation.[24] In short, the southern Democratic electorate fractured, with one group staying inside the remade Democratic Party, and another shifting to the Republican Party, at least at the presidential level. In this manner, LBJ had also remade the Republican Party.

At this point one may ask, "From where did these realigning Democrats come?" Prior to the 1964 presidential election, the Republican Party in the South was emanating from the large cities and urban sectors of the 11 states of the old Confederacy.[25] Many southern political scientists, like Donald Strong in Alabama and Weeks in Texas, observed this rising tide of urban and metropolitan Republicanism particularly during the Eisenhower years, if not before.

But the political center for the realigning southern Democrats was the Black Belt. "It is outside of these two sectors [the traditional Republican areas and the suburbs] that sizable, though erratic, gains in Republican voting have been recorded."[26] This is precisely the area that Key identified in his 1949 classic as the most racist in the region.[27] These counties, with the largest numbers of African Americans and the smallest numbers of whites, were the most intransigent and the most violent in their racism. They had been the backbone of white resistance since the era of the Civil War.[28] It was now in this area that Democrats were shifting to the Republican Party. Such a realignment meant in the long run a shift in the Republican Party's civil rights policy. This was seen in the 1964 landslide election, when the first Black Belt realignment took place.[29]

The split between the presidential and congressional Republicans made it impossible for a bipartisan approach to the regional problem to emerge. In addition, such an action was against every party tradition.

Since their inception, American parties had never had a singular approach to the race issue. Only in 1948 did a bipartisan approach emerge; but when the Republicans won in 1952, the South persuaded the Democratic leadership to moderate their 1948 approach, and finally to abandon it in 1956.[30] Since then, each party has continued to pursue a separate and conflicting path to finding a solution to racism.

LBJ stepped into the breach in 1957, and gave the Democratic Party a new approach. The Republican Party tradition emanated from Lincoln's Emancipation Proclamation and the Civil War amendments and culminated in congressional Republicans' legislative behavior on the 1964 Civil Rights Bill. The Democrats finally established their new inclusion and support for equality tradition one hundred years later with LBJ in the pivotal leadership position, thereby remaking the two-party system.

LBJ, the Remade Democratic Party, and Its Legacy: Jimmy Carter

Another southerner, Jimmy Carter, became the first Democratic president to have to confront the legacy of an inclusive party left by LBJ. Humphrey and McGovern were not southerners, and both failed to build upon LBJ's new tradition. Humphrey had come close but had lost to the Republicans' capture of the southern white backlash vote. McGovern's own political mistakes along with Nixon's "dirty tricks" doomed him across the nation, and Nixon swept the entire South. But Nixon's failure to slow desegregation and the revelations of the Watergate investigation created a wonderful political opportunity for the peanut farmer from Georgia.

In 1976, Governor Carter won the entire South except Virginia. He defeated Wallace even in the southern primaries and made an alliance with Andrew Young and the King family to win the election.[31] In this manner, he was continuing the new Democratic Party tradition. Nevertheless, Carter could not keep the remobilized South with him, losing in 1980 to a candidate who had been moving quietly in the rural South since the nomination of Goldwater in 1964. Ronald Reagan had helped with Goldwater's nomination, and since that time he had been working the small-town southern whites into the Republican Party:

> When Reagan ducked in and out of the one-horse towns referred to in Southern idiom as wide-places-in-the-road, he found no Republican organizations to speak of. But he did find sympathetic and

> satisfied listeners who could tell neighbors: "He's the kind of person we need in the White House."[32]

In November, Carter carried only one southern state, his native Georgia, and even there his support was less than what it had been in 1976.

Carter's vice president, Walter Mondale, ran for president in 1984, along with Reverend Jesse Jackson. In 1988 it was Jackson and Governor Michael Dukakis. Neither the South nor the nation responded. The Democratic Party's new tradition was being opposed. The pundits were sure that LBJ had failed. McPherson was simply one among a chorus of voices that decried LBJ's party remaking efforts. The thesis was that the Democrats should take a tactic out of the Republican Party playbook and abandon the race issue.

LBJ, the Remade Democratic Party, and Its Legacy: Enter Clinton and the "New Democrats"

When Massachusetts governor Dukakis refused to accept the "liberal" label penned for him by the Republican spin doctors, it failed to move the southern Democrats toward his electoral coalition. In fact, it even stalled the movement of the African American electorate, North and South, toward him. Later, he finally embraced the label, because his pollsters did not see any southern white Democrats moving to his candidacy, despite Senator Lloyd Bentsen's urging. In 1988 the entire South voted for another native son, George H. W. Bush. LBJ's legacy was not failing to attract southern white males as much as the Republican Party was openly appealing to their lingering, covert racism. It was playing the race card in an overt fashion. Nevertheless, political pundits and scholars blamed the Democratic Party and specifically LBJ for doing the right thing. Like McPherson, they blamed African Americans for expecting the Democratic Party to support their constitutional rights beyond the rhetorical level. As LBJ's critics saw it, it was demanding too much from the party. One neoconservative, Aaron Wildavsky, said openly that

> [a]nyone can think of problems that remain unresolved. The decisive movement of blacks into the Democratic party, for instance, is not only bad for Democracy, it is also a barrier to the potential emergence of a Republican majority able to capture not only the presidency but also both houses of Congress. Should Mexican

> Americans also become overwhelmingly Democrat, the Republicans might forever remain a minority party.[33]

Seeing this criticism in hindsight, it was wrong and baseless. Yet it continued nevertheless.

Dukakis wrote off the South after he embraced the "liberal" label and sought to expand the Democratic Party base in the East, Midwest, and West. He did, but not enough to win the 1988 election. His second action was to distance himself from African Americans and their candidate, Jesse Jackson. Dukakis would not consider Jackson for the vice-presidential spot. However, Dukakis's changes caught the imaginative eye of several Democratic hopefuls—particularly Governor William Jefferson Clinton of Arkansas.

Following their 1988 loss, several southern and western Democrats in Congress and in gubernatorial positions created the Democratic Leadership Council to shift the party back to the right of center. They took a more conservative stance on issues that could help win back what had become known as the "Bubba Democrats" or the "Reagan Democrats." Another major concern of the DLC was the question of race and what to do about African Americans. Democratic pollster Stan Greenberg found that there was strong opposition among whites to African Americans, and that whites harbored the notion that the Democratic Party had given African Americans more than it had given them. Greenberg also found that whites who felt this way had caused a surge to the Republicans throughout the South.[34] Eventually the DLC began to redirect the party away from the LBJ legacy.

In the 1988 presidential primaries, Senator Al Gore Jr. had called his version of the LBJ party legacy the "New Democrats." Gore's effort failed, but his concept was reused in 1992 by Governor Clinton. Clinton attacked Jesse Jackson and his Rainbow Coalition, and rejected his effort to become a vice-presidential candidate. Clinton's embarrassment and put down of Jackson in front of his own annual National Rainbow Coalition Convention is said to have risen his rating in the public opinion polls by 10 percentage points.[35] This tactic, which had been put forward by his political advisers, the "raging Cajun" James Carville and George Stephanopoulos, was the second strategy used in the presidential primaries to reposition the LBJ-remade party.

Clinton's third tactic to reposition the Democratic Party away from LBJ's legacy and in line with the secret poll findings of Greenberg came during the presidential election contest with President Bush. During the entire contest, from Labor Day to November, Clinton rarely mentioned "race" and appeared disinterested in the concerns of the African American community, except to use them as foot soldiers in getting out the vote. Like Dukakis before him, the political distancing of the candidate and his promises marginalized the African American community. Economics, Clinton said, was the new civil rights.

Finally, to reattract the South and let the region know that he wanted them back in the Democratic fold, Clinton nominated a vice president from Tennessee. This move broke with tradition, away from the ticket balancing of the past. This seemed to some unusual, but what analysts missed was that given what Dukakis had accomplished for the party in the East, Midwest, and West, it was only the South that was a major question mark in Democratic presidential voting. Clinton was running against a native son of LBJ's Texas, and the South had been solidly Republican.

In retrospect, the New Democrat's effort to fashion a different political image for the party by having two southerners on the ticket was a bold initiative. But in the end, it was a reaction to the achievements of LBJ and his legacy for the party.

Unlike LBJ, however, Clinton's New Democrat was a repositioning of the party toward the right of center. While he called himself a middle-of-the-road, centrist Democrat, it was an effort to make the repositioned party of LBJ win again in the South. Clinton's repositioning strategy worked, and he won not one term but two. His long-term strategy was to leave another southerner, Al Gore, in place to carry on this New Democrat party image after his two terms were over. But in the 2000 election, because of a lackluster campaign, another southern Republican native son, and the failure to carry his own home state, Gore left the Clinton reaction to LBJ's party legacy unfinished.

Yet President Clinton did leave a party legacy of its own. Not only did he show the party elites how to recapture parts of the South, for each time he captured four southern states, he also could have won the presidency without these southern states. The recent scholarly literature on this matter written by political scientist Thomas Schaller declares, "Unlike Carter and Johnson, Clinton was a southern Democrat who won the presidency on the strength of non-southern votes. In that regard, he will be remembered as the first *northern* southern Democratic president."[36] Schaller continues, "The undeniable fact is that Clinton won twice not as a result of a Democratic revival in the South but despite the absence of one."[37] And finally a new theory develops for the future of the Democratic Party that gets beyond the ruling thesis that the Democratic Party made a mistake by intervening in southern cultural values and assisting the African American electorate in attaining political and legal justice. Again, he writes, "Far too many politicians and pundits continue to repeat the conventional wisdom that the Democrats must try to recapture the South. . . . It is a dangerously self-destructive form of political myopia that, left uncorrected, will only relegate the Democrats to minority party status for at least a generation."[38] His theory urges the Democratic Party to "let go of the New Deal coalition" simply because it is not necessary and it is absurd. Senator Obama offered proof, like President Clinton, that the Republican Party in the South is not as well planted as it seems and/or believed."[39] Obama won three southern states in the 2008 presidential election.

Overall, Carter, Clinton, and to some extent Gore all reacted to the remade party that LBJ had left in place. In turn, the Republican Party has been reacting to the remade Democratic Party of LBJ. If current southern regionalism is to be understood, one must grasp the role that party leaders can play in reshaping party politics in America. LBJ was a great example of a leader who comprehended this fundamental fact.

LBJ and the Theory of the Southern Native-Son Presidential Candidate

LBJ was the pioneering southern native-son presidential candidate who broke through the glass ceiling that had limited all previous southern hopefuls to the second spot on the Democratic ticket. Prior to LBJ, the aspirations of Garner, Sparkman, and Kefauver ended at this position. Since the Civil War, southern Democrats could go no higher than the vice presidency.

LBJ rose to the presidency because of a political assassination, but he went on to win the position on his own. With that election the glass ceiling fell. Now other ambitious southerners in both parties have followed LBJ through the glass ceiling and served in the White House. Several have come from Texas, the largest electoral prize in the region. LBJ's victory paved the way for others to follow, and they did.

Johnson ran and won in a southern state where friends-and-neighbors voting behavior did not exist during his three decades in public office, unlike Carter and Clinton who came from states where it is an ingrained feature of the political process. Hence, these latter two studies could not provide a comprehensive portrait of the native-son theory because they were characterized by a voting feature that was unique to their political contexts and political history.

Analyzing LBJ in Texas, in the total absence of this localism variable, we have observed that he found a different vote and a different set of strategies to win office, to continue in that office, and to move on to higher offices. Even when the county where he was born voted overwhelmingly against him, LBJ depended upon the New Deal and his "countryside liberalism" to maintain and expand his electoral coalitions. As he moved beyond the 10th Congressional District to the U.S. Senate, he found the right combination of political bosses, conservative moneymen, and centrist ideology to hold his Senate seat and the power it brought. Thus, LBJ's election shows that southern native sons can win the presidency without a friends-and-neighbors alliance, while Carter's and Clinton's electoral stories tell us that they can win with it.

What of the southern native-son presidents and the African American coalition? The Carter and Clinton case studies offer an empirical rendering that demonstrates that African American voters can join an electoral coalition not only at the beginning of their political odyssey but also later, after they have made their electoral starts. In Georgia, African Americans came to Carter's electoral coalition by the time of his runoff election for governor. In Arkansas, they joined Clinton in his 1982 comeback effort when he reached out to them in a major way. Both rising native-son candidates had African American support from day one, but the balance-of-power type of support came in critical elections and was a mainstay of their electoral coalitions ever since.

In addition, elites in African American communities—Andrew Young and the King family in Atlanta for Carter; the African American former mayor of Little Rock, Lottie Shackelford, Ernest Green of the Little Rock Nine, and several of his own African American law school students for Clinton—legitimated these southerners to northern African American leaders and Democratic Party activists. African Americans made these southern Democratic native-son presidential candidacies viable in the urban areas of the East, Midwest, and West.

Candidates supported by African Americans worked in intrastate elections and later in national elections. However, the limitation of the Carter and Clinton case studies for a native-son theory is that both men came to power at the state level and nationally in the post–Voting Rights Act era. They offer little insight into an earlier era. It is LBJ's elections in the thirties, forties, fifties, and early sixties that add a new dimension to the theory. Because LBJ began his congressional career by running in special elections, African Americans could vote for him despite the white primary laws. By the time of the 1941 special Senate election, African American voters from outside of Texas had sought out LBJ and formed an alliance with him, which became important when he started to have competitive Republican opposition. After the white primary was outlawed, the critical 1948 primary and runoff elections saw an African American alliance with this native son. Thus, LBJ, like Carter and Clinton later, because of the state's special elections law, got African American voter support even in the pre–voting rights era.

As to African American voter support outside of Texas, LBJ sought it in the Midwest when he launched his formal campaign for the presidency in 1956. His effort to get African American leaders in Detroit to back him did not capture much attention, so he moved to a different strategy, the passage of the 1957 and 1960 Civil Rights Acts. These legislative achievements brought northern African American voters into his national electoral coalition. LBJ was the first southern native-son candidate to do this openly; previous candidates would try to persuade northern African American politicians that they would be the lesser of the evils. LBJ's efforts showed those who would follow him that they needed to make the connection. Thus, Carter used Young and the Kings. Clinton used Shackelford and the long Democratic drought of the Reagan-Bush years to motivate African American Democrats to go to the polls. Clinton's limited outreach worked because of the LBJ legacy of the major civil rights laws. There were only symbolic gestures that needed to be made, and in this area Clinton excelled. It is important to note that Gore during his unsuccessful presidential run, like Clinton, not only distanced himself from the "liberal" mantle, he too offered little, at best mostly symbolic, effort to engage African Americans. However, the appointment of African American Donna Brazile as his national campaign chairperson was a major first, and she became the outreach tool to the African American community.[40]

Again, the conservative nature of congressional Republicans, led by Newt Gingrich, pushed the African American community toward the Clinton and Gore bandwagons, which they joined without making specific demands: a Democratic victory first, and demands later. This was a limited strategy, but it played quite well for the "New Democrats" and their centrist policy.

LBJ's case study reveals that given certain contextual conditions, African Americans can effectuate an alliance with a southern native-son candidate. It also shows that such candidates can come to the alliance with substantive public policy and offer more than symbols, vague promises, and selected high-level political appointments.[41]

Finally, LBJ's case study offers the example of pioneering party leadership in support of the fashioning of a native-son theory. Southern native-son presidents after LBJ could follow his example of remaking their political party. LBJ forced the Democratic Party to break with its century-old embrace of slavery, segregation, and color discrimination. Before he left the White House, the party had dropped its antidemocratic political image. The party was no longer a party of white supremacy. LBJ had shown that the president can do more than appoint the chairperson of the Democratic National Committee. In remaking his political party, the president can leave a legacy that then reshapes the entire party system.

Because of contextual factors, Clinton, more than Carter, tried to reposition the party away from the positive portrait derived from LBJ's remaking efforts. Although the southern Republican native-son from Texas, George W. Bush, attempted to make his party a more inclusive one for African Americans, he faltered in his handling of Hurricane Katrina and the complex legacy of his educational policy, No Child Left Behind, which, although he discussed it in terms of civil rights, had severe implications for African American children and majority Black school districts.[42] However, the election of a nonsoutherner, Senator Barack H. Obama, to the White House would be the fulfillment of the Johnson legacy.

Table 13.2 offers the testable propositions that have arisen out of this empirical case study of LBJ's elections. When these are combined with those flowing out of the Carter and Clinton studies, we will have the foundation for a theory of native-son presidents. But before we conclude our discussion on the variables in this native-son theory, we must analyze the LBJ legacy for the first African American president.

LBJ and His Party Legacy for the First African American President: President Obama and the 2008 and 2012 Presidential Elections

Finally, what of LBJ's remade party legacy for the first African American president? In order for Senator Obama to win the Democratic Party's nomination and the general election there had to be an expanded Democratic electorate. That meant that the racial and ethnic electorate had to be expanded via legal voting rights. LBJ achieved this through the type of political drama and struggle that could be used by the president to secure supportive public opinion from the nation and thereby push legislation through Congress with bipartisan support: the 1965 Voting Rights Act, which was a legislative legacy of LBJ's immense legislative skills and talents, called for an "executive-centered leadership" that protected Black voting rights.[43] Often overlooked was Johnson's engagement with the civil rights movement, particularly an often forgotten telephone call to Martin Luther King Jr. shortly after he went to Selma, Alabama, to assist the African American Dallas County Voter League to empower the community. It worked. And within seven years there was a rise in presidential primary

TABLE 13.2. The Testable Propositions for a Southern Native-Son Candidate: Part II

Contextual Factors
The Southern Native-Son Candidate has been a party leader
National Factors
The Southern Native-Son Candidate has been influential in national party leadership
The Southern Native-Son Candidate has had a relative or friend influential in national party leadership
State Factors
The localism variable is and/or is not influential in local, state and national elections
The native-son variable is and/or is not related to the localism variable
The Southern Native-Son candidate has a parent and/or relative in elective office
The Parent and/or relative's political district is or has been part of the district of the Nativeson's district
The Southern Native-Son candidate has established a presence/history in the district before he runs
Racial Factors
The Southern Native-Son has established roots and connections to the African American and Latino communities
The Southern Native-Son candidate has attained electoral endorsement from the African American and Latino communities
The Southern Native-Son candidate has attained electoral support from the African American and Latino electorates
The Southern Native-Son candidate has and/or is mobilizing the African American and Latino electoral support
Electoral Factors
State election laws allows the African American electorate to vote in Special, Municipal and General elections
The Southern Native-Son candidate's election organization is willing to pay the poll taxes of African American and Latino voters
The Southern Native-Son candidate supporters and political machines and bosses are willing to pay the poll taxes of African American and Latino voters
The African American community has political/civil rights leaders and organizations that are willing to pay the poll taxes of the community

Source: Adapted as an addendum to table 11.2 in Hanes Walton Jr., *Reelection: William Jefferson Clinton as a Native-Son Presidential Candidate* (New York: Columbia University Press, 2000), 233.

Note: These testable propositions were adopted from the political context in Arkansas during Clinton's tenure in elective office. These propositions emerged from the unique variables seen in the political context in Texas during LBJ tenure in elective office.

participation for a new voting group, the African American electorate in the South. Few paid this group any attention including most political scientists, pundits, commentators, and journalists. Most of these campaign observers and experts emphasized the very limited campaign of Congresswoman Shirley Chisholm in 1972 and the audacity of Reverend Jackson's 1984 and 1988 campaigns with his limited financial support. Such campaigns were dismissed as amateurish at best. All the while the registration rates of African Americans increased and significantly affected the Democratic Party. The poorly informed media analysts and observers would focus their conventional wisdom and consensus on Senator Obama in 2008. None of these self-styled experts bothered to consider an alternate hypothesis: What if Senator Obama could unify other racial and ethnic groups in his campaign, due to the simple fact that they, too, like African Americans have faced political discrimination and voter disenfranchisement in this country? LBJ had provided the legal right to vote to African Americans and other marginalized groups in the American political process. All Senator Obama had to do was organize them behind his presidential candidacy. The huge support from the African American electorate enabled Senator Obama to win most of the southern state primaries and their delegates. Eventually, the delegate lead from these southern states allowed him to become the frontrunner for the nomination.

Utilizing a deracialized campaign message, Obama received support from African Americans by triggering a sense of group consciousness and empowerment and for other groups the sense that the American Dream belonged to all Americans.[44] The 2008 presidential campaign produced the most racially and ethnically diverse electorate in the history of presidential elections, as nonwhites cast nearly one-third of the general election votes[45] and over 65 percent (15.9 million) of voting age African Americans voted in the election,[46] compared to 66.1 percent of white voters.

The impact of the African American vote was even more evident in the 2012 election. For the first time, black voter turnout in a presidential election exceeded white voter turnout, 66.2 percent to 64.1 percent.[47] Obviously, President Obama's reelection effort contributed to this but since 2000 the gap between black and white voters has been narrowing.

LBJ's 1964 Civil Rights Act allowed African Americans to become integrated into American society and its institutions, while the Voting Rights Act integrated them into political institutions and organizations. These pieces of legislation ushered in a new paradigm in terms of the relationship of Blacks as citizens of the state.

In 1965, Johnson gave the commencement address at Howard University. This speech was not only important because Howard University is one of the leading historically Black universities in this country, but the address also indicated a significant shift in what citizens should expect from government and society. "You do not take a person who, for years, has been hobbled by chains and liberate him, bring him up to the starting line of a race and then say, 'you are free to compete with all the others,' and still justly believe that you have been completely fair." Johnson continued, "We seek not just equality as a right and a theory, but equality as a fact and as a result."[48] Johnson was giving weight to the psychological, emotional, and material loss that Blacks faced as a result of the legacy of slavery and Jim Crow racism and asserting that the government had a responsibility to redress these problems. This vision of inclusion as well as the obligation of the federal government to ensure a better social, political, and economic climate for all Americans lent itself to Johnson advancing policies to address housing, education, and poverty. Prior to the 1964 Civil Rights Act, only partial involvement and participation by the federal government could have occurred. This shift in policy and perspective gave African Americans a greater opportunity for advancement to full citizenship that would manifest itself at the ballot box especially in votes for Democratic presidential candidates.

Third, part of LBJ's party legacy for African Americans was the adoption of the 24th Amendment abolishing the poll tax. In three different referenda his own state of Texas refused to abolish the poll tax, even though it had a greater impact on whites in the state than on Texas's African American electorate. Such an obstacle and barrier had burdened the African American electorate so long due to the fact that this law in Texas placed control of voting in the hands of white county tax registrars and took it out of the hands of ordinary voters. This burden not only lowered racial and ethnic registration but turnout as well. The potential for increased turnout from these groups led to the broadening of the Democratic Party coalition that would eventually elect Obama. It lifted the first African American to the presidency.

LBJ's remarks upon the certification of the 24th Amendment again spoke to his policy agenda, which understood the complexities of oppression, poverty, and the value of the franchise:

> Today, the United States witnesses the triumph of liberty over restriction. Today, the people of this land have abolished the poll tax as a condition to voting. By this act they have reaffirmed the simple but unbreakable theme of this Republic. Nothing is so valuable as

> liberty, and nothing is so necessary to liberty as the freedom to vote without bans or barriers.
>
> Our Constitution in its 175-year lifetime has been amended but 14 times following the ratification of the Bill of Rights. A change in our Constitution is a serious event. The beneficiaries of this amendment are the people of this land.
>
> There can now be no one too poor to vote. There is no longer a tax on his rights. The only enemy to voting that we face today is indifference. Too many of our citizens treat casually what other people in other lands are ready to die for.
>
> Less than two-thirds of our eligible population cast ballots in the 1960 presidential election. Perhaps this specific act of firm resolve will turn negligence into interest. I pray that this is so.
>
> I will not let this historic event pass on without paying special tribute to my old and dear friend and former colleague Senator Spessard Holland of Florida. He led this fight from the beginning. He was in the forefront in the winning.
>
> I salute the States of South Dakota and Georgia. They raced to the wire to be the 38th and necessary State for ratification. South Dakota won that race but we are all victors. This is the first time an amendment to the Constitution has been certified in the presence of the President of the United States. I am proud that I am here. I am prouder still to place my name on this certificate.[49]

Finally, as president, LBJ made key political appointments, such as Thurgood Marshall to the Supreme Court, Robert Weaver to the newly created Department of Housing and Urban Development, and several others to subcabinet posts. This was not only innovative and would enable other presidents to do so, but it said to African Americans that, beyond the simple act of voting and political participation, they could now aspire to the highest political offices in the land. Although there were several other ways that LBJ laid the foundation for the coming of an African American president, the ways in which we have connected and linked his legacy to President Obama allows one to seek the empirical linkages.

Beyond the legal voting legacy left by LBJ, there is the matter of his political rhetoric. He adopted the theme of the civil rights movement: "We shall overcome." No president before had used these words, not have they since then. Thus, he gave the movement legitimacy, as well as embraced the ideals within the democratic principles of the nation, connecting them with justice, morality, and the values of the Founding Fathers. This moved his presidency and the federal government onto the side of the civil rights leaders and activists. Their struggle was not only recognized but put into the reform impulses and enlightened values of the nation. This gave the African American protest a value and cause that was indeed in the long tradition of the American democratic experiment. Such a positioning placed their critics and opponents outside of the human family and those who cherished America's democratic standing. It was something with a purpose, and it was not just for the African American community but also for the nation and its future generations. Civil rights have inherent value and a place inside the American democratic experiment both then and now. It became the nation's calling. But political rhetoric is not like legal voting rights; it is more abstract, and, in an era of quantitative social science, it is far more difficult to express empirically even though it is just as influential and impactful as the legal rules and regulations.

Collectively, LBJ'S legacy for the Obama presidency is not only established in institutional and legal contexts, but also in psychological ones. And clearly one saw in the Obama campaign, in both the primaries and the general election, the unique manner in which he expressed the psychological variable in his words, speeches, and debates on both the political stump and in the media. As Senator Obama debated for the reauthorization of the Voting Rights Act in 2006 and during his campaigns, he often referenced the role of persons, such as John Lewis, in seeking voting rights. And these psychological features of the campaign moved both black and white voters. LBJ was still affecting the outcome. The legacy of protecting African Americans' citizenship, increased executive power, and the expansion of the electorate are embedded in the electoral success of Barack Obama. This was probably best stated prior to Election Day 2008 by Richard Cohen: "If the polls are right, if it don't rain and the creek don't rise, the winner of the presidential election is sure to be . . . Lyndon Baines Johnson."[50]

Appendix

The Election Data—A Research Note

To develop an empirical theory of the native-son variable, this and previous case studies have had to rely upon aggregate election data.[1] There are several reasons for this. First, the native-son variable is missing from survey and polling questionnaires and their subsequent analysis and interpretations. Second, election data are the only empirical sources of information that exist for the sundry electoral races that native-son presidential candidates have entered over their entire political careers. Third, all of the earlier studies of the native-son variable rest on aggregate election return data. Finally, these data can provide testable propositions that future studies might use to perform microlevel analyses.

Edward Tufte stated, "Quantitative techniques will be more likely to illuminate if the data analyst is guided in methodological choices by a substantive understanding of the problem he or she is trying to learn about. Good procedures in data analysis involve techniques that help to (a) answer the substantive questions at hand, (b) squeeze all the relevant information out of the data, and (c) learn something new about the world."[2] Analytical procedures and models have been adopted here to enable "the investigator to compare cases which have a range of characteristics in common, but which also differ in other crucial aspects. In a very real sense, theory can only be advanced to the degree that we develop generalizations about behavior that hold in varying contexts or, alternatively, that specify the conditions under which the contextual factors interact with and modify particular relationships that obtain in other situations."[3] Aggregate election data and a demographic framework provide the continuing standard features and characteristics in the case studies of the variable that are "necessary to the development of sound theory."[4]

Texas, like Arkansas, did not have a statewide voter registration system. Poll tax receipts sufficed for, if they did not substitute for, a registration system. Voters had to present this receipt at the polling place if they wanted to vote.[5] However, this procedure was not followed systematically in Texas, and it does not provide a comprehensive paper trail as to the actual number of registered voters in the state. Poll tax payments and receipts were not retained consistently by the state of Texas, as they were in Arkansas.[6]

As for the existence of aggregate election return data for Texas, particularly in the years when LBJ was in public office, Walter Dean Burnham noted, "Texas and its neighbor Arkansas have by all odds been at the qualitative and quantitative bottom in official elections reporting."[7] Another scholar added, "Students and politicians alike have suffered from a lack of available Texas election statistics. The state does not publish official returns of general elections and does not even have a record of returns in most party primaries."[8] For the period of LBJ's political career (1937–64), as well as the years when his father Sam Ealy Johnson was in the Texas House of Representatives (1904–6, 1918–22), the official printed sources are scattered, missing, incomplete, or nonexistent. The Texas State Archives does not contain many election records simply because the state did not collect them in the first place.[9] This was a task left to the Texas Election Bureau, a nonstate agency, which calls into question the reliability of the reported election data. The Texas Election Bureau published the results of each election in the *Texas Almanac*, as the *Dallas Morning News* explained:

> The Texas Election Bureau, headquartered in the *Dallas News* Building, 801 Commerce Street, Dallas, gathers and tabulates returns from Texas elections for Texas newspapers. It is an unincorporated cooperative non-profit agency set up each election year by Texas newspapers, under supervision of a committee of five selected by the Texas Managing Editors' Association.[10]

Prior to the Bureau's move to Dallas, the *Texas Almanac* was published in Galveston, by the *Galveston News*. The *Almanac* carried only *some* of the state's election return data. During LBJ's career, the candidates themselves reported their results to the Texas Election Bureau, which subsequently reported the data in the *Texas Almanac*. A summary interpretation of the *Almanac* data has been published that reviews the problems inherent in this data reporting system and the limitations of the Bureau's collection and publication process. This compendium provides both official and unofficial totals for all the presidential races from 1848 to 1988, for senatorial primary (1912–66) and general elections (1916–90), and for gubernatorial primary (1908–90) and general elections (1845–1990).[11]

While it was a major data source for this book, the *Texas Almanac* did not contain information on LBJ's congressional elections in particular or any House of Representatives elections in general. It did carry LBJ's 1941 special election data but only for four candidates. It carried the 1948 primary data for only 11 candidates, and the 1954 data for two candidates; but the 1960 primary data are missing altogether. In terms of the general election data, it covered three candidates in 1948 and in 1954, two in 1960, and three in 1964 and 1968. Since there were more candidates than those reported on by the Bureau, or at least published in the *Almanac*, other sources had to be used to complete the present study.

The Texas Almanac can be found in the Texas public college and university libraries, and at the State Archives in Austin. The data from earlier elections must be photocopied by the researchers, although more recent years of the *Almanac* are available for sale.[12] While it is a very good source for older election data, it is a commercial publication, and therefore the absence of some data must be noted. For example, in its 1942–44 edition the following notice appeared: "Usually the *Texas Almanac* has published full details, including county-by-county tabulations, of all races for state offices. This year only the more important races are given in the county-by-county tables on the following pages."[13]

Thus, the *Almanac* failed to provide any primary election return data for LBJ. For 1942, it did give the total primary vote but no county-level breakdown. A recent effort to track down this information through the Dallas News Research Library proved to be unsuccessful. Research librarian Judy Sall told us to check with the state Democratic Party headquarters in Austin.[14] That too proved to be a dead end. Despite the *Almanac*'s notice that the "tabulations for races not reported . . . are available on supplementary sheets and will be sent free of charge by the *Texas Almanac* to anyone requesting them,"[15] this information seemingly was not kept by the *Almanac* nor reported in its recent compilation.

The Texas Secretary of State election return data are also compiled by and available at the State Archives. The data for 1857 to 1977 have been microfilmed and copies are made available to researchers. However, for many years the *Election Register* is devoid of a useful index; hence, one must scan carefully through the numerous reels to find the years and political races of interest.

The *Election Register* does not contain return data for members of the Texas House and Senate for the years of Sam Ealy Johnson's time in office. This led to a search for county election certificates for these years. The State Archives had only a small number of these certificates, as not all counties provided the Secretary of State's office with the general election returns, or at least they were not retained. Today, one finds all of the extant county election certificates tossed together in a disorganized fashion in one large lidless box.

There are no data in the *Election Register* for LBJ's 1940 and 1942 primary elections, not even total returns. In the 1948 general election some 41 counties did not even report their results; Heard and Strong compiled these data from newspaper sources and unofficial results.[16]

However, despite the existence of many compendia on presidential and senatorial elections, data on LBJ's 1948 runoff and general elections remain unavailable, simply because numerous counties did not report their results.

Nevertheless, the *Election Register* does provide the names of all the candidates who ran in these primary and general elections, even where there were 29 candidates. Such information is essential if a comprehensive statistical analysis is to be undertaken.

Finally, there are the *America Votes* series and the *Congressional Quarterly's Guide to U.S. Elections*, which proved quite helpful when it became necessary to supplement the Texas returns and provide coverage for states other than Texas. These two sources were essential to this empirically based analysis.[17] Data on the delegate votes at national conventions were taken from the *Congressional Quarterly Almanac*.

Before closing, a word must be said about the election data available in personal collections. At the Lyndon Baines Johnson Presidential Library there are collected election returns data, even down to the precinct level for some elections. However, this collection is spotty and also is missing the data for the 1940 and 1942 primary elections. After LBJ became the Senate majority leader, the librarian of the United States Senate Library requested copies of all of his election returns. Although LBJ's submission did not contain a copy of his 1938 primary election returns, a certified copy of the county-level returns from the Democratic Party were in his papers. These 1938 primary returns exist nowhere else, not in the *Election*

Register, the *Almanac*, or in a recent compilation; they exist only in the House of Representatives Box 3. We were glad that further research uncovered these missing data.

The James Allred collection at the University of Houston did not contain any additional data for these crucial missing years, but some of its clippings on W. Lee O'Daniel, his newspaper, and African Americans were invaluable. Librarian Bobby Marlin was quite helpful in guiding one in the use of this collection, and even did other research in trying to help our research forays to locate the missing LBJ election data.[18]

As the search for these missing data broadened, the Margaret Carter Papers and the Texas AFL-CIO collection at the University of Texas at Arlington filled more gaps. Especially helpful were the election returns published in George Norris Green's *The Establishment in Texas Politics: The Primitive Years, 1938–1957*.[19] Again, while there was nothing on the missing LBJ data, the precinct data for African American voters for these years were superb. These data revealed how African Americans outside of the Black Belt counties voted for the Democratic Party, and offered an urban portrait as well.

Collectively, these sources augmented each other to such an extent that it was possible to obtain a *nearly* comprehensive collection of all of LBJ's special, primary, and general election return data, except for the 1940 and 1942 primary elections. To obtain this information it was necessary to review the county newspapers in the 10th Congressional District. The Texas State Archives did not have a comprehensive collection of Texas newspapers, and none for the 10 counties that made up LBJ's district. However, the Center for American History, which is located in the Johnson Presidential Library complex at the University of Texas at Austin, has an extensive collection of state newspapers. The collection proved most helpful and included access to the *Dallas Morning News* for both of the missing years. There were three county newspapers that had the county election return data for 1940 and five for 1942. One of these was in German, but it carried the 1942 election return data for Lee County.[20] We thank a colleague, Dr. Claudio M. Ritter, for translating the July 30, 1942, issue for the book.

In order to craft a political and electoral portrait of the context in Texas and get beyond the sketchy, spotty, and missing election return data, this book used county-level data in presidential elections from the Congressional Quarterly's *Guide to U.S. Elections*, 3rd edition; Richard Scammons's *America Votes* series, volumes 1–24; Alice McGillivray and Richard Scammons, *America at the Polls*, vol. 8, 1920–56, and vol. 2, 1960–92; the Texas

Secretary of State *Election Register*; and Michael Nelson's *Guide to the Presidency*. The delegate votes at national conventions for Texas native-son presidential candidates were taken from the *Congressional Quarterly Almanac* for those presidential years. The same procedure was used for other southern native-son presidential candidates.

The Local Election Data

Research for precinct-level election data led to the Travis County Courthouse in Austin to follow the vote from African American, Latino, and white districts. Records did not exist for the missing elections, 1940 and 1942. In fact, there were few primary election records in the county for most of LBJ's congressional elections. Only general election data were available. Since LBJ had competition only in the primaries in 1944 and 1946, the extant local data offered little. It was not possible to provide a comprehensive analysis of precinct-level primary elections. However, precinct data were available in the cities of Dallas, Fort Worth, and Waco for LBJ's senatorial elections; and they have been included in this book. These data were used for the tables in chapter 6.

The African American Election Data

Previous studies on Arkansas and Georgia benefited from the existence of precinct-level data on African American voting behavior. However, election return data are not readily available for African Americans in Texas.

The initial African American voter registration was undertaken by the United States Army.[21] Senate Executive Document 53 provides *partial* county-by-county voter registration data. In addition, the Texas State Archives contain a document entitled *Voters' Registration: 1867*, which has "names of voters who registered in the period between 1867 and 1869. A few entries date from 1870, but these occur infrequently. . . . [R]ace is noted when the registrant was 'colored.' Ledger entries are grouped by county, and the names are listed chronologically in the order individuals presented themselves for registration"[22] Texas state archivist Sergio Valento generously made all of this information available for the book via the senior author.

The election data on the Black and Tan Republican candidates for president and statewide offices in 1920 were found in the State Archives' *Elec-*

tion Register and in the Archives' holding of county election certificates for these African American candidates.[23] The 1950 data were taken from the 1957 United States Civil Rights Commission Report. Other data came from academic- and foundation-based studies and from the Census Bureau's *Current Population Reports*. These data provided the basis for chapters 6 and 7.

The Survey Data

Unlike Arkansas and Georgia, Texas had a state poll called "the Texas Poll," conducted by Joe Belden. This poll was in existence during the LBJ election years, and some of the preelection polls that described electoral support for LBJ, especially in the 1948 Senate primary and runoff elections, were consulted and analyzed.

Several national polls were referenced, such as Gallup, Harris, and Roper, which captured preelection polling data on the Kennedy-Johnson and the Johnson-Humphrey tickets. These poll results are available at the Johnson Presidential Library, the Roper Center, and the Inter-University Consortium for Political and Social Research. For an analysis of LBJ's use of public opinion polls, see the book by Bruce Altschuler.[24]

These data offered interesting insights into the competitive nature of LBJ's senatorial, vice presidential, and presidential races. Nevertheless, this survey material on LBJ's elections, like his election return data, is scattered and incomplete. In addition, it is not detailed enough, nor does it provide enough cases, to capture insights about the different segments of the Texas electorate during LBJ's time in public life to be able to provide a comprehensive and systematic portrait of the Texas electorate. This task had to be undertaken using the available election return data. Overall, it is the data from LBJ's 21 elections that provide the basis for the empirical analysis of the native-son variable in Texas.

Notes

FOREWORD

1. Hanes Walton Jr., *Black Politics: A Theoretical and Structural Analysis* (New York: J. P. Lippincott, 1972), 161.

2. Hanes Walton Jr., *The Native Son Presidential Candidate: The Carter Vote in Georgia* (New York: Praeger, 1992); Hanes Walton Jr., *Reelection: William Jefferson Clinton as a Native-Son Presidential Candidate* (New York: Columbia University Press, 2000).

3. Robert A. Caro, *The Years of Lyndon Johnson: The Passage to Power* (New York: Alfred A. Knopf, 2012), 144.

4. Ibid., 155.

5. Walton, *Reelection*, 27.

6. The data for the analysis of the four Democratic southern native-son candidates in Rhode Island were gathered with the assistance of Ellen Hunter, a 2004 Brown University honors graduate in political science.

7. The outcome of the 2000 presidential election, in which "native-son" candidate Vice President Al Gore did not win a single southern state, including his home state of Tennessee, illustrated the potential limitations of this strategy.

PREFACE

1. Robert Caro, *The Years of Lyndon Johnson: The Passage to Power* (New York: Alfred Knopf, 2012), xiv–xv.

2. Angus Campbell, Phillip Converse, Warren Miller, and Donald E. Stokes, *The American Voter* (Chicago: University of Chicago Press, 1960).

3. See Mike Kingston, Sam Attlesey, and Mary Crawford, *The Texas Almanac's Political History of Texas* (Austin: Eakin Press, 1992), which is a compilation of some of the county-level almanac data for some of the top statewide elections.

4. Ibid., 34.

5. See Hanes Walton Jr., Oliver Jones Jr., and Pearl K. Ford, "African American Political Socialization: The Protest Resignations of Councilpersons Jerome Woody and Renee Baker," in *African American Power and Politics: The Political Context Variable*, ed. Hanes Walton Jr. (New York: Columbia University Press, 1997), 113–28.

6. See Pearl K. Ford, ed., *African Americans in Georgia: A Reflection of Politics and Policy in the New South* (Macon, GA: Mercer University Press, 2010).

7. See Hanes Walton Jr. et al., "The Literature on African American Presidential Candidates," *Journal of Race & Policy* (2008): 103–24; Hanes Walton Jr., Josephine A. V. Allen, Sherman Puckett, and Donald R. Deskins Jr., "The Red and Blue State Divide in Black and White: The Historic 2008 Election of President Barack Obama," *Black Scholar* 38 (2008): 19–30; Hanes Walton Jr., Josephine A. V. Allen, Sherman C. Puckett, and Donald R. Deskins Jr., "Black Politicians: Paving the Way," in *African Americans and the Presidency: The Road to the White House*, ed. Bruce Glasrud and Cary Wintz (New York: Routledge, 2010), 167–86; and Hanes Walton Jr., Josephine A. V. Allen, Sherman C. Puckett, and Donald R. Deskins Jr., "Dead Certain: The Election of Barack Obama and Its Implications for Racial Politics," in *The Obama Phenomenon: Toward a Multiracial Democracy*, ed. Charles Henry, Robert Allen, and Robert Chisman (Urbana: University of Illinois Press, 2011), 80–81.

CHAPTER 1

1. Hanes Walton Jr., *The Native Son Presidential Candidate: The Carter Vote in Georgia* (New York: Praeger, 1992), and Hanes Walton Jr., *Reelection: William Jefferson Clinton as a Native-Son Presidential Candidate* (New York: Columbia University Press, 2000).

2. See Harold F. Gosnell, *Grass Roots Politics: National Voting Behavior of Typical States* (Washington, DC: American Council on Public Affairs, 1942), 13.

3. V. O. Key Jr. described voting behavior in which candidates receive an overwhelming majority in their home counties and surrounding areas as "friends and neighbors," and also as "localism." Such voting behavior is predominantly associated with support of the "home boy," but may also be associated with an issue that directly impacts the respective area. See *Southern Politics in State and Nation* (New York: Alfred A. Knopf, 1949).

4. Angus Campbell, Phillip Converse, Warren Miller, and Donald E. Stokes, *The American Voter* (Chicago: University of Chicago Press, 1960).

5. Walton, *Native Son*, xxi–xxv. See also Betty Glad, *Jimmy Carter: In Search of the Great White House* (New York: W. W. Norton, 1980).

6. For the theoretical work on this variable, see Michael S. Lewis-Beck and Tom W. Rice, "Localism in Presidential Elections: The Home State Advantage," *American Journal of Political Science* 27, no. 3 (1983): 548–60; and Steven J. Rosenstone, *Forecasting Presidential Elections* (New Haven: Yale University Press, 1983).

7. Philip E. Converse and Donald R. Kinder, "Voting and Electoral Behavior," in *A Telescope on Society: Survey Research and Social Science at the University of Michigan and Beyond*, ed. James S. House et al. (Ann Arbor: University of Michigan Press, 2004), 70–75. See also Paul F. Lazarsfeld, Bernard Berelson, and Hazel Gaudet, *The People's Choice*, 3rd ed. (New York: Columbia University Press, 1968).

8. Converse and Kinder, "Voting and Electoral Behavior," 80. On the limitations and weaknesses of the "funnel of causality" metaphor, see Heinz Eulau, "Electoral Survey Data and the Temporal Dimension," in *Elections at Home and Abroad: Essays in Honor*

of Warren E. Miller, ed. M. Kent Jennings and Thomas Mann (Ann Arbor: University of Michigan Press, 1994), 39–70.

9. See Warren E. Miller and Teresa E. Levitin, *Leadership and Change: Presidential Elections from 1952–1976* (Cambridge: Winthrop Publishers, 1976); and Warren E. Miller and J. Merrill Shanks, *The New American Voter* (Cambridge: Harvard University Press, 1996).

10. See Jack Dennis, "The Study of Electoral Behavior," vol. 3 of *Political Science: Looking to the Future*, ed. William Crotty (Evanston, IL: Northwestern University Press, 1991), 51–89; and also Mark N. Franklin and Christopher Wlezien, eds., *The Future of Election Studies* (New York: Pergamon, 2002).

11. For a sharp critique of the series of case studies, see Pamela Johnston Conover, "Political Socialization: Where's the Politics?," vol. 3 of *Political Science: Looking to the Future*, ed. William Crotty (Evanston, IL: Northwestern University Press, 1991), 125–52; and Timothy E. Cook, "The Bear Market in Political Socialization and the Costs of Misunderstood Psychological Theories," *American Political Science Review* 79, no. 4 (1985): 1079–93.

12. M. Kent Jennings, "Survey Research and Political Socialization," in *A Telescope on Society: Survey Research and Social Science at the University of Michigan and Beyond*, ed. James S. House et al. (Ann Arbor: University of Michigan Press, 2004), 101.

13. See Warren E. Miller, *Without Consent: Mass-Elite Linkages in Presidential Politics* (Lexington: University Press of Kentucky, 1988); and Warren E. Miller and M. Kent Jennings, *Parties in Transition: A Longitudinal Study of Party Elites and Party Supporters* (New York: Russell Sage Foundation, 1986).

14. Leon D. Epstein, "National Party Conventions: Changing Functions, New Research Strategies," in *Elections at Home and Abroad: Essays in Honor of Warren E. Miller*, ed. M. Kent Jennings and Thomas Mann (Ann Arbor: University of Michigan Press, 1994), 280.

15. Ibid., 281.

16. One example of this series is Gerald M. Pomper et al., *The Election of 1976: Reports and Interpretations* (New York: David McKay, 1977).

17. Walton, *Reelection*, 233.

18. See table 3.1 in this book.

19. V. O. Key Jr., *Southern Politics in State and Nation* (New York: Alfred A. Knopf, 1949), 38, 259, 302.

CHAPTER 2

1. James David Barber, *Politics by Humans: Research on American Leadership* (Durham: Duke University Press, 1988), 442.

2. Clinton Rossiter, *The American Presidency* (New York: Harcourt, Brace and Company, 1956), 16.

3. Ibid., 44.

4. Ibid.

5. Ibid., 43.

6. Rossiter repeats and extends these insights in his second edition of *The American Presidency* (New York: Harcourt, Brace and World, 1960), 30–33, 61–64.

7. Richard E. Neustadt, *Presidential Power: The Politics of Leadership* (New York: John Wiley and Sons, 1960), 186, 187.

8. Ibid., 186. Neustadt continued this observation in his second volume. See Richard E. Neustadt, *Presidential Power: The Politics of Leadership with Reflections on Johnson and Nixon* (New York: John Wiley, 1976), 254–59.

9. Ralph M. Goldman, "Titular Leadership of the Presidential Parties," in *The Presidency*, ed. Aaron Wildavsky (Boston: Little, Brown, 1969), 384–85.

10. Ibid., 387.

11. Ibid., 385.

12. Ralph Goldman, "Titular Head of Party," in *Political Parties and Elections in the United States: An Encyclopedia*, ed. L. Sandy Maisel (New York: Garland, 1991), 1121.

13. Thomas R. Dye and L. Harmon Zeigler, *The Irony of Democracy: An Uncommon Introduction to American Politics*, 5th ed. (Monterey, CA: Duxbury Press, 1981), 249.

14. Ibid., 288, 291.

15. Thomas R. Dye, *Politics in America*, 2nd ed. (Upper Saddle River, NJ: Prentice-Hall, 1997), 402.

16. Kenneth Janda, Jeffrey Berry, and Jerry Goldman, *The Challenge of Democracy*, 5th ed. (Boston: Houghton Mifflin, 1974), 416.

17. Ibid., 279.

18. Larry Berman and Bruce Allen Murphy, *Approaching Democracy*, 2nd ed. (Upper Saddle River, NJ: Prentice-Hall, 1999), 194.

19. Benjamin Ginsberg, Theodore J. Lowi, and Margaret Weir, *We the People: An Introduction to American Politics*, 2nd ed. (New York: W. W. Norton, 1999), 517.

20. William Lasser, *American Politics: The Enduring Constitution, Second Edition* (Boston: Houghton Mifflin, 1999), 370–71.

21. Walton, *Reelection*, 237–52.

22. Barbara Bardes, Mack Shelly II, and Steffen Schmidt, *American Government and Politics Today: The Essentials* (Boston: West Wadsworth, 1998), 404.

23. W. Lance Bennett, *Inside the System: Culture, Institutions, and Power in American Politics* (Fort Worth: Harcourt Brace College, 1994), 518.

24. David V. Edwards and Alessandra Lippucci, *Practicing American Politics: An Introduction to Government* (New York: Worth Publishers, 1998), 441, table 12.1.

25. V. O. Key Jr., *Politics, Parties, and Pressure Groups*, 4th ed. (New York: Thomas A. Cromwell, 1958), 612.

26. Samuel J. Eldersveld and Hanes Walton Jr., *Political Parties in American Society*, 2nd ed. (Boston: Bedford/St. Martin's, 2000), 113.

27. Ibid., 114. For more on this point, see Samuel J. Eldersveld, *Political Parties: A Behavioral Analysis* (Chicago: Rand McNally & Company, 1964).

28. Eldersveld and Walton, *Political Parties*, 113.

29. Ibid., 102–23.

30. Paul Allen Beck, *Party Politics in America*, 8th ed. (New York: Addison Wesley Longman, 1997), 338.

31. Ibid.

32. Cornelius P. Cotter, "Eisenhower as Party Leader," *Political Science Quarterly* 98, no. 2 (1983): 256.

33. Ibid., 255, 262, 265–66, 268–69.

34. Ibid., 260.

35. Ibid., 275–78.
36. Ibid., 277.
37. Ibid., 283.
38. Ibid., 260.
39. Sean J. Savage, *Roosevelt: The Party Leader 1932–1945* (Lexington: University Press of Kentucky, 1991), 186.
40. Ibid., 129–58; See also Charles M. Price and Joseph Boskin, "The Roosevelt 'Purge': A Reappraisal," *Journal of Politics* 28, no. 3 (1966): 660–70; for a period analysis, see J. B. Shannon, "Presidential Politics in the South: 1938, I," *Journal of Politics* 1, no. 2 (1939): 146–70, and his "Presidential Politics in the South—1938, II," *Journal of Politics* 1, no. 3 (1939): 278–300.
41. Savage, *Roosevelt*, 129–58; and Shannon, "Presidential Politics in the South—1938 II," 282–88, 296.
42. Savage, *Roosevelt*, 157.
43. Ibid., 186–87.
44. Sean J. Savage, *Truman and the Democratic Party* (Lexington: University Press of Kentucky, 1997), 204.
45. Ibid., 205.
46. Ibid.
47. Sean J. Savage, "To Purge or Not to Purge: Hamlet Harry and the Dixiecrats," *Presidential Studies Quarterly* 27, no. 4 (1997): 773–90.
48. Sidney M. Milkis, *The President and the Parties: The Transformation of the American Party System since the New Deal* (New York: Oxford University Press, 1993). See also Milkis, "Franklin D. Roosevelt and the Transcendence of Partisan Politics," *Political Science Quarterly* 100, no. 3. (1985): 479–504; Milkis, "Presidents and Party Purges: With Special Emphasis on the Lessons of 1938," in *Presidents and Their Parties: Leadership or Neglect?*, ed. Robert Harmel (New York: Praeger, 1984); and Milkis, "The Presidency and Political Parties," in *The Presidency and the Political System*, ed. Michael Nelson, 2nd ed. (Washington, DC: Congressional Quarterly, 1988), 331–49.
49. Milkis, *The President and the Parties*, 123.
50. Ibid., 124.
51. Roger G. Brown and David M. Welborn, "Presidents and Their Parties: Performance and Prospects," *Presidential Studies Quarterly* 12, no. 3 (1982): 305–8, fig. 1.
52. Ibid., 308.
53. Ibid., 313.
54. Ibid., 308.
55. Milkis, *The President and the Parties*, 178–79.
56. Ibid., 179.
57. Ibid., 183.
58. Ibid., 177.
59. Ibid., 205.
60. Harold F. Bass Jr., "Presidential Party Leadership and Party Reform: Lyndon B. Johnson and the MFDP Controversy," *Presidential Studies Quarterly* 21, no 1 (1991): 97.
61. Ibid., 85–97.
62. Hanes Walton Jr., *Black Republicans: The Politics of the Black and Tans* (Metuchen, NJ: Scarecrow Press, 1975), 45–150. See also Hanes Walton Jr., *Black Political Parties* (New York: Free Press, 1972), 67–79.

63. See Leslie Burl McLemore, "The Freedom Democratic Party and the Changing Political Status of the Negro in Mississippi" (master's thesis, Atlanta University, 1965); McLemore, "The Mississippi Freedom Democratic Party: A Case Study of Grass-Roots Politics" (PhD diss., University of Massachusetts, 1971); and McLemore, "Mississippi Freedom Democratic Party," *Black Politician* 3, no. 2 (1971): 19–23.

64. Bass, "Presidential Party Leadership and Party Reform: Lyndon B. Johnson and the MFDP Controversy," 90–91.

65. Ibid., 95.

66. Ibid., 97.

67. Ibid.

68. Ibid., 96.

69. Ralph M. Goldman, "The American President as Party Leader: A Synoptic History," in *Presidents and Their Parties: Leadership or Neglect?*, ed. Robert Harmel (New York: Praeger, 1984), 50.

70. Brown and Welborn, "Presidents and Their Parties," 313. One can also find hints of this in Harold F. Bass, "The President and the National Party Organization," in *Presidents and Their Parties: Leadership or Neglect?*, ed. Robert Harmel (New York: Praeger, 1984), 59–89.

71. Rowland Evans and Robert Novak, "Later Than LBJ Thinks," *Washington Post*, December 2, 1966.

72. Rowland Evans and Robert Novak wrote a political biography of LBJ, which came out before the 1966 midterm elections and the massive Democratic congressional losses. In this volume, Evans and Novak blamed the party failures not on LBJ but on DNC chair Paul Butler, and on LBJ's presidential staffer, Marvin Watson. See Rowland Evans and Robert Novak, *Lyndon B. Johnson: The Exercise of Power* (New York: New American Library, 1966), 145–47, 572. Yet in less than three months, Evans and Novak would shift ground and make LBJ the sole culprit for the Democratic Party's significant losses. Although no one picked up on the contradiction in Evans and Novak's work, the party leadership failure argument was now afloat.

73. Harold F. Bass Jr., "Presidential Party Leadership and Party Reform: Franklin D. Roosevelt and the Abrogation of the Two-Thirds Rule," *Presidential Studies Quarterly* 18, no. 2 (1988): 303–17; and Bass, "Presidential Party Leadership and Party Reform: Lyndon B. Johnson and the MFDP Controversy," 85–101.

74. Harold Bass, "Comparing Presidential Party Leadership: Two Cases," *Presidential Studies Quarterly* 23, no. 1 (1993): 115–28.

75. Bass, "The President and National Party Organization," 59–89.

76. Milkis, *President and the Parties*, 98–124, 300–307.

77. Lester G. Seligman, "The Presidential Office and the President as Party Leader (with a Postscript on the Kennedy-Nixon Era)," in *Parties and Elections in an Anti-Party Age*, ed. Jeff Fishel (Bloomington: Indiana University Press, 1978), 295–302.

78. Peter H. Odegard, "Presidential Leadership and Party Responsibility," *Annals of the American Academy of Political and Social Science* 307 (1956): 68, 71.

79. Gary Dean Best, "Herbert Hoover as Titular Leader of the GOP, 1933–1935," *Mid-America: An Historical Review* 61, no. 2 (1979): 81.

80. Ibid., 85.

81. Ibid., 82, 85.

82. Brown and Welborn, "Presidents and Their Parties," 316n61.

83. James L. Sundquist, *Politics and Policy: The Eisenhower, Kennedy, and Johnson Years* (Washington, DC: Brooking Institution, 1968). An abbreviation of Sundquist's argument can be found in his "Political Parties and Agenda Building: Eisenhower to Johnson," in *Parties and Elections in an Anti-Party Age*, ed. Jeff Fishel (Bloomington: Indiana University Press, 1978), 263–73. This article was an excerpt from different parts of the book.

84. Sundquist, *Politics and Policy*, 389–415.

85. Ibid., 405–10. See also Robert A. Caro, *The Years of Lyndon Johnson: Master of the Senate* (New York: Alfred A. Knopf, 2002), 777–1009.

86. Sundquist, *Politics and Policy*, 386.

87. Doris Kearns, *Lyndon Johnson and the American Dream* (New York: Harper & Row, 1976), 177–219.

88. Sundquist, *Politics and Policy*, 3.

89. Ibid., 498.

90. See Dan T. Carter, *From George Wallace to Newt Gingrich: Race in the Conservative Counterrevolution, 1963–1994* (Baton Rouge: Louisiana State University Press, 1996); and Carter, *The Politics of Rage: George Wallace, the Origins of the New Conservatism, and the Transformation of American Politics* (New York: Simon & Schuster, 1995).

91. Walton, *Reelection*, 16–18.

92. For the typical textbook portrait of state and local party leadership, see John J. Harrigan, *Politics and Policy in States and Communities*, 4th ed. (New York: HarperCollins, 1991), 127–84, 251–79.

93. Walton, *Native Son*, 131–48.

94. O. Douglas Weeks, "Texas: Land of Conservative Expansiveness," in *The Changing Politics of the South*, ed. William C. Havard (Baton Rouge: Louisiana State University Press, 1972), 205.

95. Ibid., 205, 211; see also George Norris Green, *The Establishment in Texas Politics: The Primitive Years, 1938–1957* (Westport, CT: Greenwood, 1979), 198.

96. Merle Miller, *Lyndon: An Oral Biography* (New York: G. P. Putnam's Sons, 1980), 102–3.

97. James Soukup, Clifton McCleskey, and Harry Holloway, *Party and Factional Division in Texas* (Austin: University of Texas Press, 1964), 4–5.

98. Weeks, "Texas: Land," 220.

99. James R. Soukup, Clifton McCleskey, and Harry Holloway, *Party and Factional Division in Texas* (Austin: University of Texas Press, 1964), 13.

100. Ibid., 5.

101. Ibid., 13.

102. Robert A. Caro, *Master of the Senate*, 831.

103. Weeks, "Texas: Land," 230.

104. Booth Mooney, *The Lyndon Johnson Story* (New York: Farrar, Straus, and Cudahy, 1956), 48.

105. Ibid., 49.

106. Robert Caro, *The Years of Lyndon Johnson: The Path to Power* (New York: Vintage, 1983), 610–11.

107. Ibid., 612.

108. Mooney, *Lyndon Johnson*, 49.

109. Caro, *Path to Power*, 662.

110. Savage, *Roosevelt*, 129–58; see also Milkis, *President and the Parties*, 75–97; and Price and Boskin, "Roosevelt 'Purge,'" 660–70.

111. Savage, "To Purge or Not to Purge," 273–86. See also Savage, *Truman and the Democratic Party*, 204–5.

112. Kearns, *Lyndon Johnson*, 398.

113. The MFDP formed to protest the all-white segregationist Mississippi Democratic Party and they demanded to be seated at the Democratic Convention. Their presence was viewed as an embarrassment for LBJ and a challenge for civil rights leadership. For a perceptive analysis of the MFDP from the standpoint of a member who is now a political scientist, see McLemore, "Freedom Democratic Party"; McLemore, "Mississippi Freedom Democratic Party"; and McLemore, "Mississippi Freedom Democratic Party: A Case Study of Grass-Roots Politics," 19–22.

114. Walton, *Black Political Parties*, 95–105.

115. Bass, "Presidential Party Leadership," 96–100.

116. Edward G. Carmines and James A. Stimson, *Issue Evolution: Race and the Transformation of American Politics* (Princeton: Princeton University Press, 1989), 45.

117. Ibid., 50–52.

118. Ibid., 54–55.

119. Jon F. Hale, "The Democratic Leadership Council: Institutionalizing Party Faction," in *The State of the Parties: The Changing Role of Contemporary American Parties*, ed. Daniel M. Shea and John C. Green (Lanham, MD: Rowman & Littlefield, 1994).

120. Walton, *Reelection*, 11–22, 27–58.

PART I INTRODUCTION

1. Gary King, *Solution to the Ecological Inference Problem: Reconstructing Individual Behavior from Aggregate Data* (Princeton: Princeton University Press, 1997), xv, 5.

2. J. B. Shannon, "Presidential Politics in the South: 1938, I" *Journal of Politics* 1, no 2 (1939): 146.

3. J. B. Shannon, "Presidential Politics in the South—1938, II," *Journal of Politics* 1, no. 3 (1939): 297.

CHAPTER 3

1. See Sundquist, *Politics and Policy*; and also Sundquist, "Political Parties and Agenda Building."

2. Edward W. Chester, "Lyndon Baines Johnson, an American 'King Lear': A Critical Evaluation of His Newspaper Obituaries," *Presidential Studies Quarterly* 21, no. 2 (1991): 328.

3. Ibid., 322.

4. Ibid., 321.

5. Ibid.

6. Key, *Southern Politics*, 37–41.

7. Ibid., 302.

8. Ibid., 38–39.

9. Ibid., 302.

10. Ibid., 259.

11. Donald S. Strong, "The Rise of Negro Voting in Texas," *American Political Science Review* 48, no. 3 (1948): 510–22.

12. Ibid.

13. Key, *Southern Politics*, 256n1.

14. Kingston, Attlesey, and Crawford, *Texas Almanac's Political History*, 4–5, 109–11.

15. Price and Boskin, "Roosevelt 'Purge,'" 660–70.

16. Evans and Novak, *Lyndon B. Johnson*, 161–63. See also Miller, *Lyndon: An Oral Biography*, 201–3.

17. For information on the Truman purges, see Savage, "To Purge or Not to Purge." For information on FDR's purges, see Price and Boskin, "Roosevelt 'Purge,'" 660–70.

18. At the 1936 convention, FDR had the two-thirds rule ended that required the nominee to receive two-thirds of the delegates, which empowered the Southern delegate block. For the Democratic Party chairman's reaction to the removal of the two-thirds rule in nomination politics, see James A. Farley, *Behind the Ballots: The Personal History of a Politician* (New York: Harcourt, Brace and Company, 1938), 108–9, 116–19. For a scholarly analysis, see Daniel Scroop, *Mr. Democrat: Jim Farley, the New Deal, and the Making of Modern American Politics* (Ann Arbor: University of Michigan Press, 2006), 128–31.

19. Green, *Establishment*, 45–57.

20. Walton, *Native Son*, 57–58.

21. On this point, see ibid., 47, 233, fig. 2.1 and table 11.2, respectively.

22. Ibid., 131–47.

23. Ibid.

CHAPTER 4

1. Raymond Tatalovich, "'Friends and Neighbors' Voting: Mississippi, 1943–73," *Journal of Politics* 37 (1975): 808.

2. Ibid., 808–9.

3. Ibid., 809.

4. Ibid., 811, table 1.

5. See F. Glenn Abney, "Partisan Realignment in a One-Party System: The Case of Mississippi," *Journal of Politics* 3 (1969): 1102–6; and Abney, "Factors Related to Negro Voter Turnout in Mississippi," *Journal of Politics* 36 (1974): 1057–63.

6. Abney, "Partisan Realignment in a One-Party System," 1103.

7. Earl Black and Merle Black, "The Wallace Vote in Alabama: A Multiple Regression Analysis," *Journal of Politics* 35 (1973): 730–36.

8. Ibid., 733.

9. Ibid.

10. Tatalovich, "'Friends and Neighbors' Voting," 811.

11. Ibid. See also note 4, 815–16.

12. Ibid., 808. Tatalovich is critical of the Blacks' methodological approach, calling it inexact and too limiting.

13. Walter Dean Burnham, "The Alabama Senatorial Election of 1962: Return of Inter-Party Competition," *Journal of Politics* 26 (1964): 800.

14. Ibid., 818.

15. Ibid.
16. Ibid., 805.
17. Ibid., 809.
18. Ibid., 808.
19. Ibid., 829.
20. Frank Jonas, ed., *Western Politics* (Salt Lake City: University of Utah Press, 1961), vii.
21. Alfred DeGrazia, *The Western Public: 1952 and Beyond* (Stanford: Stanford University Press, 1954), 5n1.
22. Frank Jonas, "Utah: Sagebrush, Democracy," in *Rocky Mountain Politics*, ed. Thomas Donnelly (Albuquerque: University of New Mexico Press, 1940), 37.
23. Henry Peterson, "Wyoming: A Cattle Kingdom," in Donnelly, *Rocky Mountain Politics*, 134.
24. Ibid., 139, 142.
25. Thomas Donnelly, "New Mexico: An Area of Conflicting Culture," in Donnelly, *Rocky Mountain Politics*, 246.
26. Waldo Waltz, "Arizona: A State of New-Old Frontiers," in Donnelly, *Rocky Mountain Politics*, 277, 282–83.
27. Frank Jonas, "The Western Scene," in Jonas, *Western Politics*, 15–16.
28. Totton James Anderson, "California: Enigma of National Politics," in Jonas, *Western Politics*, 84.
29. Hugh Bone, "Washington State: Free Style Politics," in Jonas, *Western Politics*, 315, 330.
30. Ibid., 330.
31. Ibid., 331.
32. Raymond Wolfinger, "The Development and Persistence of Ethnic Voting," *American Political Science Review* 59 (1965): 896–908; and Wolfinger, "Why Political Machines Have Not Withered Away," *Journal of Politics* 34 (1972): 365–98.
33. Charles Beall, "Wyoming: The Equality State," in Jonas, *Western Politics*, 354.
34. Ibid., 355.
35. DeGrazia, *Western Public*, 2–3.
36. W. Eugene Hollon, *The Southwest: Old and New* (New York: Alfred Knopf, 1961), 376–79.
37. Eugene Lee and William Buchanan, "The 1960 Election in California," *Western Political Quarterly* 14 (1961): 309.
38. Ibid., 314.
39. Duane Lockard, *New England State Politics* (Princeton: Princeton University Press, 1959), vii, ix–x, 6, table 1.
40. Ibid., 22–23.
41. Ibid., 24.
42. Ibid.
43. Ibid., 24–25.
44. Ibid., 59–60.
45. Ibid., 89–90.
46. Ibid., 141–42.
47. Ibid., 142–43.

48. This held for five of the southern states where localism was not a major historical force.

49. Robert W. Speel, *Changing Patterns of Voting in the Northern United States: Electoral Realignment, 1952–1996* (University Park: Pennsylvania State University Press, 1998), 51, 117.

50. John Fenton, *Midwest Politics* (New York: Holt, Rinehart & Winston, 1966), 1.

51. John Fenton, *Politics in the Border States* (New Orleans: Hauser Press, 1957), 1–15.

52. Fenton, *Midwest Politics*, 1.

53. Ibid., 22.

54. Ibid., 191.

55. Ibid., 5, 131.

56. Walton, *Reelection*, 15, table 1.1.

57. Fenton, *Politics in the Border States*, 217.

58. Tom Rice and Alisa Macht, "Friends and Neighbors Voting in Statewide General Elections," *American Journal of Political Science* 31 (1987): 448–49. See also Rice's earlier analysis: Michael Lewis-Beck and Tom Rice, "Localism in Presidential Elections: The Home State Advantage," *American Journal of Political Science* 27 (1983): 548–56.

59. Rice and Macht, "Friends and Neighbors Voting," 448–49.

60. Ibid., 449.

61. Ibid., 452.

62. Ibid., 448n1. No data were obtained from Hawaii, Louisiana, and Maryland.

63. Matthew Potoski, "'Friends and Neighbors' Voting in Gubernatorial and Senatorial Primaries," *Southeastern Political Review* 22 (1994): 544.

64. Ibid., 547.

65. Walton, *Reelection*, 119–32.

66. Tom Rice and Alisa Macht, "The Hometown Advantage: Mobilization or Conversion?" *Political Behavior* 9 (1987): 258.

67. Ibid., 261.

68. Walton, *Native Son*, 69.

69. Walton, *Reelection*, 160.

70. Key, *Southern Politics*, 259.

71. Ibid., 261.

72. Ibid.

73. Green, *Establishment*, 14.

74. Ibid., 113.

75. Ibid., 113, 201.

76. Key, *Southern Politics*, 255.

77. Ibid., 254.

78. Monroe Billington, "Lyndon B. Johnson and Blacks: The Early Years," *Journal of Negro History* 62, no. 1 (1977): 26–42. This article is incomplete in that it leaves out African American participation in the special and general elections.

79. Ibid.

80. Letter from H. L. Mitchell, Secretary, Southern Tenant Farmers Union, to Honorable Lyndon B. Johnson, May 21, 1941, LBJ House of Representatives Papers, Box 14.

81. Billington, "Lyndon B. Johnson and Blacks," 26–42.

CHAPTER 5

1. Green, *Establishment*, 113, 201.

2. James MacGregor Burns, "Confessions of a Kennedy Man," in *To Heal and to Build: The Programs of Lyndon B. Johnson*, ed. James MacGregor Burns (New York: McGraw-Hill, 1968), 418.

3. See Julie Leininger Pycior, *LBJ and Mexican-Americans: The Paradox of Power* (Austin: University of Texas Press, 1997), 35–52, 56–57, 112–21.

4. Key, *Southern Politics*, 271–74.

5. See J. Gilberto Quezada, *Border Boss: Manuel B. Bravo and Zapata County* (College Station: Texas A&M University Press, 1999), 98–131. This book is based on letters from Congressman Johnson to County Judge Manuel Bravo of Zapata County.

6. Key, *Southern Politics*, 250.

7. Green, *Establishment*, 15–18, 59.

8. See Hanes Walton Jr., "Black Voting Behavior in the Segregation Era: 1944–1964," in *Black Politics and Black Political Behavior: A Linkage Analysis*, ed. Hanes Walton Jr. (Westport, CT: Praeger, 1994), 115–134.

9. James L. Sundquist, *Dynamics of the Party System: Alignment and Realignment of Political Parties in the United States*, rev. ed. (Washington, DC: Brookings Institution, 1983), 9–21.

10. Walton, *Reelection*, 14–18. See also Dan T. Carter, *From George Wallace to Newt Gingrich*.

11. Ralph Ellison, "The Myth of the Flawed White Southerner," in *To Heal and to Build: The Programs of President Lyndon B. Johnson*, ed. James MacGregor Burns (New York: McGraw-Hill, 1968), 214. In this one-of-a-kind work, Ellison revealed that not all white southerners' personal racial beliefs align with the historical and institutional contexts of the federal government. As demonstrated by President Johnson's leadership, changes to governmental institutions begin to address the injustices of the past.

12. Courtney Brown, "The Anatomy of a Landslide: Johnson and Goldwater in 1964," in Brown, *Serpents in the Sand: Essays on the Nonlinear Nature of Politics and Human Destiny* (Ann Arbor: University of Michigan Press, 1995), 65.

13. Walton, *Native Son*, 26–33.

14. Walton, *Reelection*, 56–48.

15. Lee and Buchanan, "1960 Election in California."

16. Black and Black, "Wallace Vote in Alabama."

17. See Tatalovich, "'Friends and Neighbors' Voting," 807–14; and Speel, *Changing Patterns of Voting in the Northern United States*.

18. See David R. Mayhew, *Congress: The Electoral Connection* (New Haven: Yale University Press, 1974).

19. See Richard F. Fenno Jr., *Home Style: House Members in Their Districts* (Boston: Little, Brown and Company, 1978); and Fenno, *Home Style and Washington Work: Studies of Congressional Politics* (Ann Arbor: University of Michigan Press, 1989).

20. Lewis-Beck and Rice, "Localism in Presidential Elections," 548.

21. Ibid., 549–50.

22. Ibid., 554.

23. Ibid., 555.

24. Miller, *Lyndon: An Oral Biography*, 188–202, 235–80, 391–402.

25. Kingston, Attlesey, and Crawford, *Texas Almanac's Political History*, 116–17.

26. See J. Morgan Kousser, *The Shaping of Southern Politics: Suffrage Restriction and the Establishment of the One-Party South, 1880–1910* (New Haven: Yale University Press, 1974); and Gerald H. Gaither, *Blacks and the Populist Revolt: Ballots and Bigotry in the "New South"* (Tuscaloosa: University of Alabama Press, 1977).

27. Alexander Heard, *A Two-Party South?* (Chapel Hill: University of North Carolina Press, 1952).

28. See Soukup, McCleskey, and Holloway, *Party and Factional Division*, 185–99; Roscoe C. Martin, *The People's Party in Texas: A Study in Third-Party Politics* (Austin: University of Texas Press, 1970), 12–14, 60–112; O. Douglas Weeks, *Texas Presidential Politics in 1952* (Austin: University of Texas, Institute of Public Affairs, 1953); Weeks, *Texas One-Party Politics in 1956* (Austin: University of Texas, Institute of Public Affairs, 1957); Weeks, *Texas in the 1960 Presidential Election* (Austin: University of Texas, Institute of Public Affairs, 1961); Weeks, *Texas in 1964: A One-Party State Again?* (Austin: University of Texas, Institute of Public Affairs, 1965); and Green, *Establishment*, 211–30.

29. Kingston, Attlesey, and Crawford, *Texas Almanac's Political History*, 7–8. For another ecological approach that uses 13 such areas instead of 8, see Soukup, McClesky, and Holloway, *Party and Factional Division*, 199. This latter work predates that of the journalists.

30. Kingston, Attlesey, and Crawford, *Texas Almanac's Political History*, 96–100.

31. Ibid.

32. Key, *Southern Politics*, 271–74, especially fig. 53. The Census data was used thereafter to track them.

33. Ibid., 273.

34. Ibid., 274–75. See also Pycior, *LBJ and Mexican-Americans*, 64–66, 83–86.

35. See Quezada, *Border Boss*, 98–131.

36. Key, *Southern Politics*, 274–76.

37. Although Key did not use Comal County as an example in *Southern Politics*, he used it in another study, *A Primer of Statistics for Political Scientists* (New York: Thomas Y. Crowell, 1954), 63–66.

38. Key, *Southern Politics*, 275.

39. Austin Ranney, "The Utility and Limitations of Aggregate Data in the Study of Electoral Behavior," in *Essays on the Behavioral Study of Politics*, ed. Austin Ranney (Urbana: University of Illinois Press, 1962), 93–96. See also Dennis, "Study of Electoral Behavior," 52–53, 82–83.

40. Evron M. Kirkpatrick, "The Impact of the Behavioral Approach on Traditional Political Science," in *Essays on the Behavioral Study of Politics*, ed. Austin Ranney (Urbana: University of Illinois Press, 1962), 18. See also Samuel J. Eldersveld, "Theory and Method in Voting Behavior Research," *Journal of Politics* 13, no 1 (1951): 70–87.

41. Irwing Crespi, *Pre-election Polling: Sources of Accuracy and Error* (New York: Russell Sage Foundation, 1988), 134–55. See also William Buchanan, "Election Predictions: An Empirical Assessment," *Public Opinion Quarterly* 50, no. 2 (1986): 222–27.

42. Ranney, "The Utility and Limitations of Aggregate Data," 91.

43. Angus Campbell, "Recent Developments in Survey Studies of Political Behavior," in *Essays on the Behavioral Study of Politics*, 31.

44. Ibid., 37.

45. Ibid.

46. Ibid., 98.

47. Christopher H. Achen and W. Phillips Shively, *Cross-Level Inference* (Chicago: University of Chicago Press, 1995), 1–3.

48. Ibid., 3–4.

49. On this matter, see Jean M. Converse, *Survey Research in the United States: Roots and Emergence, 1890–1960* (Berkeley: University of California Press, 1987).

50. State polls are less accurate. See Crespi, *Pre-election Polling*, 24–25.

51. Walton, *Native Son*, 116–19.

52. This information was retrieved from Hanes Walton Jr.'s files on "Votes in Arkansas Elections" for candidate William J. Clinton.

53. Walton, *Native Son*, 131–47.

54. Ibid., 45.

55. Ibid., 50.

56. Lewis-Beck and Rice, "Localism in Presidential Elections," 549, 551, 554–55.

PART II INTRODUCTION

1. Smith v. Allwright, 321 U.S. 649 (1944).

2. Kingston, Attlesey, and Crawford, *Texas Almanac's Political History*, 10–17.

3. Donald S. Strong, "Interviews in Texas," Southern Politics Collections, Special Collections, Vanderbilt University Archives (Nashville, TN).

4. Caro, *Master of the Senate*, 865–72. See also Herman E. Talmadge, *Talmadge—a Political Legacy, a Politician's Life: A Memoir* (Atlanta: Peachtree Publishers, 1987), 192–93.

CHAPTER 6

1. Miller, *Lyndon*, 57.

2. Evans and Novak, *Lyndon B. Johnson*, 7.

3. Ibid.

4. Key, *Southern Politics*, 272.

5. Paul Lewinson, *Race, Class, and Party: A History of Negro Suffrage and White Politics in the South* (New York: Oxford University Press, 1932), 154–55.

6. Key, *Southern Politics*, 254.

7. Ibid.

8. Ibid.

9. Ibid.

10. Ibid., 255.

11. See David Mayhew, "Why Did V. O. Key Draw Back from His 'Have-Nots,'" in *V. O. Key, Jr. and the Study of American Politics*, ed. Milton Cummings Jr. (Washington, DC: American Political Science Association, 1988), 24–38.

12. Green, *Establishment*, 5–10.

13. Key, *Southern Politics*, 255.

14. Ibid., 260

15. Ibid., 301.

16. Ibid.
17. Heard, *Two-Party*, 49–50.
18. Walton, *Black Republicans*, 62–67.
19. Heard, *Two-Party*, 222; See also Walton, *Black Republicans*, 62–67.
20. Harry Wurzbach won in the 14th Congressional District in 1920 with 56 percent of the vote and won reelection in 1922, 1924, and 1926. He lost in 1928, getting only 49.7 percent of the vote. However, in 1930 he won reelection with 59.3 percent of the vote. A Democratic, Richard Kleberg, captured the seat in 1932. Wurzbach did not run again. He had broken the Democratic Party's monopoly on the state's congressional seats.
21. Heard, *Two-Party*, 111.
22. Soukup, McCleskey, and Holloway, *Party and Factional Division*, 140.
23. Ibid., 148.
24. Ibid., 149.
25. Ibid., 162.
26. Kingston, Attlesey, and Crawford, *Texas Almanac's Political History*, 13.
27. Soukup, McCleskey, and Holloway, *Party and Factional Division*, 150.
28. Ibid., 173–74.
29. Ibid., 179.
30. Ibid., 182.
31. For a review of these books, see Hanes Walton Jr. and Daniel Brantley, "Black Southern Politics: A Look at the Tradition and the Future," in *Black Politics and Black Political Behavior: A Linkage Analysis*, ed. Hanes Walton Jr. (Westport, CT: Praeger, 1994), 278–87.
32. Lorn S. Foster, ed., *The Voting Rights Act: Consequences and Implications* (New York: Praeger, 1985).
33. Weeks, "Texas: Land," 228–30.
34. Ibid., 230.
35. Arnold Vedlitz, James A. Dyer, and David B. Hill, "The Changing Texas Voter," in *The South's New Politics: Realignment and Dealignment,* ed. Robert H. Swansbrough and David M. Brodsky (Columbia: University of South Carolina Press, 1988), 38.
36. Ibid., 49–50.
37. Ibid., 51–52.
38. James W. Lamare, J. L. Polinard, and Robert D. Wrinkle, "Texas: Lone Star (Wars) State," in *The New Politics of the Old South: An Introduction to Southern Politics*, ed. Charles Bullock III and Mark Rozell (Lanham, MD: Rowman & Littlefield, 1998), 245.
39. Ibid., 248.
40. Ibid.
41. Ibid., 249.
42. Ibid., 252.
43. Ibid., 251.
44. Ibid.
45. Ibid.
46. Ibid., 252.
47. Ibid., 257.
48. Soukup, McCleskey, and Holloway, *Party and Factional Division*, 19.
49. Idella Gwatkin Swisher, "Election Statistics in the United States," *American Political Science Review* 27, no. 3 (1933): 423.

50. Ibid., 426.

51. Walton, *Reelection*, 69.

52. O. Douglas Weeks, the leading scholar of the Texas electorate, tells us "that 2,976,967 persons were eligible to vote: 2,411,679 had paid poll taxes which were still necessary in voting for all state and local elective places for those under sixty." This meant that 81 percent of those who were of voting age population could turn out to vote. See Weeks, *Texas in 1964*, 10.

53. Walton, *Native Son*, 13; and Walton, *Reelection*, 71.

54. Walton, *Reelection*, 80–81; Walton, *Native Son*, 18–22.

55. Walton, *Native Son*, 26–33; Walton, *Reelection*, 84–87.

56. Walton, *Reelection*, 53–56.

57. The other exceptions to this trend are when third parties carried the county in 1912 and 1924.

CHAPTER 7

1. Charles Johnson, *Proceedings of the First Three Republican National Conventions of 1856, 1860 and 1864* (Minneapolis: Harrison & Smith, Printers, 1893), 83–174. For more on political abolitionism, see Hanes Walton Jr., *The Negro in Third Party Politics* (Philadelphia: Dorrance, 1969), chap. 2.

2. C. Johnson, *Proceedings*, 174.

3. Ibid., 121.

4. Ibid., 121–22.

5. Ibid., 122.

6. Ibid., 124.

7. Ibid., 124–25.

8. Virginia attended the initial 1856 Convention and had 15 votes at it; ibid., 63, 65, 80, and 172.

9. Ibid., 102–3, 124–25.

10. Ibid., 248–55.

11. Ibid., 139.

12. Walton, *Black Republicans*, 62–67.

13. Francis Edward Abernathy, "African-American Folklore in Texas and in the Texas Folklore Society," in *Juneteenth Texas: Essays in African American Folklore*, ed. Francis Edward Abernathy et al. (Denton: University of North Texas Press, 1996), 2.

14. Ibid., 3.

15. Ibid.

16. Ibid., 7.

17. Kingston, Attlesey, and Crawford, *Texas Almanac's Political History*, 24.

18. Hanes Walton Jr., *Black Politics: A Theoretical and Structural Analysis* (Philadelphia: J. B. Lippincott, 1972), 21–26. See also Harold Schoen, "The Free Negro in the Republic of Texas," *Southwestern Historical Quarterly* 39, no. 4 (1936): 292–308.

19. Georgia had a larger "Free Colored" population than did Arkansas or Texas. Arkansas had a larger "Free Colored" population than did Texas, but neither state permitted this group to vote.

20. Abernathy, "African-American Folklore," 5–7.

21. Ibid., 5.

22. Walton, *Black Republicans*, 62.

23. Quoted in ibid. See also Paul Casdorph, *A History of the Republican Party in Texas, 1865–1965* (Austin: Pemberton Press, 1965).

24. Walton, *Black Republicans*, 62.

25. *The American Annual Cyclopedia and Register of Independent Events of the Year, 1867* (New York: D. Appleton and Company, 1869), 717.

26. *The American Annual Cyclopaedia and Register of Important Events, 1868* (New York: D. Appleton and Company, 1870), 729.

27. Ibid. This data has been corrected as seen in table 7.3.

28. Ibid. This data has been corrected as seen in table 7.4.

29. Ibid.

30. Ibid., 731.

31. U.S. Senate, "Letter of the General of the Army of the United States: Communicating in Compliance with a resolution of the Senate of December 5, 1867, a Statement of the Number of White and Colored Voters registered in Each of the States subject to the reconstruction acts of Congress, with other statistics relative to the same subject," 40th Congress, 2nd Session (Washington, DC: Government Printing Office, 1868), 11–12.

32. Ibid., 2.

33. Ibid., 12. In 1867, Texas had a total of 151 counties, but 22 of them were unorganized.

34. In this document, registration and voting data are *lower* but similar turnout rates are provided by the 1868 *Annual Cyclopaedia*.

35. See the appendix on the estimating procedure.

36. Alwyn Barr, *Black Texans: A History of Negroes in Texas, 1528–1971* (Austin: Jenkins Book Publishing, 1973), and Barr, *Reconstruction to Reform: Texas Politics, 1876–1906* (Austin: University of Texas Press, 1971).

37. For a recent analysis of that data, see Hanes Walton Jr., Sharon Wright, and Frank Pryor, "Texas African American Republicans. The Electoral Board in the 1920 Presidential and Gubernatorial Elections," *National Conference of Black Political Scientists Newsletter* 17 (2003): 8–12.

38. Walton, *Reelection*, 95–99; Alexander Heard and Donald S. Strong, *Southern Primaries and Elections, 1920–1949* (Tuscaloosa: University of Alabama Press, 1950), 21, 30, 192–93, 198–99; Walton, *Black Republicans*, 177–78.

39. Walton, *Black Republicans*, 62.

40. Casdorph, *A History of the Republican Party in Texas*, 4.

41. Walton, *Black Republicans*, 62.

42. Ibid.

43. Ibid.

44. Ibid., 63. See also John Mason Brewer, *Negro Legislators in Texas and Their Descendants: A History of the Negro in Texas Politics from Reconstruction to Disfranchisement* (Dallas: Mathis Publishing Co., 1935), and Alwyn Barr, "Black Legislators of Reconstruction Texas," *Civil War History* 32, no. 4 (1986): 340–51. See also *Black Leaders: Texas for Their Times*, ed. Alwyn Barr and Robert A. Calvert (Austin: Texas State Historical Association, 1981).

45. Walton, *Black Republicans*, 63.

46. Ibid.
47. Kingston, Attlesey, and Crawford, *Texas Almanac's Political History*, 101.
48. Walton, *Black Republicans*, 64.
49. Ibid.
50. Ibid., 65.
51. Tera W. Hunter, "Introduction," in *Norris Wright Cuney: A Tribune of the Black People*, by Maud Cuney-Hare (New York: G. K. Hall & Co., 1995), xxiii.
52. Ibid.
53. Ibid., xxiv–xxv.
54. Ibid., xxiii.
55. Ibid., xxiii–xxiv. See also Carter G. Woodson, "The Cuney Family," *Negro History Bulletin* 2 (1948): 123–25, 143. See also Paul Douglas Casdorph, "Norris Wright Cuney and Texas Republican Politics, 1883–1896," *Southwestern Historical Quarterly* 67, no. 4 (1965): 455–64; and Virginia N. Hinze, "Norris Wright Cuney" (master's thesis, Rice University, 1965).
56. Maud Cuney Hare, *Norris Wright Cuney: A Tribune of the Black People* (Austin: Steck-Vaughn Company, 1968), 126.
57. Ibid., 92, 93.
58. Walton, *Black Political Parties*, 64–67.
59. Hare, *Norris Wright Cuney*, 149–50.
60. Quoted in ibid., 151–52.
61. Walton, *Black Republicans*, 66.
62. Ibid.
63. Heard and Strong, *Southern Primaries*, 132.
64. Walton, *Black Republicans*, 66.
65. Ibid., 161–63. See also Hanes Walton Jr., "Perry Wilson Howard," in *Dictionary of American Negro Biography*, ed. Rayford W. Logan and Michael R. Winston (New York: W. W. Norton, 1982), 330–32.
66. Ibid., 161. See also Donald Lisio, *Hoover, Blacks, and Lily-Whites: A Study of Southern Strategies* (Chapel Hill: University of North Carolina Press, 1985).
67. Lewinson, *Race, Class, and Party*, 220.
68. Bruce A. Glasrud, "William M. McDonald: Business and Fraternal Leader," in *Black Leaders: Texans for Their Times*, ed. Alywn Barr and Robert A. Calvert (Austin: Texas State Historical Association, 1981), 97.
69. Ibid.
70. Ibid., 98.
71. See Conrey Bryson, *Dr. Lawrence A. Nixon and the White Primary* (El Paso: Texas Western Press, 1974); and Michael L. Gillette, "Heman Marion Sweatt: Civil Rights Plaintiff," in *Black Leaders: Texans for Their Times*, ed. Alywn Barr and Robert A. Calvert (Austin: Texas State Historical Association, 1981), 156–88.
72. Miller, *Lyndon*, 56.
73. Ibid.
74. Ibid.
75. Billington, "Lyndon B. Johnson and Blacks," 31.
76. Ibid.
77. Ibid.
78. Donald S. Strong, "American Government and Politics: The Poll Tax; The Case of

Texas," *American Political Science Review* 38, no. 4 (1944): 695. See also Frederic D. Ogden, *The Poll Tax in the South* (Tuscaloosa: University of Alabama Press, 1958), 154–73.

79. Strong, "American Government and Politics," 695.
80. Key, *Southern Politics*, 587.
81. Ibid., 613–14.
82. Walton, *Reelection*, 114–16.
83. Glasrud, "William M. McDonald," 89. See also Arthur Lewis, *The Day They Shook the Plum Tree* (New York: Harcourt, Brace & World, 1963), 81.
84. Ibid., 90.
85. Ibid., 89, 91.
86. Ibid., 91.
87. Key, *Southern Politics*, 3–12.
88. Hanes Walton Jr., "Black Southern Politics: The Influence of Bunche, Martin, and Key," in Walton, *Black Politics and Black Political Behavior*, 19–38.
89. Strong, "Rise of Negro Voting in Texas," 521–22.
90. U.S. Commission on Civil Rights, *Report of the U.S. Commission on Civil Rights, 1959* (Washington, DC: Government Printing Office, 1959), 561.
91. Walton, "Black Voting in the Segregation Era," 115–34.
92. For additional data on the African American electorate vote for Latino candidates, see Strong, "Rise of Negro Voting in Texas," 518–19.
93. Holloway, "Negro and the Vote: The Case of Texas," 538–39.
94. Ibid., 542–53.
95. Ibid., 587.
96. Harry Holloway, *The Politics of the Southern Negro: From Exclusion to Big City Organization* (New York: Random House, 1969), 125.
97. Ibid., 131.
98. Ibid., 265.
99. Bullock, 377.
100. Martin, *People's Party in Texas*, 96. Throughout his book, Martin refused to capitalize the word "Negro."
101. Ibid., 95–96.
102. Ibid., 98.
103. Jack Abramowitz, "The Negro in the Populist Movement," *Journal of Negro History* 38, no. 3 (1953): 269–70.
104. Ibid., 270. Jack Abramowitz, "John B. Rayner—a Grass-Roots Leader," *Journal of Negro History* 36, no. 2 (1951): 164.
105. Ibid., 165.
106. Ibid., 165–66.
107. Judith Kaaz Doyle, "Maury Maverick and Racial Politics in San Antonio, Texas, 1938–1941," *Journal of Southern History* 53, no. 2 (1987): 199.
108. Ibid., 200.
109. Ibid., 199.
110. Ibid., 202, 207.
111. Ibid., 202.
112. Ibid., 208, table 1.
113. Ibid., 211–12.
114. Ibid., 218, table 2.

115. Ibid., 219.
116. Ibid., 220.
117. Ibid., 221, table 3.
118. Weeks, "Texas: Land," 218.
119. Ibid.
120. For those who have advanced this interpretative thesis, see Strong, "American Government," 693–709. Strong was the first to advance it in August 1944. Others simply followed his original thesis.
121. Dan Nimmo and Clifton McCleskey, "Impact of the Poll Tax on Voter Participation: The Houston Metropolitan Area in 1966," *Journal of Politics* 31, no. 3 (1969): 688, 698.
122. Allen M. Shinn Jr., "A Note on Voter Registration and Turnout in Texas, 1960–1970," *Journal of Politics* 33, no. 4 (1971): 1128. A clue as to how Texas would vote on the repeal can be seen in the 1956 vote on the segregationist school referenda. See Werner Grunbaum, "Desegregation in Texas: Voting and Action Patterns," *Public Opinion Quarterly* 28 (1964): 604–14.
123. Morris Fiorina and Paul Peterson, *The New American Democracy*, 2nd ed. (New York: Longman, 2002), 556.
124. Nimmo and McCleskey, "Impact of the Poll Tax," 683–87. The Supreme Court Case was *Harper vs. Virginia State Board of Elections, et al.* 303 U.S. 663 (1966). For the Texas case, see *Beare et al., v. Smith et al.*, 32 F. Supp. 110 (SD. Texas, 1971).
125. O. Douglas Weeks, "The Texas-Mexican and the Politics of South Texas," *American Political Science Review* 24, no. 3 (1930): 606–27.
126. Ibid., 620, 622–23.
127. Ibid.; see also O. Douglas Weeks, "The League of United Latin-American Citizens: A Texas-Mexican Civic Organization," *Southwestern Political and Social Science Quarterly* 10, no. 3 (1929): 257–78.
128. Key, *Southern Politics*, 272.
129. Ibid.
130. John Hope Franklin and Loren Schweninger, *Runaway Slaves: Rebels on the Plantation* (New York: Oxford University Press, 1999), 115–16.

PART III INTRODUCTION

1. Report of the Committee on Privileges, Suffrage and Elections, "Journal of the House of Representative of the Regular Session of 36th Legislature Convened January 14, 1919, and Adjourned March 19, 1919," 166–67.
2. *Georgia Official and Statistical Register* (Atlanta: Secretary of State, 1952), 363. The authors would like to thank State Representative Barbara J. Mobley for getting the Georgia House Research Office to assist in researching Carter's father's legislative record as well as providing a copy of her *Georgia Magazine* (April 2001), which carried an article and cover photograph of Carter when he was eight years old.
3. Jimmy Carter, *An Hour before Daylight: Memories of a Rural Boyhood* (New York: Simon & Schuster, 2001), 258–59.
4. Ibid., 67.
5. Ibid.

6. Ibid., 69.
7. Ibid.
8. Ibid., 267. See also Marvin Robertson, "'The Single Most Important Event': President Jimmy Carter Recalls Life on the Farm before Electricity," *Georgia Magazine* 67 (2001): 15–18.

CHAPTER 8

1. Milkis, *President and the Parties*, 171–83.
2. Miller, *Lyndon*, 63.
3. Walton, *Reelection*, 27, 43, 50.
4. Miller, *Lyndon*, 37.
5. Ibid.
6. Ibid., 30.
7. Ibid., 46.
8. Evans and Novak, *Lyndon B. Johnson*, 6, 9–10.
9. Mooney, *Lyndon Johnson*, 32.
10. Caro, *Path to Power*, 340.
11. Ibid.
12. Ibid.
13. Mooney, *Lyndon Johnson*, 33.
14. Law, 361.
15. Miller, *Lyndon*, 57.
16. Caro, *Path to Power*, 403.
17. Ibid., 390.
18. Ibid., 403.
19. Ibid., 398.
20. Ibid., 390, 403, 411.
21. See Kingston, Attlesey, and Crawford, *Texas Almanac's Political History*, 10–17, for a discussion of special elections in Texas.
22. Caro, *Path to Power*, 411.
23. Ibid., 438.
24. Ibid.
25. Robert Dallek, *Lone Star Rising: Lyndon Johnson and His Times, 1908–1960* (New York: Oxford University Press, 1991), 155.
26. Evans and Novak, *Lyndon B. Johnson*, 8.
27. Caro, *Path to Power*, 407–8.
28. Walton, *Reelection*, 113–18.
29. Pycior, *LBJ and Mexican Americans*, 35.
30. Ibid., 36.
31. Ibid.
32. Ibid., 38.
33. Ibid., 29.
34. Ibid., 33.
35. See Quezada, *Border Boss*, 62–67, 98–137; Evan Anders, *Boss Rule in South Texas: The Progressive Era* (Austin: University of Texas Press, 1982); John Clark, *The Fall of the*

Duke of Duval: A Prosecutor's Journal (Austin: Eakin Press, 1995); Virgil Lott and Mercurio Martinez, *The Kingdom of Zapata* (Austin: Eakin Press, 1983); Pycior, *LBJ and Mexican Americans*, 111–40.

36. Miller, *Lyndon*, 67–68.

37. Dallas Morning News, *Texas Almanac and State Industrial Guide 1941–42* (Dallas: Dallas Morning News, 1942), 384.

38. Weeks, "Texas: Land," 211–12.

39. Evans and Novak, *Lyndon B. Johnson*, 15.

40. Ibid., 17.

41. Green, *Establishment*, 46.

42. Ibid., 49–50.

43. Ibid., 58–60, 63–64.

44. Johnson Presidential Library, House of Representatives Papers, Box 47.

45. Miller, *Lyndon*, 102–3.

46. Ibid., 111.

47. Ibid., 111–12. Just prior to the 1944 primary, Oil Texas sponsored LBJ's first opposition because LBJ had voted against legislation that would have increased price supports for crude oil.

48. Ibid., 112.

49. There were 10 write-in votes for J. W. Simpson from Hays County in 1940. The former governor received three write-in votes from Williamson County, and George Hester got one from the same county in 1942. J. J. Mansfield got two write-ins from Travis County in 1944.

50. Walton, *Native Son*, 43–47, 107, 110.

51. Walton, *Reelection*, 126, 128, 130, 140, 152, 159.

52. Key, *Southern Politics*, 406–23.

53. For Carter, see Walton, *Native-Son*, 102–14; for Clinton, see Walton, *Reelection*, 147–67.

54. Jimmy Carter, *Why Not the Best* (New York: Bantam Books, 1976), 9–83.

55. See Walton, *Reelection*, chap. 8.

56. Another Texan, James Nance Garner, had moved from the House of Representatives to the vice presidency. See also George Brown, *The Speaker of the House: The Romantic Story of John N. Garner* (New York: Brewer, Warren, and Putnam, 1932); Marquis M. James, *Mr. Garner of Texas* (New York: Bobbs-Merrill, 1939); and Bascom Timmons, *Garner of Texas* (New York: Harper, 1948). In effect, Garner had crafted a partial map and politically successful one. LBJ's political map would be completely successful for other southern native-son presidential candidates.

CHAPTER 9

1. See Mooney, *Lyndon Johnson*, 51.

2. Miller, *Lyndon*, 81.

3. Caro, *Path to Power*, 688. In this special election there "were 25 Democrats, 2 Republicans, 1 Independent and 1 Communist."

4. Ibid., 677.

5. Mooney, *Lyndon Johnson*, 51.

6. Ibid., 52.
7. See White, *Making of the President*.
8. Dallas Morning News, *The 1928 Texas Almanac* (Dallas: Dallas News, 1929), 169. The *Almanac* listed the Texas senatorial succession for both senators.
9. Kingston, Attlesey, Crawford, *Texas Almanac's Political History*, 116.
10. Miller, *Lyndon*, 81.
11. Green *Establishment*, 34
12. Miller, *Lyndon*, 81.
13. Ibid., 83.
14. Walton, *Reelection*, 80–81. See also Walton, *Native Son*, 19.
15. Key, *Southern Politics*, 298–311.
16. It is equally possible that the governor's political bosses and machines could have generated even more votes to help him overcome LBJ's initial lead.
17. This total primary vote for LBJ can be found in *The Texas Almanac 1943–1944* (Dallas: *Dallas Morning News*, 1944), 258.
18. On this matter, see chapter 6.
19. Quezada, *Border Boss*, 65. Zapata County falls into our boss category and Starr into our Latino category.
20. Ibid.
21. Ibid., 66.
22. Ibid.
23. Dale Baum and James Hailey, "Lyndon Johnson's 1948 State Victory," *Political Science Quarterly* 109 (1994): 596. Their article used a multiple linear regression analysis to "estimate" voting patterns in the 1948 Senate runoff election. These estimates provide some insights into the voting behavior of the supporters of the other 27 candidates as they selected either Johnson or Stevenson. There is a problem with deriving voter estimates from regression analyses because the techniques generate numbers above 100 and below zero that are unusable. As to how Baum and Hailey dealt with this problem, see their note on page 598. For a discussion of this problem, see Achen and Shively, *Cross-Level*.
24. Letter from Mrs. C. J. Cansler, Representative for *Pittsburgh Courier*, to J. E. Kellam, State Administrator, NYA, May 27, 1941, LBJ House of Representatives Papers, Box 14.
25. Letter from Mrs. C. J. Cansler, Representative for *Pittsburgh Courier*, to J. E. Kellam, State Administrator, NYA, May 27, 1941, LBJ House of Representatives Papers, Box 14.
26. Letter from H. L. Mitchell, Secretary Southern Tenant Farmers Union, to Honorable Lyndon B. Johnson, May 21, 1941, LBJ House of Representatives Papers, Box 14.
27. Letter from Congressman Lyndon Johnson to H. L. Mitchell, Secretary Southern Tenant Farmers Union, May 28, 1941, LBJ House of Representatives Papers, Box 14.
28. Letter from J. E. Clayton, Principal, Littig High School, to Congressman Lyndon Johnson, May 21, 1941, LBJ House of Representative Papers, Box 14; see also "Our Choice for Senate: An Editorial," *The Informer* (May 17, 1941), 1, 12.
29. Letter from J. E. Clayton, Principal, Littig High School, to "Dear Friend," May 22, 1941, LBJ House of Representatives Papers, Box 14.
30. Letter from J. E. Clayton, Principal, Littig High School, to Congressman Lyndon B. Johnson, June 11, 1941, LBJ House of Representatives Papers, Box 14.

31. Letter from J. E. Clayton, Principal, Littig High School, to Dr. W. M. Drake, Chairman, Colored Division, Lyndon B. Johnson Headquarters, June 11, 1941.

32. Letter from Congressman Johnson to H. L. Mitchell, Secretary, STFU, May 28, 1941, LBJ House of Representative Papers, Box 14.

33. Letter from R. L. de Cordeva, Chairman, Latin American Democrats, to Walter Jenkins, Staff, Congressman Lyndon Johnson's Office, May 30, 1941, and from Walter Jenkins, Staff, Congressman Lyndon Johnson's Office to R. L. de Cordeva, June 6, 1941; and letter from R. L. de Cordeva, Chairman, Latin American Democrats, to "Dear Friend," May 30, 1941, LBJ House of Representative Papers, Box 14.

34. Miller, *Lyndon*, 86.

35. Robert A. Caro, *The Years of Lyndon Johnson: Means of Ascent* (New York: Alfred A. Knopf, 1990), 4.

36. Miller, *Lyndon*, 87–88.

37. Green, *Establishment*, 37.

38. Miller, *Lyndon*, 88.

39. Key, *Southern Politics*, 269.

40. Miller, *Lyndon*, 117–18.

41. Caro, *Means of Ascent*, 145–78.

42. Key, *Southern Politics*, 274.

43. Kingston, Attlesey, and Crawford, *Texas Almanac's Political History*, 150–53, 292–95.

44. Evans and Novak, *Lyndon B. Johnson*, 21.

45. Patrick Cox, "'Nearly a Statesman': LBJ and Texas Blacks in the 1948 Election," *Social Science Quarterly* 74, no. 2 (1993): 241.

46. Ibid., 252.

47. Ibid., 251–52.

48. Ibid., 252.

49. Ibid., 255.

50. Billington, "Lyndon B. Johnson and Blacks," 34.

51. The calculation of Coke Stevenson's primary and general elections means omitted the mean for the 1938 runoff election.

52. Mooney, *Lyndon*, 75.

53. Green, *Establishment*, 113.

54. Miller, *Lyndon*, 123.

55. Ibid.

56. Ibid.

57. Mooney, *Lyndon*, 76.

58. Key, *Southern Politics*, 265.

59. Green, *Establishment*, 114. See also Baum and Hailey, "Lyndon Johnson's 1948 Senate Victory," 596. See also our discussion at note 23 above, this chapter.

60. See Green, *Establishment*, 264n39, for a list of these 10 counties. See also Baum and Hailey, "Lyndon Johnson's 1948 Senate Victory," 609 and 612.

61. Harold F. Gosnell, *Champion Campaigner: Franklin D. Roosevelt* (New York: Macmillan, 1952), 105.

62. Ibid., 58–59. In explaining FDR's first electoral defeat in his run for the U.S. Senate in 1914, Gosnell declared that after that defeat FDR embraced Tammany Hall.

63. See Harold F. Gosnell, *Boss Platt and His New York Machine: A Study of the Po-*

litical Leadership of Thomas C. Platt, Theodore Roosevelt, and Others (Chicago: University of Chicago Press, 1924), and Gosnell, *Machine Politics: Chicago Model* (Chicago: University of Chicago Press, 1937).

64. Report of the Committee on Privileges, Suffrage and Elections, Journal of the Texas House of Representatives of the Regular Session of 36th Legislature Convened January 14, 1919 and adjourned March 19, 1919, 166–169. The committee held that LBJ's father, S. E. Johnson, was the winner.

65. Miller, *Lyndon*, 88.

66. William Riordan with Terrence McDonald, eds., *Plunkitt of Tammany Hall* (New York: Bedford Books/St. Martin's, 1994), 49–51.

67. Green, *Establishment*, 116.

68. Ibid.

69. Miller, *Lyndon*, 134–35.

70. Mooney, *Lyndon*, 76.

71. For a comprehensive and systematic listing of the 41 counties that failed to report or to report properly, see the book by Heard and Strong, *Southern Primaries*, 132, 184–86.

72. U.S. Commission on Civil Rights, *Report of the United States Commission on Civil Rights, 1959* (Washington, DC: U.S. Government Printing Office, 1959), 135.

73. Hanes Walton Jr., *The Negro in Third Party Politics* (Philadelphia: Dorrance, 1969), 75–78; and Steven J. Rosenstone, Roy L. Behr, and Edward H. Lazarus, *Third Parties in America: Citizen Response to Major Party Failure*, 2nd ed. (Princeton: Princeton University Press, 1996), 107–10.

74. Key, *Southern Politics*, 330.

75. Ibid., 334.

76. Green, *Establishment*, 142. See also Miller, *Lyndon*, 152.

77. Green, *Establishment*, 143.

78. Ibid., 145.

79. Ibid., 271n18.

80. Evans and Novak, *Lyndon B. Johnson*, 226. See also Mooney, *Lyndon*, 97–100.

81. Evans and Novak, *Lyndon B. Johnson*, 227–28.

82. Quoted in Miller, *Lyndon*, 160–61.

83. Ibid., 160.

84. Ibid., 161.

85. Quoted in ibid., 162.

86. O. Douglas Weeks, "Republicanism and Conservatism in the South," *Southwestern Social Science Quarterly* 36 (1955): 250.

87. Evans and Novak, *Lyndon B. Johnson*, 86.

88. Mooney, *Lyndon*, 122.

89. See Congressional Quarterly's *Guide to U.S. Elections*, 3rd ed. (Washington, DC: Congressional Quarterly, 1994), 95, 344, 565, 1173.

90. Walton, *Reelection*, 159–86.

91. Kingston, Attlesey, and Crawford, *Texas Almanac's Political History*, 326.

92. Ibid., 12.

93. Ibid., 13. See also John Tower, *Consequences* (Boston: Little, Brown and Company, 1991).

94. Walton, *Reelection*, 159, 186.

95. Ibid.

PART IV INTRODUCTION

1. Edward T. Thompson, ed., *Theodore H. White at Large: The Best of His Magazine Writing, 1939–1986* (New York: Pantheon Books, 1992), 65.
2. Ibid., 490.
3. Ellison, "Myth of the Flawed White Southerner," 216.
4. Richard Harwood and Haynes Johnson, *Lyndon* (New York: Praeger, 1973), 182.
5. T. Harry Williams, "Huey, Lyndon, and Southern Radicalism," *Journal of American History* 60, no. 2 (1973): 272.
6. Ibid., 273–74.
7. Ibid., 273.
8. Joe B. Frantz, "Opening a Curtain: The Metamorphosis of Lyndon B. Johnson," *Journal of Southern History* 45, no. 1 (1979): 3–26.
9. Robert A. Divine, "The Johnson Literature," in *Exploring the Johnson Years*, ed. Robert A. Divine (Austin: University of Texas Press, 1981), 20.
10. Eric F. Goldman, *The Tragedy of Lyndon Johnson* (New York: Alfred A. Knopf, 1974), 531.
11. William G. Phillips, *Yarborough of Texas* (Washington, DC: Acropolis Books, 1969).

CHAPTER 10

1. Yanek Mieczkowski, *The Routledge Historical Atlas of Presidential Elections* (New York: Routledge, 2001), 115.
2. Ibid.
3. David Potenziani, "Striking Back: Richard B. Russell and Racial Relocation," *Georgia Historical Quarterly* 65, no. 3 (1981): 264–65. See also Gilbert C. Fite, *Richard B. Russell, Jr., Senator from Georgia* (Chapel Hill: University of North Carolina Press, 1991).
4. For a narrative on Russell's efforts to secure the presidency, see Fite, *Richard B. Russell, Jr.*, 271–300.
5. Evans and Novak, *Lyndon B. Johnson*, 226.
6. Congressional Quarterly, *Guide to U.S. Elections*, 236.
7. "The Presidential Election—1952," in *Congressional Quarterly Almanac 82nd Congress* 8 (2nd Session, 1952), 485.
8. Ibid., 486.
9. Dallek, *Lone Star Rising*, 418.
10. Ibid. See also D. B. Hardeman and D. C. Brown, *Rayburn: A Biography* (Austin: University of Texas Press, 1987), 368–69.
11. Caro, *Master of the Senate*, 470–87.
12. Dallek, *Lone Star Rising*, 418.
13. Miller, *Lyndon*, 199.
14. Evans and Novak, *Lyndon B. Johnson*, 235.
15. Ibid., 235–36.
16. Ibid., 237.
17. Ibid.
18. "Kefauver Wins Vice President Nomination on 2nd Ballot," in *Congressional Quarterly Almanac 84th Congress* 12 (2nd Session, 1956), 764, 767.

19. Evans and Novak, *Lyndon B. Johnson*, 228.

20. Dallek, *Lone Star Rising*, 504.

21. Ibid., 503.

22. Ibid., 490–91. See also Jeff Shesol, *Mutual Contempt: Lyndon Johnson, Robert Kennedy, and the Feud That Defined a Decade* (New York: W. W. Norton, 1997), 32–33.

23. On this pivotal state primary (because it was a Protestant state that gave a Catholic candidate a victory), see Dan Fleming Jr., *Kennedy vs. Humphrey, West Virginia, 1960: The Pivotal Battle for the Democratic Presidential Nomination* (Jefferson, NC: McFarland & Company, 1992); and Harry Ernst, "The Primary That Made a President: West Virginia 1960," in *Cases in Practical Politics* (New York: McGraw-Hill, 1962), 20.

24. Ibid.

25. ". . . Kennedy Nominated on First Ballot with 806 Votes," in *Congressional Quarterly Almanac 86th Congress 2nd Session* 16 (Washington, DC: Congressional Quarterly, 1960), 773.

26. "The Vice Presidency," in *Congressional Quarterly Almanac 86th Congress 2nd Session* 16 (Washington, DC: Congressional Quarterly, 1960), 775.

27. ". . . Kennedy Nominated on First Ballot with 806 Votes," 774.

28. Weeks, *Texas Presidential Politics in 1952*, 97–99.

29. Weeks, *Texas One-Party Politics in 1956*, 47–49.

30. Weeks, *Texas in the 1960 Presidential Election*, 72–73.

31. Ibid., 47.

32. Ibid., 51–52.

33. Ibid., 69.

34. Ibid., 54.

35. Ibid., 55.

36. Ibid., 63–64.

37. Ibid., 64–65.

38. On this matter, see Donald Strong, *Urban Republicanism in the South* (Tuscaloosa: University of Alabama, Bureau of Public Administration, 1960).

39. Weeks, *Texas in the 1960 Presidential Election*, 56–57.

40. For a discussion of the influence of the religious variable in this election, see the article by Philip E. Converse, "Religion and Politics: The 1960 Election," in *Elections and the Political Order*, ed. Angus Campbell, Philip E. Converse, Warren E. Miller, and Donald E. Stokes (New York: John Wiley and Sons, 1966), 96–124, which uses national survey data. See also V. O. Key Jr., "Interpreting the Election Results," in *The Presidential Election and Transition 1960–1961*, ed. Paul T. David (Washington, DC: Brookings Institution, 1961), 150–75, which uses county-level aggregate data to study this topic.

41. Weeks, *Texas in the 1960 Presidential Election*, 19.

42. Ibid.

43. Lewis-Beck and Rice, "Localism in Presidential Elections," 548–56.

44. Rosenstone, *Forecasting*, 64–66.

45. Lyndon B. Johnson, *The Public Papers of the Presidents of the United States: Lyndon B. Johnson* (Washington, DC: United States Government Printing Office, 1965), 9.

46. Theodore H. White, *The Making of the President 1964* (New York: Atheneum, 1965), 31.

47. Ibid., 44.

48. Ibid., 10.

49. Evans and Novak, *Lyndon B. Johnson*, 350.

50. Johnson, *Public Papers*, 9.
51. Ibid.
52. Ibid.
53. Ibid.
54. Ibid., 44.
55. Miller, *Lyndon*, 340.
56. Hanes Walton Jr., *When the Marching Stopped: The Politics of the Civil Rights Regulatory Agencies* (Albany: State University of New York Press, 1988), 95–98; and Walton, *The Political Philosophy of Martin Luther King, Jr.* (Westport, CT: Greenwood, 1971).
57. Jake Pickle and Peggy Pickle, *Jake* (Austin: University of Texas Press, 1997), 92.
58. Ibid.
59. Ibid., 93–94.
60. Ibid., 92–93, 94.
61. Walton, *Reelection*, 14–19; see also Dan T. Carter, *Politics of Rage*; and John H. Kessel, *The Goldwater Coalition: Republican Strategies in 1964* (Indianapolis: Bobbs–Merrill, 1968).
62. White, *Making of the President 1964*, 257.
63. Ibid., 252.
64. Ibid., 257.
65. See Kay Mills, *This Little Light of Mine: The Life of Fannie Lou Hamer* (New York: Penguin, 1993).
66. For an account of the MFDP from its origins, see the participant observation of an African American political scientist and founding member who is now on the city council in Jackson, Mississippi: McLemore, "Freedom Democratic Party" (master's thesis); and McLemore, "Mississippi Freedom Democratic Party" (PhD diss.).
67. Walton, *Black Political Parties*, 69–79.
68. Ibid., 91–108.
69. Hanes Walton Jr., "Black Political Parties and Congress: The Role of the *Congressional Record*," in Walton, *Black Politics and Black Political Behavior*, 41–47. See also Leslie McLemore, "Fannie Lou Hamer: An Unfinished Political Portrait," paper presented at the Sixth Annual Meeting of the National Council for Black Studies, Chicago, March 17–20, 1982.
70. Shesol, *Mutual Contempt*, 216–17.
71. Mieczkowski, *Routledge Historical Atlas*, 119–20.
72. Johnson, *Public Papers*, 475. See also Patrick E. Jamieson, "Seeing the Lyndon B. Johnson Presidency through the March 31, 1968, Withdrawal Speech," *Presidential Studies Quarterly* 29, no. 1 (1999): 134–49.
73. Johnson, *Public Papers*, 477.
74. Harry Truman, *The Public Papers of the Presidents of the United States* (Washington, DC: United States Government Printing Office: 1966), 225. See also Harry Truman, *Truman Speaks* (New York: Columbia University Press, 1960), 19–30.
75. Truman, *Public Papers*, 225.
76. Ibid., 227.
77. Truman, Jefferson Jackson Day Dinner, May 29, 1952.
78. "Democrats Nominate Johnson-Humphrey at Convention Geared to Middle-Road Campaign," in *Congressional Quarterly Almanac 88th Congress 2nd Session* (Washington, DC: Congressional Quarterly, 1965), 1092.

79. Weeks, *Texas in 1964*, 25.
80. Ibid., 31.
81. Ibid., 26.
82. Ibid., 34.
83. Ibid., 33
84. Ibid., 35.

CHAPTER 11

1. Walton, *Native Son*, 132–47. For pioneering work on this subject that does not include any discussion of the former president electioneering for his vice president, see Thomas F. Schaller and Thomas W. Williams, "'The Contemporary Presidency': Postpresidential Influence in the Postmodern Era," *Presidential Studies Quarterly* 33, no. 1 (2003): 188–200; and Irina Belenky, "The Making of the Ex-presidents, 1797–1993: Six Recurrent Models," *Presidential Studies Quarterly* 29, no. 1 (1999): 150–65.
2. Walton, *Reelection*, 232, see table 11.1, which documents the percentage vote increase for the Democratic Party across the South.
3. Gerald Pomper, "The Nomination of Hubert Humphrey for Vice-President," *Journal of Politics* 28, no. 3 (1966): 639.
4. Ibid., 641.
5. See White, *Making of the President 1964*, 258–66.
6. Ibid., 260.
7. See Robert Sherrill, *The Accidental President* (New York: Grossman, 1967).
8. Shesol, *Mutual Contempt*, 208–17; White, *Making of the President 1964*, 263–75; Arthur M. Schlesinger Jr., *A Thousand Days: John F. Kennedy in the White House* (Boston: Houghton Mifflin, 1965), 39–57.
9. Among the numerous books, White's *The Making of the President 1964* is the leading exponent of this position; Shesol's work is the most recent and detailed.
10. Pomper, "Nomination of Hubert Humphrey," 644.
11. Ibid., 653–54.
12. For a discussion on presidential decision making and problem solving, see Paul Charles Light, *The President's Agenda: Domestic Policy Choice from Kennedy to Carter (With Notes on Ronald Reagan)* (Baltimore: Johns Hopkins University Press, 1983), 46–47, 51–58, 62–73, 119–20.
13. Pomper, "Nomination of Hubert Humphrey," 641.
14. White, *Making of the President 1964*, 257.
15. Pomper, "Nomination of Hubert Humphrey," 643, 649.
16. Ibid., 641, 643.
17. Ibid., 651.
18. Randall B. Woods, *LBJ: Architect of American Ambition* (New York: Free Press, 2006), 831–32.
19. Ibid., 832.
20. Ibid.
21. Johnson, *Public Papers*, book 11, 917.
22. Ibid.

23. President Johnson, "Telegram to the Texas Democratic Convention, September 17, 1968," ibid.

24. Ibid., 977. President Johnson, "Telegram to the Co-Chairman of the Campaign Organizing Workshop of the Texas Democratic Party, September 26, 1968."

25. President Johnson, "Telegram to the Co-Chairman," ibid.

26. President Johnson, "Remarks at the Astrodome in Houston at a Democratic Party Rally, November 3, 1968," ibid., 1107.

27. See ibid., 1064, 1077, 1078, 1088, 1093, and 1110 for some of the speeches that he made at sundry campaign steps.

28. See Kevin Phillips, *The Emerging Republican Majority* (New Rochelle, NY: Arlington House, 1969).

29. Walton, *Reelection*, 14–18.

30. See Carter, *From George Wallace to Newt Gingrich*, and Carter, *Politics of Rage*.

31. Weeks, "Texas: Land," 226; see also Walton, *Reelection*, 14–18.

32. Ibid.

33. Ibid., 225–26.

34. Ibid., 214.

35. Ibid., 226.

36. Ibid., 228, 230.

37. Belenky, "Making of the Ex-Presidents," 152.

38. Ibid., 153.

39. Schaller and Williams, "Contemporary Presidency," 195.

40. Ibid., 197.

41. Ibid.

CHAPTER 12

1. Mieczkowski, *Routledge Historical Atlas*, 94.

2. Walton, *Reelection*, 27.

3. Mieczkowski, *Routledge Historical Atlas*, 95.

4. Caro, *Path to Power*, 163.

5. Walton, *Reelection*, 43.

6. *Congressional Quarterly, Guide to U. S. Elections*, 1093.

7. Ibid., 500–501.

8. Ibid.

9. Ibid., 501.

10. Gosnell, *Champion Campaigner*, 119.

11. Ibid., 120.

12. Ibid.

13. *Congressional Quarterly, Guide to U.S. Elections*, 229nn1–3.

14. See Hanes Walton Jr., "African Americans, H. Ross Perot, and Image Politics: The Nature of African American Third-Party Politics," in *African American Power and Politics: The Political Context Variable*, ed. Hanes Walton Jr. (New York: Columbia University Press, 1997), 282–93.

15. Gosnell, *Champion Campaigner*, 120.

16. *Congressional Quarterly, Guide to U.S. Elections*, 502–3.

17. Gosnell, *Champion Campaigner*, 152, 154.
18. See Evans and Novak, *Lyndon B. Johnson*, 226–42.
19. Rosenstone, Behr, and Lazarus, *Third Parties*, 231–73.
20. Ibid., 18, 110–18, 142,164–65, 197, 222. See also Walton, "African Americans, H. Ross Perot, and Image Politics," 282–93.
21. See Richard K. Scher, *Politics in the New South: Republicanism, Race, and Leadership in the Twentieth Century* (New York: Paragon House, 1992).
22. Green, *Establishment*, 43–57.
23. Walton, "African Americans, H. Ross Perot, and Image Politics," 282–93.
24. Walton, *Native Son*, 116–19.
25. Ibid., 118.
26. Ibid., 116–19.
27. Melvin G. Holli, *The Wizard of Washington: Emil Hurja, Franklin Roosevelt, and the Birth of Public Opinion Polling* (New York: Palgrave, 2002), 108.
28. Ibid.
29. Quoted in ibid.
30. Walton, *Reelection*, 27.
31. For a discussion of the plans of southern delegations to revolt during the national convention, see Key, *Southern Politics*, 331–44.
32. Walton, *Black Political Parties*, 95–103.
33. Ibid. See also McLemore, "Mississippi Freedom Democratic Party," chaps. 1–5.
34. See White, *Making of the President 1964*, 277–82.

PART V INTRODUCTION

1. Mieczkowski, *Routledge Historical Atlas*, 119.
2. Ibid., 120.
3. Courtney Brown, "Anatomy of a Landslide," 55–83.
4. See Samuel DuBois Cook, "Political Movements and Organizations," *Journal of Politics* 26, no. 1 (1964): 130–44.
5. For the best analysis of this shift, see Richard K. Scher, *Politics in the New South: Republicanism, Race, and Leadership in the Twentieth Century*, 2nd ed. (New York: M. E. Sharpe, 1997). For a similar analysis but from a leadership perspective, see Carter, *From George Wallace to Newt Gingrich*. On recent southern Republican congressional electoral politics, see Earl Black and Merle Black, *The Rise of Southern Republicans* (Cambridge: Harvard University Press, 2002). On voter perception of Republicans and racial conservatism, see Tasha Philpot, *Race, Republicans, and the Return of the Party of Lincoln* (Ann Arbor: University of Michigan Press, 2007). For analysis of how racial conservatism impacted Black Republicans, see Michael Fauntroy, *Republicans and the Black Vote* (New York: Lynne Rienner, 2008).
6. Scher, *Politics in the New South*, 93–191.
7. Frank Freidel, *F.D.R. and the South* (Baton Rouge: Louisiana State University Press, 1965). See also Robert L. Riggs, "The South *Could* Rise Again: Lyndon Johnson and Others," in *Candidates 1960: Behind the Headlines in the Presidential Race*, ed. Eric Sevareid (New York: Basic Books, 1959), 280–321; Hanes Walton Jr., "Black Presidential Participation and the Critical Election Theory," in *The Social and Political Implications of*

the 1984 Jesse Jackson Presidential Campaign, ed. Lorenzo Morris (New York: Praeger, 1990), 49–62.

8. Scher, *Politics in the New South*, 102–18, 129–33; see also Courtney Brown, "Nonlinear Transformation in a Landslide: Johnson and Goldwater in 1964," *American Journal of Political Science* 37, no. 2 (1993): 582–609; Riggs, "South *Could* Rise Again," 280–321.

9. Garry Wills, *Lincoln at Gettysburg: The Words That Remade America* (New York: Simon & Schuster, 1992), 39.

10. Ibid., 38.

11. John C. Waugh, *Reelecting Lincoln: The Battle for the 1864 Presidency* (New York: Crown, 1997); Allen C. Guelzo, *Abraham Lincoln: Redeemer President* (Grand Rapids, MI: William Eerdmans, 1999).

12. Brown, "Nonlinear Transformation," 605.

13. Quoted in Gayle Montgomery and James Johnson, *One Step from the White House: The Rise and Fall of Senator William F. Knowland* (Berkeley: University of California Press, 1998), 141.

14. See Robert L. Hardesty, "With Lyndon Johnson in Texas: A Memoir of the Post-Presidential Years," in *Farewell to the Chief: Former Presidents in American Public Life*, ed. Richard Norton Smith and Timothy Walch (Worland, WY: High Plains Publishing, 1990), 105–7. See also Harry J. Middleton, "A President and His Library: My Recollections of Working with Lyndon B. Johnson," in *Farewell to the Chief*, 109–14.

CHAPTER 13

1. Harry McPherson, "How Race Destroyed the Democrats' Coalition," *New York Times*, October 28, 1988, A35. See also Thomas Edsall, "Race Continues to Be a Wild Card in American Politics," *Washington Post National Weekly* (August 1988), 12.

2. McPherson, "How Race Destroyed," A35. See also Michael Oreskes, "In Racial Politics, Democrats Losing More Than Elections," *New York Times* (November 1988), Section 4, 5–7.

3. See Ronald Radosh, *Divided They Fell: The Demise of the Democratic Party, 1964–1996* (New York: Free Press, 1996); Peter Brown, *Minority Party: Why Democrats Face Defeat in 1992 and Beyond* (Washington, DC: Regnery Gateway, 1991); Benjamin Ginsberg and Alan Stone, ed., *Do Elections Matter?* (New York: M. E. Sharpe, 1988); Carmines and Stimson, *Issue Evolution*; Thomas Byrne Edsall and Mary Edsall, *Chain Reaction: The Impact of Race, Rights, and Taxes on American Politics* (New York: W. W. Norton, 1991); Thomas Ferguson and Joel Rogers, *Right Turn: The Decline of the Democrats and the Future of American Politics* (Boston: Hill and Wang, 1987); Steven Fraser and Gary Gerstle, eds., *The Rise and Fall of the New Deal Order: 1930–1980* (Princeton: Princeton University Press, 1989).

4. William G. Mayer, *The Divided Democrats* (Boulder: Westview, 1996), 160.

5. Richard Valelly, "Vanishing Voters," *American Prospect* 1, no. 1 (1990): 141. For the key works arguing this theme, see Frances Fox Piven and Richard Cloward, *Why Americans Don't Vote* (New York: Pantheon Books, 1989); Paul Kleppner, *Who Voted?: The Dynamics of Electoral Turnout 1870–1980* (New York: Praeger, 1982); Ruy A. Teixeira, *Why Americans Don't Vote: Turnout Decline in the United States, 1960–1984* (New

York: Greenwood, 1987); Walter Dean Burnham, "The Turnout Problem," in *Elections American Style*, ed. A. James Reichley (Washington, DC: Brookings Institution, 1987), 97–133; Walter Dean Burnham, "The Democrats: Right or Left? The Eclipse of the Democratic Party," *Democracy* 2 (July 1982); Paul R. Abramson and John H. Aldrich, "The Decline of Electoral Participation in America," *American Political Science Review* 76, no. 3 (1982): 502–21; and Raymond E. Wolfinger and Steven J. Rosenstone, *Who Votes?* (New Haven: Yale University Press, 1980).

6. Valelly, "Vanishing Voters," 141.

7. William Julius Wilson, "Race-Neutral Policies and the Democratic Coalition," *American Prospect* 1, no. 1 (1990): 81.

8. Stanley Greenberg, "Reconstructing the Democratic Vision," *American Prospect* 1, no. 1 (1990): 84.

9. Ibid., 83.

10. Ibid., 84.

11. Hale, "Democratic Leadership Council," 249–63. Hanes Walton Jr., "The Political Context Variable: The Transformation Politics of the Reagan, Bush, and Clinton Presidencies," in *African American Power*, 9–32.

12. Walton, *Reelection*, 5. For a complete discussion on elections in contexts of political mandates, of changes in attributes, and of political realignment, see 3–11.

13. Robert A. Dahl, "Myth of the Presidential Mandate," *Political Science Quarterly* 105, no. 3 (1990): 363. See also Stanley Kelley Jr., *Interpreting Elections* (Princeton: Princeton University Press, 1983), because Dahl uses it as the basis of his work.

14. Dahl, "Myth of the Presidential Mandate," 364, quoting from Stanley Kelly, *Interpreting Elections.*

15. Ibid., 372.

16. On this matter, see William Gillette, *The Right to Vote: Politics and Passage of the Fifteenth Amendment* (Baltimore: John Hopkins University Press, 1969).

17. See Abraham L. Davis and Barbara Luck Graham, eds., *The Supreme Court, Race, and Civil Rights* (Thousand Oaks, CA: Sage Publications, 1995).

18. Senator Lyndon B. Johnson, "Amendment of Cloture Rule," *Congressional Record*—Senate 81st Congress, 1st Session 95, part 2 (1949), 2046.

19. Ibid., 2042.

20. Ibid., 2048.

21. See Representative Oren Harris, "Not the South's Fight Alone," *Extension of Remarks—Appendix to the Congressional Record,* 81st Congress, 1st Session, 95, part 2 (1949), 282.

22. Carter, *Politics of Rage*, 3–14, 251–56.

23. Cheryl M. Miller and Hanes Walton Jr., "Congressional Support of Civil Rights Public Policy: From Bipartisan to Partisan Convergence," *Congress & the Presidency* 21, no. 1 (1994): 11–27.

24. Brown, "Anatomy of a Landslide," 55–83.

25. Louis Seagull, *Southern Republicanism* (Cambridge: Schenkman, 1975), 149.

26. Ibid.

27. Key, *Southern Politics*, 5–6, 8–10, 531; see also Robert Fredrick Burk, *The Eisenhower Administration and Black Civil Rights* (Knoxville: University of Tennessee Press, 1984), 205.

28. Seagull, *Southern Republicanism*, 149.
29. Ibid.
30. Burk, *Eisenhower Administration*, 3–44, 204–27.
31. Walton, *Native Son*, 129–31.
32. Key, *Southern Politics*, 3–18.
33. Aaron Wildavsky, "President Reagan as a Political Strategist," in *Elections in America*, ed. Kay Lehman Schlozman (Boston: Allen & Unwin, 1987), 231.
34. See Philpot, *Race, Republicans, and the Return of the Party of Lincoln*; see also Fauntroy, *Republicans and the Black Vote*.
35. Tali Mendelberg, *The Race Card* (Princeton: Princeton University Press, 2001).
36. Thomas Schaller, *Whistling Past Dixie: How Democrats Can Win without the South* (New York: Simon & Schuster, 2006), 28.
37. Ibid.
38. Ibid., 19.
39. Ibid.
40. Walton, *Reelection*, 212. See also Bob Woodward, *The Agenda: Inside the Clinton White House* (New York: Simon & Schuster, 1994), 40.
41. Hanes Walton Jr. and Robert Smith, *American Politics and the African American Quest for Universal Freedom*, 2nd ed. (New York: Longman, 2003), 163.
42. Pearl K. Ford Dowe, "Wading in the Water: George W. Bush's Civil Rights Agenda," in *Taking the Measure: The Presidency of George W. Bush*, ed. Donald R. Kelley and Todd G. Shields (College Station: Texas A&M Press, 2013).
43. Tyson D. King-Meadows, *When the Letter Betrays the Spirit: Voting Rights Enforcement and African American Participation from Lyndon Johnson to Barack Obama* (Lanham, MD: Lexington Books, 2011).
44. Pearl K. Ford Dowe, Tekla A. Johnson, and Angie Maxwell, "Yes We Can or Yes We Did? Prospective and Retrospective Change in the Obama Presidency," *Journal of Black Studies* 40 (2010): 462–83; Valeria Sinclair-Chapman and Melayne Price, "Black Politics, the 2008 Election, and the (Im)Possibility of Race Transcendence," *PS: Political Science* 41 (2008): 739–45.
45. Pew Research Center, "Dissecting the 2008 Electorate," April 30, 2009.
46. Tasha S. Philpot, Daron R. Shaw, and Ernest B. McGowen, "Winning the Race: Black Voter Turnout in the 2008 Presidential Election," *Public Opinion Quarterly* 73 (2009): 995–1022.
47. Paul Taylor and Mark Hugo Lopez, "Six Take-aways from the Census Bureau's Voting Report," Pew Research Center, May 8, 2013.
48. President Lyndon B. Johnson, "Howard University Commencement Speech," June 4, 1965. http://www.lbjlib.utexas.edu/johnson/archives.hom/speeches.hom/650604.asp.
49. President Lyndon B. Johnson, "Remarks Upon Witnessing the Certification of the 24th Amendment to the Constitution," February 4, 1964. http://www.presidency.ucsb.edu/ws/?pid=26056.
50. Richard Cohen, "The Election That LBJ Won," *Washington Post,* November 4, 2008, A17.

APPENDIX

1. See Walton, *Native Son*, 149–56, and Walton, *Reelection*, 253–59.
2. Edward R. Tufte, *Data Analysis for Politics and Policy* (Englewood Cliffs, NJ: Prentice Hall, 1974), 1–2.
3. Jerome Clubb, William Flanigan, and Nancy Zingale, eds., *Analyzing Electoral History: A Guide to the Study of American Voter Behavior* (Beverly Hills, CA: Sage, 1981), 8.
4. Ibid.
5. For more scholarship regarding poll tax policies and their impacts, see Ogden, *Poll Tax*, 2–4, 154–67; Key, *Southern Politics*, 578–618; George C. Stoney, "Suffrage in the South: Part I, The Poll Tax," *Survey Graphic* 29, no. 1 (1940): 5–9, 41.
6. Walton, *Reelection*, 109–15.
7. Burnham, "Printed Sources," 58.
8. David Olson et al., *Texas Votes, 1944–1963* (Austin: Institute of Public Affairs, University of Texas, 1964), v.
9. Burnham, "Printed Sources," 57–58.
10. Dallas Morning News, *The Texas Almanac* (Dallas: Dallas Morning News, 1927), 360. See also Galveston News, *The Texas Almanac, 1867* (Galveston: *Galveston News*, 1867).
11. Kingston, Attlesey, and Crawford, *Texas Almanac's Political History*, 59–69, 72–95, 118–69, 200–315. Despite these limitations, the commentary on Texas politics is interesting.
12. Dallas Morning News, *The Texas Almanac, 1996–1997* (Dallas: Dallas Morning News, 1995).
13. Dallas Morning News, *The Texas Almanac, 1943–1944* (Dallas: Dallas Morning News, 1945), 249.
14. Letter, Judy Sall, Librarian, *Dallas Morning News,* to Hanes Walton Jr. (March 21, 2002), 1.
15. Dallas Morning News, *The Texas Almanac, 1943–1944*, 249.
16. Heard and Strong, *Southern Primaries*, 132, 184–86.
17. *America Votes* and *Congressional Quarterly's Guide to U.S. Elections*, 655.
18. Letter from Librarian Bobby Marlin, University of Houston Libraries, to Hanes Walton Jr. (October 16, 2000), 1.
19. Green, *Establishment*, 656.
20. *Dallas Morning News, The Texas Almanac, 1943–1944*, 249.
21. See William L. Richter, "'We Must Rubb Out and Begin Anew': The Army and the Republican Party in Texas Reconstruction, 1867–1870," *Civil War History* 19, no. 4 (1973): 334–52.
22. Jean Carefoot, *Guide to Genealogical Resources in the Texas State Archives* (Austin: Texas State Library, Archives Division, 1984), 95–97; Donaly E. Brice and John C. Barron, *An Index to the 1867 Voters' Registration of Texas* (Bowie, TX: Heritage Books, 2000).
23. Hanes Walton Jr., Sharon Wright, and Frank Pryor, "Texas African American Re-

publicans: The Electoral Revolt in the 1920 Presidential and Gubernatorial Election," *National Conference of Black Political Scientists Newsletter* 17 (2002): 8–12. For a list of the African American presidential electors in 1920 and the votes for them, see Walton, *Black Political Parties*, 220–33, table 1-A.

24. Bruce Altschuler, *LBJ and the Polls* (University Press of Florida, 1990).

Bibliography

The bibliography is organized in the following sections, in order: Books, Articles, Letters, Court Cases, Government Documents, and Library Collections.

BOOKS

Abernathy, Francis Edward. "African-American Folklore in Texas and in the Texas Folklore Society." In *Juneteenth Texas: Essays in African American Folklore*, edited by Francis Edward Abernathy, Carolyn Fiedler Satterwhite, Patrick B. Mullen, and Alan B. Govenar, 1–14. Denton: University of North Texas Press, 1996.

Achen, Christopher H., and W. Phillips Shively. *Cross-Level Inference*. Chicago: University of Chicago Press, 1995.

Altschuler, Bruce E. *LBJ and the Polls*. Gainesville: University of Florida Press, 1990.

American Annual Cyclopaedia and Register of Important Events of the Year 1867. New York: D. Appleton and Company, 1869.

American Annual Cyclopaedia and Register of Important Events of the Year 1868. New York: D. Appleton and Company, 1870.

American Cyclopaedia and Register of Important Events of the Year 1869. New York: D. Appleton and Company, 1870.

Anders, Evan. *Boss Rule in South Texas: The Progressive Era*. Austin: University of Texas Press, 1982.

Anderson, Totton James. "California: Enigma of National Politics." In *Western Politics*, edited by Frank Jonas. Salt Lake City: University of Utah Press, 1961.

Barber, James David. *Politics by Humans: Research on American Leadership*. Durham: Duke University Press, 1988.

Bardes, Barbara, Mack Shelly II, and Steffen Schmidt. *American Government and Politics Today: The Essentials*. Boston: West Wadsworth, 1998.

Barr, Alwyn. *Black Texans: A History of Negroes in Texas, 1528–1971*. Austin: Jenkins Book Publishing, 1973.

Barr, Alwyn. *Reconstruction to Reform: Texas Politics, 1870–1906*. Austin: University of Texas Press, 1971.

Barr, Alwyn, and Robert A. Calvert, eds. *Black Leaders: Texans for Their Times*. Austin: Texas State Historical Association, 1981.

Bass, Harold F. "The President and the National Party Organization." In *Presidents and*

Their Parties: Leadership or Neglect?, edited by Robert Harmel, 59–89. New York: Praeger, 1984.

Beall, Charles. "Wyoming: The Equality State." In *Western Politics*, edited by Frank Jonas. Salt Lake City: University of Utah Press, 1961.

Beck, Paul Allen. *Party Politics in America*. 8th ed. New York: Addison Wesley Longman, 1997.

Bennett, W. Lance. *Inside the System: Culture, Institutions, and Power in American Politics*. Fort Worth: Harcourt Brace College, 1994.

Berman, Larry, and Bruce Allen Murphy. *Approaching Democracy*. 2nd ed. Upper Saddle River, NJ: Prentice-Hall, 1999.

Black, Earl, and Merle Black. *The Rise of Southern Republicans*. Cambridge: Harvard University Press, 2002.

Bone, Hugh. "Washington State: Free Style Politics." In *Western Politics*, edited by Frank Jonas. Salt Lake City: University of Utah Press, 1961.

Brewer, John Mason. *Negro Legislators in Texas and Their Descendants: A History of the Negro in Texas Politics from Reconstruction to Disfranchisement*. Dallas: Mathis Publishing, 1935.

Brice, Donaly E., and John C. Barron. *An Index to the 1867 Voters' Registration of Texas*. Bowie: Heritage Books, 2000.

Brown, Courtney. *Serpents in the Sand: Essays on the Nonlinear Nature of Politics and Human Destiny*. Ann Arbor: University of Michigan Press, 1995.

Brown, George. *The Speaker of the House: The Romantic Story of John N. Garner*. New York: Brewer, Warren, and Putnam, 1932.

Brown, Peter. *Minority Party: Why Democrats Face Defeat in 1992 and Beyond*. Washington, DC: Regnery-Gateway, 1991.

Bryson, Conrey. *Dr. Lawrence Nixon and the White Primary*. El Paso: Texas Western Press, 1974.

Burk, Robert Fredrick. *The Eisenhower Administration and Black Civil Rights*. Knoxville: University of Tennessee Press, 1984.

Burnham, Walter Dean. "Printed Sources." In *Analyzing Electoral History: Guide to the Study of American Voter Behavior*, edited by Jerome Clubb, William Flanigan, and Nancy Zingale. Beverly Hills, CA: Sage, 1981.

Burnham, Walter Dean. "The Turnout Problem." In *Elections American Style*, edited by A. James Reichley, 97–133. Washington, DC: Brookings Institution, 1987.

Burns, James MacGregor. "Confessions of a Kennedy Man." In *To Heal and to Build: The Programs of Lyndon B. Johnson*, edited by James MacGregor Burns, 417–23. New York: McGraw-Hill, 1968.

Campbell, Angus. "Recent Developments in Survey Studies of Political Behavior." In *Essays on the Behavioral Study of Politics*, edited by Austin Ranney, 31–46. Urbana: University of Illinois Press, 1962.

Carefoot, Jean. *Guide to Genealogical Resources in the Texas State Archives*. Austin: Texas State Library, Archives Division, 1984.

Carmines, Edward G., and James A. Stimson. *Issue Evolution: Race and the Transformation of American Politics*. Princeton: Princeton University Press, 1989.

Caro, Robert A. *The Years of Lyndon Johnson: Master of the Senate*. New York: Alfred A. Knopf, 2002.

Caro, Robert A. *The Years of Lyndon Johnson: Means of Ascent.* New York: Alfred A. Knopf, 1990.

Caro, Robert A. *The Years of Lyndon Johnson: The Path to Power.* New York: Vintage Books, 1982.

Caro, Robert A. *The Years of Lyndon Johnson: The Passage to Power.* New York: Alfred A. Knopf, 2012.

Carter, Dan T. *From George Wallace to Newt Gingrich: Race in the Conservative Counter-revolution 1963–1994.* Baton Rouge: Louisiana State University Press, 1996.

Carter, Dan T. *The Politics of Rage: George Wallace, the Origins of the New Conservatism, and the Transformation of American Politics.* New York: Simon & Schuster, 1995.

Carter, Jimmy. *An Hour before Daylight: Memories of a Rural Boyhood.* New York: Simon & Schuster, 2001.

Carter, Jimmy. *Why Not the Best.* New York: Bantam Books, 1976.

Casdorph, Paul. *A History of the Republican Party in Texas, 1865–1965.* Austin: Pemberton Press, 1965.

Clark, John. *The Fall of the Duke of Duval: A Prosecutor's Journal.* Austin: Eakin Press, 1995.

Clubb, Jerome, William Flanigan, and Nancy Zingale, eds. *Analyzing Electoral History: Guide to the Study of American Voter Behavior.* Beverly Hills, CA: Sage, 1981.

Congressional Quarterly. *Guide to U.S. Elections.* 3rd ed. Washington, DC: Congressional Quarterly, 1994.

Conover, Pamela Johnston. "Political Socialization: Where's the Politics?" Vol. 3 of *Political Science: Looking to the Future,* edited by William Crotty, 125–52. Evanston: Northwestern University Press, 1991.

Converse, Jean M. *Survey Research in the United States: Roots and Emergence, 1890–1960.* Berkley: University of California Press, 1987.

Converse, Philip E. "Religion and Politics: The 1960 Election." In *Elections and the Political Order,* edited by Angus Campbell, Philip E. Converse, Warren E. Miller, and Donald E. Stokes, 96–124. New York: John Wiley & Sons, 1966.

Converse, Philip E., and Donald R. Kinder. "Voting and Electoral Behavior." In *A Telescope on Society: Survey Research and Social Science at the University of Michigan and Beyond,* edited by James S. House, F. Thomas Juster, Robert L. Kahn, Howard Schuman, and Eleanor Singer, 70–97. Ann Arbor: University of Michigan Press, 2004.

Crespi, Irving. *Pre-election Polling: Sources of Accuracy and Error.* New York: Russell Sage Foundation, 1988.

Dallas Morning News. *The 1928 Texas Almanac.* Dallas: Dallas Morning News, 1929.

Dallas Morning News. *The Texas Almanac, 1941–1942.* Dallas: Dallas Morning News, 1942.

Dallas Morning News. *The Texas Almanac, 1943–1944.* Dallas: Dallas Morning News, 1945.

Dallas Morning News. *The Texas Almanac, 1996–1997.* Dallas: Dallas Morning News, 1995.

Dallek, Robert. *Lone Star Rising: Lyndon Johnson and His Times, 1908–1960.* New York: Oxford University Press, 1991.

Davis, Abraham L., and Barbara Luck Graham, eds. *The Supreme Court, Race, and Civil Rights.* Thousand Oaks, CA: Sage Publications, 1995.

DeGrazia, Alfred. *The Western Public: 1952 and Beyond*. Stanford: Stanford University Press, 1954.

Dennis, Jack. "The Study of Electoral Behavior." Vol. 3 of *Political Science: Looking to the Future*, edited by William Crotty, 51–89. Evanston, IL: Northwestern University Press, 1991.

Divine, Robert A. "The Johnson Literature." In *Exploring the Johnson Years*, edited by Robert A. Divine, 3–23. Austin: University of Texas Press, 1981.

Donnelly, Thomas. "New Mexico: An Area of Conflicting Culture." In *Rocky Mountain Politics*, edited by Thomas Donnelly. Albuquerque: University of New Mexico Press, 1940.

Dowe, Pearl K. Ford. "Wading in the Water: George W. Bush's Civil Rights Agenda." In *Taking the Measure: The Presidency of George W. Bush*, edited by Donald R. Kelley and Todd G. Shields. College Station: Texas A&M Press, 2013.

Dye, Thomas R. *Politics in America*. 2nd ed. Upper Saddle River, NJ: Prentice-Hall, 1997.

Dye, Thomas R., and L. Harmon Zeigler. *The Irony of Democracy: An Uncommon Introduction to American Politics*. 5th ed. Monterey, CA: Duxbury Press, 1981.

Edsall, Thomas Byrne, and Mary Edsall. *Chain Reaction: The Impact of Race, Rights, and Taxes on American Politics*. New York: W. W. Norton, 1991.

Edwards, David V., and Alessandra Lippucci. *Practicing American Politics: An Introduction to Government*. New York: Worth Publishers, 1998.

Eldersveld, Samuel J. *Political Parties: A Behavioral Analysis*. Chicago: Rand McNally & Company, 1964.

Eldersveld, Samuel J., and Hanes Walton Jr. *Political Parties in American Society*. 2nd ed. Boston: Bedford/St. Martin's, 2000.

Ellison, Ralph. "The Myth of the Flawed White Southerner." In *To Heal and to Build: The Programs of Lyndon B. Johnson*, edited by James MacGregor Burns, 207–16. New York: McGraw-Hill, 1968.

Epstein, Leon D. "National Party Conventions: Changing Functions, New Research Strategies." In *Elections at Home and Abroad: Essays in Honor of Warren E. Miller*, edited by M. Kent Jennings and Thomas E. Mann, 265–87. Ann Arbor: University of Michigan Press, 1994.

Ernst, Harry. "The Primary That Made a President: West Virginia 1960." In *Cases in Practical Politics*. New York: McGraw-Hill, 1962.

Eulau, Heinz. "Electoral Survey Data and the Temporal Dimension." In *Elections at Home and Abroad: Essays in Honor of Warren E. Miller*, edited by M. Kent Jennings and Thomas E. Mann, 39–70. Ann Arbor: University of Michigan Press, 1994.

Evans, Robert, and Robert Novak. *Lyndon B. Johnson: The Exercise of Power*. New York: New American Library, 1966.

Farley, James A. *Behind the Ballots: The Personal History of a Politician*. New York: Harcourt, Brace and Company, 1938.

Fauntroy, Michael. *Republicans and the Black Vote*. New York: Lynne Rienner, 2008.

Fenno, Richard F., Jr. *Home Style: House Members in Their Districts*. Boston: Little, Brown and Company, 1978.

Fenno, Richard F., Jr. *Home Style and Washington Work: Studies of Congressional Politics*. Ann Arbor: University of Michigan Press, 1989.

Fenton, John. *Midwest Politics*. New York: Holt, Rinehart & Winston, 1966.

Fenton, John. *Politics in the Border States*. New Orleans: Hauser Press, 1957.
Ferguson, Thomas, and Joel Rogers. *Right Turn: The Decline of the Democrats and the Future of American Politics*. Boston: Hill and Wang, 1987.
Fiorina, Morris, and Paul Peterson. *The New American Democracy*. 2nd ed. New York: Longman, 2002.
Fite, Gilbert C. *Richard B. Russell, Jr., Senator from Georgia*. Chapel Hill: University of North Carolina Press, 1991.
Fleming, Daniel B. *Kennedy vs. Humphrey, West Virginia, 1960: The Pivotal Battle for the Democratic Presidential Nomination*. Jefferson: McFarland & Company, 1992.
Ford, Pearl K., ed. *African Americans in Georgia: A Reflection of Politics and Policy in the New South*. Macon, GA: Mercer University Press, 2010.
Foster, Lorn S., ed. *The Voting Rights Act: Consequences and Implications*. New York: Praeger, 1985.
Franklin, John Hope, and Loren Schweninger. *Runaway Slaves: Rebels on the Plantation*. New York: Oxford University Press, 1999.
Franklin, Mark N., and Christopher Wlezien, eds. *The Future of Election Studies*. New York: Pergamon, 2002.
Fraser, Steve, and Gary Gerstle, eds. *The Rise and Fall of the New Deal Order: 1930–1980*. Princeton: Princeton University Press, 1989.
Freidel, Frank. *F.D.R. and the South*. Baton Rouge: Louisiana State University Press, 1965.
Gaither, Gerald H. *Blacks and the Populist Revolt: Ballots and Bigotry in the "New South."* Tuscaloosa: University of Alabama Press, 1977.
Galveston News. *The Texas Almanac, 1867*. Galveston: Galveston News, 1867.
Gillette, Michael L. "Heman Marion Sweatt: Civil Rights Plaintiff." In *Black Leaders: Texans for Their Times*, edited by Alwyn Barr and Robert A. Calvert, 156–88. Austin: Texas State Historical Association, 1981.
Gillette, William. *The Right to Vote: Politics and the Passage of the Fifteenth Amendment*. Baltimore: Johns Hopkins University Press, 1969.
Ginsberg, Benjamin, Theodore J. Lowi, and Margaret Weir. *We the People: An Introduction to American Politics*. 2nd ed. New York: W. W. Norton, 1999.
Ginsberg, Benjamin, and Alan Stone, eds. *Do Elections Matter?* New York: M. E. Sharpe, 1988.
Glad, Betty. *Jimmy Carter: In Search of the Great White House*. New York: W. W. Norton, 1980.
Glasrud, Bruce A. "William M. McDonald: Business and Fraternal Leader." In *Black Leaders: Texans for Their Times*, edited by Alwyn Barr and Robert A. Calvert. Austin: Texas State Historical Association, 1981.
Goldman, Eric F. *The Tragedy of Lyndon Johnson*. New York: Alfred A. Knopf, 1974.
Goldman, Ralph M. "The American President as Party Leader: A Synoptic History." In *Presidents and Their Parties: Leadership or Neglect?*, edited by Robert Harmel, 19–55. New York: Praeger, 1984.
Goldman, Ralph M. "Titular Head of Party." In *Political Parties and Elections in the United States: An Encyclopedia*, edited by L. Sandy Maisel. New York: Garland, 1991.
Goldman, Ralph M. "Titular Leadership of the Presidential Parties." In *The Presidency*, edited by Aaron Wildavsky, 384–410. Boston: Little, Brown, 1969.

Gosnell, Harold F. *Boss Platt and His New York Machine: A Study of the Political Leadership of Thomas C. Platt, Theodore Roosevelt, and Others*. Chicago: University of Chicago Press, 1924.

Gosnell, Harold F. *Champion Campaigner: Franklin D. Roosevelt*. New York: Macmillan Company, 1952.

Gosnell, Harold F. *Grass Roots Politics: National Voting Behavior of Typical States*. Washington, DC: American Council on Public Affairs, 1942.

Gosnell, Harold F. *Machine Politics: Chicago Model*. Chicago: University of Chicago Press, 1937.

Green, George Norris. *The Establishment in Texas Politics: The Primitive Years, 1938-1957*. Westport, CT: Greenwood, 1979.

Guelzo, Allen C. *Abraham Lincoln: Redeemer President*. Grand Rapids, MI: William Eerdmans, 1999.

Hale, Jon F. "The Democratic Leadership Council: Institutionalizing Party Faction." In *The State of the Parties: The Changing Role of Contemporary American Parties*, edited by Daniel M. Shea and John C. Green, 249–63. Lanham, MD: Rowman & Littlefield, 1994.

Hardeman, D. B., and D. C. Brown. *Rayburn: A Biography*. Austin: University of Texas Press, 1987.

Hardesty, Robert L. "With Lyndon Johnson in Texas: A Memoir of the Post-Presidential Years." In *Farewell to the Chief: Former Presidents in American Public Life*, edited by Richard Norton Smith and Timothy Walch, 95–108. Worland, WY: High Plains Publishing, 1990.

Hare, Maud Cuney. *Norris Wright Cuney: A Tribune of the Black People*. Austin: Steck-Vaughn Company, 1968.

Harrigan, John J. *Politics and Policy in State and Communities*. 4th ed. New York: HarperCollins, 1991.

Harwood, Richard, and Haynes Johnson. *Lyndon*. New York: Praeger, 1973.

Heard, Alexander. *A Two-Party South?* Chapel Hill: University of North Carolina Press, 1952.

Heard, Alexander, and Donald S. Strong. *Southern Primaries and Elections, 1920–1949*. Tuscaloosa: University of Alabama Press, 1950.

Hinze, Virginia N. "Norris Wright Cuney." Master's thesis, Rice University, 1965.

Holli, Melvin G. *The Wizard of Washington: Emil Hurja, Franklin Roosevelt, and the Birth of Public Opinion Polling*. New York: Palgrave, 2002.

Hollon, W. Eugene. *The Southwest: Old and New*. New York: Alfred Knopf, 1961.

Holloway, Harry. *The Politics of the Southern Negro: From Exclusion to Big City Organization*. New York: Random House, 1969.

Hunter, Tera W. "Introduction." In *Norris Wright Cuney: A Tribune of the Black People*, by Maud Cuney-Hare. New York: G. K. Hall, 1995.

James, Marquis M. *Mr. Garner of Texas*. New York: Bobbs-Merrill, 1939.

Janda, Kenneth, Jeffrey Berry, and Jerry Goldman. *The Challenge of Democracy*. 5th ed. Boston: Houghton Mifflin, 1974.

Jennings, M. Kent. "Survey Research and Political Socialization." In *A Telescope on Society: Survey Research and Social Science at the University of Michigan and Beyond*, edited by James S. House, F. Thomas Juster, Robert L. Kahn, Howard Schuman, and Eleanor Singer, 98–117. Ann Arbor: University of Michigan Press, 2004.

Johnson, Charles W. *Proceedings of the First Three Republican National Conventions of 1856, 1860 and 1864*. Minneapolis: Harrison & Smith, Printers, 1893.

Johnson, Lyndon B. *The Public Papers of the Presidents of the United States: Lyndon B. Johnson*. Washington, DC: United States Government Printing Office, 1965.

Jonas, Frank. "Utah: Sagebrush Democracy." In *Rocky Mountain Politics*, edited by Thomas C. Donnelly. Albuquerque: University of New Mexico Press, 1940.

Jonas, Frank, ed. *Western Politics*. Salt Lake City: University of Utah Press, 1961.

Jonas, Frank. "The Western Scene." In *Western Politics*, edited by Frank Jonas. Salt Lake City: University of Utah Press, 1961.

Kearns, Doris. *Lyndon Johnson and the American Dream*. New York: Harper & Row, 1976.

Kelley, Stanley, Jr. *Interpreting Elections*. Princeton: Princeton University Press, 1983.

Kessel, John H. *The Goldwater Coalition: Republican Strategies in 1964*. Indianapolis: Bobbs-Merrill, 1968.

Key, V. O., Jr. *A Primer of Statistics for Political Scientists*. New York: Thomas Y. Crowell, 1954.

Key, V. O., Jr. "Interpreting the Election Results." In *The Presidential Election and Transition 1960–1961*, edited by Paul T. David, 150–75. Washington, DC: Brookings Institution, 1961.

Key, V. O., Jr. *Politics, Parties, and Pressure Groups*. 4th ed. New York: Thomas Y. Crowell, 1958.

Key, V. O., Jr. *Southern Politics in State and Nation*. New York: Alfred A. Knopf, 1949.

King, Gary. *Solution to the Ecological Inference Problem: Reconstructing Individual Behavior from Aggregate Data*. Princeton: Princeton University Press, 1997.

King-Meadows, Tyson D. *When the Letter Betrays the Spirit: Voting Rights Enforcement and African American Participation from Lyndon Johnson to Barack Obama*. Lanham, MD: Lexington Books, 2011.

Kingston, Mike, Sam Attlesey, and Mary G. Crawford. *The Texas Almanac's Political History of Texas*. Austin: Eakin Press, 1992.

Kirkpatrick, Evron M. "The Impact of the Behavioral Approach in Traditional Political Science." In *Essays on the Behavioral Study of Politics*, edited by Austin Ranney, 1–29. Urbana: University of Illinois Press, 1962.

Kleppner, Paul. *Who Voted: The Dynamics of Electoral Turnout, 1870–1980*. New York: Praeger, 1982.

Kousser, J. Morgan. *The Shaping of Southern Politics: Suffrage Restriction and the Establishment of the One-Party South, 1880–1910*. New Haven: Yale University Press, 1974.

Lamare, James W., J. L. Polinard, and Robert D. Wrinkle. "Texas: Lone Star (Wars) State." In *The New Politics of the Old South: An Introduction to Southern Politics*, edited by Charles S. Bullock III and Mark J. Rozell, 245–58. Lanham, MD: Rowman & Littlefield, 1998.

Lasser, William. *American Politics: The Enduring Constitution*. 2nd ed. Boston: Houghton Mifflin, 1999.

Lazarsfeld, Paul F., Bernard Berleson, and Hazel Gaudet. *The People's Choice*. 3rd ed. New York: Columbia University Press, 1968

Lewinson, Paul. *Race, Class, & Party: A History of Negro Suffrage and White Politics in the South*. New York: Oxford University Press, 1932.

Lewis, Arthur. *The Day They Shook the Plum Tree*. New York: Harcourt, Brace, & World, 1963.

Light, Paul Charles. *The President's Agenda: Domestic Policy Choice from Kennedy to Carter (With Notes on Ronald Reagan)*. Baltimore: Johns Hopkins University Press, 1983.

Lisio, Donald J. *Hoover, Blacks, and Lily-Whites: A Study of Southern Strategies*. Chapel Hill: University of North Carolina Press, 1985.

Lockard, Duane. *New England State Politics*. Princeton: Princeton University Press, 1959.

Lott, Virgil, and Mercurio Martinez. *The Kingdom of Zapata*. Austin: Eakin Press, 1983.

Martin, Roscoe C. *The People's Party in Texas: A Study in Third-Party Politics*. Austin: University of Texas Press, 1970.

Mayer, William G. *The Divided Democrats*. Boulder: Westview Press, 1996.

Mayhew, David R. *Congress: The Electoral Connection*. New Haven: Yale University Press, 1974.

Mayhew, David R. "Why Did V. O. Key Draw Back from His 'Have-Nots'?" In *V. O. Key, Jr. and the Study of American Politics*, edited by Milton Cummings Jr. Washington, DC: American Political Science Association, 1988.

McLemore, Leslie Burl. "The Freedom Democratic Party and the Changing Political Status of the Negro in Mississippi." Master's thesis, Atlanta University, 1965.

McLemore, Leslie Burl. "The Mississippi Freedom Democratic Party: A Case Study of Grass-Roots Politics." PhD diss., University of Massachusetts at Amherst, 1971. Order No. 7117702. http://0-search.proquest.com.library.uark.edu/docview/302623059?accountid=8361.

Mendelberg, Tali. *The Race Card*. Princeton: Princeton University Press, 2001.

Middleton, Harry J. "A President and His Library: My Recollections of Working with Lyndon B. Johnson." In *Farewell to the Chief: Former Presidents in American Public Life*, edited by Richard Norton Smith and Timothy Walch, 95–108. Worland, WY: High Plains Publishing, 1990.

Mieczkowski, Yanek. *The Routledge Historical Atlas of Presidential Elections*. New York: Routledge, 2001.

Milkis, Sidney M. "The Presidency and the Political Parties," in *The Presidency and the Political System*, edited by Michael Nelson, 331–49. 2nd ed. Washington, DC: Congressional Quarterly, 1988.

Milkis, Sidney M. *The President and the Parties: The Transformation of the American Party System since the New Deal*. New York: Oxford University Press, 1993.

Milkis, Sidney M. "Presidents and Party Purges: With Special Emphasis on the Lessons of 1938." In *Presidents and Their Parties: Leadership or Neglect?*, edited by Robert Harmel, 151–75. New York: Praeger, 1984.

Miller, Merle. *Lyndon: An Oral Biography*. New York: G. P. Putnam's Sons, 1980.

Miller, Warren E. *Without Consent: Mass-Elite Linkages in Presidential Politics*. Lexington: University Press of Kentucky, 1988.

Miller, Warren E. and M. Kent Jennings. *Parties in Transition: A Longitudinal Study of Party Elites and Party Supporters*. New York: Russell Sage Foundation, 1986.

Miller, Warren E., and Teresa E. Levitin. *Leadership and Change: Presidential Elections from 1952 to 1976*. Cambridge: Winthrop, 1976.

Miller, Warren E., and J. Merrill Shanks. *The New American Voter*. Cambridge: Harvard University Press, 1996.
Mills, Kay. *This Little Light of Mine: The Life of Fannie Lou Hamer*. New York: Penguin, 1993.
Montgomery, Gayle, and James Johnson. *One Step from the White House: The Rise and Fall of Senator William F. Knowland*. Berkeley: University of California Press, 1998.
Mooney, Booth. *The Lyndon Johnson Story*. New York: Farrar, Straus & Cudahy, 1956.
Neustadt, Richard E. *Presidential Power: The Politics of Leadership*. New York: John Wiley & Sons, 1960.
Neustadt, Richard E. *Presidential Power: The Politics of Leadership with Reflections on Johnson and Nixon*. New York: John Wiley & Sons, 1976.
Olson, David, et al. *Texas Votes, 1944–1963*. Austin: Institute of Public Affairs, University of Texas, 1964.
Ogden, Frederic D. *The Poll Tax in the South*. Tuscaloosa: University of Alabama Press, 1958.
Peterson, Henry. "Wyoming: A Cattle Kingdom." In *Rocky Mountain Politics*, edited by Thomas Donnelly. Albuquerque: University of New Mexico Press, 1940.
Phillips, Kevin. *The Emerging Republican Majority*. New Rochelle, NY: Arlington House, 1969.
Phillips, William G. *Yarborough of Texas*. Washington, DC: Acropolis Books, 1969.
Philpot, Tasha S. *Race, Republicans, and the Return of the Party of Lincoln*. Ann Arbor: University of Michigan Press, 2007.
Pickle, Jake, and Peggy Pickle. *Jake*. Austin: University of Texas Press, 1997.
Piven, Frances Fox, and Richard Cloward. *Why Americans Don't Vote*. New York: Pantheon Books, 1989.
Pomper, Gerald M., Ross K. Baker, Charles E. Jacob, Wilson Carey McWilliams, and Henry A. Plotkin. *The Election of 1976: Reports and Interpretations*. New York: David McCay, 1977.
Pycior, Julie Leininger. *LBJ and Mexican Americans: The Paradox of Power*. Austin: University of Texas Press, 1997.
Quezada, J. Gilberto. *Border Boss: Manuel B. Bravo and Zapata County*. College Station: Texas A&M University Press, 1999.
Radosh, Ronald. *Divided They Fell: The Demise of the Democratic Party, 1964–1996*. New York: Free Press, 1996.
Ranney, Austin. "The Utility and Limitations of Aggregate Data in the Study of Electoral Behavior." In *Essays on the Behavioral Study of Politics*, edited by Austin Ranney, 91–102. Urbana: University of Illinois Press, 1962.
Rice, Lawrence D. *The Negro in Texas, 1874–1900*. Baton Rouge: Louisiana State University Press, 1971.
Riggs, Robert L. "The South *Could* Rise Again: Lyndon Johnson and Others." In *Candidates 1960: Behind the Headlines in the Presidential Race*, edited by Eric Sevareid, 280–321. New York: Basic Books, 1959.
Riordan, William, with Terrence McDonald, eds. *Plunkitt of Tammany Hall: A Series of Very Plain Talks on Very Practical Politics*. Boston: Bedford/St. Martin's Press, 1994.
Rosenstone, Steven J. *Forecasting Presidential Elections*. New Haven: Yale University Press, 1983.

Rosenstone, Steven J., Roy L. Behr, and Edward H. Lazarus. *Third Parties America: Citizen Response to Major Party Failure*. 2nd ed. Princeton: Princeton University Press, 1996.

Rossiter, Clinton. *The American Presidency*. New York: Harcourt Brace & Company, 1956.

Rossiter, Clinton. *The American Presidency*. 2nd ed. New York: Harcourt, Brace & World, 1960.

Savage, Sean J. *Roosevelt: The Party Leader 1932–1945*. Lexington: University Press of Kentucky, 1991.

Savage, Sean J. *Truman and the Democratic Party*. Lexington: University Press of Kentucky, 1997.

Schaller, Thomas. *Whistling Past Dixie: How Democrats Can Win without the South*. New York: Simon & Schuster, 2006.

Scher, Richard K. *Politics in the New South: Republicanism, Race, and Leadership in the Twentieth Century*. New York: Paragon House, 1992.

Scher, Richard K. *Politics in the New South: Republicanism, Race, and Leadership in the Twentieth Century*. 2nd ed. New York: M. E. Sharpe, 1997.

Schlesinger, Arthur M., Jr. *A Thousand Days: John F. Kennedy in the White House*. Boston: Houghton Mifflin, 1965.

Scroop, Daniel. *Mr. Democrat: Jim Farley, the New Deal, and the Making of Modern American Politics*. Ann Arbor: University of Michigan Press, 2006.

Seagull, Louis. *Southern Republicanism*. Cambridge: Schenkman, 1975.

Seligman, Lester G. "The Presidential Office and the President as Party Leader (with a Postscript on the Kennedy-Nixon Era)." In *Parties and Elections in an Anti-Party Age*, edited by Jeff Fishel, 295–302. Bloomington: Indiana University Press, 1978.

Sherrill, Robert. *The Accidental President*. New York: Grossman Publishers, 1967.

Shesol, Jeff. *Mutual Contempt: Lyndon Johnson, Robert Kennedy, and the Feud That Defined a Decade*. New York: W. W. Norton, 1997.

Soukup, James R., Clifton McCleskey, and Harry Holloway. *Party and Factional Division in Texas*. Austin: University of Texas Press, 1964.

Speel, Robert W. *Changing Patterns of Voting in the Northern United States: Electoral Realignment, 1952–1996*. University Park: Pennsylvania State University Press, 1998.

Strong, Donald. *Urban Republicanism in the South*. University of Alabama, Bureau of Public Administration, 1960.

Sundquist, James L. *Dynamics of the Party System: Alignment and Realignment of Political Parties in the United States*. Rev. ed. Washington, DC: Brookings Institution, 1983.

Sundquist, James L. "Political Parties and Agenda Building: Eisenhower to Johnson." In *Parties and Elections in an Anti-Party Age*, edited by Jeffrey Fishel, 263–73. Bloomington: Indiana University Press, 1978.

Sundquist, James L. *Politics and Policy: The Eisenhower, Kennedy, and Johnson Years*. Washington, DC: Brookings Institution, 1968.

Talmadge, Herman E. *Talmadge—A Political Legacy, A Politician's Life: A Memoir*. Atlanta: Peachtree Publishers, 1987.

Teixeira, Ruy A. *Why Americans Don't Vote: Turnout Decline in the United States, 1960–1984*. New York: Greenwood Press, 1987.

Thompson, Edward, ed. *Theodore H. White at Large: The Best of His Magazine Writing, 1939–1986*. New York: Pantheon Books, 1992.

Timmons, Bascom N. *Garner of Texas: A Personal History*. New York: Harper & Brothers, 1948.

Tower, John. *Consequences*. Boston: Little, Brown and Company, 1991.

Truman, Harry. *The Public Papers of the Presidents of the United States*. Washington, DC: United States Government Printing Office, 1966.

Truman, Harry. *Truman Speaks*. New York: Columbia University Press, 1960.

Tufte, Edward R. *Data Analysis for Politics and Policy*. Englewood Cliffs, NJ: Prentice Hall, 1974.

Vedlitz, Arnold, James A. Dyer, and David B. Hill. "The Changing Texas Voter." In *The South's New Politics: Realignment and Dealignment*, edited by Robert H. Swansbrough and David M. Brodsky, 38–53. Columbia: University of South Carolina Press, 1988.

Walton, Hanes, Jr. "African Americans, H. Ross Perot, and Image Politics: The Nature of African American Third-Party Politics." In *African American Power and Politics: The Political Context Variable*, edited by Robert Y. Shapiro, 282–93. New York: Columbia University Press, 1997.

Walton, Hanes, Jr. *Black Political Parties*. New York: Free Press, 1972.

Walton, Hanes, Jr. "Black Political Parties and Congress: The Role of the *Congressional Record*." In *Black Politics and Black Political Behavior: A Linkage Analysis*, edited by Hanes Walton Jr., 41–47. Westport, CT: Praeger, 1994.

Walton, Hanes, Jr. *Black Politics: A Theoretical and Structural Analysis*. Philadelphia: J. B. Lippincott, 1972.

Walton, Hanes, Jr. "Black Presidential Participation and the Critical Election Theory." In *The Social and Political Implications of the 1984 Jesse Jackson Presidential Campaign*, edited by Lorenzo Morris, 49–62. New York: Praeger, 1990.

Walton, Hanes, Jr. *Black Republicans: The Politics of the Black and Tans*. Metuchen, NJ: Scarecrow Press, 1975.

Walton, Hanes, Jr. "Black Southern Politics: The Influences of Bunche, Martin and Key." In *Black Politics and Black Political Behavior: A Linkage Analysis*, edited by Hanes Walton Jr., 19–38. Westport, CT: Praeger, 1994.

Walton, Hanes, Jr. "Black Voting Behavior in the Segregation Era: 1944–1964." In *Black Politics and Black Political Behavior: A Linkage Analysis*, edited by Hanes Walton Jr., 115–34. Westport, CT: Praeger, 1994.

Walton, Hanes, Jr. *The Native Son Presidential Candidate: The Carter Vote in Georgia*. New York: Praeger, 1992.

Walton, Hanes, Jr. *The Negro in Third Party Politics*. Philadelphia: Dorrance, 1969.

Walton, Hanes, Jr. "Perry Wilson Howard." In *Dictionary of American Negro Biography*, edited by Rayford W. Logan and Michael R. Winston. New York: W. W. Norton, 1982.

Walton, Hanes, Jr. "The Political Context Variable: The Transformation Politics of the Reagan, Bush, and Clinton Presidencies." In *African American Power and Politics: The Political Context Variable*, edited by Robert Y. Shapiro, 9–32. New York: Columbia University Press, 1997.

Walton, Hanes, Jr. *The Political Philosophy of Martin Luther King, Jr.* Westport, CT: Greenwood, 1971.

Walton, Hanes, Jr. *Reelection: William Jefferson Clinton as a Native-Son Presidential Candidate*. New York: Columbia University Press, 2000.

Walton, Hanes, Jr. *When the Marching Stopped: The Politics of Civil Rights Regulatory Agencies*. Albany: State University of New York Press, 1988.

Walton, Hanes, Jr., Josephine A. V. Allen, Sherman C. Puckett, and Donald R. Deskins Jr. "Black Politicians: Paving the Way." In *African Americans and the Presidency: The Road to the White House*, edited by Bruce Glasrud and Cary Wintz, 167–86. New York: Routledge, 2010.

Walton, Hanes, Jr., Josephine A. V. Allen, Sherman C. Puckett, and Donald R. Deskins Jr. "Dead Certain: The Election of Barack Obama and Its Implications for Racial Politics." In *The Obama Phenomenon: Toward a Multiracial Democracy*, edited by Charles Henry, Robert Allen, and Robert Chisman. Urbana: University of Illinois Press, 2011.

Walton, Hanes, Jr., and Daniel Brantley. "Black Southern Politics: A Look at the Tradition and the Future." In *Black Politics and Black Political Behavior: A Linkage Analysis*, edited by Hanes Walton Jr., 277–99. Westport, CT: Praeger, 1994.

Walton, Hanes, Jr., Oliver Jones Jr., and Pearl K. Ford. "African American Political Socialization: The Protest Resignations of Councilpersons Jerome Woody and Renee Baker." In *African American Power and Politics: The Political Context Variable*, edited by Hanes Walton Jr. New York: Columbia University Press, 1997.

Walton, Hanes, Jr., and Robert Smith. *American Politics and the African American Quest for Universal Freedom*. 2nd ed. New York: Longman, 2003.

Waltz, Waldo. "Arizona: A State of New-Old Frontiers." In *Rocky Mountain Politics*, edited by Thomas Donnelly. Albuquerque: University of New Mexico Press, 1940.

Waugh, John C. *Reelecting Lincoln: The Battle for the 1864 Presidency*. New York: Crown, 1997.

Weeks, O. Douglas. *Texas in the 1960 Presidential Election*. Austin: University of Texas, Institute of Public Affairs, 1961.

Weeks, O. Douglas. *Texas in 1964: A One-Party State Again?* Austin: University of Texas, Institute of Public Affairs, 1965.

Weeks, O. Douglas. "Texas: Land of Conservative Expansiveness." In *The Changing Politics of the South*, edited by William C. Havard, 201–30. Baton Rouge: Louisiana State University Press, 1972.

Weeks, O. Douglas. *Texas One-Party Politics in 1956*. Austin: University of Texas, Institute of Public Affairs, 1957.

Weeks, O. Douglas. *Texas Presidential Politics in 1952*. Austin: University of Texas, Institute of Public Affairs, 1953.

White, Theodore H. *The Making of the President 1964*. New York: Atheneum, 1965.

Wills, Garry. *Lincoln at Gettysburg: The Words That Remade America*. New York: Simon & Schuster, 1992.

Wolfinger, Raymond E., and Steven J. Rosenstone. *Who Votes?* New Haven: Yale University Press, 1980.

Woods, Randall B. *LBJ: Architect of American Ambition*. New York: Free Press, 2006.

Woodward, Bob. *The Agenda: Inside the Clinton White House*. New York: Simon & Schuster, 1994.

ARTICLES

Abney, F. Glenn. "Factors Related to Negro Voter Turnout in Mississippi." *Journal of Politics* 36, no. 4 (1974): 1057–63.

Abney, F. Glenn. "Partisan Realignment in a One-Party System: The Case of Mississippi." *Journal of Politics* 3 (1969): 1102–6.

Abramowitz, Jack. "John B. Rayner—A Grass-Roots Leader." *Journal of Negro History* 36, no. 2 (1951): 160–93.

Abramowitz, Jack. "The Negro in the Populist Movement." *Journal of Negro History* 38, no. 3 (1953): 257–89.

Abramson, Paul R., and John H. Aldrich. "The Decline of Electoral Participation in America." *American Political Science Review* 76, no. 3 (1982): 502–21.

Barr, Alwyn. "Black Legislators of Reconstruction Texas." *Civil War History* 32, no. 4 (1986): 340–51.

Bass, Harold F., Jr. "Comparing Presidential Party Leadership Transfers: Two Cases." *Presidential Studies Quarterly* 23, no. 1 (1993): 115–28.

Bass, Harold F., Jr. "Presidential Party Leadership and Party Reform: Franklin D. Roosevelt and the Abrogation of the Two-Thirds Rule." *Presidential Studies Quarterly* 18, no. 2 (1988): 303–17.

Bass, Harold F., Jr. "Presidential Party Leadership and Party Reform: Lyndon B. Johnson and the MFDP Controversy." *Presidential Studies Quarterly* 21, no. 1 (1991): 85–101.

Baum, Dale, and James Hailey. "Lyndon Johnson's 1948 Senate Victory." *Political Science Quarterly* 109 (1994): 595–613.

Belenky, Irina. "The Making of the Ex-Presidents, 1797–1993: Six Recurrent Models." *Presidential Studies Quarterly* 29, no. 1 (1999): 150–65.

Best, Gary Dean. "Herbert Hoover as Titular Leader of the GOP, 1933–1935." *Mid-America: An Historical Review* 61, no. 2 (1979): 81–97.

Billington, Monroe. "Lyndon B. Johnson and Blacks: The Early Years." *Journal of Negro History* 62, no. 1 (1977): 26–42.

Black, Earl, and Merle Black. "The Wallace Vote in Alabama: A Multiple Regression Analysis." *Journal of Politics* 35, no. 3 (1973): 730–36.

Brown, Courtney. "Nonlinear Transformation in a Landslide: Johnson and Goldwater in 1964." *American Journal of Political Science* 37, no. 2 (1993): 582–609.

Brown, Roger G., and David M. Welborn. "Presidents and Their Parties: Performance and Prospects." *Presidential Studies Quarterly* 12, no. 3 (1982): 302–16.

Buchanan, William. "Election Predictions: An Empirical Assessment." *Public Opinion Quarterly* 50, no. 2 (1986): 222–27.

Burnham, Walter Dean. "The Alabama Senatorial Election of 1962: Return of Inter-Party Competition." *Journal of Politics* 26 (1964): 798–829.

Burnham, Walter Dean. "The Democrats: Right or Left? The Eclipse of the Democratic Party." *Democracy* 2 (July 1982).

Casdorph, Paul Douglas. "Norris Wright Cuney and Texas Republican Politics, 1883–1896." *Southwestern Historical Quarterly* 68, no. 4 (1965): 455–64.

Chester, Edward W. "Lyndon Baines Johnson, an American 'King Lear': A Critical Evaluation of His Newspaper Obituaries." *Presidential Studies Quarterly* 21, no. 2 (1991): 319–31.

Cohen, Richard. “The Election That LBJ Won.” *Washington Post*, November 4, 2008: A17.

Cook, Samuel DuBois. “Political Movements and Organizations.” *Journal of Politics* 26, no. 1 (1964): 130–44.

Cook, Timothy E. “The Bear Market in Political Socialization and the Costs of Misunderstood Psychological Theories.” *American Political Science Review* 79, no. 4 (1985): 1079–93.

Cotter, Cornelius P. “Eisenhower as Party Leader.” *Political Science Quarterly* 98, no. 2 (1983): 255–83.

Cox, Patrick. “Nearly a Statesman: LBJ and Texas Blacks in the 1948 Election.” *Social Science Quarterly* 74, no. 2 (1993): 241.

Dahl, Robert A. “Myth of the Presidential Mandate.” *Political Science Quarterly* 105, no. 3 (1990): 355–72.

“Democrats Nominate Johnson-Humphrey at Convention Geared to Middle-Road Campaign.” In *Congressional Quarterly Almanac 88th Congress 2nd Session* 20 (Washington, DC: Congressional Quarterly, 1965): 1092.

“Dissecting the 2008 Electorate.” *Pew Research Center*, April 30, 2009.

Dowe, Pearl K. Ford, Tekla A. Johnson, and Angie Maxwell. “Yes We Can or Yes We Did? Prospective and Retrospective Change in the Obama Presidency.” *Journal of Black Studies* 40 (2010): 462–83.

Doyle, Judith Kaaz. “Maury Maverick and Racial Politics in San Antonio Texas, 1938–1941.” *Journal of Southern History* 53, no. 2 (1987).

Eldersveld, Samuel J. “Theory and Method in Voting Behavior Research.” *Journal of Politics* 13, no. 1 (1951): 70–87.

Evans, Rowland, and Robert Novak. “Later Than LBJ Thinks.” *Washington Post*, December 2, 1966.

Frantz, Joe B. “Opening a Curtain: The Metamorphosis of Lyndon B. Johnson.” *Journal of Southern History* 45, no. 1 (1979): 3–26.

Greenberg, Stanley B. “Reconstructing the Democratic Vision.” *American Prospect* 1, no. 1 (1990): 83–89.

Grunbaum, Werner. “Desegregation in Texas: Voting and Action Patterns.” *Public Opinion Quarterly* 28 (1964): 604–14.

Jamieson, Patrick E. “Seeing the Lyndon B. Johnson Presidency through the March 31, 1968, Withdrawal Speech.” *Presidential Studies Quarterly* 29, no. 1 (1999): 134–49.

Johnson, Senator Lyndon B. “Amendment of Cloture Rule.” *Congressional Record Senate 81st Congress 1st Session* 95, part 2 (March 9, 1949): 2046.

“Kefauver Wins Vice President Nomination on 2nd Ballot.” In *Congressional Quarterly Almanac 84th Congress 2nd Session* 12 (1956): 6–7.

“. . . Kennedy Nominated on First Ballot with 806 Votes.” In *Congressional Quarterly Almanac 86th Congress 2nd Session* 16 (Washington, DC: Congressional Quarterly, 1960): 773.

Lee, Eugene C., and William Buchanan. “The 1960 Election in California.” *Western Political Quarterly* 14, no. 1 (1961): 309–26.

Lewis-Beck, Michael S., and Tom W. Rice, “Localism in Presidential Elections: The House State Advantage.” *American Journal of Political Science* 27, no. 3 (1983): 548–56.

McLemore, Leslie Burl. “Fannie Lou Hamer: An Unfinished Political Portrait.” Paper presented at the Sixth Annual Meeting of the National Council for Black Studies, Chicago, March 17–20, 1982.

McLemore, Leslie Burl. "Mississippi Freedom Democratic Party." *Black Politician* 3, no. 2 (1971): 19–22.

McPherson, Harry. "How Race Destroyed the Democrats' Coalitions." *New York Times*, October 28, 1988.

Milkis, Sidney M. "Franklin D. Roosevelt and the Transcendence of Partisan Politics." *Political Science Quarterly* 100, no. 3 (1985): 479–504.

Miller, Cheryl M., and Hanes Walton Jr. "Congressional Support of Civil Rights Public Policy: From Bipartisan to Partisan Convergence." *Congress & the Presidency* 21 (1994): 11–27.

Nimmo, Dan, and Clifton McCleskey. "Impact of the Poll Tax on Voter Participation: The Houston Metropolitan Area in 1966." *Journal of Politics* 31, no. 3 (1969): 682–99.

Odegard, Peter H. "Presidential Leadership and Party Responsibility." *Annals of the American Academy of Political and Social Science* 307 (1956): 66–81.

Philpot, Tasha S., Daron R. Shaw, and Ernest B. McGowen. "Winning the Race: Black Voter Turnout in the 2008 Presidential Election." *Public Opinion Quarterly* 73 (2009): 995–1022.

Pomper, Gerald. "The Nomination of Hubert Humphrey for Vice-President." *Journal of Politics* 28, no. 3 (1966): 639–59.

Potenziani, David. "Striking Back: Richard B. Russell and Racial Relocation." *Georgia Historical Quarterly* 65, no. 3 (1981): 263–77.

Potoski, Matthew. "'Friends and Neighbors Voting' in Gubernatorial and Senatorial Primaries." *Southeastern Political Review* 22 (1994): 543–48.

"The Presidential Election—1952." In *Congressional Quarterly Almanac 82nd Congress 2nd Session* 8 (1952): 485.

Price, Charles M., and Joseph Boskin. "The Roosevelt 'Purge': A Reappraisal." *Journal of Politics* 28, no. 3 (1966): 660–70.

Rice, Tom W., and Alisa A. Macht. "Friends and Neighbors Voting in Statewide General Elections." *American Journal of Political Science* 3 (1987): 448–52.

Rice, Tom W., and Alisa A. Macht. "The Hometown Advantage: Mobilization or Conversion?" *Political Behavior* 9 (1987): 257–62.

Richter, William L. "'We Must Rubb Out and Begin Anew': The Army and the Republican Party in Texas Reconstruction, 1867–1870." *Civil War Quarterly* 19, no. 4 (1973): 334–52.

Robertson, Marvin. "'The Single Most Important Event': President Jimmy Carter Recalls Life on the Farm before Electricity." *Georgia Magazine* 67 (2001): 15–18.

Savage, Sean J. "To Purge or Not to Purge: Hamlet Harry and the Dixiecrats." *Presidential Studies Quarterly* 27, no. 4 (1997): 773–90.

Schaller, Thomas F., and Thomas W. Williams. "'The Contemporary Presidency': Post-presidential Influence in the Postmodern Era." *Presidential Studies Quarterly* 33, no. 1 (2003): 188–200.

Schoen, Harold. "The Free Negro in the Republic of Texas, I." *Southwestern Historical Quarterly* 39, no. 4 (1936): 292–308.

Shannon, J. B. "Presidential Politics in the South: 1938, I." *Journal of Politics* 1, no. 2 (1939): 146–70.

Shannon, J. B. "Presidential Politics in the South—1938, II." *Journal of Politics* 1, no. 3 (1939): 278–300.

Shinn, Allen M., Jr. "A Note on Voter Registration and Turnout in Texas, 1960–1970." *Journal of Politics* 33, no. 4 (1971): 1120–29.

Sinclair-Chapman, Valeria, and Melayne Price. "Black Politics, the 2008 Election, and the (Im)Possibility of Race Transcendence." *PS: Political Science* 41 (2008): 739–45.

Stoney, George C. "Suffrage in the South: Part I, The Poll Tax." *Survey Graphic* 29, no. 1 (1940): 5–41.

Strong, Donald S. "American Government and Politics: The Poll Tax: The Case of Texas." *American Political Science Review* 38, no. 4 (1944): 693–709.

Strong, Donald S. "The Rise of Negro Voting in Texas." *American Political Science Review* 48, no. 3 (1948): 510–22.

Swisher, Idella Gwatkin. "Election Statistics in the United States." *American Political Science Review* 27, no. 3 (1933): 422–32.

Tatalovich, Raymond. "'Friends and Neighbors' Voting: Mississippi, 1943–73." *Journal of Politics* 37, no. 3 (1975): 807–14.

Taylor, Paul, and Mark Hugo Lopez. "Six Take-aways from the Census Bureau's Voting Report." Pew Research Center, May 8, 2013.

Valelly, Richard. "Vanishing Voters." *American Prospect* 1, no. 1 (1990): 140–42.

"The Vice Presidency." In *Congressional Quarterly Almanac 86th Congress 2nd Session* 16 (Washington, DC: Congressional Quarterly, 1960): 775.

Walton, Hanes, Jr., Josephine A. V. Allen, Sherman Puckett, and Donald R. Deskins Jr. "The Red and Blue State Divide in Black and White: The Historic 2008 Election of President Barack Obama." *Black Scholar* 38 (2008): 19–30.

Walton, Hanes, Jr., Josephine A. V. Allen, Sherman Puckett, Donald R. Deskins Jr., and Billie Dee Tate. "The Literature on African American Presidential Candidates." *Journal of Race & Policy* (2008): 103–24.

Walton, Hanes, Jr., Sharon Wright, and Frank Pryor. "Texas African American Republicans: The Electoral Board in the 1920 Presidential and Gubernatorial Elections." *National Conference of Black Political Scientists Newsletter* 17 (2003): 8–12.

Weeks, O. Douglas. "The League of United Latin-American Citizens: A Texas-Mexican Civic Organization." *Southwestern Political and Social Science Quarterly* 10, no. 3 (1929): 257–78.

Weeks, O. Douglas. "Republicanism and Conservatism in the South." *Southwestern Social Science Quarterly* 36 (1955): 248–56.

Weeks, O. Douglas. "The Texas-Mexican and the Politics of South Texas." *American Political Science Review* 24, no. 3 (1930): 606–27.

Williams, T. Harry. "Huey, Lyndon, and Southern Radicalism." *Journal of American History* 60, no. 2 (1973): 272.

Wilson, William Julius. "Race Neutral Policies and Democratic Coalition." *American Prospect* 1, no. 1 (1990): 81.

Wolfinger, Raymond E. "The Development and Persistence of Ethnic Voting." *American Political Science Review* 59 (1965): 896–908.

Wolfinger, Raymond E. "Why Political Machines Have Not Withered Away." *Journal of Politics* 34 (1972): 365–98.

Woodson, Carter G. "The Cuney Family." *Negro History Bulletin* 2 (1948): 123–43.

LETTERS

Cansler, C. J. Representative for *Pittsburgh Courier*, to J. E. Kellam, State Administrator, N.Y.A., May 27, 1941. House of Representatives Papers, Box 14.

Clayton, J. E. Principal, Littig High School, to Congressman Lyndon B. Johnson, May 21, 1941, House of Representatives Papers, Box 14.

Clayton, J. E. Principal, Littig High School, to "Dear Friend," May 22, 1941, House of Representatives Papers, Box 14.

Clayton, J. E. Principal, Littig High School, to Congressman Lyndon B. Johnson, June 11, 1941, House of Representatives Papers, Box 14.

Clayton, J. E. Principal, Littig High School, to Dr. W. M. Drake, Chairman, Colored Division, Lyndon B. Johnson Headquarters, June 11, 1941.

de Cordeva, R. L. Chairman, Latin American Democrats to "Dear Friend," May 30, 1941, House of Representatives Papers, Box 14.

de Cordeva, R. L. Chairman, Latin American Democrats, to Walter Jenkins, Staff, Office of Congressman Lyndon Johnson, May 30, 1941.

Jenkins, Walter. Staff, Office of Congressman Lyndon B. Johnson, to R. L. de Cordeva, June 6, 1941.

Johnson, Lyndon B. Congressman, to H. L. Mitchell, Secretary, Southern Tenant Farmers Union, May 28, 1941, House of Representatives Papers, Box 14.

Johnson, Lyndon B. Congressman, to H. L. Mitchell, Secretary, STFU, May 28, 1941, House of Representatives Papers, Box 14.

Marlin, Bobby. Librarian, University of Houston Libraries, to Hanes Walton, Jr., October 16, 2000.

Mitchell, H. L. Secretary, Southern Tenant Farmers Union, to Honorable Lyndon B. Johnson, May 21, 1941, House of Representatives Papers, Box 14.

Ritter, Dr. Claudia. Institut Fur Politische Wissenchaft, to Hanes Walton, Jr., November 16, 2001, 2.

Sall, Judy. Librarian, *The Dallas Morning News*, to Hanes Walton, Jr., March 21, 2002.

COURT CASES

Beare v. Smith, 32 F. Supp. I 1 0 (SD. Texas, 1971).

Brown v. Board of Education, 347 U.S. 483 (1954).

Harper v. Virginia State Board of Elections, 303 U.S. 663 (1966).

Nixon v. Condon, 286 U.S. 73 (1932).

Nixon v. Herndon, 273 U.S. 536 (1935).

Smith v. Allwright, 321 U.S. 649 (1944).

Sweatt v. Painter, 339 U.S. 629 (1950).

GOVERNMENT DOCUMENTS

Georgia Official and Statistical Register. Atlanta: Secretary of State, 1952.

House of Representatives. Oren Harris, "Not the South's Fight Alone." Extension of

Remarks—Appendix to the Congressional Record, 81st Congress, 1st Session 95, part 2 (1949), 282.

Report of the Committee on Privileges, Suffrage and Elections. "Journal of the House of Representatives of the Regular Session of 36th Legislature Convened January 14, 1919, and Adjourned March 19, 1919."

Senator Lyndon B. Johnson. "Amendment of Cloture Rule." Congressional Record—Senate 81st Congress, 1st Session, vol. 95, part 2 (March 9, 1949), 2046–48.

U.S. Commission on Civil Rights. *Report of the United States Commission on Civil Rights, 1959.* Washington, DC: United States Government Printing Office, 1959.

U.S. Senate. "Letter of the General of the Army of the United States: Community in Compliance with a Resolution of the Senate of December 5, 1867, A Statement of the number of white and colored voters registered in each of the states subject to the Reconstruction Arts of Congress, with other statistics relative to the same subject." 40th Congress, 2nd Session. Washington, DC: United States Government Printing Office, 1886.

LIBRARY COLLECTIONS

Strong, Donald S. "Interviews in Texas." Southern Politics Collections, Special Collections—Vanderbilt University Archives, Nashville, Tennessee.

Index